The Irish Revival

Irish Studies

Kathleen Costello-Sullivan, *Series Editor*

For a full list of titles in this series,
visit https://press.syr.edu/supressbook-series/irish-studies/.

The Irish Revival

A COMPLEX VISION

Edited by Joseph Valente
and Marjorie Howes

SYRACUSE UNIVERSITY PRESS

First Edition 2023
23 24 25 26 27 28   6 5 4 3 2 1

∞ The paper used in this publication meets the minimum requirements
of the American National Standard for Information Sciences—Permanence
of Paper for Printed Library Materials, ANSI Z39.48-1992.

For a listing of books published and distributed by Syracuse University Press,
visit https://press.syr.edu.

ISBN: 978-0-8156-3801-8 (hardcover)
978-0-8156-3794-3 (paperback)
978-0-8156-5579-4 (e-book)

Library of Congress Cataloging-in-Publication Data
Names: Valente, Joseph, editor. | Howes, Marjorie Elizabeth, editor.
Title: The Irish revival : a complex vision / edited by Joseph Valente and Marjorie Howes.
Description: First edition. | Syracuse, New York : Syracuse University Press, 2023. |
Series: Irish studies | Includes bibliographical references and index.
Identifiers: LCCN 2022057446 (print) | LCCN 2022057447 (ebook) |
ISBN 9780815638018 (hardcover) | ISBN 9780815637943 (paperback) |
ISBN 9780815655794 (ebook)
Subjects: LCSH: English literature—Irish authors—History and criticism. |
Irish literature—History and criticism. | Literature and society—Ireland—History. |
Nationalism and literature—Ireland—History. | Politics and culture—Ireland—History. |
LCGFT: Literary criticism.
Classification: LCC PR8750 .I78 2023 (print) | LCC PR8750 (ebook) |
DDC 820.9/9415—dc23/eng/20230316
LC record available at https://lccn.loc.gov/2022057446
LC ebook record available at https://lccn.loc.gov/2022057447

Manufactured in the United States of America

For our mothers:

Elizabeth Jane Valente

Lidie McKinney Howes

Contents

Illustrations

Acknowledgments

We would like to thank our acquisitions editor Deborah Manion for her guidance and enthusiasm. We are grateful as well to assistant editor Kelly L. Balenske and marketing coordinator Lisa Renee Kuerbis for their patience and efficiency. Much appreciation to the series editor of Irish Studies, Kathleen Costello-Sullivan, for shepherding the project throughout. We also owe thanks to the anonymous Syracuse University Press readers for their helpful assessments and insightful commentary. Kezia Whiting gave us invaluable help in preparing the manuscript. Finally we would like to thank our contributors for their illuminating research, hard work, and unflagging collegiality. The cover art is by Christina Valente.

The Irish Revival

Introduction

A Complex Revival

Joseph Valente and Marjorie Howes

In his 1923 Nobel Prize lecture, "The Irish Dramatic Movement," W. B. Yeats famously located the origins of the Irish Revival in the fall of Charles Stewart Parnell, the ensuing paralysis of his Irish Parliamentary Party, and the gradual collapse of the constitutional politics for which he stood. Citing the "Gaelic League of Dr. Hyde," his own "literary movement in English," and the theater project of the lecture's title, Yeats proposed that "when Parnell fell from power in 1891 . . . [a] disillusioned and embittered Ireland turned from Parliamentary politics" toward a cultural nationalism that was "romantic and poetical" instead.[1] Yeats's formulation was so powerful, and so consonant with what would become the traditional nationalist genealogy of Irish liberation—from Parnell to Pearse to de Valera—that his historical analysis went largely unchallenged for the next seventy-odd years, until the publication of R. F. Foster's magisterial biography of him. In it, Foster argued that the defining projects of the Revival were already underway during Parnell's time and, moreover, that they had emerged in anticipation of Parnell's success in achieving Home Rule. The Revival originated, he contended, as preparation for self-governance, not in frustration at its deferral.

Foster disputed both Yeats's chronology and his postulated causality for the emergence of the Revival, and these crucial insights helped enable a subsequent flourishing of scholarly work in which the Revival has been repeatedly revisited, reappraised, and reimagined. This work is richly varied in its goals and procedures, but several general patterns have emerged. Much scholarship has revised an earlier era's assumptions of Irish exceptionalism to focus on the Revival's mutual imbrication with other intellectual currents and traditions, both in Ireland and elsewhere.[2] The cast of recognized revivalist thinkers and activists now extends well beyond Yeats and his circle, as scholars have unearthed neglected figures, many of whom were well known in their time but were subsequently written out of cultural history.[3] The contributions of women have been illuminated, and regional variations of the Revival explored.[4] Other work, such as P. J. Mathews's groundbreaking *Revival*, has enlarged the proper scope of revivalist activity beyond language and literature to encompass political movements, industrial and agricultural societies, and cultural pursuits from sports to handicrafts.[5] In two related but very different efforts, Sinead Mattar's *Primitivism, Science, and the Irish Revival* and Abby Bender's *Israelites in Erin: Exodus, Revolution and the Irish Revival* illuminate how revivalist discourses drew upon fields and discourses that were not traditionally (or reasonably) characterized as revivalist.[6]

Overall, the general tenor of recent scholarship has involved an emphasis on inclusion. This is both natural and valuable. More material is available, archives have come to light, and previous standards and canons are being revised. Including previously neglected figures often restores to the historical record work that revivalist contemporaries were aware of, and helps illustrate the significance of international frames and connections and local variation. Much of this work, however, tends to see the various revivalist figures and projects as part of a fairly unified ideological endeavor. Mathews, for example, sees the strains of the Revival he analyzes as coalescing under the umbrella of the popular Victorian ethos of "self-help." Thus even as he expanded and recontoured the terrain of the Revival, he sustained the assumption, held by both Yeats and Foster, of a unified field whose elements were organized around a single point of reference. But a tension has emerged between the unity suggested by the term "Revival" and the myriad differences uncovered by the ever-expanding capaciousness of the phenomenon. Indeed, the rubric of revivalism itself has come under increasing pressure. As James Murphy and Betsey Taylor FitzSimon put it, "The phrase, Irish Revival, is like a net that has been cast over a whole series of movements that swept across the cultural landscape of Ireland at the end of the nineteenth and the beginning of the twentieth century."[7]

Rather than simply include more and cast the Revival's net over a wider and wider area, this volume seeks to refigure and retheorize the field as a whole. Instead of seeking a basis for the presumptive unity of revivalism—whether in the agendas of political resistance, devolutionary self-management, or cultural self-help—we take the Revival to exemplify the specialized notion of complexity recently developed in the information and biological sciences.[8]

A complex system may be defined as follows: a mobile assemblage of several or many interacting objects which transpires without any central control or coordination or fixed rules of operation, and gives rise to self-organizing, self-adapting forms of collective behavior.[9] Such systems can be found in nature, for example in insect colonies, and in the human body, for example in our immune systems or the neuronal pathways of the brain. The key to these complex systems is that the individual components or agents follow their own respective paths, toward their own respective aims or for their own gain, without binding consideration of or even reference to the larger manifold of which they turn out, in the last analysis, to be a part. They act, that is to say, not in concert with one another, but in the unplanned, yet ultimately coherent articulation of their differences. Appearing as if magically yet organically, this congruence has been dubbed "emergent."

The phenomenon of emergence depends upon an intricate series of feedback mechanisms, in which the adaptations each agent makes in response to environmental input has indirect, involuntary, but nontrivial effect on the other agents, resulting in a continual recursive process affecting, and thereby consolidating, the entire collective.[10] Such independent yet interactive adjustments respond to forces both internal and external to the operation of the assemblage; i.e., to the alterations wrought by their own individuated pursuits and to the impact of the larger ecosystem upon them. As a consequence, the state of ongoing autopoesis, which all complex systems produce, simultaneously defines the individual agents in their relation to each other and the group thus formed in its relation to an outside.

Complex systems, accordingly, are not just self-organizing and self-adapting; they are self-organizing in and through their self-adaptation, a properly evolutionary as well as emergent phenomenon. And like all evolutionary developments, complex dynamics unfold in an uneven manner. The interactions among the agents are uniform neither in magnitude nor saliency. Rather, they eventuate in a network, comprising a series of nodes of differing degrees of interlinkage, differing densities of the actions and reactions that intersect there. The highest degree nodes, called hubs, serve as "major conduits for the flow of information in the networks," allowing for the decentered mode of coordination that characterizes complex systems.[11] However prominent any given hub within a network might be, its deletion, failure, or breakdown does not incapacitate the entire collective, as would the default of a central control. The advantage thus enjoyed by complex systems, termed resiliency, is especially marked in so-called "small world" variants—such as the Irish Revival—with "relatively few long distance connections" and a "small average path-length" for information transfer.[12]

Looking at the Revival, we can discern that its various branches grew into a network of interactive relationships without any over-arching center of authority or intentionality. Nothing like a bureau of revivalism existed or could have existed. Its constituent organization, like the GAA, the Gaelic League, the creamery movement, the Irish Literary Theatre, etc., pursued their own aims in relative autonomy from the others and modulated in accordance with their own feedback mechanisms, each of which affected and was affected by the others in a fashion that could not have been and yet must seem, in retrospect, purposeful. That is the very essence of an emergence phenomenon, where the several self-adaptations of discrete agents eventuate in a self-organization unforeseeable in advance but entirely legible as it materializes. Internally, the emergence of the Revival from the feedback loops of its member-groups took shape as a series of dialectical relationships of contest and cooperation, alliance and antagonism, dialogue and disruption among their various agendas. Externally, the several ventures seemed to have come together at points in their joint sense of an overriding objective, decolonization broadly construed, but they divided on what that aspiration implied and hence on the ultimate aim to be achieved: here ethnic authenticity, there political autonomy, elsewhere neither of these, but instead a greater collective prosperity and well-being. But even on the last of these, divisions obtained over whether the good life sought was one of effective modernization or diligently preserved agrarianism, whether it entailed national sequestration or partnership with a greater Europe, whether it was to be secular in the main or fully theocratic. By the same token, the various branches of the Revival came together at points in their resistance to British domination, a crucial aspect of revivalist "emergence," but the persistence of sectarian differences, a key element in the separation of those branches, gave rein to disagreements over the nature of the resistance to be mounted, the form of decolonization to be achieved, and the proper understanding of both the indigenous, precolonial past and the consummate postcolonial futurity. The enhanced power and influence enjoyed by certain wings of the Revival (such as the Gaelic League), their role as hubs linking the other nodes in the network, allows even these questions, the signature, animating questions of the movement, to remain unresolved without condemning the Revival itself to crippling irresolution, without destroying its potent if unguided efficacy, and without fracturing beyond repair its freeform integrity. As a heuristic paradigm, the complex adaptive system enables this volume to respect the independent character of the sundry revivalist institutions and projects it treats while at the same time remarking the specific structure whereby that character is inflected, not to say constituted, through the inter-agitation of the others, resulting in a preternaturally successful, paradoxically unplanned plan of campaign.

Essays here adopt varying senses or forms of complexity and varying methods for articulating that delicate balance between irreducible differences and resonant points of connection. Greg Dobbins's argument that AE's theosophy is "ripe for critical rediscovery" describes such a balance within the writings, activism, and life of one revivalist, George Russell, in two distinct but related ways. First, he illuminates the complex relationships among Russell's myriad interests and pursuits: journalism, social activism, political activity, painting, literature, and alternative spirituality. In addition, Dobbins compellingly reads theosophy itself as offering a theory of the revivalist project overall, one that complements and refigures complexity theory. Theosophy, Dobbins explains, "begins with the recognition of the complexity of the material world, and seeks to align the various particularities within it—not to suppress such differences, but to celebrate and acknowledge them as unique instances of the sacred—in order to apprehend a greater organizational principle lurking behind it." Similarly, Anne Fogarty's essay also focuses on a single figure, Eva Gore-Booth. And she also stresses both the interconnectedness of her work as a poet, playwright, philosopher, and activist, and her self-conscious theoretical insistence on the inseparability of feminism, nationalism, and workers' rights.

Other essays find the nexus of difference and alliance on scales that are both larger and smaller than the scale a focus on the work of a single figure affords. Gregory Castle examines the expansive ecosystem he calls the media habitus, the network of print publications and the practices of reprinting and reframing individual texts that characterized the Ireland of the period. Marjorie Howes identifies complexity in the media on a much smaller scale, in the ambiguities and contradictions inherent to the project of examining individual texts in relation to the print culture context in which they appear. Karen Steele, in contrast, looks to a larger scale than Castle, one that extends beyond Ireland, arguing that two newspapers' content and editorial policies worked to place Ireland alone, according to the principle of Sinn Fein, but also in a transnational frame. Her essay shows that they did so, however, in strikingly different ways.

The pro-independence *United Irishman* tended to compare Ireland to other small nations, in order to advance the cause of separatism, while the *Irish Independent*, which favored Home Rule and later Dominion status within the empire, emphasized the economic forces of globalization instead.

Part of the richness of complexity theory lies in its ability to grapple with the role of contingency, rather than strict causality, in writing cultural history, allowing scholars to uncover histories of the possible, of what might have been, and of the forgotten. Brian O' Conchubhair's essay on William Rooney and the Celtic Literary Society analyzes several overlapping but independent factors that contributed to the survival of the Gaelic League and the fading away of the Celtic Literary Society. He also speculates intriguingly how those histories might have played out differently if Rooney had not died at age twenty-seven. Paige Reynolds's essay also offers a form of counter-history, arguing that the idea that the Revival was dominated primarily by male writers did not originate with those writers themselves, but rather emerged in the accounts of later scholars. By examining two prose genres written by women (utopian fiction and realism) as part of the revivalist project, and by highlighting their depictions of the everyday, Reynolds restores to the record writers, genres, and themes erased by previously dominant cultural histories. Similarly, in a corrective to accounts of the Revival that stress the exclusion or limited participation of women, Tina O'Toole's essay shows that women's experiences and feminist ideas were in fact an important shaping element of the period's revolutionary discourses.

O'Toole emphasizes the affiliations between activism and writing and the confluence of nationalism, feminism, and aesthetic innovation in the works of writers like Rosamond Jacob. Such variety, overlap, and interdisciplinarity are phenomena that complexity theory is well suited to capture, and other essays also pursue different forms of linkage across a range of disciplines and discourses. Steele employs recent network theory and examines the importance of "weak ties" among people, in Ireland and beyond, who participated in revivalist activities in various spheres, such as journalism, sport, culture, and politics. Kelly Sullivan, on the other hand, invokes the forms of linkage the Irish manifestation of the international Arts and Crafts movement sought to create as part of a vernacular Irish material culture connecting printing and book making, clothing, furniture, and architecture. Her chapter on Harry Clarke's stained glass windows positions Clarke as part of that movement, calling Clarke's work a "visual corollary of the Irish Revival."

Sullivan's essay notes that the inescapably public nature of Clarke's work—church windows—offered both constraints and opportunities for him. Confined to the traditional narratives and figures deemed acceptable for church windows, Clarke also effected radical aesthetic innovations in his depictions of them; many of these innovations are still prominently on display in Irish churches today. Issues surrounding institution building and the public sphere were, of course, central to the Revival, and appear in a number of other essays in this volume as well. Mary Mullen's essay on George Moore identifies in his work a dynamic she sees as central to the Revival overall: the impulse to create institutions versus the impulse to critique and resist institutionality. Such questioning of institutionality is echoed by O'Toole, who casts the Revival itself as an institution that sought to exclude some women writers. In a different vein, O' Conchubhair's chapter argues that, by creating bilingual public monuments, William Rooney made salient contributions to a revivalist public sphere. Both Castle and Howes raise questions surrounding the reception history of print culture, and Howes broaches the idea of a counter-public sphere in the literary and material culture of the native Irish.

Art, architecture, texts, and material practices could all signify publicly as part of a complex set of revivalist projects. So, too, could human bodies. Joseph Valente's essay brings disability studies into dialogue with Irish studies, and uncovers the deep-seated and thoroughgoing ableism that underpinned revivalist literature and its culminating political demarche, the Easter Rising. This insight leads him to propose the innovative and revealing term "rehabilitationist" as a more accurate descriptor than "revivalist" for the literature of the period. Abby Bender's examination of Patrick Pearse's deployment of images of breastmilk and nursing mothers shows that this imagery expresses the profound contradictions attaching to the Revival's widespread ideology of sacrifice even more effectively than his more famous use of blood imagery: it "exposes, and indeed clarifies, the central tension around the sacrificial narrative: that is, its ironic anti-natalism, its anti-futurity, its biological, generational nihilism."

Both Bender and Valente also offer compelling ways of queering revivalism. Bender's characterization of Pearse melds the feminine/maternal and the masculine/sacrificial, while Valente identifies a queering of the sovereignty myth in the eroticization of male bodies that are both perfectly intact and already doomed to extinction. In a related vein, O'Toole's essay uncovers in Jacob's work forms of sexuality that are ambiguous and fluid, difficult to categorize or define. And Fogarty sees Gore-Booth as espousing a queer ethos that rethinks conventional definitions of concepts such as love, essence, agency, and the nonhuman world. More broadly, the volume as a whole seeks to rethink categories and concepts that scholars have traditionally employed to understand the Revival, whether by inventing new terms (Valente), or reconceptualizing existing terms, such as realism (Mullen), simultaneity (Dobbins), remediation (Castle), or the everyday (Reynolds), to demonstrate their previously unappreciated importance to revivalist discourses.

The paradigm of complexity poses a unique challenge for the organization of an essay collection such as ours. Typically, a volume of this sort prioritizes the individual valence of each essay by arranging them seriatim, without explicit reference to the gestalt of which they are part, or it prioritizes the conceptual unity and structural integrity of the volume by the use of certain annotational devices, such as titled sections and subsections, which locates the essays within a schematic design. Complexity theory, as we have elaborated, delineates how individual items in a manifold exert independent force, pursue their own line, and yet generate through their unplanned, unintended interplay a collective structure and community of purpose. That is to say, a complex system can be understood to combine the two conventional approaches to arranging an essay collection without in any way synthesizing them. Taken on its own, then, either approach violates the distinctive impetus of complexity that our volume looks to capture. Where complexity is dynamic and flexible in the extreme, allowing for myriad forms of external association among the units in a group, the format for a scholarly text of this genre is relatively fixed, static, and governed by the logic of either-or.

The way we have organized the volume, accordingly, and the headings we have chosen, should not be taken as a mimetic exercise, a diagram of how the Revival is to be represented on the complexity model. Rather, the order provided here indicates just one of many possible ways for readers to think of the essays as fitting together. As this introduction hopes to have shown, other assemblages, and other ways of drawing connections and differences among the essays, are not only possible but encouraged. This kind of flexibility and multiplicity, not just within essays but also between essays and in the organization of the volume as a whole, stands as yet another instance of how complexity theory can aid in developing our understanding of the Irish Revival.

Part One

The Revivalist Symbolic

Recovery and Remediation

1

The Celtic Literary Society

A Political and Secular Gaelic League?

Brian Ó Conchubhair

Now largely forgotten and effaced from the collective memory, the Celtic Literary Society, as distinct from the Irish Celtic Society,[1] provides a useful point of reference to measure the radicalism, conservatism, growth, and influence of Conradh na Gaeilge/the Gaelic League and assess the complexity and "messiness" of the Irish language movement during the Revival. Drawing on Paul Ricoeur, scholars may be better served to approach the Revival as a subject which was never a given at the beginning; rather it may be more beneficial to comprehend it as an evolving and devolving organism that only gathered meaning and significance in the fullness of time as the narrative story unraveled, and was told, recorded, and archived.[2] The Celtic Literary Society's less than a decade-long existence offers a more complex counternarrative, sheds light on what might have happened had the Gaelic League followed a different path, and adds color and perspective to the League's actions, statements, and policies. Ultimately, the Celtic Literary Society's willingness to integrate with other cultural and political groups, rather than form strategic alliances, damaged it, as did a lack of "political connections, especially with the Irish Parliamentary Party, characteristic of organizations with similar

My thanks to Brendan Kane and Daniela Thein for feedback on this paper.

concerns, such as the Fenian Young Ireland Societies of the 1880s or the Gaelic League."[3] The decision to merge with other organizations, such as Maud Gonne's radical Inghinidhe na hÉireann, and affiliate with Cumann na nGaedheal, founded in September 1900,[4] was no less decisive. The combination of these factors saw the Society lose its distinctive identity and specific focus; simultaneously, it rendered the Gaelic League the primary Irish-language organization not only in Dublin, but throughout Ireland and further afield. It also solidified the League's position as defender and sole voice of the some one million Irish speakers on the island. The Society's slippage from cultural memory may be attributed to a combination of the aforementioned factors as well as, in no small part, to the early death of its founding member, William Rooney.[5] In sketching the Society's arc, this essay illuminates the complexity, interdependency, and overlapping agendas that existed during the Irish Revival. Rather than a simple binary narrative, such as the one offered by Yeats in his Nobel Prize acceptance speech, in which a disillusioned Ireland turned away from parliamentary politics and Dr. Hyde founded the Gaelic League while Yeats began a movement in English, the reality appears multifarious as much recent scholarship on the Gaelic League and the Irish-language Revival shows.[6] Explanations, such as that offered by Yeats, endeavor to make simple, easy, and neat that which is complex, difficult, and inherently messy. Such explanations are indeed eminently preferable, and have the advantage of offering a linear, simplistic, yet reductionist account of what was in reality a series of complex multifaceted social, political, cultural, artistic, literary, linguistic, and intellectual movement.[7]

The Celtic Literary Society is essential not only to understanding the Gaelic League's development, but to how the League understood and rationalized itself within the wider Irish-Ireland cultural nationalist project. As an alternative to the vision offered by the Catholic Church, the GAA, Douglas Hyde, or W. B. Yeats, the Celtic Literary Society further reveals the Irish Revival's complexity and diversity. Reintroducing the Celtic Literary Society into the narrative of the Irish Revival both disturbs the simple narrative proposed by Yeats in his famous Nobel Prize acceptance speech, and also buttresses recent efforts to reveal the complexity and interconnectivity of numerous organizations with overlapping membership. It suggests that the Irish-language revival more closely corresponds to a chaotic discourse, and in reconstructing the internal rivalries, tensions, and alliances between various organizations—the Society for the Preservation of the Irish Language (SPIL), Gaelic League, Gaelic Union, Celtic Literary Society, and the Leinster Literary Society—we are forced to consider their competing and over-lapping agendas and motivations and recognize the complexity and diversity of revivalist discourse.

William Rooney: The "Common Man" Who Could Have Been Hyde

The Celtic Literary Society is indistinguishable from William Rooney. Writing in the *Irish Press* in 1967, T. P. O'Neill wrote of Cumann na nGaedheal: "Rooney was a guiding spirit in its activities . . . It was not a cultural society alone for it also had a political policy . . ."[8] Some fifty years later, in 2007, Nelson Ó Ceallaigh Ritschel posited that "Arthur Griffith's papers, especially the *United Irishman* (1899–1906) and *Sinn Féin* (1906–14), may have been more radical had the working-class Rooney lived and remained at Griffith's side."[9] Best known in popular culture as the author of once-common songs such as "The Men of the West," "Ninety Eight," and "An tSeanBhean Bhocht," Rooney, at the time of his premature death in 1901, represented the great hope of nationalist Ireland. If he is now largely forgotten or deemed irrelevant, that was not the case while he lived or at the time of his death. Indeed, had he lived, he may well have emerged a central figure in Irish cultural and nationalist politics. As Shovlin remarks, "What role he might have played in the new Ireland must remain moot, but it is likely that he would have become a significant actor in the move toward independence: his best friend Griffith, after all, became the Free State's first leader in 1922."[10]

William Rooney was apparently born in October[11] 1873 at 39 Mabbot Street, a tenement building in Dublin's Monto district.[12]

According to Connolly, he was the eldest of a family of seven, with four brothers and two sisters.[13] The 1901 census records his father Patrick (fifty-nine years old and a speaker of Irish and English) as a Dublin tradesman and coachbuilder.[14] He had participated in the 1867 Fenian uprising and served as a leader of the veterans' Old Guard Union.[15] In 1901 the family resided at Leinster Avenue, North Dock, Dublin, and consisted of Patrick (fifty-eight); Theresa (fifty-three); Patrick[16] (twenty); John (twenty-four); Luke[17] (eighteen) and Judith (twenty-two). Educated by the Christian Brothers in Dublin's Great Strand Street, and for a short period at the Brothers' Richmond Street School,[18] according to Bradley, at about twelve years of age William became a junior clerk in a solicitor's office in Dame Street,[19] but continued night-time education to complete the 1887 Intermediate Examination (Junior Grade).[20] He achieved honors in English and algebra, and a pass in arithmetic, chemistry, philosophy, and drawing.[21] Reluctant to apply for a position in the Civil Service in case of an overseas posting, he also, at his mother's behest, rejected a position with a Limerick newspaper.[22] Soon after commencing in Dame Street, he switched to a new clerical position in a North Strand office with the Midland Great Western Railway. Later, he unsuccessfully applied for a position as a schools' attendance officer.[23]

Typical of his generation, he joined the Fireside Club,[24] "the largest children's association in Ireland in the late 1880s."[25] Cultural nationalism shaped its teachings: the academic study of the Irish language, history, and literature, as well as social instruction concerning equality of the sexes, self-sufficiency, independence, and unity as a prerequisite for social progress.[26] These activities introduced him to Arthur Griffith, who become his confidant.[27] With Henry Egan Kenny ("Sean-Ghall"), Rooney established the City of Dublin Branch of the Irish Fireside Club in late 1888.[28] Their meetings convened initially at Dame Street and subsequently at Clarendon Street.[29] The club soon decided to establish an Irish-language class and wrote to the Society for the Preservation of the Irish Language seeking an instructor. Consequently, Richard Joseph O'Mulrenin became the club's Irish-language instructor. O'Mulrenin, who wrote for the Gaelic Union's journal *Irisleabhar na Gaedhilge* as "Clann Conchubhair," had previously taught Irish in Louvain in Belgium. Returning to Ireland in 1876, he worked as the "Agricultural Editor" for *Freeman's Weekly* and is frequently presumed to be the source for Joyce's famous line in *A Portrait of the Artist as a Young Man* that "John Francis Mulrennan has just returned from the west of Ireland. European and Asiatic papers please copy." Whatever the certainty of this connection, there is no doubt that Rooney proved an able student and O'Mulrenin a competent teacher. In 1889, Rooney read two papers to the Club on the topics of "Some Minor Irish Litterateurs" and "Illustrious Irishmen," which, according to Bradley, "both in style and treatment, and in the evidence they exhibit of research and wide reading, were far above the average work of a boy who had not yet completed his sixteenth year."[30] Bradley's account sees Rooney joining the Leinster Literary Society in 1890 where he also read papers, and in June 1891 he published his first poems in *United Ireland*.[31] His earliest collaborations with Griffith appeared in the *Evening Herald* in early 1892 when they coauthored a series of articles on "Notable Irish graves in and around Dublin."[32]

In addition to participating in the pro-Parnell Young Ireland League and leading excursions to sites of national importance, he featured prominently in the '98 Committee, established in early 1897 to commemorate the centenary of the 1798 Rebellion, and delivered a speech in Irish at the laying of the foundation stone of the Wolfe Tone statue on August 15, 1898. This project brought Rooney throughout Ireland and, as Bradley claims,

> to him the greater credit is due for the impetus which the Irish Language movement received in the country districts during those years. He would frequently leave his work on a Saturday evening, take a train West or to some other portion of Ireland, address a meeting in Irish on Sunday, travel back to Dublin again by the night train, and return to work as usual on Monday morning.[33]

In addition to proselytizing for the language in the Irish-speaking districts, Rooney's lasting legacy may be the prominence of the Irish language on 1798 memorials.[34] Typical in this regard is the 1798 memorial in Graigue, Carlow, where the majority of the fifty-three-word inscription is in Irish followed by a twenty-two-word English translation.

> I gcuimhneamh ar sé céid fear agus dá fhichid d'fhearaibh Éireann d'imir a n-anam agus do dhoirt a gcuid fola ag troid mórchatha ar an láthair seo in aghaidh gall an dá ficheadh do Bhealtaine san mbliadhain d'Aois an Tighearna Míle Seacht gCéid nócha a hocht. Suaimhneas síorruidhe go dtugaidh Dia dhóibh.

> Amen. In memory of the 640 United Irishmen who gave their lives for their country at the Battle of Carlow May 25th 1798.

Other bilingual monuments include the Anne Devlin statue in St. Michan's Park, Dublin. Such Irish-language inscriptions in the Gaelic font represent the first manifestations of the Irish Revival in the public sphere. While the Society for the Preservation of the Irish language (SPIL), the Gaelic Union, and the Gaelic League published academic and popular materials, these permanent structures erected in public places were highly visible and elegant in design and execution. They mark the reappearance of the Irish language in post-famine Ireland and its reemergence in the public sphere, as well as its introduction into the cultural politics of commemoration.[35]

When the Belfast-based newspaper the *Shan Van Vocht*[36] closed, to be replaced by the Dublin-based *United Irishman*, the directors offered Rooney the editorship. He declined, hoping instead to tempt his exiled friend Griffith back from South Africa.[37] The *United Irishman* first appeared on March 4, 1899—the same time that Conradh na Gaeilge replaced *Fáinne an Lae* (first issued on January 8, 1898, by Bernard Doyle) with *An Claidheamh Soluis*—and ran until 1906. But the *United Irishman*, under Rooney's guidance, offered a different perspective toward literature written in English than *An Claidheamh Soluis*.[38] Between leading excursions, editing *Seanchuidhe*, working for the Midland Great Western Railway Company,[39] and being the *United Irishman*'s "most prolific writer"[40] from March 1899 to March 1901, he became engaged to Máire Ní Chillín/Máire Killeen (1874–1956).[41] Their marriage, scheduled for May 1901, never occurred. A "serious cold" contracted in March 1901 led to a rapid deterioration of his health.[42] Tuberculosis caused his death on May 6, 1901; a death, according to Yeats, that "plunged everybody into gloom."[43] His close friend Griffith "was desolate and for many weeks his pen recorded little but his grief. His family and Rooney's had lived in the same house . . ."[44] He was buried at Glasnevin, where allegedly more than thirty floral wreaths garnished his coffin,[45] and the national newspapers mourned his premature death. The *Southern Star* lamented that:

> in the death of William Rooney at the age of twenty-seven, Ireland has lost, as a contemporary well puts it, "The Davis of the National Revival." For the past two years his contributions to the Gaelic and extreme Nationalist journals, under the signatures of a.k.a.—Fear na Muintire, Criadhaire, Sliabh Ruadh, Clann an Smoil, Shel Martain, Knocksedan, Killester, Feltim, Ballinascorney have awakened true nationality in the hearts of thousands.[46]

Máire Ní Chillín/Máire Killeen, his Mayo-born fiancée, a leading member of the Ard-Chraobh of Conradh na Gaeilge, was among the Gaelic League's most active female members and was a vice president of Inighidhe na hÉireann. In June 1904, three years after Rooney's death, she married Donegal-born Patrick Bradley/Pádraig Ó Brolcháin (1876–1934), who had edited Rooney's ballads and poems and provided a highly hagiographic account of his wife's former lover in a volume entitled *Poems and Ballads: William Rooney* (1901). On Lady Gregory's advice, the *Daily Express* editor E. V. Longworth offered this volume for review to a young Irish writer about to depart Ireland for Paris. The volume and its damning review might well have sunk into the mists of time had the reviewer not been James

Joyce. Griffith, among others, never forgave him for his slight on their dear dead friend.

> Though Rooney's poetry had been acclaimed in patriotic circles, it didn't warrant such honours according to Joyce. Rooney "has no care . . . to create anything according to the art of literature," Joyce wrote, because "patriotism has laid hold of the writer." Instead of literature, all Joyce found was "a weary succession of verses, 'prize' poems—the worst of all." . . ."[T]hey have no spiritual or living energy, because they come from one in whom the spirit is in a manner dead . . . a weary and foolish spirit, speaking of redemption and revenge, blaspheming against tyrants, and going forth, full of tears and curses, upon its infernal labours." Though he admired a translation Rooney had made from a poem by Douglas Hyde, Joyce found there was "no piece in the book which has even the first quality of beauty, the quality of integrity, the quality of being separate and whole . . ." Joyce's sense that patriotism made bad poetry was made explicit in his comment that Rooney "might have written well if he had not suffered from one of those big words which make us so unhappy." Arthur Griffith, on the other hand, saw Rooney's patriotism as being what made his poetry significant, and used this line of Joyce's in an advertisement for the book, inserting the word patriotism in brackets after "one of those big words."[47]

Ó Luing interprets Joyce's action as

> Éireannach ag scríobh i bpáipéar Sasanach ag lochtúchán ar shaothar náisiúnta Éireannaigh eile, ba leor san chun Art Ó Gríofa a ghríosadh chun feirge, ach nuair b'e a chara ionmhain a bhí i gceist ina theannta san ba dheacair dó an gníomh a mhaitheamh agus is rud cinnte nár mhaith.[48] [An Irishman writing in for English paper faulting the nationalist work of another Irishman, such was suffice to enrage Arthur Griffith, but the fact that it was his dear friend made it difficult for him to forgive the deed, and he certainly never did.]

Given Joyce's disparagement of Rooney's verse, it is ironic, as Frank Shovlin argues convincingly, that the title character of Rooney's poem

"The Priest of Adergool: An Incident of the Connacht Rising"—a poem that won a prize offered in 1898 by the *Weekly Freeman* for the best poem written on an incident in the 1798 rebellion—is the origin for Fr. Conroy, Gabriel's brother and a senior curate in Balbriggan, in Joyce's famous story "The Dead."[49]

The Celtic Literary Society:
A (Broadly) Political Gaelic League?

Rooney, shaped by the Fireside Club, joined the pro-Parnellite Leinster Literary Society that assembled at Marlborough Street.[50] While Griffith was at the fore in issuing statements of support for Parnell as president and vice president, Rooney began attending meetings in early 1891, before joining as a member on February 13, 1891. On February 27, he read a paper on "Art M'Morrough O'Kavanagh." He soon became editor of *Eblana*, the Society's manuscript journal, and as vice president signed the minutes. Despite his claim that he was "never a supporter of Parnell but an indifferent nationalist," Griffith issued another "Address to C. S. Parnell" that Rooney also signed in 1892. The 1892 split ruptured the Society, which dissolved on December 9, 1892.[51] Some members reconstituted themselves as *Comh-Chumann Gaedhilge Éigseach*/Celtic Literary Society, and convened for the first time in September 1893 at 32 Lower Abbey Street.[52] The decision to establish the Society apparently occurred at a meeting at Rooney's North Strand home on February 3, 1893.[53] Its most active members other than Rooney, as Seamus MacManus recalled, were Griffith, Denis Devereax, Peter White, Pádraig Ó Brolcháin, and Tom Cuffe.[54] Rooney served as the Society's president and the editor of its manuscript journal, *An Seanachuidhe*.

The Celtic Literary Society aimed "to educate every inhabitant to the errors of the past; the needs of the present and the possibilities of the future."[55] The *Freeman's Journal* reported the Society's objectives were "to spread as much knowledge of their own country amongst the working youth of Dublin, as the utilitarianism of the time had obliged them to know about others, and by creating an appetite for

native literature prepare the way for the works promised by the pro-
jectors of an Irish Library."[56] The *Flag of Ireland* reported "the main
object of the society, which was provide for the working youth of
Dahlia society that would make them acquainted with the literature
and history of their country."[57] Its goals were fourfold: (1) The study
and cultivation and support of the Irish language, (2) The extension of the knowledge of the Irish language, history and antiquities,
(3) The popularizing of Irish music, and (4) The encouragement of
Irish industries. The stated principles of the Society were "broadly
National, being Non-Sectarian and Non-Partisan." The key words
"broadly National" and "non-partisan" were of tremendous significance: they distinguished the Society from the Gaelic League, which
was both nonpolitical and nonsectarian. This distinction allowed the
Society to discuss and engage in politics—and the overlap between
the Society and the Pro-Boer Transvaal Committee is marked—while
simultaneously allowing the League to declare itself as nonpolitical
and above politics. Accordingly, it made the Society a natural fit for
Griffith's An Comhairle Náisiúnta/National Council and, later, Sinn
Féin. It also marked the League as a more appealing proposition for
Irish-language Unionists, Irish-speaking Protestants, and Quakers,
and consequently allowed the League to present itself as a nonsectarian organization whose members practiced a diversity of religions.
With Rooney elected president for the first season,[58] the inaugural
meeting occurred on October 4 at Costigan's Hotel, 38 Sackville
Street/Upper O'Connell Street, where Rooney delivered the opening address entitled "Sir Samuel Ferguson."[59] Griffith had joined the
Society before emigrating to Africa and, on his return to Dublin, was
elected vice president in September 1899 and president the following
year.[60] The Society subsequently announced its meetings were "open
to ladies, who do not require tickets."[61] If ladies, with or without
tickets, were welcome as guests at meetings, the issue of female membership of the Society would soon surface.

Relevant here is the issue of timing. This is early October 1893.
Douglas Hyde would deliver "The Necessity for De-Anglicising Ireland" to the Irish National Literary Society several weeks later on

November 25, 1892. Subsequently published in *The Revival of Irish Literature*[62] by Fisher Unwin in 1894, the lecture led to the creation of the Gaelic League/Conradh na Gaeilge at Martin Kelly's civil service academy at 9 Lower Sackville Street, Dublin, on July 31, 1893. The League's aims were twofold: (1) The preservation of Irish as the national language of Ireland and the extension of its use as a spoken language and (2) The study and publication of existing Gaelic literature, and the cultivation of a modern literature in Irish. In addition to the Roscommon-born and university-educated Hyde, the founding members included Charles Percy Bushe (Dublin-born civil servant in the Four Courts), Thomas Walker Ellerker (Yorkshire-born senior official at the Four Courts), Rev William Hayden S. J. (Waterford-born Jesuit, university educated), Martin Kelly (native speaker from Clare, civil servant in the Four Courts), John McNeill (Antrim-born civil servant in the Four Courts), Patrick O'Brien (Cork-born native speaker, printer), T. O'Neill Russell (West-Meath-born Quaker and commercial traveler in the United States), James Michael Cogan (Dublin-born civil servant in the Four Courts), and Patrick J. Hogan (Limerick-born barrister and civil servant in the Four Courts).

While Rooney and Griffith were working-class Dublin Catholics and largely self-educated, the League's founders were an assortment of Catholics and Protestants, rural and university-educated men. In accounts of Society meetings, the absence of clerics, Catholic or Protestant, is striking and in stark contrast to the ubiquitous presence of Catholic priests and conservative Catholics at all levels of Gaelic League activity. The League embraced women as full members at all administrative levels including the national executive.[63] It also established an impressive network of branches throughout urban and rural Ireland as well as overseas. Despite annual elections, Hyde retained the presidency from 1893 until 1915, and the League's leadership structure remained largely stable with Hyde serving as president for twenty-two years from 1893 until 1915 when the IRB-inspired coup led him to resign on the grounds that the League was no longer nonpolitical.[64] Such stability in leadership ensured continuity in procedure and consistency in policy. The League had become "Hyde's

League" and as such linked the League in the public mind and media to a particular individual who came to personify the organization. The Society, on the other hand, never achieved that consistency of leadership or national profile.

Having expanded membership to women in 1894, they admitted non-Dublin members in 1895. Such corresponding members paid a fee of 2s 6d per year that entitled them "to all the privileges of ordinary membership" whenever they were in Dublin.[65] This fee later rose to 4p per week for Dublin-based members and ½ crown per year for country members. In terms of membership fees it was lower than peer organizations: the Gaelic League 5 shillings[66] ($2 for Americans); SPIL 10 shillings (Associates 1 shilling); the National Literary Society 10 shillings; the Irish Texts Society 7s 6d ($2 for Americans); and the London-based Irish Literary Society 21 shillings.[67] The Society evidently saw itself initially as Dublin-based only rather than following the Gaelic League or GAA model of establishing numerous local branches scattered throughout the provinces. This lack of a geographical spread not only reduced its overall influence, but limited membership and restricted revenue.

Unlike the fractious relationship between the Gaelic League and the Society for the Preservation for the Irish Language (SPIL), the Society's 1900 report testifies to close links with the Gaelic League. The Society's choral class, "as well as assisting on all occasions in the gaiety, aided the Central Gaelic League in making the evening concert of the Feis Laighean a success, rendering the choruses in Gaelic, and assisting also later on in the chorus organized for the Oireachtas."[68] The Society also boasted that its language classes "have all but outgrown the facilities provided, and are amongst the best attended in the city," and congratulated itself that "many of the classes at present held in connection with the Gaelic League branches are being taught by scholars who gained their knowledge of Irish mainly in the society's classes, and point to the fact that we possess the only class which has existed without a week's interruption for the past seven years."[69] Not only did the Society maintain a productive relationship with SPIL, but also "the relations of the society with the League have been most friendly, and will, we trust, remain so while one enemy of an Irish-Ireland remains to be combatted. The committee desire to thank the Society for the Preservation of the Irish language for the gift of prizes for the classes."[70]

Given his engagement to a leading Gaelic Leaguer, Rooney's interaction with Gaelic League officials, and the lack of hostility between the Celtic Literary Society and the League, why did Rooney never become a senior figure or official in the Gaelic League of which he was a member or, more pertinent, why did the Celtic Literary Society never affiliate with the League and become a branch? The answer, it appears, is politics:

> Of the Gaelic League he was always an enthusiastic supporter and worker, though with its policy in some respects he was not in agreement. He thought the term "non-political" was too narrowly construed by the League, and that its policy, to really raise the enthusiasm of the people, must be strongly national in its highest sense—must, in fact, recognize Ireland's claim to complete nationhood, and work with the idea before and towards that ideal.[71]

Kelly discerns that most revivalist organizations "tended to identify themselves as politically non-aligned, but it would be a mistake to equate this with the apolitical principles of the Gaelic League."[72] Unsurprisingly, given the overlap between the Gaelic League and the Society, Rooney was coopted as a League member in May 1896.[73] When he was nominated for the Gaelic League Executive, however, his bid proved unsuccessful.[74] McGee suggests "[a]lthough Rooney had been co-opted as a member of the League's committee for organizing Oireachtas meetings, he was always denied membership of its executive council."[75] The Gaelic League's refusal to participate in the 1798 centenary because it violated its nonpolitical, nonsectarian policy led to tensions with the Celtic Literary Society. While Kelly argues "much of Rooney's thought derived from Hyde's brilliant intervention,"[76] Rooney believed "that a Gaelic League agenda without an explicit separatist dimension would prove to be yet another 'West British' illusion."[77] Yet Bradley, in keeping with the glorification of his subject, states "while holding these views, and giving expression to them when occasion arose, [Rooney] ardently supported the League, and during his tours in the West he placed a large number of branches on a foundation."[78]

On the other hand, the Celtic Literary Society and the Gaelic League found themselves in direct opposition when competing for funds in 1894 from the Mullen Bequest,[79] a considerable amount of money an Irish gun maker in the United States had left for the promotion of Irish in Ireland.[80] By early November 1893, the Young Ireland League and the Celtic Literary Society successfully petitioned the governors of the City of Dublin Technical Schools to provide Irish-language classes in their schools and to appoint a professor of Irish.[81] The same month, the Society opened membership to ladies.[82] The catalyst for this enfranchisement appears to have been Maud Gonne, whose request for membership was initially rejected.[83] The November 1893 report provides a taste of the weekly meetings:

> The routine business having been disposed of the chairman called on the editor to read the current number of the *Seanachie*, the society's MS journal. The contents were numerous and varied, and were very warmly received. They included articles on "Ellen O'Leary, poetess and Fenian," by Ossian; "National Education, Here and Elsewhere," by Sliabh-Martin; "Spranger Larry," by Shanganus; "Inspiration from Mitchel," by Shawn Duin; "Can the Orangemen be Converted?" by Fireghan; "Nationality v Cosmopolitanism," by Kilmaeanogne; and "Wolfe Tone," by Los; "Three Songs—The Little Brown Berry, Rosie Flaherty, and To Die for Motherland," by Anemoe, Ballynagois and Glendhu respectively; "Connaught," a piece of verse, by Hi Fiachra; "Found," some verses by Shemus; the third and fourth chapters of the society's composite novel "The Sons of Cain," and two sketches, "On the Long Car" (Cluain Tarbh), and "A Beautiful Legend" (Kilgobbin) . . . On Wednesday next Mr. John R. Whelan will read a paper entitled "From Freedom to Serfdom" dealing with Ireland from the landing of St. Patrick to the English invasion.[84]

Matters of a political nature frequently appeared as topics for debate. December saw the Society discuss the motion "Could the Irish Nation exist independent?"[85] while other topics included "Will the Celtic become the Ruling Race"[86] and "That English Rule has benefited Ireland."[87] Such subjects conform to Kelly's contention that cultural nationalism offered separatists opportunities to disseminate ideals of Irish self-reliance and the incompatibility of British state authority with Irish progress and prosperity.[88]

Debating was not the Society's sole activity. By early November, Michael Cusack (1847–1906) conducted an Irish-language class every Monday evening at 8 p.m., after the regular meeting. Pádraig Óg Ó Conaire contends that this class, taught initially by Pádraic Mac An Fhailinghe/P. Nally,[89] and subsequently Michael Cusack, existed from the beginning.[90] Cusack's role offers a fascinating cross-over between the Celtic Literary Society, the Gaelic League, the SPIL, and the Gaelic Athletic Association, and shows how interconnected these disparate revivalist organizations were. A nominal charge for membership—2d per week—met the language class's expenses.[91] The Irish language featured again in early 1894 when representatives of the Young Ireland League, the Gaelic League, and the Celtic Literary Society met at 15 D'Olier Street. With Griffith presiding, they discussed an Irish-Language Congress based on the 1882 Irish-Language Congress.[92] Among the bodies represented at the March 27 Easter Congress that convened in the Mansion House's "new" ballroom were clergymen, members of the Christian Brothers' community, and a large number of National schoolteachers.[93] The lord mayor presided, and among those present were representatives of St Patrick's Training College; Marlborough Street Training College; Christian Brothers; and teachers from Clare, Kerry, Galway, Tipperary, Cork, Mayo, Carlow, and Sligo; as well as representatives of the Sheridan Literary Society;[94] the Young Ireland League; the Gaelic League; and the Celtic Literary Society. Several of the speakers addressed the meeting in Irish as well as in English.

The Gaelic League representatives included Michael Cusack, J. MacNeill, T. O'N[eill] Russell, J. J. Barrett, William Byrne, J. Casey,

Thomas Corless, P. Conway, P. Nally, J. Nally, H. A. MacNeill, Miss O'Donovan, Rev. P. O'Leary P. P., William Colbert, Patrick O'Brien, and J. Burgess. The Celtic Literary Society representatives included Wm. Rooney, Joseph Doyle, John R Whelan, M. J. Quinn, P. Morgan, T. Wilson, J. Tinnains, J. M'Cally, P. Nally, John Doras, John Clegg, P. J. Gregan, and S. J. Barrett.[95] The crossover in membership is conspicuous: Cusack (the Society's teacher and GAA founder) and P. Nally (publisher of the Society's textbook) both represented the Gaelic League, while S. J. Barrett (SPIL member and future Gaelic League treasurer) represented the Society. The remarkable interconnectivity and fraternization of people in the Gaelic League and the Celtic Literary Society, as well as the Gaelic Union and the SPIL, reveals the involvedness, intersection, and overlap of this period. The lord mayor, in the course of his address, referred to the 1882 Congress circular and noted among their victories that Irish could now be taught, outside school hours, in national schools; Irish now had a status, along with the dead languages, on Royal University and Intermediate Education curricula; and Irish-language professors had been appointed at Maynooth College, at Clongowes College, and at the St. Stephen's Green University College. The Christian Brothers, as ever, provided classes in many of their schools. Yet, he noted:

> . . . while the advances were so few the deficiencies, which still existed in making the Irish language a useful and a living language, were numerous, and, as far as he could see, they were practically pretty much in the same condition in the year '94 as in the year 1882. No professors had been appointed in the teaching colleges. Out of 8,500 National schools, only 50 schools taught Irish. Prizes were not given in the National schools, and no class books were published. No diocesan colleges, grammar schools, or collegiate institutions, with the exception of Maynooth, Clongowes, Blackrock College, St. Jarlath's College, Rockwell College, and a few others, taught the language . . . no arrangements had been issued for training teachers or for securing that the various persons holding public appointments throughout the country should have that knowledge of Irish which in some parts of the country

at all events would be of great use in communicating with a large section of the people. He hoped that the Congress of '94 would be attended with a greater need for success than that which followed the Congress of '82.[96]

In the summer of 1894, the Society's language class met at 81 Great Britain Street (Parnell Street).[97] A history class was added in the fall of 1894 to teach "Irish history to the youths of the city."[98] In December 1894, Joseph Doyle, the Society's president, proposed a motion at the annual general meeting

> that the teaching of Irish in the primary schools is the surest sign of making its use universal through the country, and as that can only be accomplished by the teachers being thoroughly acquainted with the language, that we call on the managers of the Training Colleges to take immediate steps to make Irish an essential item in their curricula.[99]

The language class, studying O'Growney's books, continued to meet on Monday evenings in 1895 with attendance "open to non-members of the society, of both sexes, on the payment of 1d weekly."[100] The *Freeman's Journal* reported in September 1901 that the Society's Irish classes continued "their success of previous years, and the numbers attending have so largely increased that it is now considered advisable, if not imperative, to assign two nights for the teaching of Gaelic. Perfect unanimity exists between the Gaelic League and the society . . . The committee have again to express their gratitude to the SPIL for their gift of book prizes to our Irish classes."[101]

This collegiality is at odds with the animosity frequently on display between the Gaelic League and SPIL regarding orthography, syntax, grammar, and the very nature and purpose of the Irish language. The Celtic Literary Society seemingly navigated a steady path through the choppy linguistic and sociolinguistic waters of the early Revival. In 1899 Bernard Doyle, based at 9 Upper Ormond Quay, published P. Nally's *Gaduidhe Dubh Ó Dubháin* on behalf of the

Celtic Literary Society.[102] Described as "Gaelic texts, Vol I," this slim folktale, "edited for the Society, with a complete Vocabulary of all the words in the Text," appeared in Gaelic font and in dialectical, rather than classical, Irish. The anonymous preface explains the desire to meet "the want of a reading book and vocabulary, at a low price, which would be suitable for students who had mastered the four books written for the Gaelic league by Father O'Growney, or the three books of the Society for the Preservation of the Irish language." Once again, we see the Society at the fore in editing and publishing vernacular Irish-language texts, as well as providing textbooks that address the needs of those not met by O'Growney's *Simple Lessons*.

A heated debate in 1895 concerning the role of Young Ireland League members led to accusations that the Society served as nothing more than that organization's rump. After one member's resignation, the committee strove to increase membership and, consequently, Rooney recommended Griffith, who was duly elected in November 1895.[103] If the Society limited itself initially to the metropolitan center, by 1900 it was diversifying. In that year, the committee congratulated the Society on the establishment of kindred organizations in Cork,[104] Limerick, Derry, and Mountmellick (Laois) within the previous year, and expressed the desire to cordially cooperate with them in all their undertakings.[105] The Celtic Literary Society in Castlebar also produced a version of *O'Donnell's Cross*, a dramatic adaption of L. McManus' novel *In Sarsfield's Days*.[106] Politics again featured prominently at the Society's seventh annual general meeting, with the president T. P. Fox in the chair. Fox remarked that while the Boers' struggle had commanded members' attention, the session's literary program had been adhered to with fidelity.[107] He recalled how the session opened on Friday, October 6, 1899, with an inaugural lecture on "The Definition of an Irish Nation" presided over by Maud Gonne, and reported that

> [t]he National anniversaries of the session were fittingly honoured. Through the courtesy of the Committee of the Workmen's Club, York street, the Davis anniversary was celebrated there by a lecture

and concert of Davis' songs, rendered by members of the society's choral class. The Mitchell anniversary was commemorated by a lecture delivered by Mr. W. J. Ryan: the Manchester Martyrdom was commemorated by a lecture also delivered in the hall of the Workmen's Club, and the birth of Emmet was commemorated by the usual lecture and concert of songs associated with his memory. . . . The society, through its members, has taken an active part in the informing of public opinion on the merits of the war against the Transvaal, and has been instrumental in exhibiting to the world the opinion of Dublin on the question. Similarly, in the organisation and management of the Patriotic Children's Treat, the members of the various classes of the society were unsparing in their efforts to prove that Irish Nationality has an abiding place in the hearts of Dublin's boys and girls. The committee congratulate the ladies' committee on the magnificent success of its undertaking.[108]

Yet the Society's independent days were numbered. On August 30, 1900, Griffith and Rooney, following up on Griffith's article in the *United Irishman* in March 1900 calling for a new association to unite disparate nationalist groups, established Cumann na nGaedheal as a political organization and umbrella cultural and educational society for advanced nationalist/separatist groups. Collectively, Arthur Griffith, William Rooney, and Maud Gonne[109] fashioned Cumann na nGaedheal's program as "a kind of hold all, its objects were deliberately vague so that any appropriate organization could be included."[110] W. B. Yeats described Cumann na nGaedhael's aim as "[t]he rooting of the whole Irish people in Ireland, the weakening of every force and influence that tends to drive them into exile or makes them unworthy of their fathers while they remain at home."[111] In October, Inghinidhe na hÉireann affiliated and accepted representation on the governing council. If the lines between the Celtic Literary Society and politics were previously somewhat blurred, the Rubicon had now been crossed: the Society joined the new umbrella group on October 19 to "advance the cause of Ireland's National independence."[112] Further integration, and a blurring of identities, followed on January 2, 1901, when the newly founded Cork branch of Cumann na nGaedhael titled itself the Cork Celtic Literary Society. Its attitude on political neutrality was clear and several of its members would figure prominently in subsequent Irish history:

> Seven of the young men who had been in the Young Ireland Society met to form a new society, as a branch of the National Organisation, Cumann na nGaedheal. It was decided to call the Society "The Cork Celtic Literary Society." So that there would be no ambiguity regarding its aim, it put as its object: "To Strive For The Establishment Of An Irish Republic." Immediate means proposed were: 1 A.—Adopting and propagating the principles of the United Irishmen. 1 B.—Working for the restoration of the national language. 2—The study and teaching of Irish History. In another matter the Society adopts the objects of Cumann na nGaedheal. The seven young men were: Terence MacSwiney, Dan Tierney, Batt Kelleher, Fred Cronin, Bob Fitzgerald, Michael Radley, Liam Roche.[113]

Griffith informed the 1901 annual general meeting of the Celtic Literary Society Branch on September 6 that

> the society has sustained the heaviest blow that could possibly have been inflicted on it by the death of its founder and inspirer, William Rooney . . . The death of William Rooney in the dawn of his manhood deprived the society of its bravest labourer. While his hand held the helm we knew all was safe, but now that we are to know him no more, that we are never to hear his voice again urging us to be confident of the future, it behoves us all to persevere more determinedly in the work to which he devoted his life if it is to be carried to fruition.[114]

In 1902, the Cork Celtic Society operated at rooms in Great George's Street, where a very large attendance including many members of Inghinidhe na hÉireann discussed the tenth number of *Éire Óg*, the Celtic Literary Society's manuscript journal.[115] By now the Society was clearly integrated into Cumann na nGaedheal. In 1903, the Liverpool Cumann na nGaedheal branch advertised a series of lectures on Irish history and culture organized by the Celtic Literary Society. The *Southern Star* reported that the "Celtic Literary Society of Cumann na nGaedheal" passed a resolution calling on "Cork Country Council, Cork Corporation, and other public bodies, to reject any address to the English King."[116] In 1904, the usual Dublin weekly meeting learned that Seamus MacManus would deliver the 1905 inaugural address on the topic of "Idealism in Ireland."[117]

On November 28, 1905, Cumann na nGaedhael merged with the Dungannon Clubs and An Comhairle Náisiúnta/the National Council to form a new political party called Sinn Féin.[118] An Comhairle Náisiúnta/the National Council's founding manifesto was a bilingual document with the organization's name in Irish only, but with a subtitle in parenthesis as "The National Committee"—Rooney's legacy was not forgotten. This political organization represented Griffith's policy of national economic, cultural, and political self-reliance and aimed "to establish in Ireland's capital a national legislature endowed with the moral authority of the Irish nation." Despite securing 27% of the vote in the 1908 North Leitrim by-election, it failed as a political party until 1916 when the British authorities mistakenly named the IRB Easter Rising a Sinn Féin rebellion. In 1917, republicans rallied under the banner of Sinn Féin, and the party, in various guises, has participated in Irish and British politics ever since.[119] The same cannot be said of the Celtic Literary Society. Now forgotten, its role in the Irish-language and cultural Revival is disremembered—as is often the fate of minor parties when they merge with larger entities in the pursuit of power.

Conclusion

A consideration of the Celtic Literary Society role sheds critical light on the Gaelic League, messes linear narratives of cause and effect, and lays bare the Revival's messiness. Following Paul Ricoeur, we can envision the Revival as a "subject" was never a given at the beginning; rather it unfolded in the fullness of time as the narrative story unraveled and was told, recorded, and archived.[120] A study of the Celtic Literary Society reveals the overrepresentation of Catholic clerics, for obvious reasons, in rural and provincial League branches, but also the League's active and successful cultivation of Catholic bishops and Cardinals as influencers and guiders of public opinion. Nonetheless, the League proved broad enough to accommodate members of different religions who occupied leading roles within the League, especially at the national level. In contrast, recognition of and participation by clerics appear conspicuously lacking in the Society where priests, ministers, parsons, and nuns are markedly absent. While the Society accepted women after Maud Gonne's intervention, women do not appear to have held leadership roles, unlike the League which accepted women from the start. Unlike the Society, the League ultimately grew beyond Dublin and urban centers, and developed a network of branches throughout Ireland and beyond.[121] With Hyde reelected as president from 1893 to 1915, the League benefitted from a high-profile leader who commanded respect and authority at home and abroad. The university-educated Hyde shrewdly took advantage of his network of academic contacts at the 1898 Commission on Intermediate Education to challenge and embarrass Trinity College. In the process, he raised the League's profile nationally and internationally. Recognizing the importance of publicity, the League established a weekly newspaper and a publishing house, and issued propaganda and promotional pamphlets. Hyde's social origins, academic education, and scholarly reputation facilitated the 1905–6 American fund-raising tour that involved public academic lectures at Harvard, Yale, and the University of California, Berkeley, and two visits to the White House. The League's ambitions were always national, i.e., political, and preserving the language in the Irish-speaking districts was critical. It initiated several successful high-profile events such as Oireachtas na Gaeilge, Irish-Language Week, the Irish-Language Fund, and Hyde's North American tour. The League allied itself with other organizations (GAA, cycling clubs), but retained its own distinctive identity and particular goals.

   In contrast, the Celtic Literacy Society's legacy includes bilingual 1798 memorials, the Irish-language component of Cumann na nGaedheal, the early Sinn Féin, and the establishment of the Irish Literary Theatre. It was the Society that proved instrumental in Alice Milligan writing "The Deliverance of Red Hugh" as a play to celebrate Samhain.[122] The production apparently inspired W. B. Yeats to see his own plays performed with a Dublin accent; the result was *Cathleen ni Houlihan*.[123] The Society's decline may be attributed to Rooney's death and its incorporation within Cumann na nGaedheal. The Society remained prominently a Dublin city-based organization that made little effort to expand beyond the capital or create a network of rural branches. Its Dublin members were regarded as pro-Parnell and pro-IRB. Its rotating presidency, while democratic, prevented the emergence of a strong dominant leader—such as Hyde—who could shape the organization over time and become its public face. The Society's decision to be "nonpartisan" rather than "nonpolitical" allowed for cooperation with political groups, but also made it sympathetic to the IRB. Conversely and critically, the League's nonpartisan clause allowed it, and Hyde, to assert their "nonpolitical" status—a distinction they stressed often and frequently, even after the Society's demise, but the Society's existence allowed for that key distinction to be made long after Sinn Féin subsumed the Society. The Society comprised largely Dublin-based working-class males: the noticeable absence of Catholic clerics in the minutes and newspaper accounts is striking and underlines, by contrast, how comfortable the League was with Catholic clergy and correspondingly the Catholic hierarchy for clergy to be involved in the League. In addition to being urban and working-class, the Society's membership tended to be non-university educated. While widely read and well informed, they tended in large part to be self-educated through extensive use of public libraries.

Whereas the Gaelic League influenced Irish dancing, Irish music and singing, folklore, and place names as well as fashion and design, the Society offers a vision of an Irish-language organization that quickly abandoned its specific agenda and merged with other groups following a broader, vaguer, more generalized political objective. This policy is very similar to that which the League ultimately adopted in 1915 when the IRB forced Hyde's resignation.[124] Yet we may ponder what would have happened had the Society rather than the League blossomed in the nineteenth century's closing years. How different might history be had the League abandoned its nonsectarian, nonpolitical stance much sooner? What if the League had participated in the 1798 commemorations and merged with the National Council and, later, with Sinn Féin? How dissimilar were the later P. H. Pearse's attitudes toward Synge, and Rooney's attitudes toward literature in English? What would have been lost in terms of the Irish-speaking districts and the production of Irish-language literature? Had the League merged with the Society and Inighidhne na hÉireann, what role would Hyde, MacNeill, and Peter O'Leary have played? Had Rooney lived, would he have been the IRB's choice to replace Hyde as president in 1913 and 1915, as it sought control of the League? What role would Rooney have played in the Irish Volunteers or in the cultural politics of the Free State?

The Celtic Literary Society further disrupts the simplistic revivalist narrative that critics have successfully undermined and complicated in recent years. Additionally, it suggests that the Revival may be read as an antinarrative that more closely corresponds to a chaotic discourse than the linear and binary explanation proposed by Yeats. If "narrative" implies a form of discourse in which sequenced events are meaningfully connected (Parnellite splits leads to creation of a cultural group by Yeats and Hyde results in the creation of Irish Free State) an "antinarrative" is a chaotic discourse form "of time without sequence, telling without mediation, and speaking about oneself without being fully able to reflect on oneself."[125] Acknowledging the Society's role in shaping the Conradh na Gaeilge/the Gaelic League and in turn the Revival forces a consideration of the various language organizations' competing, overlapping agendas and motivations. This essay maps those individual revivalist components that follow their own respective paths and aims without binding consideration of, or reference to, the larger manifold of which they form a part, be they individuals or local Gaelic League branches. Through the articulation of their differences, they directly and indirectly shaped each other as part of a larger continual recursive dynamic that was the Revival. Rooney is important for offering a more nuanced and complicated understanding of the politics of the Revival than that binary version offered by Yeats in his acceptance speech. His role in the 1898 commemorations, his success in bringing the Irish language into the public sphere and before the public gaze, and his articulation of an alternative to the Gaelic League and Irish-Ireland's prescriptions of what constituted Irish national literature are critical aspects of the Revival that require elucidation and clarification.[126] Regardless of what Yeats said in his Oslo acceptance speech, the Revival and the Irish-language revival were more complex than he claimed. The story of the Irish-language revival is as much the story of the Society for the Preservation of the Irish Language, the Gaelic Union, and the Celtic Literary Society as it is of Hyde's Gaelic League. When we honor "in song and in story the names of the patriot men, whose valor has covered with glory full many a mountain and glen," we should "[f]orget not William Rooney nor the Celtic Literary Society, who marshalled their bravest and best."

2

Revival, Remediation,
and the Irish Media Habitus

Gregory Castle

In an 1892 lecture for the Irish Literary Society, Charles Gavan
Duffy claimed that "the aim of this society, and of kindred societies,
and of the literary revival[,] . . . is to begin another deliberate attempt
to make of our Celtic people all they are fit to become."[1] First issued
as a "live" statement, then published, along with lectures by Douglas
Hyde and George Sigerson, Duffy's "deliberate attempt" is, in both
instances, a performance: it *does what it calls for*, that is, it educates
the Irish people, attempts to raise them up to what "they are fit to
become." An Irish-Ireland nationalist, Duffy was part of a larger
Revival movement that has only recently come to light, though in
the period I will be focusing on, the 1890s, the Irish-Ireland Revival
was more widely known and influential than the Literary Revival
associated with W. B. Yeats and Augusta Gregory, which was then
in its infancy. Recent trends in Irish studies scholarship have uncovered a wide variety of movements and counter-movements under the
aegis of Revival;[2] missing from these studies, however, is a theory of
what makes possible such a wide variety of projects and practices—
vital manifestations of a larger cultural movement—and what makes
them cohere or constellate under the heading Revival. I offer here, as
a complement to these studies, an understanding of Revival as a complex system, a dynamic social field of production and reproduction,
constituted by statements, texts, and performances, and operating

in terms of interrelation (in a constellation, in dialectics) rather than opposition (in a system of domination). What matters is not the harmony of expressions but the facilitation of emergences, not the steady forward motion of historical progression but the dialectical dynamic of feedback mechanisms. The social practices and aesthetic projects that constellate around the term *Revival* make sense (literally) by virtue of the media habitus in which this dynamic is both encouraged and perpetually altered.

Pierre Bourdieu describes habitus as a social field of production in which "acquired, socially constituted dispositions" take the form of "socialized subjectivity."[3] It is a structure of mobile limits, of "durable, transposable dispositions" that function "as principles which generate and organize practices and representations that can be objectively adapted to their outcomes without presupposing a conscious aiming at ends or an express mastery of the operations necessary in order to attain them."[4] In the "dialectic between habitus and institutions,"[5] "bastard institutions," such as artistic salons and coteries, enable "genuine articulations" between social fields, between "those who hold political power" and the artists who write for the "literary press": "acting as solicitors and intercessors, or even sometimes as true pressure groups, [writers and artists] endeavour to assure for themselves a *mediating control* of the different material or symbolic rewards distributed by the state."[6] Distinction accrues to those who exploit the symbolic potential of the habitus; the result is cultural capital, typically in the form of status and prestige.[7] In order to counter the closed nature of the habitus, as Bourdieu describes it, I introduce Michel de Certeau's critical response to it; that is, I introduce as part of the logic of the habitus a number of tactical approaches to its strategic limitations. These approaches have principally to do with remediation, which I understand to be a process of republication with a rectifying intent (I thus draw on both senses of remediate).[8] Revival discourse emerged in a habitus in which writers and artists found an audience for debate; but more important, they found the means to create that audience within a shared media environment, using many of the same rhetorical and visual tools.

They modeled the idea that feedback in a discursive system takes the form of remediation—both as input (that is, statements, texts, and performances reentering the system in an amended form) and as remedial education. I look at texts by Duffy, Hyde, Padraic Pearse, D. P. Moran, Yeats, and John Eglinton, all published in the 1890s, in the first rush of Revival activism, to see how each illustrates the process of remediation in the habitus and how each reinforces a message about self-improvement for the sake of a future Irish nation.[9]

Ronan McDonald, referring to Yeats's desire to "keep the Gaelic tongue and Gaelic memories and Gaelic habits of mind," writes that "[t]he yearning for a pre-modern organic society must deploy modern media to disseminate itself. And the revival in all its modes suffuses through a burgeoning *fin de siècle* ecology of periodicals, newspapers, and theatres, together with the expanding literate readership generated by education reform in the 1870s and '80s."[10] McDonald's "ecology" corresponds roughly with my conception of the habitus under Irish conditions, that is, an indigenous discursive community in which the distinction accrued by virtue of one's ability to negotiate that environment and its habitués has a powerful rectifying intent. Revivalists found common cause in revolutionary attitudes toward the nation-state, individual freedom, the body as a site of political expression and solidarity, and gender as the contested performative space in which recalcitrant subjects reaffirm the nation by virtue of their necessary resistance to the process of national *Bildung*. Gaelo-Catholic and Anglo-Protestant men dominated this performative space, in part because of the way nationalist discourse valorized and legitimized a form of Irish Republican masculinity, which had arguably come to characterize the subject as such in the habitus. My aim is to show how this subject, and the concept of national Bildung it supported, emerged amid a chorus of dissenting voices. What Moran says of the Gaelic Revival applies as well to the habitus that conditioned its emergence: it "has no definite objective; it is a stirring up, portending no one knows exactly what."[11] But far from ungovernable, the contest and conflict ("stirring up") that was, in fin de siècle Dublin, a daily occurrence in the press and a nightly one in the theater, cohered as a complex system of feedback mechanisms that enabled the rectifying spirit of Revival.

Revival, National Bildung, and the Media Habitus

The rectifying spirit that kindles the enthusiasm of widely disparate revivalists emerged out of the project of national Bildung. Grounded in Hegel and lately explored in a postcolonial context by Pheng Cheah, national Bildung refers to the way nation-states develop, specifically along lines roughly commensurate with those that characterize classical Bildung at the individual level: the harmonious unity of an individual's aspirations and the social world in which they are achieved.[12] Wilhelm von Humboldt's concept of Bildung alluded to here lies at the foundation of a teleological understanding of development that prized organicism and totality, but under the conditions of freedom. His insistence that "[f]reedom is the first and indispensable condition which the possibility of such development presupposes" is echoed in D. P. Moran's call for "the free and full development of every individual" and in Pearse's for the "development of the individual bents and traits of each [pupil], the kindling of their imaginations."[13] The dialectical pleasures promised by the concept of classical Bildung are forestalled in a process that continually reintroduces the forces that dialectical closure must suppress, the *negative term*, the persistence of which Hegel himself recognized.[14]

In the tradition of negative dialectics associated with Theodor Adorno and Slavoj Žižek, this persistence constitutes a form of nonidentity, a refusal to be subsumed into or subordinated to the dominant force in a social totality. The critical difference for colonial nationalism lies in a form of tactical (which is to say, provisional) totalization based on individual experience. "The totality of the nation," Frantz Fanon writes, must be "a reality to each citizen."[15] Totality, then, is not an ideal to be grasped, but the sum of the colonial subject's experience. This "knowable totality," Anjali Prabhu explains in her study of Fanon and Levinas, was "unambiguously oppressive to colonized subjectivity" and stood in bold relief

against infinity, the "unknowable entity" that lies outside conceptual thought.[16] Prabhu's phenomenological understanding of totality
allow us to think of the subject of national Bildung in terms other
than annihilation in dialectical closure. For to understand and communicate the "crushing realities" of the colonized other "involves not
only an empathetic, but also ethical, and therefore completely intelli-
gible, articulation of that other's needs within the *unequal structure
of colonial totality.*"[17] This, I contend, is what happens in the Irish
habitus, where national belonging is a function of a multitude of
voices articulated in a system that organizes disparity, conflict, divergence, and factionalism. In such a system, belonging is not a matter of submission to colonial totality and its unequal and oppressive
structures of feeling. Rather, it is a matter of *disposition*, in the dual
sense of temperament and arrangement, a *feel* for the nation that is
not limited to any geopolitical or historical boundary. As Bloom says
in *Ulysses*, "a nation is the same people living in the same place. . . .
Or also living in different places."[18]

Bloom's apparent confusion might be profitably read as an up-
ending of assumptions about what constitutes a nation, for it uncovers an important aspect of Irish-Ireland Revival: the belief that
the Irish alone should determine what it accommodates, in culture
and in politics. Moran's hardline Irish-Ireland position was founded
on this power of the excluded: "The Gael must be the element that
absorbs,"[19] he claimed, and thereby presented an alternative to the
compromises of parliamentary party nationalism. In the destabiliz-
ing process of a dialectic that fails to totalize, that remains open and
perpetually dissatisfied, the recalcitrant subjects of national Bildung
achieve a kind of positive agency by virtue of their resistance to the
cancellation of their existence in the formation of a "knowable"
social totality. This contradiction, in which the dialectical unfold-
ing of the idea of the Nation is forestalled by recalcitrant negative
elements (which David Lloyd has christened "non-modern" and
Cheah "ghostly"), solicits increasingly sophisticated efforts on the
part of dominant nationalist groups to co-opt and assimilate them.[20]
As Cheah notes, "any project of national Bildung, no matter how

popular, radical, or rational and progressive in its original conception" remains "internally susceptible to ideologization and state manipulation."[21] It also remains susceptible to the "ghost" of what the
nation cannot assimilate, "a defective form of mediation that does
not return to and augment the nation's proper body."[22] The relation
of the ghostly or unmediated other to this body takes the symbolic
form of a haunting that serves to remind those in power that their
ideas of totality can never be realized.

By "tarrying with the negative," to use Žižek's provocative phrase,
the inassimilable elements of the national body—"the remainder
of some *real*, some nondiscursive kernel of enjoyment" that erupts
"into the social field"—confirm both their own freedom and the
ideal of the nation that they have refused.[23] If, in the Irish colonial
context, the hero of personal Bildung is isolated and disconnected
from meaningful opportunities for social cooperation, if formation
is a matter of disharmony and misrecognition, then national Bildung
offers a consolatory vision of Irishness in which the alienated colonial subject is reinvented, through indigenous modes of education, as
a national subject.[24] But while the hero of the classical bildungsroman surrenders heroically to (is negated by) the will of the state (say,
Weimar in the age of Goethe) that underwrites his formation, the
hero of national Bildung in a colonial setting improves himself *for
the nation to come.*

Revival's drive toward national Bildung challenges the distinction between self and society, so vital to Goethe and other Weimer
theorists of Bildung, on the grounds that such a distinction is impossible to maintain, except under conditions of radical misprision. The
freedom and material grounds for social advancement and aesthetic
education, the prerequisites for classical Bildung, do not exist in a
colonial society, except in distorted and phantasmal forms. The pedagogical dynamic of this challenge is not so much *edifying* as *rectifying*, a form of historical and political revisionism subject to a whole
range of ideological commitments—all of which find an airing in the
same media habitus, where traditional temporal tropes (for example,
precolonial, legendary, primeval), are mobilized as alternatives to the

historical field of national development. Such alternatives to modernity bring into prominence the motif of the past's subversive coexistence with the present and its persistent futurity. Revival writers, artists, politicians, and journalists explored the emancipatory power of rectification, particularly in the form of deliberate anachronism, canny use of nostalgia, and other tactical forms of misprision. We might regard these forms of the backward glance as motifs for avoiding more insidious (that is to say, instrumental) forms of historicism that condemn the colonial subject to an ahistorical existence.[25]

The key question for many revivalists was the care of the individual whose commitment, even sacrifice, to national Bildung creates an embodied space bearing the mark of self-improvement projects aimed at solidifying the individual as a *national* subject. Irish-Ireland revivalists exhorted a marginalized and oppressed people to improve itself, promoting, as an exemplar of the people, the healthy Irishman whose heroic masculinity was the expression of national identity. As a result of the perceived degeneration of Irish manhood, a discourse of heroic self-improvement emerged out of the pragmatic concern for the bodies and minds of Irish men, a discourse that often comported uneasily with an anticolonial movement that was strongly feminist at the grass roots.[26] To some degree, the process of sublation whereby the healthy and heroic man embodies the nation parallels a similar (and much more familiar) process by which the figure of woman had come to stand for an ancient people; in both cases, the agency conferred on the iconic figure is bound up with the search for a viable alternative future for Ireland. It must be said, however, that the pragmatic options offered in the name of Irish men prevailed in the habitus over the options founded on the idealism of such figures as Cathleen ni Houlihan, if only because the former were more easily co-opted into Irish-Ireland political platforms.

National health, national development, national Bildung—all depended on sound Irish men. For Moran, the Gaelic League was exemplary; it was a "reasonable and masculine movement" that had the potential of "stirring up the intellect of the people" and making them "sober, moderate, masculine."[27] By the 1890s, a "hyper-masculine republican identity" (as Nancy Curtin puts it), rooted in the republican ideals of Wolfe Tone and the United Irishman, but modified by the ideology of Young Ireland and the Fenians, was readily available to nationalists of every stripe. This form of masculinity was characterized by a cluster of values—civic virtue, chivalry, militant citizenship ("all citizens must behave like soldiers") and sacrifice—that signaled its successful appropriation of imperial forms of "masculine virtue."[28] Far from being the bounty of a rediscovered essence, it was in fact an effect of the habitus: an organically derived, if not necessarily authentic, sense of self conditioned by the media environment in which it arose and flourished. At the same time, deep-rooted uncertainties about the significance of colonial history to an era of national self-determination were assuaged by projects of self-improvement and political education, projects that found their horizon in the same habitus.

This horizon takes the form of a productive disruption to historical time and to standard historical accounts of Irish national aspirations. Habitus, as Bourdieu says, is "a product of history," but it also "produces individual and collective practices—more history—in accordance with the schemes generated by history."[29] It operates on a system of temporality that "ensures the active presence of past experiences, which, deposited in each organism in the form of schemes of perception, thought and action, tends to guarantee the 'correctness' of practices and their constancy over time, more reliably than all formal rules and explicit norms." Habitus does not encourage or valorize a return to the past or its revival as it once was; instead, as a "system of dispositions" it guarantees a kind of "internal law," "a present past that tends to perpetuate itself into the future by reactivation in similarly structured practices."[30] In an Irish context, this guarantee, like the totality that Fanon sees as the sum of each person's national experience, arises in the recognition of the past's "active presence" in the fight against colonial oppression.

It must be noted that Bourdieu's emphasis on an "internal law" alerts us to a general problem in his conception of habitus, that it is "a finished discourse, to which the subject of practice must submit."[31] If habitus is in some ways a closed or bounded "system of cognitive and motivating structures," the "practical work" within the system "is a world of already realized ends."[32] This world acquires its status as a "finished discourse" through "regularities": "Yet these 'regularities' (repetitions) are not *rules*."[33] Partly in response to Bourdieu, Michel de Certeau developed a theory of everyday practice within systems, "a general semiotics of tactics" that subverts strategic thinking and its "mastery of time through the foundation of an autonomous place."[34] For de Certeau, mastery forecloses the subversive potentialities of *tactic*, which resists the constraints of institutional and spatial "localization" and relies "on a clever *utilization of time*."[35] He requires a sense of space that is more fluid and open than the habitus; but his description of this space resonates with a similar sense of "durable dispositions" within a "finished" system. Like the habitus, it is "actuated by the ensemble of movements deployed within it [and] occurs as the effect produced by the operations that orient it, situate it, temporalize it, and make it function in a polyvalent unity of conflictual programs or contractual proximities."[36]

The Irish media habitus exhibits just this "polyvalent unity," a structure of bounded openness, self-correcting and self-legitimizing, which governs a fluid set of dispositions, multiple sites of power and prestige in a variegated media environment, concentrated in Dublin, which included newspapers, book series, lectures, pamphlets, and so on. In the context of colonial Ireland, the habitus necessarily "tarries with the negative"; unruly and unassimilable elements of the social totality gain a hearing, mainly in the press, the dominant institution in the habitus. Cheryl Herr has written of the Irish press at this time that it "was an institution marked by contradictory stances, some of them from other institutions, some self-generated, but all struggling to gain cultural supremacy." Her reading of the "Aeolus" episode of *Ulysses*—which takes place on the premises of the *Freeman's Journal*—emphasizes the links between form and "institutional power" and suggests that the "truth" about Irish culture "is to be found . . . in the complexities and complicities of cultural coding—in the social institutions that create 'subjects' and explain to them their domination *masked* as history."[37]

The "contradictory stances" Herr mentions can be explained by reference to a media habitus that maintains them in a kind of productive equilibrium. If the press, as an institution, "explained" domination by inviting readers to misrecognize it as the transcendent engine of history, it also entertained alternative explanations, in which the mask is thrown off. For while the nationalist press often served, through compromise, the dominant power, the *advanced* nationalist press served a constituency that sought to overcome domination and compromise.[38] Nevertheless, both served an educational ideal, which, according to Mark Hampton, prevailed in the early days of print culture and peaked at the turn of the century in the radical and working-class press in England that sought to promote education as the means "to attain representation."[39] Maud Gonne described the Irish press in similar terms as "as 'a great educative force,' and as a primary source for cultural regeneration and civic instruction."[40] The press came to exhibit the "practical consciousness of language," as Cheah describes it, which functions as a "self-recursive mediation that facilitates the subject's self-proximity or presence to itself, thereby maintaining at the collective level the national organism's integrity."[41] The remedial aim of the media habitus would thus be "to resurrect the national spirit through the formation of a critical public sphere that continually presses against the state in order to inspirit it and transfigure the degraded present."[42]

Revival institutions in the habitus—particularly universities, literary societies, the Gaelic League, the Abbey Theatre[43]—produced lectures, magazines, and in-house publications with this "inspiriting" aim in mind. However, as Christopher Morash points out, no significant media innovation originated in Ireland.[44] So the distinction must lie elsewhere, in the way the media and its innovations were actually used, particularly in a complex and contentious environment in which political opinion, social commentary, and aesthetic expression drew on many of the same themes, the same tropes, and the same enthusiasm for Irish national self-determination. Amid a factionalized and ideologically varied field of production, and in "bastard institutions" that co-opted imperial technology, the habitus created, to modify Benedict Anderson's phrase, an endlessly *reimagined* community.[45] At times, the self-consciousness of opinion and debate, the centrality of public performance in the cultural life of the city, gave the media habitus the quality of a social drama, one in which misrecognition and rectification were staged as part of a community's articulation of its own social mores and moral values.[46] Central to many of the debates in the media were classrooms and lecture halls, libraries, museums, and other institutional spaces that were not only sources of knowledge for texts and statements but also locations for the performance of this knowledge. A good example of this performativity is Joyce's account, in *Ulysses*, of Stephen Dedalus's Shakespeare "lecture" in the National Library, which takes on a theatrical quality that emphasizes the social distinction of Joyce's cast of characters and Shakespeare's importance as a normalizing force in the habitus.[47]

By the late nineteenth century, the Irish media habitus—a diffused and disunified yet tightly interconnected network—was caught up in the general project of modernity. A transnational web of communication links (the so-called "Victorian internet"[48]) created unique opportunities for anticolonial nationalism to further both its cause and its institutional presence beyond Dublin, Belfast, and the larger provincial cities. Revivalists and nationalists across the spectrum took advantage of these opportunities and produced a long tradition of nationalist journalism (beginning in earnest with the *Nation*) that had undergone, in the 1890s, a transformation as the publishers in Dublin and London came to recognize the impact and influence not only of Revival but of the media habitus that subtended it. Articles that once might have whipped up enthusiasm, only to disappear from view in the daily papers, could reach a broader audience in a republished and recontextualized form, one that more explicitly and formally sought to educate that audience. In this way, Revival confronted colonial modernization with tactical appropriations of

existing institutions and technologies for indigenous and anticolonial ends, the "alternative modernity" that P. J. Mathews discerns in
Revival at large.[49]

Media and Remediation in the Habitus

Misrecognition requires recognition, logically and temporally; the relationship is similar to what we find in the media habitus between
mediation and remediation. On the one hand, it is a simple matter of
initial publication (or performance) and subsequent republication in
the daily press. On the other hand, it is a much more complex matter of
understanding the habitus as the site of remedial actions, attempts to
rectify misunderstandings and deliberate falsifications—all the forms
of misprision that characterize the colonizers' transformation of the
colonized into an absolute other. Remediation introduces a delay between iterations of a work and in this duration arises complexities and
nuances that serve as correctives or amplifications to a prior version of
a discourse (its first-order mediation); in Bourdieu's terms, elements of
the discourse reactivate familiar "structured practices" at a later time
and under new conditions of enunciation. By reorienting perspectives,
clarifying and rectifying earlier statements, remediation clears out a
more substantial ground, within the habitus, for that great collective
assemblage, the Nation. This was prominently the case in the texts I
examine in the following sections: Moran's *Philosophy of Irish Ireland*; Pearse's *Three Lectures on Gaelic Topics*; the lectures by Duffy,
Hyde, and Sigerson in *The Revival of Irish Literature*, and the articles
by Yeats, Eglinton, Russell, and Larminie in *Literary Ideals*.[50] In the
space of about eight years, these texts (and others like them)—first as
articles and lectures, then as books or pamphlets—redefined Revival
for the twentieth century, moving away from the idea of antiquarian
preservation toward the project of national Bildung. Understood in
this way, Revival is less a matter of recovering an ancient birthright
than of securing a foothold in the future.

Moran's *Philosophy of Irish Ireland* explicitly links this urgent
sense of futurity to the need for republication. His preface to the first

edition (1905) aligns the Irish-Ireland perspective of his past writings with the newspaper he would come to edit. The articles that make up the volume were first published in the *New Ireland Review*, 1898–1900 and "contain the reflections, the arguments, and register the convictions that led up to the starting of the *LEADER*." He makes a point of mentioning, several times, that *Philosophy of Irish Ireland* is a republication, as if that fact were essential to understanding its full message. "The author believes that the republication is opportune at the present time, and that the volume will be welcomed by the serious and sincere thinkers who are the inspiration and the mainstay of all intellectual and moral movements." Yet the opportunity referred to did not require emendation: "I have added nothing to the articles, and the total amount of the subtractions would equal only about four or five lines."[51] What matters is that the articles have been *republished together*, and in this new form they seek to overcome or *remedy* a variety of misrepresentations and misunderstandings about the Gael.

The project of remediation suggested here, driven by an educational ideal, proved popular, as indicated by Moran's preface to the second edition (also 1905). Stressing remediation in its most material sense, he confesses that the printers "had broken up the type," not realizing that the volume would sell, and then remarks that "the mere running out of print would not induce me to go to the expense of having the text re-set," were there not demand for the volume. What he notices in the preface is a continuation of interest, over five years, in writings that were, strictly speaking, ephemeral, but were also carefully archived (the broken and reset type serves as an apt symbol of this paradoxical condition). Their republication makes them more accessible (for those who could afford the book) but it also markedly different, despite Moran's claim that he did not significantly alter them. They fly now under a different flag; as texts of political philosophy, they reenter the habitus at a crucial turning point in the years leading up to the Rising. His central question, raised again in the aftermath of King Edward VII's visits in 1903–4, can only seem more urgent:

The condition of a country might appear quite hopeless at the first glance, but if there were a real and virile national spirit left in it it would be too soon to say that the nation was dying. That reflection brings us to the question: Is there such a national spirit in Ireland at the present time?[52]

If such a spirit has suffered at all, it would appear that history is to blame. For while Moran wouldn't "dare to find fault with [his] countrymen," he imagines that anyone who did would be "instantly told that there are historical causes which explain all our defects."[53] He points out that "any attempt on the part of the people to make Ireland Irish, to restore her language, to resurrect her old customs and modernise them" is "tortured into an attack upon politicians, a danger to the country, and a wile of the devil."[54] It is against this distortion and misrecognition of the people's will that he issues his call for "the free and full development of every individual [which] will in no wise endanger or weaken any political movement."[55]

Indeed, only through such freedom can Ireland become the "absorbing power" that historically had made it "a strong, positive entity."[56] "The foundation of Ireland is the Gael," Moran famously wrote, "and the Gael must be the element that absorbs."[57] This idea of Ireland is echoed, in a less triumphant vein, by Hyde when he speaks of north-east Ulster, "where the Gaelic race was expelled and the land planted with aliens, whom our dear mother Erin, assimilative as she is, has hitherto found it difficult to absorb." What "the battleaxe of the Dane, the sword of the Norman, and the wile of the Saxon were unable to perform," Hyde concedes, "we have accomplished ourselves. We have at last broken the continuity of Irish life."[58] *Philosophy of Irish Ireland* is an attempt to repair this broken continuity, to reassert the right of the Irish people to determine what influences and alters its national identity. This inclusive geopolitical thesis is complemented by the spiritual-moral argument for Gaelic literature put forward by Pearse in *Three Lectures on Gaelic Topics*,[59] which brings together lectures Pearse gave between March 1897 and January 1898 as president of the New Ireland Literary Society. Their publication changes the mediation from performance (in which he *speaks* in the company of others) to text (in which his statements are *read* by others). In remediation, genre, mode, and authorial intention undergo a shift. Pearse refers, in his preface, to the "lectures or papers" he is presenting, as if he wishes not to establish a clear line of distinction between performance and text; moreover, the lectures were "not originally intended to see the light of publication," but publication, he recognizes, would shed new light on the questions raised in them. Like Moran, he insists that only a few "emendations" were made, because he wanted to "send them forth as nearly as possible in their original forms."[60] He is noting, as Jacques Lacan did in a similar situation, that his text "will be halfway between" an oral performance and a written text. The only way *in* to the former is through the latter.[61] And though remnants of Pearse's oral performance linger in a style that is at once self-effacing—he can make only "a few rapid and tentative remarks"[62]—and assertive—"No Mr. Chairman, emphatically no"[63]—these remnants attach to a new original, a written artifact subject now to the "structured practices" of the media habitus.

Pearse recognizes that his written text will be quite different from his lectures, but he is canny enough also to recognize that, through his written text, his voice will be heard by many *for the first time* (the event of remediation); readers are reminded—in the preface and footnotes, in the numerous asides, in the cadence and flow of the author's rhetoric—of the living moment in which they were first uttered (the event of a first mediation). The author establishes a need for republishing when he writes in the preface that his "main object . . . has been to assist, in some little degree, in spreading the reputation of the Society."[64] His object is part of a larger pedagogical goal, the restoration of Gaelic as a living language with a living literature, and his lectures are meant to educate the "ordinary reader."[65] That they retain something of their vital oral character means that the remediation process does not transform them so much as *open them up* so that their pedagogical value can be recognized and exploited.

In the first lecture, Pearse examines a long tradition of romantic prose literature—part of it a mixture of genuine history and fiction—and notes that in the preceding three centuries there was "a period of decline, fall, and finally, resurrection."[66] For him, resurrecting Gaelic literature, and the bardic sensibility that created it, entails not a revival of the bardic era but a vision of the future built on the values and spirituality found therein—a vision that he confesses may be "far too rosy."[67] The future of the "Gaelic race" hinges on noble ideals and a sense of manly fortitude, but even when these are strongly in evidence, so too is the paradox of this futurity—"Gaelic literature, like the Gaelic race, has long been dying, but it is 'fated not to die'"—which leavens the "extravagance of our enthusiasm."[68] If the Gael is "fated not to die," it is because of the idealism indigenous to Gaelic culture. "In his folk-songs the Gaelic peasant reveals himself in a new light to us," Pearse writes in the second lecture. "We behold him wandering in an ideal world of his own."[69] A durable future, even a conception of eternity, can be discerned in the folk song's "simplicity of language and beauty of thought," which guarantee the future of the Gael, for "if they live, then, too, will our race live 'go *bruinn an bhrátha*'" [to the brink of doom].[70]

In the third lecture, on "The Intellectual Future of the Gael," Pearse exploits the performative nature of his rhetoric to drive home the point that the Gaelic ideal, however imperfect its acquisition, is a necessity if the future is to be defined by freedom, self-determination, and spiritual unity. As with the footnote to the previous lecture, the introduction and address to the chairman are retained for no other reason than to establish the performative context of the written text; it is a trope of the habitus, a way of accounting for, and exploiting, remediation, granting to the published text something of the authority and emotional appeal of the initial performance. This leavening of the written form with traces of oral performance gives a greater sense of urgency to Pearse's enthusiastic proposal for an "intellectual future" grounded in Gaelic literature, a proposal which asks to do nothing less than to create the conditions for Bildung on a national scale. These conditions cannot be created out of modern literature, whose "unnatural senility" is the antithesis of the Gaelic temperament: "Now, this may be modern, and up-to-date, and all that; but, I ask, is it pure, good, healthy, natural literature? Is it literature which tends to exalt the soul, to make us better, holier, happier? No, Mr. Chairman, emphatically no."[71] Like Standish James O'Grady, who sought to resuscitate the heroic ethos subtending the legend of Cuchulain and the Red Branch of Ulster, Pearse wants to find in literature the *soul* of the Gael, "his love for nature and his veneration for his heroes," which is "a soul-lifting and an ennobling thing."[72] The spirit of the "mighty heroes" is not dead, he insists; it lives on in "our irresistible, overmastering conviction that we, as a nation, are made for higher things."[73] The "vague longings" for these "higher things" are bound up with an intellectual force: "Nothing seems to me so certain, nothing seems to me so logical a *consequence of our temperament*, of our history, of our present circumstances, as that, if we are to have any future, *it must be an intellectual future*."[74]

Perhaps this is why Pearse sought to republish his lectures, for by doing so he took a step toward the very future for which he advocated. Like Moran, he believed that previous generations of nationalists—from the United Irishmen to O'Connell's Repeal Association to Young Ireland—did not seek in the essential Gael the very things they desired.[75] *Three Lectures*, like the other texts under consideration here, underscores the importance of indigenous intellectual traditions, hence Pearse's insistence on the importance of Gaelic literature understood as an artifact not of a distant past but of present thought and expression. And hence the necessity of his "far too rosy" picture of the future of Gaelic artistic and intellectual life. "I *am* an enthusiast," he tells the chairman of the Society, in closing his third lecture,

> and I glory in being one. To those who would object that the sketch I have attempted to give of the intellectual future of our race is a mere ideal picture, I would reply that it is *intended* as an ideal picture. If you wish to accomplish anything great place an ideal before you, and endeavor to live up to that ideal.[76]

Pearse's *Scoil Éanna* (St. Enda's School) was just such an ideal, a radical experiment in revolutionary pedagogy that rejected the norms of the British school system in Ireland. "There is no education system in Ireland," Pearse writes in "The Murder Machine." "The English have established the simulacrum of an education system, but its object is the precise contrary of the object of an education system. Education should foster; this education is meant to repress."[77] His "education system of a people" would develop a "national consciousness enshrined mainly in a national language"[78] and do so by "reactivating" the indigenous practice of fosterage as an alternative to state-sponsored education, which he regarded as the "universal provider of ready mades, aiming at turning out all men and women according to regulation patterns."[79] Like Humboldt, Pearse believed that individual formation was possible only under the conditions of freedom. "I plead for freedom within the law, for liberty, not license, for that true freedom which can exist only where there is discipline, which exists, in fact, because each, valuing his own freedom, respects also the freedom of others."[80] This meant honoring the inclinations of his pupils,

> the formation of [their] characters, eliciting and development of the individual bents and traits of each, the kindling of their imaginations, the placing before them of a high standard of conduct and duty, in a word, the training up of those entrusted to its care to be strong and noble and useful men.[81]

In this programmatic statement, Pearse aligns his Humboldtian pedagogical theories with the "too rosy" nativist picture he had painted a decade earlier. In the years between *Three Lectures* and "The Murder Machine," he had refined his sense of the "national factor in education," in part by absorbing the lessons of the Montessori system and bilingual education in Belgium.[82]

The concern for "national consciousness," as articulated through stages of mediation in the habitus, links Moran and Pearse in a common Irish-Ireland project of national *Bildung*. What made their statements, texts, and performances durable and authoritative (if not necessarily authentic) was their intercalation in the media habitus, where they resonated across the ideological spectrum, linking disparate institutional associations and coteries through the tactical use of tropes and images (for example, the Gael, the bard, the fosterling, Cuchulain) that sustained long-standing indigenous modes of expression. Through the technique of remediation—which is, in essence, the creation of new grounds for recognition—each of these authors generated feedback within the habitus, which was itself reframed in terms of revised statements, enlarged and restructured texts, and performances that opened up to include responses to them.[83]

A Battle of the Books

Pearse's St Enda's School represents an institutional approach to education, but it is an institution of revolution, established to inculcate a vision of nature-love and hero-love that would glorify "beauty, strength, manhood, intellect, and religion."[84] The Irish-Ireland politics reflected in Moran's and Pearse's writings predicate a vision of education as an instrument of national Bildung attuned to both political and moral improvement. In Pearse's lectures, Gaelic-language literature emerges time and again as a touchstone for one indigenous future; in Moran's *Philosophy of Irish Ireland*, the geopolitical principle of Gaelic absorption prepares for another. Now I wish to shift the focus of analysis to Duffy, Hyde, Yeats, and Eglinton, who marshal some of the same arguments—for indigenous literary traditions, for the heroic ethos of legends, for the spirit of the Gael—outside of the Irish-Ireland political framework.

In 1893, Duffy, Hyde, and Sigerson brought out *The Revival of Irish Literature*, in which Duffy and Hyde argued strenuously for the reformation of Irish education and culture, while Sigerson argued for the importance for Revival of Irish legend and literature. These lectures were first heard as addresses to the Irish Literary Society in London, which Duffy chaired, in the period 1892–93. Though first read and, shortly thereafter, published in London, they had a powerful impact in Ireland, especially Hyde's "The Necessity for De-Anglicising Ireland," which called for a return to the Irish language, Irish names, and all manner of Irish cultural practices. Duffy and Sigerson represented a branch of the Literary Revival that was sustained by the ideals of Young Ireland (Duffy edited the *Nation* in the 1840s and Sigerson was later a contributor). They were more interested in establishing the criteria for a national literature than in making a case, as Moran and Pearse attempt to do, for linguistic essentialism and the soul of the Gael.

Duffy's two addresses were early salvos in the Revival struggle for the right to decide what counted as authentic Irish literature, art, and culture. In the first, he proposed a book series that would help young Irishmen regain the cultural capital that years of colonialism had depleted. "The Celts are among the most teachable of races," he notes. "[T]o be wise and successful [Ireland] must harmonise with the nature of the people, and correct it where correction is needful."[85] He emphasizes discipline and practicality in educational matters and praises political and historical figures ("great men") as "representative Irishmen"—a form of misrecognition that precariously occupies the middle ground between naiveté and canniness. When he contrasts "young men accustomed to the dram-drinking of sensational literature" with "young fellows whose first business in life is to make some way in the world,"[86] he indicates not only the precise nature of the emasculation that he perceived all over Ireland—the influence of "sensational literature"—but also the extent to which such influence stood in the way of the young Irishman's Bildung-process.

In the second lecture, which reports, one year later, on the success of the book series, Duffy insists strenuously on the continuing need for national self-improvement: "What writers ought to aim at, who hope to benefit the people, is to fill up the blanks which an imperfect education, and the fever of a tempestuous time, have left in their knowledge, so that their lives might become contented and fruitful."[87] Like his Irish-Ireland peers, he swerves from the program of aesthetic education advocated by Humboldt and Friedrich Schiller in the direction of more pragmatic self-improvement projects.

He urges his readers to attend more vigorously to their mental and moral training and their physical hygiene—elements of national life that, in his view, literature ought to promote and defend. In a meeting of the Literary Society in 1892, Duffy remarked that "the training of books was the best training a young man could get, and if they formed a library they should publish books of a practical character. . . . Formerly people were stimulated with poetry, but the condition of the country was now too serious for madrigals."[88] The library here proposed is precisely what Duffy's first lecture describes: a "serious" plan of national self-improvement that would forego "madrigals" in favor of practical subjects like history, oratory, and politics, on the assumption that "the Celts"—despite their "imperfect education"—"are among the most teachable of races."[89] Publications on great events and personages of the recent Irish past would solidify and legitimize a Young Ireland vision of the Irish nation and the Irish people.

To some extent, Duffy's lectures—particularly the form they take in republication alongside Hyde's polemical "De-Anglicising Ireland"—are a riposte to Yeats, the up-and-coming revivalist who had the same idea for a book series, but with a different vision and reading list: Duffy favored history, biography, and criticism, while Yeats favored imaginative literature grounded in ancient legends.[90] The conflict between them, ostensibly over titles, illustrates a larger divergence within Revival ranks between the cosmopolitanism of the Literary Revival and the provincialism of Young Ireland and its fin de siècle adherents in the Irish-Ireland movement. At the same time, this "battle of the books" is a battle of generations, in which Duffy plays the role of a storied and somewhat notorious eminence grise. John F. Taylor, a barrister, writer, and orator, spoke for many moderate nationalists when he claimed that Duffy would act as a "safeguard" against national enthusiasm: "the danger is lest the new company should be used as a propagandist machine for sectional ideas and principles in conflict with the sentiment of the people."[91] Yeats, who at this time claimed to embrace the radicalism of John Mitchel, clearly understood the subtext of Taylor's message and responded in the *Freeman's Journal*, saying that he had no intentions of manipulating a book series for "sectional" purposes. What concerned him were the criteria for selection: will the series "publish the right books on the right subjects, and if it does so, will it be able to put them into the hands of a sufficient number of Irish readers?" Yeats thought the goal should be "to interest the people of Ireland in intellectual matters by giving them books of the kind they seek for."[92] Yeats held that Irish literature was rooted in an ancient legendary tradition whose heroic ethos would strain at the limitations imposed by the Young Irelander's moralistic pedagogy. As he put it in an essay for the *United Irishman* in October 1891, "[i]magination, and not learning, is the centre of life," and in the books he recommends "dwells the best imagination of National Ireland."[93]

Like Duffy, Yeats understood the importance of "bring[ing] books, and the movements and 'burning questions' of educated life, to the doors of a people who are scattered through small towns and villages."[94] And, also like Duffy, he was not entirely immune to masculinist ideology, "heroism, the love of true manhood and so on."[95] Where he differed, I think, was in his rejection of the need for the Irish to be more "practical" and in his studied misrecognition that it was precisely the "serious" condition of the country that called for madrigals. In the end, Duffy became editor-in-chief, and Yeats left the field of battle "reduced to arguing about the quality rather than the fact of [the Dublin society's] support for the New Irish Library."[96] The lack of attention to literature, Yeats warned later in a letter to the *United Irishmen* in September 1894, would have dire consequences for the nationalist movement, for it "drives from us those very educated classes we desire to enlist" so "let us bow our heads in silence and talk no more of a literary renaissance, for we can, at least, cease to be imposters."[97]

Duffy may have won the "battle of the books," but Yeats won the war; for in the end, it was the Literary Revival, and especially the theater Yeats cofounded and wrote for, that more successfully altered the terms of Irish cultural debate in the habitus. The irony, of course, is that, as an author and as a political educator, he elicited just the sort of assent to "romantic Ireland" that he accused Duffy of giving to Young Ireland, with the crucial difference that he asked for an assent to imaginary and literary rather than historical and political texts. Duffy wished to promote the lives of great Irishmen, while Yeats sought, in his essays and articles and in journals like *Samhain*, to teach people how to understand art, the imagination, and the worlds they create. However much they may have differed, they worked within a media habitus in which they both commanded respect—Yeats as an upstart, Duffy as a stalwart—and in which they both found ample opportunities to engage in the kind of popular polemics that fitted so well a logic of misrecognition, which thrives on the agonism of statement and counterstatement, error and rectification.

Ad Victus Ire Spolia

At the end of the decade, Yeats and a few other Literary Revivalists of the new generation convened in the habitus to discuss the nature and function of a national literature. The result of this virtual round-table was *Literary Ideals in Ireland*, a collection published in 1899 that reprinted articles published in the daily press by Yeats, John Eglinton, George Russell (A. E.), and William Larminie.[98] According to the editor's note, the reprinted articles "constitute a controversy which was not intended when the first article was written but which spontaneously grew from week to week in the Saturday issues of the *Daily Express*, and developed, as will be seen, a certain organic unity."[99] The instance of the habitus formed here is a metrocolonial conjunction (the *Express* was a Unionist paper[100]) that enabled, among a variety of cultural nationalists, a "certain organic unity"— that is to say, a tactical unification around the idea of the nation. In *Literary Ideals*, the question of national Bildung is recast in terms of a larger temporal development, one that reaches back to prehistorical—and over into *non*historical—epochs. The collected articles were published by the London firm T. F. Unwin, which was known for bringing out new and controversial works, in collaboration with the *Daily Express*.[101] Joyce at least twice invokes the same newspaper to make a point about ambiguous loyalties. In "Aeolus," Bloom notes that J. J. O'Molloy "does some literary work for the *Express* with Gabriel Conroy" and Molly Ivors, the outspoken revivalist in "The Dead," roundly and somewhat teasingly condemns Gabriel for writing in a "rag like that. . . . Now aren't you ashamed of yourself?"[102]

This web of connections, like the roster of authors in *Literary Ideals*, is part of a small and ex-centric domain within the habitus, one that was frequently misrecognized, according to Clare Hutton, as the purview of a "haughty, self-involved Protestant minority."[103] However, the point is not that the authors and publisher of *Literary Ideals* took a minority position, but that the interconnectedness of the habitus enabled a small coterie to accrue distinction through the tactical use of a single institution (the *Daily Express*), one that afforded a number of different sites of literary and cultural production—including those related in Joyce's texts, which level a critical gaze at the operations of the habitus. It also affords the opportunity to remedy potential misreadings of the initial articles. After all, readers may not have seen either their "organic unity" or the full dimensions of the "controversy" that they excited, which could only be understood properly once all the articles were published together; that is, in the form of a retrospective totality.

The controversy had to do with the relation of tradition—folklore, legends, mythology—to modern literary movements. Yeats and Eglinton make the main points. Yeats argues that a national literature must be founded on the old legends "and should always, even when it makes new legends about traditional people and things, be haunted by places. It should make Ireland, as Ireland and all other lands were in ancient times, a holy land to her own people."[104] In response, Eglinton draws out the remedial implications of the Revival use of legend and tradition:

> Finn and Cuculain, if they are to appear once more in literature—
> and I, for one, shall welcome them—must be expected to take up
> on their broad shoulders something of the weariness and fret of

our age, if only to show how lightly they may be carried, and to affright with shadowing masses of truth, such as mortals hurl not now, the uneasy seats of error.[105]

Eglinton plainly sees the legends as a rectifying force, nearly Gothic in its ferocity, which could unleash upon the "uneasy seats of error" (that is, the sites of misrecognition in the habitus) a terrible truth about the "weariness and fret" of the present. In this strange alchemy, truth takes on a fantastic and uncertain shape; it becomes itself a kind of error, an interpretation offered as something given. This Nietzschean move, which demonstrates an artistic approach to truth, seems to distinguish Eglinton's view from Yeats's. The legends, the former writes, "can only be made to live again by *something new added to them* out of the author's age and personality."[106] However, I think Yeats's recognition that "new legends" can be made "about traditional people and things" aligns him more closely with Eglinton than either one admits.[107] This alignment is arguably realized nearly twenty years later when he completed his sequence of Cuchulain plays, in which it is clear that he has come over to Eglinton's position by offering us the legends, but with *something new added to them* that comes from his development as a modernist artist practiced in what Nietzsche calls "good deception."[108]

The renovation of the legends was an explicit element of the Abbey Theatre's public outreach, represented not only by Yeats's attempt to educate audiences about modern drama but also Augusta Gregory's desire to use her *Cuchulain of Muirthemne*[109] to interest children and young people in the ancient Irish past. Her version of the legends was commercially and critically successful, not least because it bore the imprint of her Kiltartan background and produced a version of the Cuchulain legends whose style conveys the ancient past in the cadences and phrases of contemporary speech.[110] Like O'Grady and Eleanor Hull before her, Gregory parlayed her position in the habitus to further her artistic and pedagogical ends through yet another remediation of the Cuchulain story.[111] In this way, a bloodthirsty Iron Age warrior, whose heroic ethos was inimical to modernity, assumed a prominent, even privileged place in the media habitus: from retellings of the Cuchulain story by O'Grady, Hull, and Gregory to Yeats's dramatic cycle to Oliver Sheppard's statue, "The Dying of Cuchulain" (1911), perhaps the most famous icon of Irish national self-determination, which was installed in the Dublin General Post Office in 1935.

The question of national literature and the role of legends, as it was posed in *Literary Ideals*, acquires a significance that transcends the ideology of the newspaper in which it took shape. For we might well regard the responses to it by Yeats and his colleagues as an attempt to forge a unity quite apart from what the *Daily Express* or Unwin might sanction: "a possible chapter of Irish literary history."[112] This "possible chapter" chimes with the efforts of early revivalists, like O'Grady, Yeats, and Gregory and with Joyce's stated purpose in *Dubliners*: "My intention was to write a chapter in the moral history of my country and I chose Dublin for the scene because that city seemed to me the center of paralysis."[113] But Dublin was also the center of media production, and I think Joyce understood the ironic situation in which he found himself: trying to find an Irish publisher for a work that pressed against the "regularities" of the habitus when it comes to representing the truth about Ireland.

The Literary Ideals of Ireland did much to help define the Literary Revival in its earliest days. Like the other volumes examined here, it capitalized on republication, which made possible the differential repetition of statements, texts, and performances rearranged into "a certain organic unity" that not only gives Revival a form of conceptual validity but also replicates, in the ecumenical coming together of variant discourses, the dialectical operation of the habitus itself. As I have tried to show, the tactical operations of the habitus, while embedded in the productive forces of empire, remain mobile and resistant, ready to score, as de Certeau puts it, "lucky hits in the framework of a system."[114] Such "lucky hits" are sometimes camouflaged by the misrecognitions they seem to encourage, as when Yeats, in *Literary Ideals*, emphasizes that "our little romantic movement" is founded in the old legends and a poetry wrought "out of dreams that were dreamed before men became so crowded upon one another."[115] The cultural conversations in the volumes I have been discussing, mediated in the newspaper and lecture hall, then *remediated*, republished under new conditions of recognizability (first as editorial, then as debate), exemplify the media habitus, even as they redefine its limits and the "structured practices" that open them up for those who still dream in the crowds.

Part Two

Revivalism in Print

At Home and Abroad

3

Yeats, Gregory, and the Revival's Print Cultures

Marjorie Howes

Over the last several decades studies of periodicals and other print culture contexts have been central to scholarship on late Victorian literature, modernism, and the Irish Literary Revival. Such work has done much to deepen our sense of the Revival's complexities and its mutual imbrication with other contemporaneous literary trends. Scholarship on print culture is part of what Peter Brooker and Andrew Thacker characterized as the "materialist turn;"[1] it examines how different physical instantiations of texts produce varying meanings even when the linguistic codes do not change. It can examine a wide range of elements, such as bibliographic codes, periodical codes, editorial policies, layout and design, typeface, economic factors, circulation, and readership. Scholars read individual periodicals or volumes as distinct material and ideological enterprises; they also explore how attending to the original publication context can enrich our reading of particular texts.[2]

Yug Chaudhry's *Yeats, the Irish Literary Revival and the Politics of Print* is a thoroughly researched and elegantly argued example that does both, producing a newly complex portrait of the Revival, and W. B. Yeats's participation in it, in two important respects. First, Chaudhry offers a compelling reading of the original meaning and function of "September 1913" in its initial material print context in the *Irish Times*. In doing so, he outlines an interpretation of the poem that counters, without simply replacing, a number of later interpretations, including those offered or encouraged by Yeats himself. Second, Chaudhry shows how the early Yeats, "often with his conscious connivance and sometimes unconsciously,"[3] shaped his journalistic output in accordance with the editorial politics of a wide array of publications, ranging from the advanced nationalism of *United Ireland* to the imperialist and anti-Irish periodicals the *Scots* and *National Observer*.

Chaudhry rightly suggests that individual poems have different meanings in various print culture contexts, and that Yeats's writings varied ideologically based on the particular periodical he was targeting. Such claims, however, tend to identify material print culture contexts with ideological and interpretive coherence; they imply that such contexts provide additional information that can help produce more accurate and/or more complete interpretations of individual texts, periodicals, or other publications. In contrast, this essay seeks to build on, but also to complicate, work like Chaudhry's by arguing that the material elements of some print culture contexts offer nothing as straightforward as information or coherence. Instead, they can embody kinds of complexity that raise as many questions as they answer. I will explore this idea in relation to some examples of texts by Yeats and Augusta Gregory.

The Wind among the Reeds and the Revival

I will begin with a print culture context that has been often mentioned but seldom studied in depth: the original publication of Yeats's *The Wind among the Reeds* in 1899. As is well known, this volume differed substantially from the way it appears in later editions of Yeats's works. The cover displayed an intricate Celtic design created by Althea Gyles. The titles of most of the volume's poems indicated that each one was spoken by a particular figure in a series of personae: Michael Robartes, Hanrahan, Aedh, and Mongan. To explain these figures and other references to Irish mythology and folklore, Yeats appended forty-three pages of notes to the volume's sixty-two pages of poems. In later publications Yeats altered the volume, cutting the notes and replacing the names with abstractions like "he," "the poet," and "the lover."

The Wind among the Reeds represents a bibliographic context that Yeats had a good measure of control over; he was not forced to accommodate an editor's political bias, as was the case in the publications Chaudhry examines. So, Yeats's choice to include such an extensive paratext should provoke study. Somewhat surprisingly, however, even scholars who have studied the volume in depth, such as Alan Grossman and Stephen Putzel, have largely ignored the notes.[4] I argue that attending to this particular publication context reveals a certain incoherence in Yeats's definition of Irishness during this period, an incoherence that reflected how his revivalism drew upon, and was structured by, a number of wider late Victorian discourses of the time. It also reveals a tension between readings of print culture that seek to identify the bibliographic or periodical codes of a publication, and those that study the reception history of how contemporary readers actually interpreted it.

Obviously, the cover design, personae, and notes were meant to indicate the Irishness of the volume and its author. But the precise shape and sources of this Irishness remained unclear, ambiguously suspended between the scholarly and the poetic. In the notes, Yeats cites a wide range of authorities, including the *Encyclopaedia Britannica*, Standish O'Grady, Dr. Joyce, Professor Rhys, Douglas Hyde, and Frazier's *Golden Bough*. These references position the author of the volume as a scholar, and, more specifically, a comparativist: the notes place Irish folklore and mythology in the context of Greek, Eastern, English, and Scottish culture. This stance sits uneasily alongside other features of the notes that characterize Yeats as a dreamy, unscholarly poet. Yeats repeatedly claims that he is writing away from his books or that he has forgotten where he read something or who told him a particular story. The poet figure constructed by the notes may be unscholarly, but he is also authoritative and self-promoting. Yeats places the volume's poems in the context of his own other work, mentioning that he has written about Niamh in

"The Wanderings of Oisin" and about Clooth na Bear in *The Celtic Twilight*, and promising to write "a great deal elsewhere" about people who are enchanted by the fairies. Largely missing from the notes are the occult sources that Yeats was deeply immersed in at this time, and which are clearly relevant to the poems in the volume; including them, we may surmise, could have alienated readers and certainly would have violated the injunctions to secrecy that informed many of Yeats's magical endeavors.[5]

Taken together, these elements of the notes provide a specific print culture context that constructs a complicated, even conflicted, characterization of the volume's Irishness. This Irishness is coded as elaborate, obscure, needing the meditation of expert commentary, and worth a good deal of effort to recover. It is also coded as something more like national temperament: imaginative, imprecise, and impractical, something akin to the description of the Irish in Matthew Arnold's "The Celtic Element in Literature." The notes variously position each individual poem in *The Wind among the Reeds* as potentially part of several larger systems: the volume itself and its symbolic system, Yeats's other works, the world of Irish folklore and mythology, and the system of world cultures. Thus the 1899 volume embodies not "a" print culture context, or "a" set of codes, but several possible contexts or codes, reflecting in a concrete manner how different strands or facets of revivalism—literary, anthropological, romantic, scientific—mingled in the thinking and texts of Revivalists.

Moreover, whether we conclude that a single code or multiple, even conflicting codes were embedded in the text, when we turn to the actual reception history of the volume there is little evidence that contemporary readers saw either of those things. Reactions to the notes were mixed. A few of Yeats's contemporaries praised them. Fiona Macleod (William Sharp) called them "the prose equivalent of the verse" and saw them as important sources for the poems, "where the roots grow and the fibres fill with sap."[6] John Davidson's review quoted two of the notes and praised Yeats for having "a living and intellectual regard for what is to most only a faded mythology."[7]

Other readers and reviewers, on the other hand, including Yeats's father,[8] were baffled and irritated by the notes.[9] Yeats himself predicted that critics would probably "spend half of every review in complaining that I have written very long notes about very short poems."[10] In a review essay on "A Group of Celtic Writers," Macleod directly contradicted her review of *The Wind among the Reeds*, writing that the "obvious fault" of Yeats's poems was that "they frequently require commentary; for sometimes they are no more than exquisitely versified folklore."[11]

Thus, the specific material features of this publication context can be interpreted in a number of ways. On a general level, one can posit a single context or code: most of the bibliographic elements of *The Wind among the Reeds* were concerned with signifying Irishness, and most contemporary readers and reviewers all agreed that the notes were a significant and unusual feature of the volume. On a closer level of scrutiny, two kinds of multiplicity or conflict emerge. The single context or code and the Irishness it signifies break down into multiple elements, such as the scholarly and the poetic. And Yeats's contemporaries interpreted the volume's physical features in ways that differed among themselves and were at variance with current scholarship's reading of those features. The original material print culture context of the volume provokes contradictory conclusions.

The *Savoy* and Decadence

To make matters even more complicated, that print culture context was not "original"; a number of poems in the volume had appeared in different publication contexts before 1899. Focusing on one, the short-lived London periodical the *Savoy*,[12] will allow me to explore the mutual imbrication of Yeats's version of revivalism with a late Victorian discourse that later came to appear to many scholars as opposed to it: decadence. The "tired hedonism" of the decadents might seem otherwise quite incompatible with the earnest self-help ethos of the Revival. But Joseph Valente has argued persuasively that aestheticism and decadence were foundational to Yeats's revivalism, rather than opposed to it.[13] This section will build on Valente's argument to examine how the *Savoy* embodies that relationship and the dialectical tensions that shaped it.

The *Savoy* began publication in January of 1896; it was defunct by the end of that year. It was designed to compete with the decadent magazine the *Yellow Book*, whose title was meant to evoke the yellow covers of supposedly risqué French novels. During the trials of Oscar Wilde in 1895, the publisher of the *Yellow Book* fired Aubrey Beardsley, the art editor of the journal, who was notorious for his grotesque and often sexually explicit drawings. A rumor had circulated that Wilde was involved with the *Yellow Book* and that Wilde had a "friendship" with Beardsley, and the *Yellow Book* fired Beardsley to try to distance itself from the scandal. Yeats's friend Arthur Symons edited the *Savoy*, and Beardsley became its art editor.

The *Savoy*'s opening issue claimed, "We are not Realists, or Romanticists, or Decadents" and insisted "For us, all art is good which is good art." But, although it has been described by Roy Foster as Pre-Raphaelite rather than decadent, this distinction, like the function of Yeats's notes, would certainly have been lost on most contemporary readers. Beardsley's association with it was one factor; another was the Wildean echoes of "all art is good which is good art." A third was the magazine's title, which, according to Laurel Brake, invoked the "luxurious Savoy Hotel, resplendent with the new technology of electric lights throughout" for everyone, but also invited more "intelligent" readers to remember Wilde's association with both the hotel and the Savoy Theater.[14] The *Savoy* put forward a self-consciously coherent editorial stance. Its contributors and its readership were largely male, but it also targeted a segmented readership in which some male readers appreciated the connection with Wilde.

Other readers, of course, would be scandalized by it, and the *Savoy*'s decadence and its association with sexual transgression would have been clear to many readers, even in the absence of an editorial policy devoted to highlighting them, because it began life in the aftermath of the Wilde trials. Other features of the publication encouraged this characterization as well. Its publisher, Leonard Smithers, specialized in selling illegal pornography and other exotica, including, according to one of his catalogues, two books bound in human skin.[15] He was notorious for his degeneracy, even among his friends. The magazine explicitly rejected conventional respectability and popularity. Symons wrote proudly in the preface to the second issue to thank the "critics of the press" for the "flattering reception" they had given to the first issue, a reception which he claimed "has been nonetheless flattering because it has been for the most part unfavorable" because any really new endeavor provokes the disapproval of large numbers of people.[16] In the final issue, he concluded loftily that "art cannot appeal to the multitude."

Yeats had some ambivalence about the magazine; he considered Smithers "a scandalous person"[17] and when Althea Gyles became Smithers's lover in 1899, Yeats was so horrified that he forbade her to bring Smithers with her when she came to his house. But the *Savoy* paid well, and he endorsed its project to explore everything, as he wrote later, "especially what has been long forbidden." Yeats was one of its most regular contributors; of the eight issues published, he contributed to six. Others included Havelock Ellis, who was busy founding the modern field of sexology and producing his study of homosexuality, and other literary figures such as Symons, Ernest Dowson, Beardsley, Selwyn Image, and Lionel Johnson. Besides the aestheticist logic Valente identifies as central to Yeats's revivalism, another set of connections between revivalism and decadence lay in the *Savoy*'s participation in regionalism and the local color movements of the 1890s that were foundational to both revivalism and decadence.

The decadent movement was more interested in far-away, exotic places like the West of Ireland than is often recognized. The *Savoy* developed something of a Celtic bent in its last few issues, and not just because of contributions from Yeats. In August of 1896 Yeats and Symons, together with George Moore and Edward Martyn, went to the Aran islands. That same summer saw Yeats's decisive meeting with Augusta Gregory and the beginning of their long friendship and collaboration. After their visit, Symons wrote several essays for the *Savoy* about the West of Ireland, with titles that included "In Sligo: Rosses Point and Glencar" and "The Isles of Aran." These pieces are fairly typical examples of the regionalism of the time, and represent a species of literary tourism. Symons described Sligo as a gentle, dreamy, otherworldly place, one that also contained "the treachery which is always one of the allurements of voluptuous things." On his way to Aran, he recounts, he did his homework by reading Emily Lawless's novel *Grania*, which he says "is supposed to be the classic of the islands;" he also read a 17th century text on the West and looked at maps. He found Aran to be a place of mystery and tranquility, the people "primitive" but like "placid animals, on whom emotion has never worked, in any vivid or passionate way." Symons wrote that on Aran he was "far from civilization, so much further out of the world than I had ever been before."

The *Savoy* provided a print culture context that was intimately connected to the revivalist context of *The Wind among the Reeds*, but also differed from it substantially. Like *The Wind among the Reeds*, the *Savoy* suggested an elite readership capable of appreciating somewhat obscure meanings, but this capacity was based more on cultural and especially sexual sophistication than on knowledge of folklore or of printed sources. Early issues of the *Savoy* displayed the decadent yearning for far-off places without specifying Ireland; later issues represented Irishness in a quaintly exotic form, easily consumable by visitors, both actual and literary. Understanding the Irishness of the *Savoy* did not require expert scholars, the *Golden Bough*, or footnotes; a copy of Emily Lawless and a couple of maps would be sufficient. Beardsley's cover for the November 1896 issue of the magazine pictured two grotesque, Beardsley-esque men, clearly not Irish peasants, walking along a country road. One of them is wearing glasses and reading from an open book, a perfect figure for the kind of elite literary tourism embodied in the *Savoy*'s representations of Ireland, which emphasized a lack of civilization rather than the rich and strange Irish cultural difference suggests by Yeats's notes to *The Wind among the Reeds*.

While on one hand the *Savoy* embodies the overlapping of decadence and revivalism, on the other hand, within this print context, individual poems signify differently than they do in Yeats's volume. In the November issue Yeats published two poems that would eventually appear as "Hanrahan Reproves the Curlew" and "To My Heart, Bidding it have no Fear" in the 1899 volume. In the *Savoy* their titles were "O'Sullivan Rua to the Curlew" and "Out of the Old Days," and both of them appeared under the general title "Windle-Straws." Literally, a windle-straw is a dry, thin, withered stalk of grass, especially one that is left over after flowering and harvesting are over. Metaphorically, it can mean a flimsy, slight, or insignificant thing, or a tall, lanky person who is weak in health or character. As a title for the two poems, it invokes the English literary tradition rather than the Irish. It signals the decadent tropes of exhaustion, the harvest of youth and love gone or squandered. This makes the sexual content of the poems, emphasizing lost love, "passion-dimmed eyes," and the "trembling heart," stand out, rather than their Irishness. So do other contents of the issue, such as Havelock Ellis's essay on Casanova, the famous, and infamous, lover of women. The point of the essay is that moral condemnation of Casanova is beside the point; Casanova was just a fully natural human being, more fully human than civilization could handle. The title "Windle-Straws" also characterizes the poems themselves as slight, ephemeral productions; small, isolated texts rather than parts of a larger mythological or literary system, in sharp contrast to the multiple larger systems of *The Wind among the Reeds*.

As in my first example, a comparison between these two material print culture contexts generates conflicting conclusions rather than ideological or interpretive coherence. First, these early Yeats poems look different in each context: one emphasizes an Irishness that is (partly) a complex, arcane system that needs to be deciphered by scholarly experts, while the other either does not feature Irishness (as in the earlier issues of the *Savoy*) or features Irishness according to the less demanding, more quaintly exotic and more potentially scandalous conventions of decadent sexuality and travel writing. Second,

Yeats's revivalism and decadence shared several underlying ideological structures, including the logic of aestheticism, a conviction that English civilization was exhausted and corrupt, and an interest in regionalism. My first point about the meanings of Yeats's poems depends upon separating decadence and the Revival to some extent; in contrast, my second point, which grows out of the same print culture material, insists that they are inseparable.

The *Cornhill Magazine* and Versions of the Popular

One difference remaining between decadence and the Revival was how ideas about popularity and unpopularity functioned within them. The *Savoy*'s (ultimately fatal) embrace of unpopularity in some respects accorded with Yeats's experience of his reception and his increasing conviction that he should not try to be popular, but it was a simpler issue for Symons than for the cultural nationalist Yeats. While decadence could be fairly consistently contemptuous of the popular, the idea of the popular remained a central and ambiguous issue for Yeats and other revivalists. One of the fundamental principles or goals of the Revival was that Irish literature should have an intimate connection with the Irish people. What kind of intimate connection this was to be, and how the Revival should conceptualize "the people" formed the basis of many classic debates and questions during the Revival. My final example examines how concepts of the popular appear in two important essays by Yeats and Augusta Gregory, respectively, in a print culture context that would seem to be ideologically opposed to them, raising yet another kind of complexity for the study of such contexts. While this example treats two essays that look out of place in the original context in which they appear, they do so for different reasons. Including Gregory also allows me to highlight the complex internal range and variation that characterize the print culture context of a single publication: the *Cornhill Magazine*.

Gregory published "The Felons of Our Land" in the *Cornhill Magazine* in May of 1900, and Yeats published "What Is 'Popular

Poetry'" there in 1902.[18] At first glance, the *Cornhill Magazine* was a surprising venue in which to publish anything written as part of a revivalist project. It was also a very different enterprise from the *Savoy*. By the turn of the century, the *Cornhill Magazine* had been around for forty years. When it began in 1860, according to Barbara Quinn Schmidt, it "revolutionized" magazines by providing a "monthly miscellany of 128 pages aimed through its shilling price at the expanding number of middle-class leisure readers." William Thackeray, by then a prominent man of letters, was its prestigious first editor, and he wrote that "we shall suppose the ladies and children always present." Its publisher George Smith was an influential and widely respected arbiter of literary value, as opposed to the disreputable Smithers, and the magazine was named after the London street where its offices were located. It was aimed at a growing readership of middle class people who wanted to read for entertainment, education, and the cultivation of their own gentility and cultural sophistication. In Schmidt's words, its purpose was to help those readers "learn about manners, current topics, attitudes, and mores from more knowledgeable writers."[19] The *Cornhill Magazine* sported a striking orange cover and was meant to be displayed, as well as consumed, as a sign of one's taste. Its contents were by no means confined to literature. Alongside fiction, poetry, and articles about literature, the *Cornhill Magazine* featured essays on a wide range of topics, from foreign places to politics to bird watching to family budgets. References to Ireland were mostly of the humorous variety. It had something for everyone, and was filled with advertisements for a range of products and services, mostly books.

Perhaps the *Cornhill Magazine*'s most visible feature was its determination to combine quality literature with popularity, and respectability with commercial success. By Yeats's time it was no longer the unique blockbuster with extraordinary sales it had been during the first decade of its life, and it was edited by Smith's son-in-law Reginald John Smith. But it was still popular, and Andrew Maunder observes that by the turn of the century "cultural criticism could still cite the pervasiveness of the *Cornhill Magazine* and its connections with popular pleasure reading."[20] Debates over the magazine were largely debates over its popularity; some readers and reviewers looked down on what they saw as the vulgarity of the magazine and its readership. Others criticized it for its substantial numbers of female readers. The *Cornhill Magazine* inspired admiration, but it also provoked anxieties about "popular literacy and social barriers."[21] The editorial policy appeared to be similarly ambivalent. It contained gestures toward inclusiveness and the transcending of class divisions, but it also harbored impulses toward exclusiveness and the reinstalling of such divisions.

Yeats's essay, for example, shared space with an article by "Lady Grove" called "Social Solecisms" that discussed questions of etiquette and proper speech.[22] The article struck a delicate balance between class rigidity and class mobility, explaining that standards do change over generations but that identifying and maintaining current standards was important. She suggests that readers could, by following the tips she gave them, effectively enter the more exclusive sectors of society even if they were not born into them. This formulation gave readers the chance to advance socially and culturally, and it also reassured them that such advances would differentiate them from the less advanced. Her encouraging conclusion was that "No plant flourishes without cultivation except where it is indigenous to the soil, but care and cultivation will produce specimens which it needs all the inherent advantages of time and place to rival." Other articles in the *Cornhill Magazine* around the turn of the century addressed questions of taste, such as distinguishing a good book from a bad one, proper manners, and questions about public culture and the public sphere, including an assessment of the state of the French press, and a December 1901 essay by Andrew Lang entitled "The Reading Public."[23] Lang criticized the public's poor taste in literature, while also acknowledging that elite literature was a specialized sphere that would not interest everyone. He included a supposed letter from a "working man" describing his high culture reading habits and concluded "I think my friend's description applies to every class of society . . . to know Shakespeare by heart is as rare in Universities as in railway-works and factories." His distinction between the portion of the reading public that appreciates good literature and the portion that does not rejected traditional class divisions but replaced them with a different kind of distinction, which was very much in keeping with the *Cornhill Magazine*'s overall project.

It was also partly in keeping with Yeats's "What is 'Popular Poetry'?", which Yeats had originally intended to publish in the *Speaker*, but for unknown reasons ended up placing in the *Cornhill Magazine* instead. The essay is an important statement of his developing artistic and revivalist principles. And, as Roy Foster points out, it also "interrogat[es] his own relation to 'popularity'."[24] Yeats did this by rejecting one conception of "popular poetry"—poetry that was actually popular—and substituting another definition of "popular poetry"—one that yoked together folk culture and elite literature. He criticized the kind of popular poetry represented by the Young Ireland poets and commercially successful writers like Longfellow, Hemans, and Burns. These, Yeats argued, were the poets of "a predominant portion of the middle class, of people who have unlearned the unwritten tradition . . . and who have not learned the written tradition which has been established upon the unwritten." In contrast, he concluded, "There is only one kind of good poetry, for the poetry of the coteries, which presupposes the written tradition, does not differ in kind from the true poetry of the people, which presupposed the unwritten tradition."

Yeats's redefinition of the "true poetry of the people" was part of his larger efforts to engage the problem of how to create or reveal a popular audience for the Revival without pandering to popular tastes, and it solved his problem rather brilliantly in one way. It married the undeniably Irish folk culture he and other revivalists were busy unearthing and disseminating to the elite literature he was producing, but which was often failing to find an audience among large portions of the reading public. It banished from a legitimate conception of the "popular" the middle classes against whom he would increasingly, and famously, define his own work, and his idea of Ireland. But the *Cornhill Magazine* seems like an odd venue for a pro-Irish diatribe against the middle classes: Yeats appears to be rejecting the magazine's core readership and asking readers to see Ireland as culturally sophisticated rather than crudely amusing.

On the other hand, Yeats and the *Cornhill Magazine* were both seeking to perform the same sleight of hand, in which social differentiation could be simultaneously maintained and transformed into a shared and consciously cultivated culture, whether Irish nationalism or cultural sophistication. I have found no evidence of how *Cornhill* readers responded to Yeats's essay. Were they put off by his denigration of "a new class and a new art without breeding and without ancestry" created by "the counting house"? Or did their aspirations to upward mobility induce them to see in that description the people they hoped to display their superiority to? Did Yeats see an exciting opportunity in the diminished but still evident popularity of the *Cornhill Magazine* to gain a wider audience? Or did he publish there out of necessity? All these questions await further research. In any case, it is clear that determining whether or not a given article accords with the general editorial bent of a publication, whether consciously or unconsciously, is not necessarily a straightforward business.

However, it is possible to draw some conclusions about how Yeats's essay might have appeared in the context of the *Cornhill Magazine*'s major preoccupations. Yeats's effort to craft an alternative conception of the popular in Irish literature that would alter, rather than simply reflect, the actual tastes of the reading public was published in a magazine whose most visible feature was its claim to combine actual popularity and high cultural taste. The dilemma Yeats's essay addressed was central to the *Cornhill Magazine*'s place in the turn of the century print landscape; read alongside essays like Lady Grove's and Lang's, Yeats's preoccupation with social class and hierarchies of discernment, rather than his Irish nationalism, would likely have been the most visible elements of the essay to *Cornhill* readers.

Yeats's reformulation of the popular was heavily oriented toward the past, and depended upon the antiquity of tradition, on the idea that good literature uses words that "borrow their beauty from those that used them before." The written tradition borrows from the unwritten tradition, and the unwritten tradition in its turn can be traced back to "ancient religion." By ancient religion Yeats means not Christianity but a more ancient paganism, and he claimed that "the people" "cannot separate the idea of art or a craft from the idea of a cult with ancient technicalities and mysteries. They can hardly separate mere learning from witchcraft, and are fond of words and verses that keep half their secret to themselves."

For Yeats, the important characteristics of the people and the culture they share with other classes, such as the castle, the cloister, and the poet, are located in a past that is removed from contemporary Ireland. He did not incorporate into his conception of "the popular" elements of living, contemporary popular culture in Ireland, which, like Young Ireland's popular ballads, was drawn from both the English and the Irish traditions rather than being rooted solely in a purely Irish folk culture. But this is precisely what Gregory had done in "The Felons of Our Land," which appeared in the *Cornhill Magazine* two years earlier. At first glance, Gregory's essay, like Yeats's, appears an odd fit for the *Cornhill Magazine*, but for different reasons.

Gregory's essay shared space in the May 1900 issue with an article critiquing developments in contemporary theater like the long run, the star system, the use of elaborate sets, and the decline in productions of Shakespeare. Also appearing in that issue were a reminiscence by a former colonial official in Natal, South Africa, a short story by Henry James, an essay on the American South, a satirical piece on John Bull's troublesome empire, including the "shocking bad tenant" "Paddy Gilhooly" on Hibernia Road, and an article on what we now call helicopter parents. In the midst of this mélange, Gregory's essay stands out for its overtly anti-imperial politics, something that was unusual for the *Cornhill Magazine*. The essay was also unusually political for Gregory herself. Foster describes it as the moment when she came out as an Irish nationalist, and doing so made her nervous. In her diary for April 30, she recorded that a friend had read it and told her she had gone too far away from the opinions of her husband (now dead, of course) and son. Gregory concluded that she had "determined not to go so far toward political nationalism in anything I write again."

The essay offers conceptions of the people and popular culture that differed strikingly from those in Yeats's essay. Gregory defined "felony" as a crime in the eyes of the law, but not in the eyes of the people, and she examined how Irish nationalists—treated as felons by the British—have been memorialized by the Irish people as heroes. Unlike Yeats, she approached Irish popular culture through the living traditions of the people, many of which embody subaltern strategies for resisting and rewriting official imperial history: "Irish history," she wrote, "having been forbidden in the national schools, has lifted up its voice in the streets." She invoked the kind of popular poetry Yeats had scorned and emphasized its circulation within the commercial nexus of contemporary small-town Ireland: "At little Catholic bookshops, at little sweet and china shops in country towns, one finds the cheap ballad books, in gaudy papers, red, yellow, and green." Gregory included actual popular reading practices, citing the popularity of *Speeches from the Dock*, a volume of the last public words of political prisoners. Whereas Yeats opposes good literature to commercially successful literature, Gregory flaunts the commercial and even vulgar nature of the cheap and gaudy ballad books. Yeats's peasants are located in the ancient past; Gregory's are located in contemporary Ireland. The people, in Gregory's formulation, are dominated by England but also create and inhabit an anti-imperial counterculture, a dynamic also evident in her plays such as *Spreading the News*, *Hyacinth Halvey*, and *The Rising of the Moon*.

This popular counterculture included a range of popular practices that represented active negotiations with, and appropriations of, British culture and power. For example, she claims that "The chief ornament of many a cottage is the warrant for the arrest of a son of the house framed and hung up as a sort of diploma of honor." The idea of using the way one's house was decorated to signify one's social, political, or cultural capital would have been familiar to *Cornhill* readers, many of whom were women, and who were accustomed to displaying the magazine on their coffee tables, and displaying their taste in other aspects of their homes, their shopping, and their entertainments.

Other elements in "The Felons of Our Land" seemed calculated to offend *Cornhill* readers. Locating a cultural artifact that displayed a particular sensibility in a peasant's cottage, and embracing the status of a law-breaking felon, would have violated the *Cornhill Magazine*'s commitment to middle class status and respectability though I have found no record, apart from the concerns expressed in Gregory's diary, of how readers might have actually responded. Unlike Yeats, Gregory also highlighted the people's Catholicism, which also would have been likely to provoke disapproval. She cited another popular practice: treating the clothing and bodies of men executed by the government as religious relics. She recounts finding a letter in her husband's papers in which an army colonel recommends to his government that, when people are executed, "Not even a shoe should be given to the family, for all the cloths the deceased had on are considered as relicks," a word with specifically Catholic religious connotations. She also includes other material practices allied with popular Catholicism, such as funeral processions and popular pilgrimages to Wolfe Tone's unofficial grave site.

Both Yeats's and Gregory's essays engaged the important revivalist question of how to conceptualize the Irish people and Irish popular culture in a British print culture context that was overtly hostile to Irish nationalism. The two writers produced very different versions of the popular. Yeats's was literary, purist, folkloric, and largely rooted in the past; Gregory's was more anthropological, embracing the hybrid vigor of living popular traditions. Both essays seem calculated to upset readers of the *Cornhill Magazine*, each in a different way. "What is 'Popular Poetry'?" explicitly denigrated the middle class commercial world many of them inhabited, while Gregory praised contemporary Irish culture using terms—felony, Catholicism, commodity culture—that they would have found unrespectable. And yet both essays found a home in the magazine, perhaps because each essay offered something that the *Cornhill Magazine* did endorse: a standard for discerning literary value in Yeats, and a model of everyday culture and practices as embodying political views and social status in Gregory. Setting these two examples by Yeats and Gregory beside one another helps illuminate the complex and varied ways that individual texts could simultaneously accord with some elements of a print culture context and clash with other elements.

All of the examples examined here demonstrate that such contexts can be confusing and difficult to interpret, but also illuminating. Grappling with such print culture contexts in which revivalist texts appear can help us explore the Revival's embeddedness in multiple late Victorian and early modernist discourses, the proliferation of competing definitions of Irishness, and the combination of various definitions within individual volumes or texts. It allows us to see surprising connections, as well as substantial differences, between Revivalist authors and the British print culture landscape of the time. And emphasizing that these print culture contexts generate as many questions as they answer helps us appreciate not just the role of overlapping discourses and conflicting codes, but also the importance of ambiguity, contingency, and uncertainty in producing a vision of the Revival in all its complexities.

4

Ourselves (Transnationally) Alone

Globalism and Nationalist Journalism during the Revival

Karen Steele

During the Revival years, Irish literature, politics, and public life turbulently coexisted in hundreds of different nationalist newspapers and periodicals circulating over a varied marketplace. This print culture, as Christopher Morash maintains, "was not simply the vehicle for the literary revival; it was a constituent part of it."[1] R. F. Foster has recently emphasized that the "little newspapers and magazines of the nationalist fringe," more than High Culture, "galvanized the imaginations and opinions of young radicals" who would go on to shape Ireland's literary and political future.[2] This chapter proposes that to understand Ireland's revolutionary generation, and the Irish Revival more broadly, one would do well to investigate both radical and mainstream journalism *side by side* to appreciate how the networks of "nationalist journalism" operated in the Revival years.

   Two outstanding examples of revivalist print culture—one radical weekly and one mainstream daily—had an outsize influence on cultural and political debates of the day: the weekly *United Irishman* (1899–1906), which was edited by one of Ireland's preeminent journalists, Arthur Griffith (1871–1922), who later founded Sinn Féin and was president of the first Dáil; and the revitalized, post-Parnellite *Irish Independent* (1905–), Ireland's first mass market daily newspaper, edited by Timothy R. Harrington (1866–1937) and owned by William Martin Murphy (1844–1919). While each of these periodicals promoted distinctive, often competing, ideas about the industry and practice of the newspaper business and its vision for Ireland's political and cultural future, the two papers shared unmistakable optimism about the role of the press to enact change—and conveyed this through the use of a surprisingly similar conceit, "ourselves alone," an unfaithful translation of *Sinn Féin*, to advocate for a particular version of Irish political and cultural autonomy. Yet alongside this ostensible motto of "ourselves alone," Irish periodicals, like Irish literature and politics, proved ready to employ methods, styles, funds, and subscription lists from abroad.

This chapter explores how these two distinctive Irish nationalist newspapers circulating during the Revival cultivated likeminded readers but also established alternative and overlapping networks connecting cultural and political organizations; such organizations, while firmly focused on fostering Irishness and establishing an Irish state, continuously crossed geographical, political, and linguistic boundaries. In tracking the tensions present in each journal's commitment to "ourselves," then, I examine global and local networks of Irish journalism, whether in terms of business practices, models for political separatism, pragmatic organizing principles, or abstract philosophy concerning the imagined communities that were a primary readership for each journal. Ultimately, studying Irish media's distinctive reactions to the separatist message "ourselves alone" helps us recognize the persistence of a complicated nationalist perspective that locates Ireland "alone," yet within a transnational frame.

"Networks" in the Irish Nationalist Press

In *Forms: Whole, Rhythm, Hierarchy, Network*, Caroline Levine advances a new methodology for apprehending culture in relation to social life, modeling how a given form simultaneously empowers and limits its user. In examining networks as form, Levine draws on both the vocabulary and insights of network theorists such as Patrick Jagoda, Patrick Joyce, and Franco Moretti to understand networks in terms of "defined patterns of interconnection and exchange that organize social and aesthetic experience."[3] As media historians have also observed,[4] print networks of the past were facilitated by proximity to other writers, activists, editors, publishers, and printers through pubs, clubs, salons, editorial offices, news agents, even tobacco shops. Indeed, as Laurel Brake sees it, "networking can be considered a part of the *structure* of journalism" in the nineteenth century.[5]

While access to such networks was often controlled by gender, class, geography, political stance, or language fluency,[6] Revivalist Dublin, with its compressed, modest urban population of 300,000, afforded these two nationalist newspapers easy access to multiple networks. Lucy McDiarmid notes that even celebrities faced close interactions with everyday citizens of the city during these years: "'intimacy' seemed not only possible but almost unavoidable."[7] And Foster describes the "geographical concentration" in Dublin as "an intimate but complex city, with certain areas defined by political subcultures: a geography of radical Dublin," ensuring that proximity inevitably shaped the discourse of each periodical.[8] Just as Fenians gravitated to Tom Clarke's paper-shop and then joined Inghindhe na hÉireann members at a Gaelic League lecture or céildh in the evening,[9] so too, newspaper editors at the *United Irishman* exchanged nods with their counterparts at the *Irish Independent*, walking to and from their offices on Upper Ormond Quay and Middle Abbey Street, located only a few minutes' walk from one another. Another kind of geography was at work in the network of Irish diasporic readers; newspapers sustained their national, political, and religious identity through advertisements, correspondence columns, meeting notices, and reports of lectures and speeches.

Newspaper networks can be glimpsed through material elements of each paper, too. A periodical's format, size, pagination, illustrations, advertising, and pricing reveal connectivity and the capacity to create links between disconnected nodes. When Murphy relaunched his new daily *Irish Independent*, he imported innovations from London's *Daily Mail* while also adopting an eight-page format similar to Griffith's weekly *United Irishman*; in comparison to Griffith's penny weekly, Murphy crammed more columns onto each page of his half-penny daily in an effort to demonstrate its good value and provided visual relief with headlines, crossheads, and plenty of photographs and hand-drawn illustrations. When another advanced national-ist periodical, the *Irish Citizen*, joined the market in 1912, more than a decade after the *United Irishman*'s first issue, its weekly price matched the one-penny cost of *Sinn Féin*, the *United Irishman*'s sep-aratist successor. Some of the same advertisers in Griffith's weeklies later appeared in the *Irish Citizen*; yet the *Irish Citizen*'s adoption of new journalist techniques such as rhetorical uses of photographs, political cartoons, and bold crossheads reveals how Irish suffrage journalism, like Murphy's commercially minded daily journalism, were both influenced by Alfred Harmsworth, W. T. Stead, and trans-national innovations in the newspaper business.[10] The editorials and correspondence columns of both the *United Irishman* and the *Irish Independent* carefully monitored how the Dublin and international press covered the news. Laurel Brake describes this monitoring and discussion of the competition as a form of journalistic "dialogue." As a structural feature of the Victorian press, these networks are rendered visible to readers through a paper's "cross-referencing to fellow writers, issues past and to come, to correspondents, to rivals, and its personifications, pseudonyms, and insistent anonymity or signature."[11]

Perhaps one of the most suggestive benefits in tracking networks in the nationalist press is their capacity to cultivate weak ties. Yeats's "Easter 1916" tellingly opens by illustrating such weak ties that were inevitable in Revivalist Dublin, with the speaker remember-ing quotidian, nearly forgettable experiences passing rebels on the streets "with a nod of the head / Or polite meaningless words." So too, newspaper networks connected people who knew one another only slightly, bringing a paper or reader access to a wider range of information and resources than that provided by like-minded indi-viduals. The broad assortment of nationalist dailies, weeklies, and monthlies circulating in Revivalist Ireland sustained a wide range of answers to the Irish question, from Home Rule, de-Anglicization of

Ireland, parliamentary abstentionism, agricultural or trade revival, militant separatism, or "suffrage first, above all else."[12] If "nationalist press" is an inadequate predictor of ideology, we would do well to remember that their networks are "neither consistently emancipatory—freeing us from a fixed or dominant order—nor always threatening—trouncing sovereignty or dissolving protective boundaries."[13]

The nationalist media's reflections on Ireland's transnational affiliations are a case in point, for both papers refused to consider Ireland's relation to the world solely within the political networks of the British Empire. Where the *United Irishman* studied the continental press and highlighted another "little nation," Hungary, as providing a model for Ireland's decolonization, the *Irish Independent* systematically tracked business developments in North and South America while consistently advocating Dominion status for Ireland, rather than separation from the Empire. In what follows, I consider both papers as examples of transnational Irish culture, "invested in the multiple points of identification and belonging that result from a writer's commitment to Ireland, to other countries, and to the world at large."[14] Although both papers articulated different versions of nationalist sensibility in response to the long history of colonization by Great Britain—and thus emphasized the need to focus on Ireland "alone"—each paper also looked outward beyond the metropolitan "center" of London, with distinctive results. As Françoise Lionnet and Shu-mei Shih influentially argue, when we focus on these latter exchanges, what they describe as "minor transnationalisms," we are better able to witness "the multiple relations between the national and transnational, including a varied terrain of minority interactions with both majority cultures and other minorities."[15]

"Ourselves" in the *United Irishman*

"Minor transnational" exchanges in periodical networks are particularly visible in moments of transition, such as when new titles emerge from older, or soon-to-be defunct, ones. This is especially true of the *United Irishman*, which is most closely associated with the motto

"Sinn Féin" and its exigency as a political movement. Both the paper and the movement can be traced to the advanced nationalist newspaper network established by Alice Milligan and Anna Johnston's *Shan Van Vocht* (1896–99), a short-lived literary monthly based in Belfast. As Padraic Colum first noted, the phrase *Sinn Féin* emerged in an Irish-language poem published in the *Shan Van Vocht* by Douglas Hyde, a frequent contributor to the monthly.[16] When the *Shan Van Vocht* folded in April 1899, its concluding editorial acknowledged the negative impact of "unfortunate sectional policies" among Dublin nationalists, yet praised the networks of support in the United States, Canada, and Argentina; many of these networks would continue to support the new Dublin weekly *United Irishman*.[17]

In print from 1899 to 1906, the *United Irishman* was edited by Arthur Griffith and William Rooney, until Rooney's untimely death on May 6, 1901. Initially a four-page, half-penny weekly, it quickly grew to an eight-page, one-penny weekly starting in July 1899. The *United Irishman* took its name from the late eighteenth-century parliamentary reformists who organized the 1798 rebellion, as well as the mid-nineteenth century advanced nationalist weekly edited by Young Irelander John Mitchel.[18] In choosing to name their Dublin-based separatist journal the *United Irishman*, Griffith and Rooney acknowledged their shared network with the *Shan Van Vocht*, whose editors passed along their subscription list to Rooney and Griffith upon the folding of their Belfast journal.[19] Whereas the *Shan Van Vocht* dedicated extensive coverage to remembering the leadership and activism associated with the United Irishmen, building up to the frenzy of separatist centenary commemoration activities in 1898, the weekly *United Irishman* cited, instead, the example of Young Irelanders, who edited and contributed to the separatist weeklies the *Nation* (1845–47) and its more openly seditious successor, the *United Irishman* (1848). On page two of each issue, next to the subscription information of the new *United Irishman*, Griffith and Rooney included the quote, "We must have Ireland, not for certain peers or nominees of peers, in College Green, but Ireland for the Irish," by Young Irelander John Mitchel, whose craggy, blunt style influenced the journalistic voice of Arthur Griffith.[20] The first individual featured in the Man of the Week column, the Young Irelander James Fintan Lalor, signaled the *United Irishman*'s desire to align its political and cultural project with the advanced nationalist journalism of Young Ireland. Indeed, numerous Young Irelanders were featured in the Man of the Week column, from John Mitchel to Thomas Devin Reilly.

In its early years, the paper experimented with a range of features, eventually settling into a familiar pattern that helped readers access a range of overlapping nationalist networks: an All Ireland column (written in the first year and a half by Rooney, then by Máire Butler)[21] that highlighted the diverse Irish political and cultural activities ongoing throughout the island; Man of the Week, which profiled Irish men (never women) from the past and present whose writings and activism contributed to the Irish cause; Coming Events, which focused on Gaelic and separatist meetings and events located in Ireland and on the continent; Democratic Notes, which covered legislative efforts in Ireland and abroad on the "development of the national ideal"; Ireland in London, written by Henry Egan Kenny; Over the Frontier, which surveyed the continental press; Correspondence (for letters to the editor, a spirited section); Dublin Stage, one of the few signed columns, written by Frank Fay; sporting columns, almost all of which were written by Michael Cusack;[22] and various columns and reports on the Gaelic Athletic Association, National Associations, and Northern Notes (written by "an Shan Van Vocht," possibly a pseudonym for Alice Milligan). Each number concluded with a page (later stretching to two pages) of advertisements.

It is perhaps no surprise that Arthur Griffith, who would later found Sinn Féin, launched his first successful Irish newspaper using the business model of self-reliance. From youth, Griffith had trained in various dimensions of the Irish newspaper business, preparing him to wear virtually every hat when he assumed sole editorship of the *United Irishman*. As the son of a printer, Griffith apprenticed, first, as a compositor and, later, as a copyreader for the venerable advanced nationalist weekly the *Nation* before moving on to work as copyreader at the pro-Parnellite *Irish Daily Independent*, a proof-reader at Dublin's *Evening Telegraph*, and a compositor at Thom's Printing. His first editing position in journalism occurred not in Ireland, however, but in South Africa, where he emigrated in 1897 to edit the short-lived weekly *Courant*; he returned to Ireland expressly to join Rooney in launching the *United Irishman*.[23]

In the early years of the *United Irishman*, Griffith and Rooney wrote nearly all of the copy, using a host of pseudonyms to conceal the collaborative authorship of the paper.[24] In later years, even when the paper could count on high profile, talented contributors such as W. B. Yeats, George Moore, Oliver St. John Gogarty, John Eglinton, Edward Martyn, Frank Fay, and others, Griffith would step in, if necessary, to write what they pledged but failed to deliver on time. As James Stephens later acknowledged, if a promised column was late, Griffith "would write the missing articles himself and write them much better than anybody else could."[25] After Rooney's death, Griffith assumed responsibility for nearly all the copy for an issue, while assuming three additional duties as editor, copywriter, and compositor, for which he drew the modest salary of twenty-five shillings a week.[26] In a telling indication of the quixotic nature of Griffith's motto of self-reliance, his salary was occasionally supplemented by the trust-funded Maud Gonne, who contributed her personal funds and the proceeds from her US lecture tours. Indeed, Griffith understood that his separatist enterprise required financial support from, as well as dissemination to, locations abroad; the paper, by 1906, had agents in Belfast, London, Paris, Brooklyn, and Philadelphia.

The rhetorical style and editorial voice of the *United Irishman* conveyed, from its outset, a resonantly Irish, satirical panache, helping us witness how literary and political writers in Ireland's past provided another network for Griffith, whom Foster describes as "the most rhetorically powerful Irish journalist of his time, and an original and creative political thinker."[27] F. S. L. Lyons detected, for example, "both the savagery of Swift and the ruggedness of John Mitchel but to these he added his own intensity and his own intimate knowledge of the political and economic environment about him."[28] While the *United Irishman* promoted a rich assortment of revivalist activities—Gaelic music, historical and mythological retellings, book and theater reviews, games, literary events—its editorials proved uncompromisingly separatist: "Lest there might be a doubt in any mind, we will say that we accept the nationalism of '98, '48, and '67 as the true nationalism and Grattan's cry 'Live Ireland—perish the Empire' as the watch-word of patriotism."[29] Due to the scathing candor of Griffith's nationalist, anti-British stance, the paper was seized and confiscated twenty-three times and publicly suppressed three times, and eventually folded in April 1906 as a result of a libel suit by an Irish priest who took issue when the paper critiqued a parish for canceling a feis planned on a Sunday.[30]

Even a cursory glance at an issue of *United Irishman* provides readers with an impression of the rich, multifaceted political and cultural networks across Ireland, with meeting notices and minutes, reports on Gaelic sporting events, and invitations to céilí, book launches, musical festivals, and new plays. With its tiny readership and frequently univocal authorship, the *United Irishman* publicized rather than dispassionately reported on these various strands of separatist activity. If, according to Glandon, it "accelerated the separatist movement and drew it together, gave it a voice, and served as its 'secretary and organizer,'" this "organizing voice" of multiple networks was, more often than not, emerging out of one man's mouth.[31] In fact, less than two years into the paper's run, the paper formalized this consolidating impulse by announcing, on November 25, 1900, the formation of Cumann na nGaedheal (Federation of the Gaels), with the sole purpose of "advance[ing] the cause of Ireland's national independence."[32] This umbrella organization, a precursor to Sinn Féin, assumed responsibility for one of *United Irishman*'s central missions, circulating the various ways that Irish citizens could stand apart from Great Britain economically, culturally, socially, politically, and legislatively. Cumann na nGaedheal supported Irish industries; promoted the study and teaching of Irish history, literature, Gaelic language, music, and art; cultivated Irish games and the physical education of Ireland's youth; and, following Douglas Hyde's seminal proposal in 1892, resisted the Anglicization of Ireland. As Glandon explains, Cumann na nGaedheal not only disseminated information about the myriad efforts to de-Anglicize Ireland but also developed Irish foreign policy and started the process of nationalizing public boards.[33]

The *United Irishman* carefully documented fin de siècle newspaper networks within and beyond Irish shores—unsurprisingly, as it was written and edited by Ireland's preeminent journalist. Using its own columns, as well as the Correspondence section, the *United Irishman* incessantly tracked the newspaper business in Ireland, in the United Kingdom, and on the continent, to find fault with Irish (especially Dublin) papers that failed, in the editor's estimation, to promote Ireland, its culture, and its industries. A favorite target was the *Irish Times*, which was repeatedly described as a promoter of "west Britonism,"[34] but nationalist weeklies and dailies such as the *Freeman's Journal*, the new *Irish Independent*, and the *Evening Herald* received heavy criticism, too. In the Correspondence column, other readers of the paper chimed in, adding to the chorus of condemnations when Dublin dailies and weeklies failed to live up to the pledge of "ourselves alone." Letters by "Hibernicus" frequently highlighted instances when the press occluded Irish nationality, misidentifying the nationality of Irish men and women as English or describing Queen Victoria as the monarch of Ireland.[35] Griffith also paid close attention to the mechanics and industry of the trade and viciously critiqued instances when a printer, such as Browne and Nolan, employed non-Irish compositors.[36]

From its inception, the *United Irishman* benefitted from a network of advanced nationalists who organized, in 1898, a series of centenary commemorations of the United Irishman Uprising. A secret, nonsectarian republican movement, the late eighteenth-century Society of the United Irishmen was a prototype of minor transnationalism, marked by "creative interventions that networks of minoritized cultures produce within and across national boundaries."[37] The Society aimed to eliminate British rule through studying transnational revolutionary examples in the United States and France and developing political and military collaborations with France for the insurrection that took place in 1798. Drawing on his experiences in South Africa, Arthur Griffith cofounded and used his paper to publicize another transnational political movement, the Irish Transvaal Committee, to canvass against army recruitment in Dublin. Griffith was familiar with the latest developments in journalism—especially the incisive, direct editorial voice associated with the new journalism—and studied continental papers carefully. Indeed, so important was the foreign (and later, French) press that the *United Irishman* featured a weekly column in its first three years, "Over the Frontier"—located on the left column of page two, sometimes occupying just shy of half of this page—that tacitly conveyed the editors' estimation that Irish separatism must be understood in a comparative mode.

The "Over the Frontier" section functioned separately from that of the foreign news coverage, which by July 1899 had its own section, "Foreign Notes," on page one. The "Over the Frontier" column, by comparison, contained a series of short commentaries, based on the editors' reading of parliamentary reports, national dailies, and international papers, and touched on international developments, with special attention to France, England, the United States, Germany, Russia, and India. Each brief snippet began in medias res, with the assumption that readers were already conversant with these foreign stories. With little to no attempt to provide context about which "drama in France" was referenced, or the particulars of "the agreement between France and England," the *United Irishman* cultivated a network of politicized newspaper readers through modeling how to read the news and piece disparate international stories into a guide for Ireland's separatist future. Reading "Over the Frontier" in many ways reproduces the interpersonal interpretation of the news depicted in Henry MacManus's mid-nineteenth-century painting *Reading the Nation*, with its engaged circle of Irishmen and women, who listen, respond, question, whisper, and laugh as the advanced nationalist paper the *Nation* is read aloud.

Perhaps the most significant, and lasting, example of how the *United Irishman* navigated its separatism in a transnational comparative mode is Griffith's influential polemic "The Resurrection of Hungary," which was serialized for twenty-seven weeks, from January 21, 1904, to July 22, 1904. (Griffith reprinted the serial as a pamphlet, which sold over 30,000 copies; some were translated for readers on the Indian subcontinent.)[38] Griffith's contemporary Padraic Colum described the "Resurrection of Hungary" as "constitutional without being Parliamentarian . . . and militant without being insurrectionary."[39] While Griffith's examination of Hungary's dual-monarchy under the Austrian Empire was his most influential comparative study, his longstanding interest in foreign politics, evident in the "Over the Frontier" column, routinely prompted Griffith to "employ imaginative parallels from abroad."[40] In "Resurrection," Griffith proposed a route to Irish independence from the British Empire through the establishment of a dual monarchy, a vision that most scholars agree was based on a profound misreading of Austro-Hungarian history.[41] In addition to advocating an economic boycott of British goods, Griffith proposed what would later become a key plank of Sinn Féin parliamentarianism: that elected members of parliament refuse their seat in Westminster and convene a competing body at home.[42] As Lyons concedes, Griffith's sophomoric reading of Hungary tells us more about his skills as a propagandist than as a historian: "For he had grasped the central lessons of the Ausgleich for Ireland—that it had been won for the Hungarians by a masterly display of parliamentary non-cooperation."[43] Yet it is telling that Griffith looked to another country, rather than the many homegrown historical examples that were available to him, for his influential theory of how to stand alone politically. Daniel O'Connell, Thomas Davis, Charles Lever, Michael Davitt, and Charles Stewart Parnell had each, in turn, proposed a similar set of policies.[44]

A consummate journalist and theorist of journalism, Arthur Griffith ceaselessly read, synthesized, critiqued, and crabbed about local, national, and international currents in the press. It was hardly surprising, then, that when William Martin Murphy bought out the old Parnellite *Independent* and introduced Irish readers to the *Independent and Nation* in September 1900, Griffith would cite Murphy's paper, which employed "Parliamentarian vultures," as a pointed contrast to his own paper, which he saw as the due inheritor of Parnellite journalism.[45] Yet if Murphy's vision of journalism sharply differed from Griffith's, both men forged their respective ideals for Ireland's future on experiences, lessons, and for Murphy, capital, from abroad.

Ownership as Authorship in the *Irish Independent*

Griffith declaimed that it was "from the little countries Ireland must learn the way to steer her course," and his paper incessantly studied political and imperial systems abroad to see how Ireland could chart its own political and economic independence from Great Britain.[46] The owner of the *Irish Independent*, William Martin Murphy (1844–1919), looked broadly across the continents—and oriented his new nationalist daily to do so as well—but with one crucial distinction: Murphy aimed to enhance his own bottom line. A transportation tycoon, Murphy expanded on his family inheritance by building light railways and tramways in Ireland, Britain, Africa, and South America.[47] As Patrick Maume observes, Murphy's global business experience "encouraged his belief that a self-governing Ireland's interests lay with the British empire," prompting his reputation, among Irish Irelanders, as a "West British cosmopolitan."[48]

Murphy took full advantage of networks facilitated by geography, family, and business to transform the *Independent* into a highly profitable venture that both channeled and shaped public opinion on Ireland's future. A native of Castletownbere and a close family friend of A. M. and T. D. Sullivan, proprietors of the *Nation* and part of the venerable "Bantry band" of newspapermen, Murphy understood from an early age the cultural capital of the newspaper business. Both his own marriage to Mary Julia Lombard (daughter of James Fitzgerald Lombard, a leading merchant in Cork with extensive business interests in Dublin) and the marriage of one of his daughters to the Chance family provided him access to additional revenue and professional networks for starting or expanding his commercial enterprises. In transforming the business of the daily news when he took over the *Independent*, he richly profited by his efforts, establishing himself as Ireland's first press baron.[49]

Prior to Murphy's ownership, the *Irish Independent* emerged in the wake of the "newspaper war" that broke out during the Parnellite split. Founded in 1891, just after the death of Parnell, whose cause it championed for a brief spell, the *Irish Independent* soon fell into decline. Murphy purchased the paper in 1900, merging it with the *Daily Nation*; in 1904, he bought out the *Independent*'s shareholders and hired a new editor, Timothy (T. R.) Harrington, like Murphy, a native of Castletownbere, Co. Cork.

Whereas Griffith (and indeed, most editors and writers for the advanced nationalist press) understood the press as a persuasive medium for grappling with Ireland's political and cultural awakening, Murphy had a sharply different vision of how journalism could shape Ireland's future. He conceived of the new *Irish Independent* as a non-party organ, "the first halfpenny popular paper in Ireland," expressly designed to emulate English new journalism.[50] In 1904, a year prior to the paper's relaunch, Murphy and Harrington traveled to London to study the business practices of Alfred Harmsworth's *Daily Mail*; its relaunched format made these influences immediately apparent in the extensive use of photographs, color print, and eye-catching headlines and crossheads. Within days of its relaunch, the *Irish Independent* claimed a daily circulation of 30,000; by 1910, the paper brashly reported that its circulation numbers were independently audited, bolstering its claim that it was the first Irish newspaper to prove the size of its readership. By World War I, daily circulation was over 100,000, and it was turning a sizable profit.[51]

In its relaunched format, the paper was similar to the *United Irishman* at eight pages, but it cost half as much and crammed eight columns of print onto each page. Whereas the *United Irishman* placed ads on the final page, the *Independent*'s advertisements were located on page one, similar to "English quality" papers (and Harmsworth's *Daily Mail*), telegraphing another distinction between mainstream nationalist dailies and advanced nationalist periodicals. In the next few years, the paper expanded its advertisements, dedicating page one and page eight to advertisements, with many more featured throughout other pages of each issue; it included up to five different typefaces in its ads to capture readers' attention.[52] Over its first decade, the *Independent* continued to broadcast its circulation numbers and proclaim its "limitations" in ad space as a way to heighten the value of advertising in its pages. By 1908, with the hiring of advertising manager T. A. Grehan, the paper introduced even more dynamic marketing and noticeably new styles of advertising.[53]

Where the *United Irishman* looked to the "little countries" in its advocacy of Irish separatism, the *Irish Independent* prioritized the economic forces of globalization. Its organization and prioritization of sections reinforced Ireland's interconnections with an increasingly global British Empire. Page two, "Finance and Commerce," contained daily updates on Dublin, London, and New York stocks. Market reports covered Dublin, Cork, Limerick, Cambridge, Birmingham, Hull, Newcastle, Leeds, and Salford. Mining markets and mining reports tracked developments in South Africa, West Africa, Western Australia, New Zealand, British Columbia, and Egypt, while rail reports focused on Britain, America, and Canada. The *Independent* also regularly covered land exploration in Rhodesia, West Africa, New Zealand, British Columbia, Siberia, and Egypt, as well as shipping, rubber, and oil shares.

The new masthead of the paper, a sunrise with a harp in the foreground, conveyed to readers that, despite its imported innovations and global business interests, the *Independent* was written for Irish readers awakened to the distinctiveness of their nationality. The title of the paper's first editorial notice on January 2, 1905, "Ourselves," surely was intended to reach Irish separatists who recognized this word as the English translation of Sinn Féin, by now a byword for separatist thinking.[54] If, as Felix Larkin remarks, Griffith regarded Murphy's commercially minded *Independent* (and its competitor, the *Freeman's Journal*) as "prostitute journalism," it may be, in part, because the *Independent* aimed to attract Griffith's and the *Freeman*'s network of readers.[55] Harrington's first editorial professed to be "a national journal in fact as well as in name" while holding to an impossibly neutral standard: "To the Irish Language and Industrial Revival Movements, as to every movement for the National rights of Ireland the 'Irish Independent' will be neither offensive nor aggressive in its style of advocacy, and as a newspaper will be found acceptable by every class and creed."[56]

T. R. Harrington also worked to establish editorial independence from the proprietor of the *Independent*, and there is ample evidence on its pages and in his private letters to Murphy that he both demanded and was given "a free hand as regards the policy of the *Independent* on political questions."[57] Indeed, while William Martin Murphy was openly antagonistic toward both Parnell and the post-Parnellite Irish Party, T. R. Harrington's editorial writing hewed closely to the views of his middle-class Catholic nationalist readers.[58] As Maume explains, the paper expertly navigated the nationalist waters, ostensibly supporting the Irish Party while keeping dissidents Healy and William O'Brien at arm's length.[59] Although the paper was not successful in covering some subjects with neutrality (most notoriously, the Dublin Lockout and the Easter Rising), Harrington aimed for an approach to journalism to which few newspapers in early twentieth-century Ireland aspired.

The *Independent* demonstrated its commitment to the "Irish language and Industrial Revival movements" by featuring, from its first issue in 1905, a daily Irish-language column, titled "Irish Ireland," written by Eoghan Ó Neachtain. (Previous to its relaunch, the *Irish Daily Independent* featured a weekly Irish-language column by Máire de Buitléir.) In his first column, Ó Neachtain broadly distilled the familiar motto "ourselves transnationally alone":

An rud a gcuireann an duine suim an cuireann an tÉireannach suim ann; acht imtheachta nah hÉireann, nach bhfuil sui mag daoinigh eile ionnta & nach raigh sui mag a lán dár muinntir féin ionnta go dtí le goirid annuas, sin iad a bheas mar ughdar cainte san roinn seo, thar éinnidh eile.[60]

That which interests all men interests Irishmen; but Irish affairs, which don't interest others and which didn't interest a lot of our own people until recently, will be the main talking point of this section, above all else. (Translation by Aoife Uí Fhaoláin)

Ó Neachtain's opening column carefully balanced Ireland and the world in this brief excerpt: acknowledging that world politics and foreign affairs would necessarily be of interest to Irish readers, he insisted that his focus on "Irish affairs" sought to correct a disparity in how infrequently the media represented Ireland in its pages. Such a complaint, of course, was expressed repeatedly during the Revival: both the founders of the Irish literary theater and the initial editors of the suffrage weekly the *Irish Citizen* highlighted the exigency of "correcting" negative or nonexistent representation of Irish people, politics, and culture, whether on the stage or in the press. In its early years, Ó Neachtain used his column to educate readers about Irish history, Gaelic culture, nationalist heroes, and Gaeltacht traditions.[61] Much of this content echoed subjects and themes already well-established in other advanced national periodicals, such as the "From the Old Land" columns in the *Shan Van Vocht* or the Inghinidhe na hÉireann meeting minutes in the *United Irishman*. Nevertheless, the linguistic return to Irish in this column, as well as its consistent placement on page four, sandwiched between each day's editorial and the "London Letter," reinforced this opening manifesto about Ireland's cultural and historical place in the world—connected yet alone.

The *Irish Independent* conveyed an ambivalent message regarding the British Empire. Prior to its relaunch in 1905, the paper was a frequent critic of Great Britain, championing the Boers during the South African War and maligning Queen Victoria's Irish visit in 1900.[62] Starting in 1905, however, the relaunched *Independent* supported Home Rule; by 1912, with the release of Erskine Childers's *Framework of Home Rule*, the *Independent* modified its stance, advocating Dominion status, based on the economic shortcomings for Ireland in a Home Rule solution.[63] As Patrick Maume documents, Murphy's vast global business interests shaped his political outlook; once he became proprietor of the paper, he "exerted an influence over the line taken by the *Independent* on Irish Home Rule and, in particular, the idea of Dominion status as a solution to Ireland's unsatisfactory constitutional position."[64]

The *Independent*'s increasingly global coverage of the news showcased its growing reliance on professional networks of journalists across Europe and North America, courtesy of new technologies such as the train, telegraph, and telephone. Its "London Letter" column carried the byline "By our special Wire," a Reuter's dispatch. Its news from France came courtesy of the "Paris correspondence wire." One consistent column on the "World News" pages, "Items of Interest (By Wire and Dispatch)," collected, trimmed, and arranged such wire postings from home and abroad to heighten the experience for Irish readers that they lived in a global village. Featuring pithy human interest stories from Ireland, Great Britain, Canada, and the United States, the column replicated the kinds of gossip and news that, in an earlier era, would be exchanged at the market or post office: a bribery sentence in Oregon, a jewelry theft in East Sussex, a freak death aboard a train to Birmingham, an attempt to swim across the Channel, military appointments and promotions, births, deaths, and health turns of the socially prominent. The *Independent*'s heavy reliance on using wire reports eventually earned it the nickname, coined by D. P. Moran, of "snippy bits."[65]

From its relaunch, the *Independent* aimed to reach an audience "composed of those who enjoyed or aspired to a middle-class consumerist lifestyle."[66] This readership—members of a global empire, of middle-class or aspiring middle class backgrounds—informed what Aoife Uí Fhaoláin has described as the *Independent*'s "hybrid identity."[67] For example, while the *Independent* featured Irish language or bilingual content in its daily "Irish Ireland" column, as well as some news reports, individual articles, letters, reviews, birth, marriage and death notices, and advertisements, it also promoted links with the British Empire, through vocally supporting Home Rule and international trade, and highlighting the social affairs of the Irish gentry.[68] The *Independent* typically dedicated two pages to "World News," though news about British parliamentary debates on Home Rule and Ireland's thirty-two counties was included on these pages and frequently took up at least half of the stories in this section. Indeed, if Murphy afforded his editor a level of editorial autonomy that was unusual for its day, he undoubtedly influenced the *Independent*'s expectation that Ireland would preserve its bond with the British monarchy and the British Empire. The *Independent*, thus, advocated a different version of "ourselves transnationally alone." It provided consistent space on its pages for its transnational network of Irish readers, featuring telegrams from Australia, Canada, and the United States supporting the *Independent*'s editorial message, initially in favor of Home Rule and later for Dominion status. Telegrams from expatriates in Australia, Argentina, and America were reprinted in its pages, proclaiming "unanimous demand" for Home Rule for Ireland.[69]

Adapting and ideologically transforming "ourselves alone" to benefit another important network for the *Independent*—the capitalist class—the *Independent* provides us with a useful vantage point by which to understand the "worlding" of the nationalist press: a paper made to exist—and to flourish—as part of global networks of print capital. Within a year of the paper's relaunch, the *Independent* dedicated considerable column space to debating the value of Dublin hosting its first International Exhibition, despite fierce opposition by separatists, who voiced objections to the exhibition's likely impact on Irish home industries.[70] Murphy succeeded in landing the exhibition through securing the support of King Edward and that of influential Irish business tycoons such as Lord W. J. Pirrie, the shipbuilding magnate and owner of Harland and Wolff.[71] The *Independent* covered the International Exhibition as an exemplary moment of "ourselves transnationally alone": through bringing international trade to Dublin, the six-month exhibition, from May 4, 1907, through November 9, 1907, was meant "to promote Ireland's agricultural and industrial resources and to improve productivity and standard of living in rural Ireland." The paper also kept the topic ever-present in its readers' minds, dedicating over a hundred columns in 1905–6 and over four hundred separate columns in 1907.

On May 1, 1907, the opening day of the exhibition, the *Independent* dedicated a significant portion of the issue to covering multiple aspects of the event: the official program, a detailed description of the procession through Dublin streets, a drawing illustrating Lord Lieutenant reading a message from the king declaring the Exhibition open, a fashion column describing some of the dresses of those in attendance, and, in keeping with its new journalist innovations, an entire page, titled "The Exhibition in Pictures," of drawings and photographs of this first day. In addition to drawings of the Hall of Industries and Palace of Arts and photographs of the exhibition grounds, showing a great water chute and an interior from the Irish exhibitors' section, the paper featured a prominent photograph of William Martin Murphy together with the Marquis of Ormonde, who was president of exhibition.

In its coverage of the opening day of the world exhibition, the *Independent* emphasized repeatedly the Irishness of this international event of commerce. One well-placed article, written by "an Irish-Glaswegian" with an "Irish-Ireland spirit sharpened by a residence amongst Britishers," established his ethos through posing as an experienced archeologist of nations:

> Here was a bit of one of the Earl's Court Exhibitions, there a reminder of the Crystal Palace, and on all sides, the fibrous plaster granite blocks by which one best remembers the last huge Exhibition in Glasgow. But with all these similarities I found the Irish International Exhibition dissimilar to any in my experience—it was Irish and in Ireland and that was everything.[72]

This Irishman-in-exile stressed that the distinctively Irish International Exhibition—"Irish and in Ireland"—proved that Ireland was ready for Home Rule. Its success should not, the author averred, lead to premature separation from the British empire: "Gazing on the huge displays from foreign countries, [. . .] one could not help looking back on the rival project of a National Exhibition [. . .], I was forced to turn my mind from the National Exhibition idea—I had almost said fiasco—with the thought, 'not yet, not yet.'" For the *Irish Independent*, then, this World Exhibition provided it with another opportunity to advance its version of "ourselves transnationally alone": home rule, foreign investment, and an enhanced Irish commercial bottom line. Indeed, the owner of the *Independent* personally benefitted from the message and the success of the exhibition. He was offered a knighthood by Edward VII, who opened the exhibition. While Murphy publicly declined the knighthood to maintain his nationalist credentials, he gained considerable stature among the network that his paper had been assiduously cultivating: the Protestant unionist-oriented business class. The exhibition launched Murphy's public career in the Dublin Chamber of Commerce, which he eventually led as its president.[73]

Conclusions

Studying nationalist periodicals of the Revival—radical and mainstream—tests a longstanding assumption about the inward gaze of revivalist writers, a view influentially articulated by Declan Kiberd in *Inventing Ireland*, that "if many—perhaps a majority of—Irish writers and nationalists were slow to identify with movements elsewhere, this was because their minds were unresponsive to the comparative method, having been attuned to the revivalist idea that the Irish were unique, 'like no other race on earth.'"[74] As we have seen, both separatist and Home Rule nationalist papers paid careful attention to movements elsewhere—to advance Ireland's political independence and to develop its commercial practices. As we also have seen, Levine's insights into network theory help us appreciate the work of new approaches in Irish Studies, such as *Yeats and Afterwords*, which return to formal lines of analysis without forgetting the insights of historicism.[75] By tracking the "affordances" (latent uses or potential actions) in newspaper networks, we can appreciate the cultural richness of newspapers—written for Irish readers, about Irish gossip, news, and politics—to draw in readers and react to events, policies, party politics, cultural enterprises, personalities, that were not only local but increasingly from well beyond Irish shores.

Part Three

The Revivalism of Everyday Life

Novel Forms

5

School Stories

George Moore, Realism, and Revival

M a r y L . M u l l e n

The more I was taught the stupider I became, and perhaps, the more unwilling to learn.
—George Moore, *Hail and Farewell*, 98.

George Moore was almost invariably forgotten. That was due, perhaps, to the fact that he belonged to no school in England.
—Ford Madox Ford, 135.

Looking back at his collaboration with George Moore during the Irish Revival, W. B. Yeats laments that Moore was "more simple, more naive, more one-idea'd than a Bank holiday schoolboy."[1] To mock his immaturity and downplay his importance to the Revival, Yeats goes on to suggest that although Moore had written "five great novels," he was ruined by their collaboration because it encouraged Moore to seek a style. As Yeats purportedly tells Moore, style "is colored glass and you need a plate-glass window."[2] A dig at Moore's realism, this advice suggests that Moore's need for clarity forever separates him from Irish authors like Standish O'Grady, James Joyce, and J. M. Synge whose disparate works are united precisely through "the formation of a style."[3]

Adrian Frazier warns readers against taking this portrait too seriously, or, worse, echoing Yeats's mockery of Moore.[4] He suggests that in order to understand Moore's importance to the Irish Revival, we need to move beyond Yeats's unfair characterization of him in *Dramatis Personae*. Like Frazier, I seek to reassess Moore's contribution to the Irish Revival. But I argue that Yeats's portrait of Moore, however dismissive and unfair, actually provides the language through which to do so. Yeats minimizes Moore's writing by provocatively combining two dimensions of the word "school"—school as a site of institutional education and school as a style or approach to literature. As a "Bank holiday schoolboy," Moore appears at odds with formal schooling, while as someone who needs a "plate-glass window" he seems incompatible with the literary style of Yeats's Irish school. But, in the process of mocking Moore, Yeats raises questions about the relationship between formal schooling and literary schools. To what extent was the Irish Literary Revival an institutional movement? And was realism with its "plate-glass window" actually at odds with the new Irish literary school?

For a long time, critics, like Yeats, associated the Revival with poetry and drama and saw realism, especially the realist novel, as antithetical to the newly emerging literary school. As early as 1916, Ernest Boyd asserted that revivalists were not interested "in the novel as such."[5] He celebrates Moore's short story collection *The Untilled Field* (1903) and his novel *The Lake* (1905) as distinct accomplishments only to suggest that they are anomalies given the social factors in Ireland that "tend to retard the evolution of the Irish novel."[6] John Wilson Foster's account of the fiction of the Revival reassesses the place of prose within the movement but continues to identify realism as a reply *to* the Revival rather than a genre *of* the Revival.[7] Recently, Joe Cleary builds on this approach as he historicizes the emergence of Irish naturalism.[8] In his account, Irish naturalism responds to the institutions of the Revival while Moore's experiments with realism and naturalism remain "directed at a securely institutionalized conservative English Victorian literary world."[9] For Cleary, Moore's Revival writing remains too English—and too tied to English institutions—to inaugurate an Irish genre tradition.

By contrast, I argue that Moore's Revival realism actually contributes to larger trends within the Revival precisely because it questions institutionality even amid a period of institution building. Specifically, I suggest that by yoking together these two meanings of the word "school" Yeats provides the vocabulary through which to understand the complexity of Moore's Revival realism and, by extension, the complexity of the Revival itself. Moore, a vocal opponent to formal schooling who had vexed relationships to literary schools, does not merely reply to the Revival; he shows the tensions within the Revival between institution building and institutional refusal, the invention of a self-consciously Irish style and literary experiments that work across genres and encompass disparate modes of writing. Although, as Claire Hutton persuasively argues, the literary Revival worked through institutional structures, the literary aesthetics of the Revival also questioned institutionality.[10]

Following Roderick Ferguson, I define institutionality as a mode of social organization that incorporates difference while minimizing the "ruptural possibilities" of that difference.[11] Emerging from his study of the growth of interdisciplines such as ethnic studies, Black studies, and gender studies in the university, Ferguson's definition interrogates the unintended consequences of institutional incorporation. While new institutional formations seek to disrupt existing institutions by representing and protecting what he calls "minority difference," they actually extend established networks of power in ways that undermine this very difference.[12]

Ferguson's definition helps explain the Revival's contradictory relationship to institutions and institutionality. On the one hand, revivalists worked to build institutions precisely because the "ruptural possibilities" of difference were all too active in Ireland. In founding institutions that anticipated the nation-state to come, such as the Irish Literary Theatre, the Gaelic League, Inghinidhe na hÉireann, and St. Enda's school, revivalists sought to cultivate a national public and national unity through new institutions.[13] On the other hand, revivalists offered a powerful critique of institutionality as they criticized existing English institutions because they reduced the possibilities of political action and aesthetic experimentation. The Revival both sought to transform social difference into national unity through institutions, and adopted a critical attitude that questioned what Ferguson calls "the will to institutionality"—or the desire to absorb social difference through institutions.[14]

In what follows, I trace Moore's opposition to literary schools and formal schooling both before and during the Revival in order to make two related arguments. First, Moore's short-lived participation in the Irish Revival, like his celebration and then rejection of Émile Zola's naturalism, demonstrates that Moore abandons literary movements when they begin to feel institutional. Second, in its representation of contingent moments of ruptures that revive life and art, his short story collection, *The Untilled Field*, captures the central contradiction of the Revival: building new institutions versus criticizing institutionality. More than simply a response to the Revival, Moore's Revival realism demonstrates that the Irish Revival is not only defined through competing and overlapping institutions, it is also defined through contradictory approaches to institutionality as a mode of social organization.

School Stories

One of the most surprising things about Moore's relationship to the Irish Revival is that he affiliated himself with an emerging Irish school in the first place. A Catholic landlord from county Mayo, he made his name as an author by serving as "Zola's ricochet in England."[15] He sought to translate Zola's novels into English and presented his early novels, such as *A Mummer's Wife* (1885), as naturalist novels in the style of Zola. In this role, he famously attacked the circulating libraries for censoring fiction—his first of many public attacks on institutions that govern literary production. When Moore turned his attention to Ireland in *A Drama in Muslin* (1886) and *Parnell and His Island* (1887), he ruthlessly criticized landlords and peasants alike as he distanced himself from his native land. Given Moore's desire to intervene in an English literary scene and his critical writing on Ireland, his decision to leave London for Dublin in 1901 remains, as Frazier concludes, "a complicated mystery even to himself."[16]

But Moore did move to Dublin, where he often found himself in comical and contradictory positions as he contributed to the newly formed Irish Literary Theatre and became a zealous advocate for the Irish language movement. Declan Kiberd describes Moore's uneasy relationship to the very institutions Moore tries to support: he wants his nephews to learn Irish but does not learn it himself; he supports the Gaelic League by hosting the most English of events—a lawn party.[17] Early reviewers of Lady Gregory's *Ideals in Ireland* (1901) shared Kiberd's suspicion of Moore's conversion to the revivalist cause. Questioning Moore's inclusion in the volume, one reviewer calls his article advocating the return to the Irish language "ridiculous" and his participation in the Revival a mere passing "hobby."[18] Moore's humorous, if cutting, memoir of the Revival, *Hail and Farewell*, encourages such criticism by explaining his desire to join the Revival as a compulsion to "thrust my finger into every literary pie-dish" as opposed to a serious shift in either his thinking or his art.[19]

For many critics, Moore could not be a sincere contributor to the new "Irish school" because he had already been such a vocal participant in the debates about realism and naturalism in England. It is easy to see him as an opportunist merely seeking publicity: he stopped writing about the scandal of the circulating libraries' censorship in England only to begin writing about the scandal of the British empire's drive toward uniformity in Ireland.[20] But, I suggest that Moore's short-lived participation in Zola's French school of writing can teach us about his short-lived participation in the Irish school of the Revival precisely because they take similar forms. In both instances, Moore declares himself to be a disciple of a new school of literature only to publicly break with the school. And, in both cases, Moore justifies his departure from the literary school by associating the literary movement with institutions—especially educational ones. When Moore breaks with Zola, he casts him in the role of schoolmaster. In turn, when he breaks with the Irish Revival, he questions its increasing institutionalization—the way it serves schools rather than life. In *Hail and Farewell*, he warns, "If you aren't very careful,

Yeats, the Academic idea will overgrow the folk" before leaving Ireland and the Irish Revival.[21] For this reason, Yeats's mocking portrait of Moore is in many senses, right: Moore acts as a "Bank holiday schoolboy" who relishes his freedom as he actively resists institutions and the discipline they imply. Moore departs from literary schools at the very moment that they begin to feel institutional.

Moore uses the language of school to explain his break from Zola despite the fact that Zola explicitly rejected this language. In his own work, Zola insisted that "naturalism is not a school" and instead characterized it as a method.[22] He explains that methods can be practiced by anyone but schools suggest the "genius of one man" or "the ravings of a group of men."[23] But when Moore publicly broke with naturalism, he portrayed Zola as a schoolmaster to undermine this emphasis on method. In his 1894 essay, "My Impressions of Zola," Moore recalls how he and Zola move upstairs to discuss Moore's recent criticism of naturalism: "He led the way, I followed, feeling very much as I used to feel at school when I had been ordered a flogging. The master lay on the sofa."[24] Zola appears as a schoolmaster: not only the leader of a literary school, but an all-powerful teacher who can order a flogging. At the end of the meeting, Zola, schoolmaster, expels Moore from his literary school. Moore's public account of this conversation, by contrast, casts himself as incapable of being schooled. He wants to please "the master," but cannot. While Zola believes firmly in naturalism, Moore only has "fugitive contradictory thinking."[25]

By casting Zola in the role of schoolmaster, Moore transforms the experimental novelist who inspired him to fight the circulating libraries in England into an institutional figure to reject. Moore makes similar rhetorical moves throughout his career, voicing his discontent with contemporary literature by comparing novels to "schoolbooks" and authors to "schoolmasters."[26] In his attack on Mudie's Library, which refused to carry a few of his novels, Moore suggests that Mudie's practices relegate novels to the "school-room"—claiming that the English novelist "is read there or nowhere."[27] Moore criticizes English novels' didactic and moralizing content, suggesting that there should be a shift away from the sanitized literature of mid-century to a more aesthetic literature detached from questions of use, morality, and convertion. Later in his career, Moore began attacking schools and universal education because of their deadening influence, declaring his one talent to be a "determination not to be taught."[28]

In fact, the possibility of a new literary school at odds with existing institutions initially attracts Moore to the Revival. Tellingly, when championing the Irish language in the midst of the Irish Revival, Moore celebrates the fact that "the Irish language [. . .] has never been to school."[29] Although Moore did not collect folklore or study Irish mythology, he, too, was intrigued with what Yeats calls "that peasant mind their schoolmasters had taught them to despise."[30] In the preface to the revised 1926 edition of *The Untilled Field*, Moore presents the literary innovations of the Revival as an alternative to the conventional language of the schoolroom. He particularly remembers "how Synge had sprung at once out of pure board-school English into a beautiful style, finding it in an idiom that had hitherto been used only as a means of comic relief."[31] Synge's style is beautiful to Moore precisely because it is living, while "pure board-school English" is sterile and empty. For Moore, revivalist writers find style in the language and forms of thinking that schoolmasters despise and seek to root out.

Many revivalists shared Moore's resistance to existing institutions. Lady Gregory's editor's note to *Ideals In Ireland*, like many of the essays in the collection, clearly identifies the institutions at odds with the flourishing of new thought in Ireland: commissioners of education "engaged in cutting veins that unite the present and the past" and Trinity College, which remains separate from Irish culture.[32] Douglas Hyde suggests that "bad teaching" is the "chief cause" of Ireland's problems as he condemns existing schools and their English-language curriculum in his contribution to the volume.[33] Echoes of Patrick Pearse's *The Murder Machine* occur throughout these essays, as they, like Pearse, approach the existing educational system in Ireland and England as artificial machinery that ruthlessly destroys art and thought instead of "fostering the growth of things."[34]

Revivalists questioned educational institutions because of their colonial effects and, more broadly, because they perpetuate existing social arrangements rather than inspiring social change. Maud Gonne, for instance, links Irish National Schools to asylums and workhouses, calling them "the sombre factories for the destruction of our race" and she suggests that institutions ostensibly founded to educate and aid people actually work to eradicate Irish difference.[35] Gonne criticizes these institutions because they are English but their Englishness is not their only problem: they impose form rather than fostering growth. Tellingly, Yeats, Gonne, and Moore all indicate that their lack of formal education enables their revivalist work in their autobiographies. Yeats notes that if he had gone to a university instead of an art school, he "should have had to give up my Irish subject-matter."[36] Gonne nostalgically portrays how she was "allowed to run wild" as a girl—free from the rigors and discipline of school—while Moore celebrates his expulsion from Oscott College.[37] Whether critiquing existing school structures or celebrating their informal education, these writers imply that formal schooling integrates students into institutions in ways that ensure the endurance of the same rather than ruptures of difference.

And yet, unlike Zola, revivalist writers self-consciously represented themselves as a literary school rather than a method that others could adapt. In 1895, Yeats concludes his essay on contemporary Irish prose writers with the hopeful declaration, "We have for the first time in Ireland, and among the Irish in England, a school of men of letters united by a common purpose."[38] The term "school" also appears in the founding statement of the Irish Literary Theatre in 1897, which asserts a desire "to build up a Celtic and Irish school of dramatic literature."[39] Adopting the language of a "school" suggests that the literature of the Revival was more than an aesthetic project—it was an institutional one.[40]

Not surprisingly, one of the lasting effects of the Revival is institutional: twentieth- and twenty-first century critics often return to the Revival in order to justify their own critical project. Vivian Mercer's 1956 article, "An Irish School of Criticism?" celebrates Yeats's criticism and anthologies as a model and, more recently, Edna Long-ley claims that the growth of Irish Studies programs "vindicates Yeats's original critical project."[41] While the literary experiments associated with the Revival exceeded these attempts to define and call into being an identifiable group, "united by a common purpose," such statements nevertheless indicate an institution-building impulse that continues to shape the study of Irish literature today.

Moore never fully contributed to shaping the Irish literary school, but his participation in the Revival did briefly change his relationship to formal schools. In a stark departure, Moore presents *The Untilled Field* as a schoolbook—the criticism he usually reserved for conventional realist novels. In *Hail and Farewell*, he claims that the stories, written in English but translated into Irish, will be accepted "as a text-book by the Intermediate Board of Education" and fill the increasing need for Irish language books.[42] Of course, it never succeeded as a textbook and reviewers criticized the Irish language collection for being too English.[43]

While this claim may simply be another performance by Moore—after declaring that the collection will be a textbook, he emphasizes how difficult it was for him to write stories suitable for schoolchildren—it nevertheless reveals the contradictions within his revivalist work. Moore was drawn to the Revival as a way of resisting literature that smacked of the schoolroom, but his Irish-language textbook sought to contribute to the institutionalization of the Irish language in schools. Moreover, although *The Untilled Field* celebrated the Irish language, it did not draw on a native Irish tradition of storytelling but instead adapted forms from Ivan Turgenev's 1852 collection, *A Sportsman's Sketches*. And, finally, although Moore presents the collection as a schoolbook, the stories within this book tend to criticize schooling. I suggest that the hybridity at the heart of *The Untilled Field*—the way it is both literary and institutional, Irish and international—not only expresses Moore's contrarian nature or uneasy relationship to the Irish Revival but reveals an important dynamic at work in the Revival: to build new institutions while being critical of institutionality; to create and question schools.

Revival Realism

How does Moore's Revival realism fit in this dynamic of building institutions while being critical of institutionality? To answer this question, I think about how realism, as a literary form, functions in relation to institutions and institutionality. For many Irish studies scholars, realism is so firmly entrenched with English institutions that it is necessarily at odds with the intellectual energy of the Revival.[44] For others, realism functions like institutionality—a mode of social organization that integrates differences in ways that reinforce social norms.[45] But Moore's Revival realism, specifically *The Untilled Field*, models forms of institution building where the "ruptural possibilities" of difference endure. Instead of integrating difference to contain it, Moore celebrates how ruptures of difference revive life and art. Moore does not simply challenge the institution of English realism in these stories; he rethinks the relationship between realism and institutionality, highlighting disruptive moments that do not cohere into generalized lessons or uphold social norms.

Anna Kornbluh's recent argument that realism "designs and erects socialities"—that it produces rather than simply represents social space—helps us see how *The Untilled Field* engages with institutions.[46] For Kornbluh, realism functions as architecture by imagining new social forms, structures, blueprints. In Henry James's novels, the focus of Kornbluh's study, this architecture creates coherence, even conveys a sense of totality. When thinking about *The Untilled Field* in terms of the architecture it represents and imagines, by contrast, one is confronted by ruin, disrepair, and failure. In "In the Clay," Father McCabe builds churches that his parishes cannot afford to repair; in "A Letter to Rome," Father MacTurnan is troubled by relief-work roads that go nowhere; and in "A Play-House in the Waste," the community builds a play-house only for the roof and walls to crumble. Through this failed architecture, *The Untilled Field* criticizes what Robert Welch calls the Catholic Church's "dreary institutionalism"—the way it suppresses life, art, and thought.[47] Alluding to the title of the collection, the narrator within "Julia Cahill's Curse" suggests that these broken buildings are central to understanding Ireland, writing, "What was more significant than the untilled fields were the ruins."[48] While older ruins tell the story of eviction, these new ruins indicate that "the inhabitants must have left voluntarily" (203). The abandoned homes are not simply representations of the Irish landscape, they are visible symbols for the failing social system: there are structures but little life in Moore's Ireland.

Against the background of this pervasive ruin emerge moments of rupture that reanimate social possibilities. In "A Letter to Rome," Father MacTurnan's isolation allows him to imagine a new future for the Church where priests marry and share their relative wealth with their parishioners. Paying attention to the particular problems his parishioners face, he is able to reject the Cardinal's "narrow ways" (180). In "The Wedding Gown," Margaret Kirwin lends her wedding gown to her grand-niece, Molly. This act of generosity at once restores Margaret to her senses—she understands her surroundings for the first time since she has moved in with Molly's family—and transforms their relationship from one of fear and familial responsibility to one where they act through each other. In turn, "Almsgiving" unsettles the narrator's assumption that the blind beggar's life is one of privation as it reveals the beggar's robust social life. These moments produce what Alison Harvey calls an Irish realism of "minor figures" that pushes against social conventions and disrupts social structures.[49]

Together, *The Untilled Field*'s failed architectural projects and its moments of rupture express the tension within the Revival between the "will to institutionality"—the desire to integrate difference through institutions—and the "ruptural possibilities" of social difference. Whereas the ruined buildings depict the existing social structures that, for Moore, prevent Revival, the new building projects—many of which quickly fall into disrepair—represent the institutional projects of the Revival. These projects sometimes advance the aesthetics of the Revival—Father McCabe attempts to revive ancient Irish architecture in "In the Clay"—and sometimes are more pragmatic—as an agent of the Irish Industrial Society, the narrator in "Julia Cahill's Curse" acquires land to build schools for lacemaking. In both forms, they are institutional, for they contribute to a new "Irish school" or build new schools. By contrast, the moments of rupture within the stories point to forms of revival—moments of reawakening and restoration—that never assimilate into a larger movement. Representing the Revival and imagining revivals, Moore produces a ruptured realism that uses particular, embodied experience to revitalize social structures through social difference.

Take for instance the opening story of the 1903 collection, "In the Clay," which dramatizes the conflicts between Father McCabe's failed architectural projects and John Rodney's art. Father McCabe, who commissions Rodney's work, ruins parishes by building new churches, and ruins churches by using poor designs. As the narrator asserts, Father McCabe "had begun life by making an ancient abbey ridiculous by adding a modern steeple" (12). Father McCabe's architectural visions echo many of the aesthetic trends of the Revival—he happily discusses "the Celtic renaissance" and presents his architectural projects as an attempt to return to and reanimate the "origins of art" (18).[50] But because the parish cannot afford these projects, they do not serve his parishioners. For Rodney, a sculptor who Father McCabe enlists to realize his visions, Father McCabe's failed architectural projects suggest more pervasive national failure. He sees Ireland as "a country where there had never been any sculpture nor any painting, nor any architecture to signify" (5–6). Although Father McCabe attempts to revive art, he only extends social structures that impede life.

Although Rodney is critical of Ireland and the Irish Revival, he is able to transform his art through a radical act of mimesis as he models Lucy. In a country without artistic models (Father McCabe does not know that the statue of the Virgin and Child requires a nude model), Rodney happens upon Lucy, the daughter of a cheesemonger. With Lucy sitting as a model, Rodney does his best work: "He had never had such a model before, not in France or in Italy, and this time he had done the best piece of work he had ever done in his life" (16).

The success of this statue shows that mimetic representation—here, representing the nude Lucy—transforms conventional religious sculpture: the "Virgin and Child in the sense suggested by the capital letters" becomes a "piece of paganism" that evokes vitality and life (5). This form of mimesis differs from the "plate-glass window" that Yeats associates with Moore's style, for its force emerges not from its clear representation of reality, but from the unstable merger of reality—Lucy's singular figure—with a more familiar, and more idealized religious figure. Such art does not suggest either documentary realism or grand architectural designs but rather shows how the embodied presence of ordinary, everyday people can restore life to lifeless structures.

Thus, while the story represents Revival as an institutional endeavor through Father McCabe, it shows the possibilities of multiple, small-scale revivals through Rodney. Sometimes understood as a figure that represents Moore's own critical attitude to the Revival, Rodney actively distances himself from the emerging Irish school and, eventually, Ireland itself: "He had never believed in any Celtic renaissance and all the talk he had heard about stained glass and revivals did not deceive him" (12).[51] And yet, what is at stake in art for Rodney is revival: art restores vitality to lifeless forms. For this reason, the story represents the destruction of Rodney's statue as the destruction of life. After Lucy's brothers demolish the statue because they overhear Father McCabe's criticism of it, Rodney thinks of the statue, once so full of life, "as one thinks of a corpse"—a dead form once more (22). Implicitly linking art and life, Rodney's sculpture celebrates revival while also demonstrating how the very institutional project of Revival can suppress, even destroy, both life and art.

Lucy Delaney, the model who restores life to Rodney's art, complicates this relatively neat division between Father McCabe and Rodney. Although she, like Rodney, questions deadening institutions, she is reabsorbed into institutions by the end of the collection. In a powerful anti-institutional act, she sets fire to her school and leaves Ireland in "The Way Back." Mirroring her brothers' destruction of Rodney's statue, Lucy's act of destruction refuses institutional authority rather than channeling it. But despite her forcefulness, she is not able to live the life that she desires: her family reasserts their control over her by making her marry a mathematical instrument maker, and Rodney suppresses her disruptive potential by viewing her through the lens of national myth rather than as a distinct individual. As he laments her marriage he recasts her as a national type, a "Grania" (221). In his words, "It is well she has gone; for it is many years since there was honor in Ireland for a Grania" (221). Rodney's statement playfully undermines the recent reworking of the Grania myth by revivalists. It implies that despite Moore's own work with Yeats to represent Grania in *Diarmuid and Grania* and Alice Milligan's engagement with the myth in *Last Feast of the Fianna*, Ireland is not ready to honor Grania.[52] But through this allusion, Rodney's statement also defines Lucy as a woman caught between two men rather than a woman seeking an independent life (in this story, the two men are Rodney and the critic, Harding).[53] When Lucy models for Rodney, he traces her singular figure, transforming the "Virgin and Child" by representing a particular, embodied woman. When Lucy marries, however, Rodney minimizes her disruptive potential as an individual woman and, instead, mythologizes her. However critical of the institutions of the Revival that Rodney may be, he also uses them to contain Lucy's anti-institutional force.

Although Lucy is in many ways a marginal figure within *The Untilled Field*—a muse who does not narrate her own story, a symbol for Ireland's inability to reckon with its own desires—she reveals how gender shapes the revivalist's relationships to institutions and institutionality. She more actively resists institutions than Rodney— she sets fire to her school, while he only passively declares "that he would sooner die than go on teaching" (200). But she is also more easily integrated into institutionality—her disruptive force is suppressed first through marriage and then through revivalist myth. By exposing Rodney's contradictions, Lucy's story shows how revivalists navigated conflicting dynamics within and between institutions rather than adopting a coherent position either for institutions or against institutionality. But, just as importantly, Lucy's story suggests that men who otherwise celebrate the "ruptural possibilities" of social difference work to integrate women into institutions in ways that delimit their disruptive potential. Lucy exposes how the aesthetics of the Revival often represented women in ways that made it more difficult for women to represent themselves.

The second story of the collection, "Some Parishioners," features similar tensions between architecture and art, institution building and criticisms of institutionality in its narration of Father Tom's interactions with his parishioners.[54] Father Tom is one of the most narrow-minded priests within the collection and uses institutional spaces, such as the schoolhouse, to rein in the robust social life of his parishioners. Father Tom does not share Father McCabe's architectural visions, but he nevertheless faces an architectural dilemma: the church walls are not secure and he must either raise two hundred pounds to fix them or three or four thousand pounds to build a new church. Another symbol of a failed social structure that cannot endure, this crumbling church drives the plot of the story. Needing to find money "to have the church made safe," Father Tom endangers his parishioners (49). He refuses to marry Mary Byrne and Ned Kavanagh because they do not have the five-pound fee, forcing them to have a wedding without a religious ceremony. While Father Tom is shocked by their sin and his role in it, the story implies that the parishioners are just fine without the structure of the church—more happy, even.

Biddy M'Hale, another parishioner, further complicates Father Tom's attempt to rebuild the church because of her commitment to her own architectural visions: she wants to build a stained glass window for the church but will not contribute to restoring the structure of the edifice. Although the image of the Virgin in the window that Biddy installs is entirely conventional—the agent has a window just like the one that Biddy envisions in stock—this image, like Rodney's sculpture, reanimates Biddy in surprising ways. Sharing her vision for the window, she suggests that she'd "like the Virgin to wear a blue cloak" (103). The meaning of this blue cloak differs for Biddy and the agent who supplies the window. For the agent, blue is appropriate because it "signified chastity," but for Biddy it evokes her youth—a time when she "used to go blackberrying with the boys" while wearing a blue ribbon (103, 89). The blue color resuscitates a time when Biddy's "woman's hopes" were still alive—when she did not yet know that she would live a celibate life (89). Tellingly, she begins to wear the blue ribbon of her youth once more and after her window is installed, she, like the Virgin, wears "a bright blue cloak" (110).

Ultimately, the window transforms Biddy's reality and she begins to see religious visions that awaken the hopes of her youth while simultaneously celebrating her faithfulness: visions of Jesus taking her in his arms as well as images of a "beautiful young man" (115). By the end of the story, "The things of the world are no longer realities to [Biddy]. Her realities are what she sees and hears in that window" (114). Creating a reality rather than reflecting it, the stained-glass window ultimately represents what mimesis cannot capture: Biddy's rejuvenation. Tellingly, unlike Lucy, Biddy is never reintegrated into institutions but rather shows the spirit that institutions lack. The story closes with Father Maguire and a visitor "looking at her, trying vainly to imagine what her happiness might be" (115). This final line both validates Biddy's visions and suggests that they exceed realist representation, alluding to forms of spirit that do not translate back into structure.

Throughout its stories, *The Untilled Field* uses repetition to capture contradictory institutional dynamics within the Revival—Father McCabe's stained glass windows that extend Church authority and Biddy's stained glass window which revives spiritual life, Lucy's brothers' act of destruction that channels institutional power and Lucy's act of destruction that demolishes the school. In the process, it encourages an understanding of Moore's Revival realism *as* a dynamic: a force as well as a form. For despite the attention to architecture throughout the collection, Moore's representation of Ireland does not cohere into shared social space or convey the sense of totality that Kornbluh locates in Henry James's realist architecture.[55] Instead, he undercuts social coherence—and social convention—by dramatizing moments of rupture as sources of renewal, for both life and art. Sometimes these moments emerge from architecture that creates new realities: Biddy's window allows her to access the dreams of her youth. Other times, these moments emerge by representing existing realities: using Lucy as a model for the Virgin Mary revitalizes Rodney's art. Refusing to offer a prescription for Revival, Moore's realism instead draws attention to contingent moments of renewal.

Moore's Revival realism demonstrates how realism expresses the contradictions of the Revival rather than simply functioning as a reply to the Revival. In the process, his realism pushes against our own tendency to narrate the Literary Revival as a school story, or to feel entirely at home in an "Irish school of criticism" that defines itself as an extension of the Revival. For the Revival did not only seek to create unity out of difference—forming a shared literary style that imagined a unified nation or establishing a shared critical practice—it was also a moment of institutional critique. As a "Bank holiday schoolboy" who relishes his freedom from schools, Moore imagines forms of revival that celebrate the ruptural possibilities of social difference as he narrates the limits of institutionality as a mode of social organization.

6

An Ordinary Revival

Yeats and Irish Women Novelists

Paige Reynolds

One of the sine qua non of revivalist literary culture has been the privileging of poetry and drama over fiction. In John Wilson Foster's *Fictions of the Irish Literary Revival*, the major study of revivalist fiction, Foster asserts that "the novel as a recognizable and autonomous form received a setback at the hands of the revival and its aims and aspirations" and thus reduced the novel to "a middlebrow tributary" of the period's artistic production.[1] Rather than adapt the novel's form to the aims of the Revival, as we see in the innovative drama of this period, Foster argues, the novel seems to hang on to the "tired, conventional form" of social realism and popular romance.[2] In recent decades, scholarship on the Revival has showcased the rich diversity of aesthetic forms and practices integral to this movement, as well as underscoring the contributions of previously neglected figures.[3] But our understanding of literary genre during this period remains largely unchanged: we still tend to regard the Revival as a movement defined almost exclusively by its poetry, folklore, and drama.

The dismissal of the novel is a particular problem when we try to understand the place of women writers in the Revival. During these years, an impressive group of Irish women wrote hundreds of novels on Irish themes for audiences at home and abroad. They include Jane Barlow, Emily Lawless, Somerville and Ross, Katharine Tynan, Miss L. MacManus, M. E. Francis (Francis Blundell), Rosa

Mulholland (Lady Gilbert), Charlotte Riddell, L. T. Meade (Elizabeth Smith), Katherine Cecil Thurston, and W. H. Letts, among others. Some of this fiction overtly engages the Revival's desire to recuperate Irish myth or history, such as Nora Hopper's *Ballads in Prose* (1894), or to convey the social and political characteristics of the Irish people and their culture through the native rural landscape, as is evident in Emily Lawless' *Grania* (1892). Some of these novels directly address the political foment of the era; for example, a number of popular romances are set amid the political conflicts of the 1916 Rising, and portray a young Irish woman in a love triangle with an Irish rebel and an English soldier. Yet other novels by Irish women writers must be read more carefully to identify the subtle ways that they engage and advance revivalist concerns. In order to recognize the astonishing variety of revivalist fiction, we have to attend to genres such as the popular romance, children's fiction, and the Catholic novel, genres often dominated by women writers.

A more capacious understanding of Irish fiction during these decades not only expands the revivalist canon to include more women writers; it also acknowledges the central importance of reading audiences to the Revival's aims because many of these women were astonishingly prolific and popular worldwide. It also allows us to interrogate long-accepted critical claims about the movement. What role, for example, have Yeats and the literary critics writing in his wake had on the understand of genre during the Revival? While the neglect of women writers in the Irish tradition has become a familiar refrain, how might the Revival's particular antipathy to the middle classes, and more generally to ordinary experience, influence our subsequent perspective on Irish fiction during the Revival? To explore these topics, this essay will focus on two novels written by women during the Revival: Jane Barlow's 1891 utopian novel *History of a World of Immortals without a God: Translated from an Unpublished Manuscript in the Library of a Continental University*, written under the pseudonym Antares Skorpios (and perhaps authored in tandem with her father James Barlow), and Rosa Mulholland's 1910 realist novel, *Father Tim*, which like George Moore's novel *A Drama in Muslin* (1886) explores rural poverty, though Mulholland's novel also depicts the urban poverty infecting Dublin.

That these two novels are largely unknown, and that these two writers fall largely outside of critical conversations about the Revival, are not obvious historical problems. The Revival has long been represented as engineered by Irish men such as Douglas Hyde, George Russell, and W. B. Yeats. But the contents of the Revival's major publications suggest the movement was not inherently sexist. In *Representative Irish Tales* (1891), Yeats's two-volume anthology of the Irish short story, two of the ten writers, Maria Edgeworth and Rosa Mulholland, were women.[4] Of the eight young Irish poets published in Russell's collection *New Songs* (1904), fully half were women: Eva Gore-Booth, Alice Milligan, Susan Mitchell, and Ella Young.[5] Katharine Tynan's anthology *A Cabinet of Irish Literature* (1902–3) offered in its fourth volume an evaluation of the Revival and included ninety-one authors, forty-three of whom were women, a ratio, as Margaret Kelleher notes, "unique in the history of Irish anthologies."[6] And in 1905, the American critic Horatio Sheafe Krans wrote a short study entitled *Yeats and the Irish Literary Revival*, noting "Mr. Yeats's recent visit to this country has called special attention to the work in drama, poetry, and fiction, of a group of young Irishmen," but he name-checks Augusta Gregory, Nora Hopper, Emily Lawless, Jane Barlow, and Moira O'Neill in his overview of revivalist writers.[7]

The notion of the Revival as almost entirely dominated by male writers is not necessarily about revivalists themselves. Instead, it surfaces in subsequent critical assessments of the movement. W. P. Ryan's *The Irish Literary Revival* (1894) includes a generous listing of women writers in its account of the early Revival. However, accounts written after Yeats's ascension to fame—such as Ernest Boyd's *Ireland's Literary Renaissance* (1916), Daniel Corkery's *Synge and Anglo-Irish Literature* (1931), and Richard Fallis' *The Irish Renaissance* (1977)—focus almost exclusively on male writers. George J. Watson's *Irish Identity and the Irish Literary Revival* (1979) confines Gregory to footnotes, mining her writing largely to assert once more the dominant role of Yeats. This tendency is not simply a problem of boys versus girls. In volume five of *The Field Day Anthology of Irish Writing*, Antoinette Quinn asserts women did not "create a recognizable female tradition within literary nationalism" and were, in her estimation, a "presence" rather than a "tradition."[8]

This pattern suggests that one reason women novelists, and the work they produced, fall outside of our understanding of the Revival may stem from the fact that critics assiduously read the period through Yeats. This critical perspective is valid given that Yeats's singular vision, talent, and initiative indisputably make him a central force of the Revival. But it also means he can be blamed partially for the neglect of these women novelists. For instance, Yeats successfully advocated poetry and drama over fiction. There is an easy justification for his stance: realism, with its attention to the faithful representation of ordinary life, was at odds with the lofty idealism of the Revival. Propagated by English writers, the realist novel easily could be represented as a pernicious imperialist form to which Irish poetry and drama provided the riposte. Like the popular melodrama of the English theater, which Yeats regularly maligned, the Victorian novel provided a useful strawman for the Revival. His disdain for fiction also may be, as frequently it is with Yeats, a matter of personal talent and taste. His lone realist novella *John Sherman* (1891) was, by his own admittance, a failure.[9] Yet if we step away from the estimations of Yeats and his critics, it becomes obvious that the realist novel might well serve the aims of the Revival. It critiques existing social, economic, and political structures; it attends to civic and moral responsibility; it represents those frequently unrepresented. Plus, the realist novel had an established audience at home and abroad, which might have served as a valuable tool for a nationalism seeking to produce a shared sense of culture and values in pursuit of political autonomy.

With Yeats, the "women" part of the neglected women novelists of the Revival is a trickier issue. As critics and biographers have noted, he had a complex and contradictory relationship with women writers of the period, even with those whom he championed.[10] Yeats's achievements in poetry and drama may be superseded only by his excellent taste in women writers. He directly identified and promoted the talents of Eva Gore-Booth, Maud Gonne, Augusta Gregory, Winifred Letts, Dora Sigerson Shorter, and Katharine Tynan, among others. He famously collaborated with Tynan, with whom he coedited *Poems and Ballads of Young Ireland* (1888), and Gregory, with whom he cofounded the Abbey Theatre and coauthored several plays. His judgments of talent were strong and influential, and not always easily understood. For instance, he published and commended Rosa Mulholland as "the novelist of Catholic Ireland"[11] and published her work in his *Representative Tales of Ireland*, but dismissed Emily Lawless for being "in imperfect sympathy with the Celtic nature."[12]

The genre and gender politics of the Yeatsian Revival, most powerfully articulated by literary critics writing in his wake, have sidelined Irish women novelists. But something else may have precluded these novelists from making their way into our understanding of the Revival more generally—the movement's express antipathy to the everyday. This claim might raise hackles, given the detailed accounts of quotidian rural peasant life offered by Hyde, Gregory, Synge, Yeats, and other leading lights of the Revival, but hear me out. In her luminous study of the ordinary in French modernism, *Spoiled Distinctions* (2015), Hannah Freed-Thall describes the ordinary as a "slippery term," as "that which always eludes set categories of distinction; like its sister term the everyday, the ordinary is what escapes."[13] These are the objects, practices, modes of attention, habits, and customs that do not call attention to themselves, that seem unworthy of note or reflection. Of course, once something does draw attention to ubiquitous and overly familiar objects, practices, or beliefs, they are no longer ordinary. And that to some degree explains the project of those revivalists who carefully depicted the lives and stories of the indigenous Irish peasants. In large part, the Revival's agenda was deliberately to recalibrate attention. It rendered the Irish ordinary extraordinary by highlighting its uniqueness, its authenticity, its purity; by depicting its exceptional particularity through dialect, innovative form; by describing its distinctive landscapes, customs, and people. Even the Revival's celebration of poetry and drama reflects its investment in the extraordinary. The concentrated form and magnified attention of poetry renders its subjects extraordinary, and theatrical spectacle serves a similar purpose for drama. A moment from J. M. Synge's *The Playboy of the Western World* (1907), the quintessential revivalist text, exemplifies such a scorn for the ordinary. In this play, the protagonist Christy Mahon is attacked and almost set on fire when Pegeen Mike and the Mayoites discover that, rather than a heroic parricide with a murderous loy, he is merely a farm boy with lousy aim.

To some degree, the Revival was about granting attention and thus awarding dignity to the everyday Irish experience maligned by the English. It gave worth to objects, behaviors, and beliefs—largely associated with the Irish past—that had been dismissed by colonialism and its notion of progress. It drew attention to the handmade furnishing in the peasant cottage, clothes made from Irish tweed, native dance and music, oft-repeated folktales, Irish-language phrases and syntax. These were deliberately revived and accentuated for populations rapidly losing touch with the Irish quotidian, both real and imagined, thanks to encroaching modernity and centuries of colonial policies and practices. However, the representation of the Irish ordinary as extraordinary ceased when the work focused on detailing the everyday lives of an emergent middle class whose ordinary was infused with Anglicized habits, spaces, and objects that infected the drawing room, modern fashion, domestic routines, courtship, or childrearing. In many works of Irish women's fiction, the narrative centers on ordinary domestic experience, seeking to reflect accurately the life of its intended readers. These narratives are packaged in a familiar literary form because the commercial success of these books rests on accessibility and easy recognition.

This embrace of the ordinary, in both content and form, helps to explain further the marginalization of women's fiction of this period. As critics including Henri Lefebvre and Michel de Certeau remind us, the everyday is feminine terrain.[14] The feminized everyday in the feminized popular novel becomes a particular problem for Irish cultural nationalism that represented women, in the words of

Tina O'Toole, through "a passive femininity that would be of strategic value to the anti-imperialist cause," and depicted them largely as mythic goddesses, passive victims, hags, or mourning mothers.[15] The intricate and contradictory masculinist logics of empire identified and critiqued by Joseph Valente were compounded in a nation dominated by nationalist and religious discourses that confined women to secondary roles and domestic spaces.[16] Where in revivalist literature might there be a place for the representation of everyday tasks of the bourgeoisie: parenting, cleaning the house, going to church, working on a farm or in a shop? Only modernism, with its insistence on new methods, could accommodate these novels; it alone could give voice to the ordinary, as evident in Joyce's celebrated representation of the everyday.

Interestingly, Yeats's practical work on behalf of the Revival complicates the idea that his sense of the movement could not accommodate the feminine everyday. In her study *Modernism and the Ordinary*, Liesl Olson suggests that the commonplace provided the fabric of collectivity in a modernism generally characterized by individual, alienation, and isolation.[17] This proves true in the way that Yeats effectively consolidated talent and advanced the Revival through coteries and salons organized and frequented by women. The almost ubiquitous presence of Yeats among Irish salon culture of the period allowed him to identify talented writers who might contribute to cultural nationalism. He visited Lissadell in 1894 and encouraged Eva Gore-Booth to write on Irish themes; he frequented Gregory's Coole and there helped to foster Irish writers of the period; he regularly encountered Tynan and Dora Sigerson Shorter at their weekly salons. He also understood the practical workaday value of organizations and institutions in fostering the movement's ideals: the preliminary meeting of the Irish (National) Literary Society in Dublin was held at the Yeats home in 1891, and he helped found the Irish Literary Society in London in 1893 with Charles Gavin Duffy at the Caledonian Hotel and the National Literary Society with Hyde as president in 1892. Yeats was a poet well aware of the mundane activities necessary to realize the vision of the cultural revival, even as he rendered these activities both intriguing and arduous in the poetry of "The Fascination of What's Difficult."

If Yeats understood the value of the everyday in practice, he was less in tune with the everyday as the focus of Irish writing. His relationship with Katharine Tynan provides the perfect example. He cultivated Tynan, collaborated with her, and promoted her work—particularly her early poetry. As Aurelia Annat demonstrates, Tynan's prose was often in lockstep with the revivalist "cult of the rebel-hero and the trope of Irish history as narrative of resistance to Irish rule," as evidenced in *Katharine Tynan's Book of Irish History* (1918) or her historical novel *Lord Edward: A Study in Romance* (1916).[18] Yet following her marriage in 1893, Tynan lived in England where she was no longer active in Irish politics or in institution building, nor did she continue to write exclusively about Irish themes. Yeats ultimately marginalized her, a bias that arose in sync with her increased attention to the everyday. As Donna Potts observes, "The qualities that [Yeats] consistently praised in Tynan—her nationalism, her religious devotion, her loving descriptions of nature, her naivete, her sentimentality, and even her popularity—were precisely those qualities that later eliminated her from the modernist canon as well as the consideration of later scholars of the Irish Literary Revival."[19] Yeats's relationship with Tynan, and his antipathy toward the everyday as represented in her later writing, meshes neatly with the marginalization of the ordinary evident more generally in modernism cited by Olson and others. But it worked both ways. The bias against the everyday during these decades is so pervasive that in her autobiography *Twenty-Five Years: Reminiscences*, Tynan curses the practical demands of the "Irish Theatre" for distracting Yeats from the real work of his poetry.[20]

By reading women writers and the everyday through Yeats, I may appear to recapitulate the same blinkered logics I have identified in other criticism that understands the Revival primarily through his articulated aims and ideals. But there is no escaping the fact that Yeats was, and remains, the most influential figure in the Revival and in subsequent considerations of the movement. His particular antipathy to the ordinary is crucial to our understanding of women's revivalist fiction, as well as to the Revival more generally. In "The Celtic Element of Literature," his consideration of Matthew Arnold's *The Study of Celtic Literature* (1867), Yeats condoned Arnold's celebration of the Celt's otherworldly qualities and asserted that all folk literature, including that produced during the Revival, "delights in immortal and unbounded things."[21] Many of his poems—such as "The Lake Isle of Innisfree," "Reconciliation," and "Byzantium"—celebrate the move from the quotidian to the world of imagination and romantic love and art. Likewise, plays such as *The Countess Cathleen* (1899) and *Cathleen ni Houlihan* (1902) stage protagonists who abandon the quotidian for greater aims, often at the cost of their lives—an exchange represented as entirely worthwhile and validated in these plays. For Yeats, the everyday is something to be abandoned or shed. But as Michael Sheringham notes, "the everyday . . . is where we already are: to find it, we cannot 'arise and go there,' in Yeats's phrase, but have somehow to bring about a transformation that will make it visible or palpable."[22]

That very commitment to a visible and palpable everyday, I would argue, is what many Irish women endeavored to provide in their novels. Can we start to think about the Revival in such a way that allows us to see more clearly the contributions that women fiction writers made to the project of early-twentieth-century cultural nationalism in Ireland? Such a recalibrated focus provides us a richer understanding of the Revival, as revealed by the consideration of two sorely neglected novels by two sorely neglected Irish women writers that illuminate the complex place of the everyday in revivalist discourses.

Jane Barlow and the Utopian Ordinary

This analysis of the ordinary commences with a somewhat surprising popular form—a utopian novel set on the planet Venus written by Jane Barlow (1857–1917) and titled *History of a World of Immortals without a God: Translated from an Unpublished Manuscript in the Library of a Continental University*. Barlow was best known for her novels, poems, and sketches about Irish peasant culture, including the enormously popular *Irish Idylls* (1892), *A Creel of Irish Stories* (1897), and *Irish Ways* (1909). These studies of rural Irish life embody the picturesque primitivism that characterized much revivalist writing. They detail the everyday practices of the rural Irish, albeit whitewashing their economic hardships; the dialogue seeks to capture the brogue of native inhabitants; a focus on nature dominates the narrative. And in fact, Barlow's writing was so popular and innovative that Gregory cited her reading of *Irish Idylls* as one inspiration for her first trip to the Aran Islands.

In *The Irish Literary Revival: Its History, Pioneers and Possibilities*, published in 1894, W. P. Ryan celebrated Barlow's realistic accounts of rural life as the epitome of revivalist writing: "Miss Jane Barlow's *Irish Idylls* are a luminous index to young Irish authors of that world of appealing humanity which is still to be found by observant eyes in Irish local life."[23] However, a year later, Yeats "regretfully excluded Miss Barlow's *Irish Idylls*" from his list of the best thirty Irish books "because, despite her genius for recording the externals of Irish peasant life, I do not feel that she has got deep into the heart of things."[24] This assessment is telling. His dismissal of Barlow rests on her commitment to representing the "externals" over the "heart of things," with the assumption that these two elements are necessarily at odds. In *The Bookman* that same year, he wrote of Barlow:

> She is master over the circumstances of peasant life, and has observed with a delightful care no Irish writer has equaled, the coming and going of hens and chickens on the doorstep, the gossiping of old women over their tea, the hiding of children under the shadows of the thorn trees, the broken and decaying thatch of the cabins, and the great brown stretches of bogland; but seems to know nothing of the exultant and passionate life Carleton celebrated, or to shrink from its roughness and its tumult.[25]

Here Yeats gives faint praise to Barlow's capacity to record with unique detail the banal "circumstances of peasant life"—but his condescension is evident, culminating in his critique of her knowing "nothing of the exultant and passionate life" he sees depicted in William Carleton's sketches. He represents her sketches as full of conviction, but lacking in passionate intensity.

Barlow's invocation of the ordinary that Yeats cites in her rural sketches appears as well in her utopian novel, *History of a World of Immortals without a God: Translated from an Unpublished Manuscript in the Library of a Continental University*, written under the pseudonym Antares Skorpios. This 1891 novel follows the Dutch doctor Gervaas van Varken who, inspired by his reading of Swift's *Gulliver's Travels*, voyages to the planet Hesperos (Venus), where he encounters a utopian society inhabited by "one hundred millions of rational and highly-cultured beings."[26] The narrative begins when the misanthropic Van Varken journeys to Bombay in 1729, where he befriends an English-speaking Parsee (an Indian follower of Zoroaster), who encourages him to travel to Tibet to consult with Koot Homi, "a man endowed with many and strange gifts" (8). Homi awards van Varken "the power of instantaneous passage from one terrestrial point to another" (14), and the doctor travels to Hesperos—his bag packed, as he details, with "sundry small articles for the toilet, also my silver watch, and an ingenious instrument for measuring quantities of heat" (18).

As its title promises, the novel offers van Varken's record of Hesperian history and contemporary practices, though the document is mediated and occasionally interrupted by the obtrusive voice of the translator. Science fiction may seem far from the ordinary, and also far from revivalist literature, which asked its authors to turn to native traditions in Ireland. But Barlow invokes the utopian novel, a genre used with surprising regularity by writers of this period in England and America, to posit what a free Ireland might look like. As a popular form, the utopian novel imagines alterative societies and offers readers a detached and detailed record of an ideal society, one that highlights the social and political failures of contemporary society. For all of their imaginative settings and practices, authors of utopian novels are, according to Amy Boesky, "chiefly interested in the particularities of their own here and now."[27] The detailed account of ordinary life in *History of a World*, delivered in a detached tone by the scientist van Varken and his academic translator, thus offers readers an interstellar "imagined community" predicated on a rational atheism and socialism—a critique of society akin to other utopian works ranging from Thomas More's *Utopia* to Charlotte Perkins Gilman's *Herland* to Oscar Wilde's *The Soul of a Man under Socialism*.

History of a World "de-anglicizes" its content, as well as distilling it of Irishness by focusing on the continent, the east, and outer space. The history of the development of Hesperian society is not the tale of preindustrial or preliterate peoples, but instead of an evolved and educated socialist utopia, burdened only by the mystery of faith. Rather than the lives of the Irish primitive, Barlow recounts the ordinary lives of the rational and forward-thinking citizens of Venus. The novel's emphasis on rationality and decorum pushes against essentialist representations of Irish as wild and uncivilized, and because there are no children on Hesperos, it also refuses depictions of women as constrained by the "natural" roles of wife and mother. Although Barlow's utopia is set far from Ireland, she aggressively embraces revivalist practice and form in this novel. Seemingly outside the ambit of revivalist literature, *History of a World* employs the observational tactics of the literary sketch and the travelogue, and due to its rich anthropological detail and its recounting of Hesperian oral history, seems no less fantastic in its approach and form than Synge's *The Aran Islands* (1907) or Gregory's *Visions and Beliefs in the West of Ireland* (1920). It provides an objective account of an idealized (and uncorrupted) peoples, describing their unique and superior lifestyle for modern audiences. It recuperates a lost historical narrative, albeit a fictional one, to shed light on the present day. In its quest to preserve an eighteenth-century record, it reflects the Revival's antiquarian impulse, and the translation of this found document into English from Dutch points to the era's interest in bilingualism.

The utopian novel thus fits into the revivalist canon and usefully recalibrates our understanding of the movement. For example, Alice

Milligan wrote her own utopian novel entitled *A Royal Democrat: A Sensational Novel* (1890) in which the Prince of Wales is shipwrecked in Ireland and lives as a nationalist. Barlow's *History of a World* provides a valuable instance exposing how the Revival failed to accommodate a popular form focused on the everyday. The novel records the ordinary lives of the Hesperians, with a focus on the planet's enlightened cultural and political life, which is enabled in part by a stable population of immortal citizens. The Hesperians are not Yahoos: they resemble humans dressed in Eastern costumes, all with "a look indicative of immense and profound knowledge" (30), and they are eager to learn Dutch, as well as to share their various discoveries and practices. Horseless vehicles run through their city streets, houses are "elaborately and tastefully ornamented" (28), and the food "resembled in taste various kinds of flesh-meat, very delicately cooked" (31). Van Varken carefully describes their landscape and atmosphere, their plant and animal life, and their total lack of "the loathsome cockroach" and other annoying insects (44). Their daily lives are limned for readers, though details about sex are redacted by the translator, who announces: "I suppress all details in these notes, as public opinion, very rightly, does not permit the discussion of such matters" (68).

One logic for excluding the popular novel from the Revival rests in its focus on the middle classes. The utopian novel, however, sneaks its way into the Revival, which was orchestrated largely by Anglo-Irish anxious about a rising Catholic middle class. Through her depiction of Hesperian society, Barlow offers her readers a classless meritocracy predicated on creativity and meaningful labor of what looks like an educated middle class with no private property. They have eradicated lawyers, bankers, stockbrokers, policemen, tax men, and coastguards, who are "now at liberty for more directly useful professions" (158). They share one language and a world parliament, and van Varken recounts a Hesperian modern history that culminates in the eradication of violence and the establishment of socialism (150). As van Varken confirms, "The Hesperian system was founded on the fair and rational doctrine of give and take, honestly carried out" (153). Many of the conflicts dividing a colonial Ireland, such as those based in religion, language, class, property ownership, and regional identity, have been eradicated.

A Protestant member of the Anglo-Irish gentry, Barlow imagines in this novel a society less motivated by religious ideology and practice. As van Varken reports, "There are no clergy, for there is no known God" (155). The Hesperians, one hundred million creatures of different ages, were called into being all at once by a silent "Unknown Power" (48). The lifecycle exempts them from death. Instead, Hesperians instantaneously dissolve, according to the "Law of Evanescence" (57), when their suffering exceeds their happiness, so there is no physical decay. His history reveals that these rational and eternal beings are distressed only by their inability to encounter directly their unknown god, in whom they have faith (81). Many of their discoveries and innovations results from the pursuit of their Supreme Maker. However, their inability to commune directly with their Maker burdens these citizens. The novel concludes with a summary of lectures offered by Dr. van Varken, in which his misanthropy colors his account of Earth with its terrible climate, its violent peoples, its contradictory religions. These lectures intensify the "gloom" (167) of the Hesperians, and his portrayal of Earth's Maker fails to "raise any enthusiastic delight" (167). The editor notes that van Varken's documentation of his experiences peters out with "a few incoherent jottings" (176) and suggests that he fled back to Earth because the Hesperians were entertaining the notion of dissecting him for study. The narrative concludes with the editor's bleak conjecture that these "Godless Immortals" continue to suffer the "World-Weariness and Sorrow which was plainly settling down upon them like a heavy pall" (177).

Nonetheless, Barlow's depiction throughout of ordinary people, objects, and practices renders life on this entirely different planet discovered during Earth's eighteenth century an obtainable ideal. Van Varken repeatedly invokes the word "extraordinary"—and yet his report of life on Hesperos seems fairly banal in part because there is no reproduction, no disease, no cataclysmic interruptions for good or ill. The everyday here is not a colorful pastiche of details, but instead an amalgamation of facts about how life on Hesperos unfolds, how its history came to be—a kind of guidebook for the incipient Irish nation. In the depiction of this socialist utopia, Hesperian society embodies the Revival's self-help logic, and its cooperative ideals mesh neatly with those advanced by George Russell's *Irish Homestead* and by the Irish Agricultural Organisation Society, founded in 1894, that advocated for agricultural cooperatism. *History of a World* also engages with the scientific discourses that Sinéad Garrigan Mattar argues shaped the Revival: evolutionary theory, comparative anthropology, European scientific discourse. Barlow's novel recounts the Hesperian's remarkable innovations in shipbuilding, mineralogy, medical science, engineering, and astronomy, as well as discoveries like the creation of a Sympathetic Telegram to communicate between the planet's two hemispheres. As such, Barlow is in sync with Yeats, Synge, and Gregory and their use of comparative science to produce work that differed from romantic primitivism.[28] However, *History of a World*, like many utopian novels, celebrates the liberating promise of technology and reflects an enthusiasm for modernity that Yeats's Revival represses but can be seen in Milligan's and Pearse's use of slideshows, Martyn's interest in gramophone recording, or Synge's photography. If the question at the core of revivalist literature is how to imagine and construct Irish culture and nationality, then *History of a World* is a revivalist novel. Barlow provides a blueprint for the new state, harnessing the tactics if not the content of revivalist writing.

Rosa Mulholland and the Social Realist Ordinary

Rosa Mulholland's *Father Tim* (1910) is in many ways the polar opposite of *History of a World*. Set in late nineteenth- and early twentieth-century Ireland, *Father Tim* is a social realist novel that formally looks much like other late Victorian popular fiction. However, like Barlow's utopian novel, *Father Tim* is deeply critical of established political, social, economic, and cultural structures in

Ireland and seeks to imagine alternatives for a new nation. Among
the most notable aspects of this novel is its representation of everyday
practices and concerns across variant economic and social classes
in both rural and urban Ireland, insights obtained only through the
mobility allowed to a priest such as its protagonist, Father Tim. The
implicit critique registered through his observations of and encounters with the quotidian suggests that intimate knowledge of the everyday practices and concerns of all Irish people, not the heroic deeds
of the past or merely the everyday life of the Irish rural peasantry,
is necessary to produce a healthy nation. If Barlow advocated for
socialism and atheism, Mulholland valorizes Catholicism, demonstrating the constructive role its beliefs and practices play in a rapidly
changing Ireland.

The novel follows the life of the titular Father Tim Martin. Like
Barlow, Mulholland offers readers a male protagonist at a remove
from the culture he observes, describing everyday life as he travels
to new sites and observes local practices with a largely, though not
consistently, objective eye. Father Tim ministers to the rural and
urban poor, and Catholicism is represented as the organizing and
unifying moral force of the many social groups among whom he
circulates. *Father Tim* showcases the ordinary lives of Irish characters across classes, as in the chapter entitled "The Widow Langan."
As a young priest, Father Tim is preoccupied with everyday tasks:
visiting mountain homes, reading his Office, planting potatoes and
cabbage, as well as a rose, in his back garden, and reading in the
evenings.[29] These everyday tasks convey his laudable ideals: ministry,
prayer, and reading, as well as planting food for sustenance and a
rose for beauty. He is inspired by studying the great deeds and beliefs
of "prophets and teachers, from before the Orient" (72), and when
he closes his book, the Irish rural landscape further stirs him. In this
chapter, his normal daily routine is interrupted by the brogue of the
Widow Langan, who has returned home with her son after her husband's death of the "yella fever in the Brazils" (74).

Mulholland distills from her account of Brazil "the exotic and
passionate life" that Yeats extolls, just as Barlow had with Hesperos.

The Widow Langan provides in *Father Tim* a vivid account of everyday life for poor Irish emigrants working on Brazilian coffee plantations. She is treated like cattle with nothing to eat but "a little rice, and a dust of what they called floriline, and two or three bananas" (75); she finds herself in "a town called St. Paulo [where] all the people were black, an' couldn't speak a word to us, but laughed at us" (75); she encounters "real lizards" and "centre-pieces"—"cratures, the size of a rabbit, with hundherts of scrabby claws, that would run over you and tear you" (76). Abetted by an Irish priest, the widow returns to Wicklow, and she asks Father Tim to help her obtain work with a wealthy local family. In the next chapter, Father Tim visits this family's estate, observing "an abode of that happiness and prosperity of the world" (84), with a drawing room "of shaded lamps, a glowing fire, the rich colour of chrysanthemums, and three or four smiling faces" (84). The juxtaposition of the Irish quotidian for rich and poor troubles Father Tim, and its vivid rendering conveys to readers that political nationalism must take into account the radical disjunction among socioeconomic groups. This novel insists that oppression in Ireland is neither a singular national experience, nor one strictly political and imposed by outsiders.

This same logic attends even more vividly in the city, where Father Tim ministers to Dublin slum dwellers. Like many popular novels, *Father Tim* sentimentalizes the poor. But its vivid depiction of poverty draws particular attention to the fact that what is ordinary for the slatternly mother in the slums, for instance her limp baby dangling in her dirty arms, is categorically not ordinary for the targeted reader. The common deprivations and sufferings shared among the poor in Ireland are rendered, by this novel's attention, extraordinary and worthy of close consideration. Poverty here is not ennobling, as one might argue it is in Synge's writing. Mulholland's novel slots neatly into the logic of "self-help" that characterizes revivalism, providing religion as the universalizing "ordinary" that might uplift all citizens, not only through ministry to the poor and through philanthropy, but also by stemming the ills of excessive drinking and emigration that plague the incipient nation.

A social realist novel, *Father Tim* offers a tonally restrained, objective perspective similar to that found in Barlow's utopian novel. Father Tim moves easily among the various social classes, detailing their strengths and weaknesses and their universal need for God. Science and religion work in concert, and throughout the novel advances a message celebrating moderation by focusing on how different economic contexts shape an individual's relationship to alcohol or money. Mulholland piles on the details, which helps to explain Charles Dickens's affinity for her writing. But throughout *Father Tim*, the larger goal is to demonstrate the sacrifice and generosity of its priest protagonist, in particular his refusal to judge or condemn his followers. Rife with cautionary tales of drunkenness, promiscuity, and suicide, the novel simply records the positive impact of Father Tim's ministrations. He is a protagonist remarkable in his equanimity. Neither saint nor superhero, Father Tim is not even particularly charismatic: he is no Cuchulain. Instead, Mulholland celebrates him for being observant, for moving easily among different social classes. He can comfort and console; he can teach; he can converse. He stands at a clear remove from the rural peasantry and urban poor whom he ministers, as well as from the gentry and the urban bourgeoisie. By drawing attention to the many social and economic groups that compose Ireland, and reporting on their strengths and weaknesses as manifest in everyday life, Mulholland gives us a different form of revivalist literature. She seeks to educate and uplift, securing the ideals in which Yeats and the revivalists whom he championed evinced little interest, such as religion, urban experience, domestic life, and the middle classes.

Traditionally, realism has been regarded as a form outside, even explicitly at odds with, the ambit of both revivalism and modernism. It is easy to sympathize with arguments claiming that the formal constraints of popular realist fiction oppose modernism's quest to make it new, even in light of Suzanne Clark's still-compelling reading of sentimental literature as modernism's "unconscious" thanks to its status as the "excluded other."[30] But it remains unclear why a novel like *Father Tim* cannot find its place within a more broadly defined, and thus more accurate, revivalist canon—especially since critics have found a spot within the Revival for George Moore and even Cork Realists such as T. C. Murray. The novels of Irish women writers of the period frequently mimic the popular form of the English novel, but a number of them push back against its constraints. *Father Tim*, for instance, has a provocatively hybrid form. The vivid detail of everyday life suggests it is a social realist novel, and its focus on religion might categorize it as Catholic fiction, a genre adeptly employed by subsequent Irish women writers such as Kate O'Brien and Mary Lavin. The early chapters of *Father Tim* promise a bildungsroman, as we follow young Tim's spiritual development and his decision to pursue his vocation as a priest. It then flirts with becoming a religious tract, as one chapter directly quotes biblical passages and cites the words of Canon Keating (29). Later, the novel offers a morality tale when it follows a young peasant woman whose desire for autonomy in the city results in an illegitimate child. And despite its focus on the underclasses, this is not strictly a naturalist novel: there is none of the Darwinian survival of the fittest here, the predetermination we associate with naturalism. Catholicism, in tandem with the indomitable Irish spirit, provides the real possibility for uplift in Mulholland's novel.

Passion and Detachment in Revivalism

Barlow's *History of a World* and Mulholland's *Father Tim*, two novels quite different in form and content, both demonstrate that Irish women's fiction, which has languished outside our understanding of the Revival, does in fact embody and enact the movement's principles. They also expose how Yeats's predilections have influenced our understanding of the Revival. In particular, they suggest that his stated antipathy to the everyday may help explain why works focused on the ordinary such as these have been marginalized in understandings of the Revival.

In closing, I want to revisit Yeats's critique of Barlow's fiction as lacking in "the exultant and passionate life." The ongoing lionization of these intense feeling states as emblematic of the revivalist literature, I would argue, is problematic. Both *History of a World* and *Father Tim* offer protagonists whose signal characteristic is detachment. In Barlow's *History of a World*, a balanced narrative voice takes the extraordinary—life on Venus—and renders it ordinary and recognizable, and thus possible for readers to imagine and imitate. Van Varken, despite his occasional fits of misanthropy, is a trained scientist, and his reasoned observations are further mediated by the narrative structure of the novel, in which a translator and editor further contextualize this found manuscript for its readers. Likewise, Mulholland's *Father Tim* offers vivid snapshots of ordinary life across all classes in Ireland. Despite its detailed exposure of the vulnerabilities and sufferings of these individuals, Father Tim is depicted through a deliberately dispassionate narrative voice, and represented as simply one good priest among many, a judicious man objectively noting the flawed world around him.

Rather than agitate readers through sensational depictions of the extraordinary, these novelists deliberately mute the "passion" and "exuberance" that their narratives might stimulate. In doing so, these women are trying to rejuvenate popular fiction and retrain its readers. Their detachment is in part about pushing back against the bad "passion" that infected popular fiction. They represent the ordinary in a form and voice that recalibrate the assumed function of popular fiction and render it valuable to the aims of Irish cultural nationalism. The Revival sought to educate and uplift Irish readers by exposing them to their literary and cultural heritage. Barlow and Mulholland share a similar optimism about the potential of reading publics, and their novels instruct readers on how this everyday practice of reading widely available popular novels—the type of work they published and readers actually purchased—might advance national interests.

In the final chapter of Barlow's *History of a World*, a compilation of "curt and jejune memoranda" (173) describes urban life in Australis, the imperial metropolis of Hesperos. The narrator cites van Varken's particular interest in the city's "great magazines or depots of all sorts of articles . . . abundantly supplied by the communistic labor" (173). He admires the culture, citing its museums, its architecture, and the temple of the Unknown God. But the translator interrupts the narrative to express anxiety about reading publics on earth who might encounter this history:

> Should this book, by any mischance, have fallen into the hands of any habitual consumer of the style of literature known as "Shilling Shockers," or "Penny Dreadfuls," the Shocked or Terrified is earnestly exhorted to waste none of his valuable time on the pages that follow. He may rely on it that, although up to this point he may have been able to comprehend the narrative, the remainder of the work is utterly beyond his tether. I will now proceed with my translation. (45)

The translator distinguishes this work from popular literature infected by the "shock" and "terror" sought by readers of lowbrow literature.

In *Father Tim*, Mulholland likewise evinces an interest in the role that reading plays in stimulating intense feeling and prompting behavior. When the Widow Langan explains how she managed to return to Ireland from Brazil, she tells Father Tim,

> It was a good Irish priest that came around, an' he saw the way the Irish an' English people were treated, an' he wrote home to the newspapers. But och! I declare, I'm not learned, but no newspaper on earth would hold all I've been through, your reverence. However, they wrote an' gave us our passages home. (79)

Here, the mass press enables a reversal of the emigration the novel excoriates throughout. Later in this novel, one sign of Dublin's degradation can be observed in the reading habits of the urban poor, "story journals full of exciting pictures of elegant personages passing through dreadful experiences attired in the magnificent, if disheveled, evening dress of the rich which the factory girl or the basket-hawker has no other opportunity of ever beholding" (173). In contrast, upright members of the Dublin working class read the

Quarterly Review, to sate "a taste for keeping pace with the leading thought of the day as to art and literature" (208).

How, these novels ask, can the ordinary that characterizes popular fiction for the mass public be rendered in a way that stimulates rational thought, innovation, critique—rather than simply default to stimulating empty vicarious passion in its readers? The revivalists imagined that Irish exceptionalism might generate a shared sense of national pride, which would in turn engender real political change. They sought to banish from literature the commonplaces represented in and by much of Irish women's fiction. And this logic worked— only, of course, to have the Catholic middle class later impose its own aggressive norms on a newly independent populace. As we know, with the establishment of the Free State, the ordinary came to serve less promising ends. In his accounts of the everyday, Ben Highmore discusses how the term "ordinary" is used to protect state norms, how the concept provides a prophylactic against outside threats to ordinary family life from nonnormative sexuality and other hazards.[31] It might be possible that the refusal to engage the ordinary, as represented in Irish women's fiction during the Revival, had long-term, deleterious effects on the national imagination. Ignoring this body of work prevented a wide-ranging imaginative engagement with and conversation about an important aspect of Irish culture. Women's fiction of the Revival imagines how the ordinary—everyday things, practices, emotions—might serve national interests. By not engaging with the quotidian these writers represented, the Revival, as we came to know it, may have enabled the oppressive versions of the normative, the ordinary, the mainstream that came to define daily life across much of twentieth-century Ireland.

In recalling her friend Jane Barlow, Katharine Tynan wrote of the Revival: "There was a sharp division at that time between Realists and Idealists. The Realists stood for all that was ugly. We chose to be Idealists."[32] This claim falls neatly in line with a recognizable revivalist ethos, but we need to open up the category of Idealists to include utopian fiction, social realism, popular romance, and other genres of fiction. Barlow's utopian novel and Mulholland's social realist novel disrupted the affective norms of popular fiction, in part to explore how popular forms (and their large audiences) might serve the aims of revivalism. Their use of the ordinary expands our obdurate gendered and generic presumptions about the Revival, and suggests that they were doing the work that Maurice Blanchot would one day clamor for in their knowledge that "The everyday is no longer the average, statistically established existence of a given society at a given moment; it is a category, a utopia and an Idea, without which one would not know how to get at either the hidden present or the discoverable future of manifest beings."[33]

Part Four

Revivals of Spirit

7

"The Politics of Time and Eternity"

A. E., Theosophy, and the Temporality of Emergence

Gregory Dobbins

A.E. as Theorist of the Revival

Out of all of the foundational figures associated with the beginning of the Revival, the writing of George William Russell—better known by his pseudonym "A. E."—presents one of the more difficult cases for critical recuperation.[1] This is not exactly because of historical neglect, since it is not as if the singular importance of the role A. E. played within the period has become obscured over time. An older historical understanding of the Revival identified with W. B. Yeats's autobiographical recollection of the period held that it presented a moment in which cultural activity displaced politics as a consequence of the general disillusionment brought about by the fall of Parnell in 1890. The intensification of cultural activity which followed in turn formulated an imagined form of cultural nationality which would motivate subsequent political movements two decades later.[2] As a writer of poetry and prose fiction, literary critic, and painter, A. E.'s prominence as an artist confirms older understandings of the Revival as an essentially cultural event. In recent years, however, scholarship has effectively challenged this long influential teleological interpretation of Irish cultural history. In addition to the archival recovery of different types of political and social activism simultaneous to the heyday of the Irish Literary Theatre, such scholarship has often asserted that the Revival should be understood as a larger historical process engaged with virtually every aspect of Irish society beyond a cultural register alone.[3] A. E. was also a socio-political activist, agrarian reformer, and self-taught economist, and some of his more polemical writing motivated by such diverse commitments even anticipates a more expansive understanding of the Revival; as he asserted in an essay published in 1910 entitled "Ideals of the New Rural Society," "nations are not built up by the repetition of words, but by the organizing of intellectual forces."[4] Perhaps more than any other figure, A. E. demonstrated a unique capacity to forge and organize the various institutions necessary for the Revival to occur in the first place—and more recent reassessments of the period continue to account for the significance of his deeds.[5] The various contributions A. E. made between the mid-1890s and his death in 1935 are dazzling in their variety. They include: journalism as editor of the *Irish Homestead* and the *Irish Statesman* and as contributor to a number of other periodicals; economic/social activism on behalf of the Cooperative movement as assistant secretary for Sir Horace Plunkett's Irish Agricultural Organisation Society (IAOS); political interventions through his unofficial role as intermediary between the Cooperative movement, Sinn Féin, different nationalist groups, organized labor, and the socialist movement; and a commitment to the development of alternative forms of spirituality in Ireland through his early membership in the Irish Theosophical Society, expositions of mysticism for the *Irish Theosophist* and other esoteric publications, and as founder and leader of the Dublin Hermetic Society. Moreover, through these various institutional roles A. E. served as a crucial source of support for younger writers. Figures as diverse as James Joyce, James Stephens, Liam O'Flaherty, Lord Dunsany, Sean O'Faolain, Frank O'Connor, P. L. Travers, and Patrick Kavanagh, among others, benefited early in their careers from his patronage.

A. E.'s personal qualities as mentor and activist have long been recognized—though often at the expense of a closer consideration of his writing. In *Ireland's Literary Renaissance* (1916), likely the very first full-length critical history of the Revival which considered it as a distinct period, Ernest A. Boyd takes note of A. E.'s singularity within the context of the time:

> A. E. is that most essential requisite in Ireland—a personality. It is no exaggeration to say that almost every Irish writer of value to-day owes something to the poet, painter and economist, who has become a centre of ideas which are freely at the command of all who seek them.[6]

Boyd's description of A. E. indicates some sense of exactly why it continues to be necessary to account for his place within the Revival. However, Boyd's focus on his "personality" gestures toward some of the difficulties one faces in the critical recuperation of A. E.'s writing. Early literary accounts of the Revival dating from the end of that period focus on his personality to a greater degree than anything else. In a work notorious for its bitter satire and personal attacks upon almost every figure of note associated with the Revival, George Moore concedes near the end of *Hail and Farewell* that his representation of A. E.'s character was ultimately beyond his literary abilities; A. E.'s unqualified support and unstinting energy were such that Moore found it impossible to find any fault with him.[7] Yeats, whose relationship with A. E. was much more ambiguous and occasionally strained through a friendship that began during their teenage days as students at the Metropolitan School of Art and continued until A. E.'s death in 1935, regarded him as "the one masterful influence among Dublin men and women who love religious speculation but have no historical faith."[8] While he admired A. E.'s passionate commitment to visionary experience, Yeats depicts him in *The Trembling of the Veil* as yet another point of negative juxtaposition against himself as he tracks his own personal development as an artist and an intellectual. To Yeats, A. E. exemplified "The Conditional Man"—the sort of fanatic identified with Phase Twenty-Five of the historical cycles described in *A Vision* whose "imaginative intensity" on behalf of their beliefs limited their capacity for self-expression.[9] Joyce's depiction of A. E. in *Ulysses* acknowledges his support for younger writers, commitment to social reform, and fascination with mysticism—but ultimately he serves as a strawman for Stephen Dedalus' rejection of neo-Platonic and *volkish* perspectives regarding the positions concerning creativity and literary production negotiated throughout "Scylla and Charybdis." In all of these cases—and even if the perspectives they demonstrate toward A. E. are somewhat different—Moore, Yeats, and Joyce each deploy elements of A. E.'s personality in order to construct a foil for them to advance their own respective projects rather than to present more prolonged engagements with his actual positions. These various influential works appear to help inaugurate a critical understanding of A. E. in which his eccentric personal qualities inevitably take precedence over the substance of his thought. Even the most appreciative accounts of A. E. follow this model of placing personality before larger intellectual project. In two laudatory biographical accounts of his life by John Eglinton and Monk Gibbon which appeared not long after his death, A. E. emerges as an exceptional friend and mentor, a crucial figure necessary for the foundation and administration of many of the various institutions and organizations associated with the Revival, and an unyielding advocate of political and social reform—yet all of these personal characteristics appear more significant than the aesthetic qualities of his writing or the novel facets of his philosophical commitments.[10]

To be fair to all of these earlier representations of A. E.'s life and career as an intellectual, perhaps his creative writing isn't the best place to find evidence for the justification of a deeper critical recuperation, and this essay does not propose to recover A. E.'s literary output in order to insist on its misperceived aesthetic value.[11] As Yeats writes in *The Trembling of the Veil*, "if I had any influence upon him—and I have little doubt that I had, for we were very intimate—it may not have been a good influence," and in comparison to the sorts of innovation evident in the work of many other writers associated with the Revival, A. E.'s writing can seem remarkably dated even within its own historical context.[12] Writing from a much more sympathetic position than Yeats, Gibbon concedes that A. E.'s literary works were often "wordy and rhetorical," and that while they were motivated by "beauty of thought and sincerity of utterance," in many of them "the form seems inadequate and the imagery a little vague."[13] Gibbon argues that the fault lies partly in A. E.'s mysticism, for while "Theosophy unquestionably developed and disciplined his mind, its influence upon his style was bad, and some of his worst and vaguest writing belongs to the days when he regarded himself as the apostle of a cause."[14] Yet—as Gibbon goes on to paradoxically suggest—since a familiarity with Theosophy is required to make sense of A. E.'s writing at its best, a deeper engagement with the terms of esoteric mysticism is required to appreciate it: "What is needed most in the reader is a kindred insight or illumination which will enable him to follow the thought behind these apparently simple phrases, which nevertheless open up endless vistas before the mind."[15] Gibbon's position is indicative, for it identifies one of the larger obstacles for a consideration of A. E.'s importance to the Revival beyond the acknowledgement of the merits of his personality: there is something unsettling and even possibly embarrassing about his lifelong belief in Theosophy and his earnest devotion to the philosophical positions of Madame Helena Petrovna Blavatsky. The single consistent position which lay behind A. E.'s shifting understanding of Irish culture and politics over four decades of prolific activity remained a steadfast faith in a supersensible and intangible understanding of the universe that a wide variety of perspectives—both then and now—would consider farfetched and unusual. Moreover, that esoteric belief system had been widely discredited by contemporaneous organizations which took such positions seriously even *before* A. E. first made his commitment to Theosophy. Recent scholarship has treated A. E.'s relationship to Theosophy with greater respect than once might have been the case given that movement's reputation, but it tends to present it as a historical *symptom* rather than as the basis for a credible theoretical position in its own right. Various critics, for example, have argued persuasively that the Irish Theosophical Society presented progressives like A. E. from evangelical Ulster Protestant backgrounds the means to rebel against that formative influence while also expressing dissent from competing forms of sectarian identity; that its circulation of sacred materials from Asia fostered the development of an "Irish Orientalism" which articulated the relationship between the political struggle for national self-determination to a larger global anti-imperialist historical trajectory; that it made available distinctions between self-interest, individualism, and collectivity useful to the practical needs of political organizational work; and that Theosophy helped to inspire A. E.'s individual actions on behalf of Ireland by confirming a sense of an assured personal and collective sense of destiny.[16] Without countering any of those compelling attempts to historicize in rational terms the significance of A. E.'s relationship to Theosophy, it is worth asking whether the esoteric positions formulated by Blavatsky and reiterated by A. E. might contribute something further on their own terms. A deeper consideration of A. E.'s mystical writing might raise the possibility that he be regarded more as an eccentrically motivated theorist rather than as the sort of theoretically minded eccentric who regularly appears in accounts of the Revival dating back to earlier depictions of him by Moore, Yeats, and Joyce.

The goal of my essay is to recover what Gibbon refers to as the "illumination" provided by A. E.'s commitment to Theosophy—not, necessarily, in order to make the case for a belated appreciation of the aesthetic qualities of his writing nor to make claims for the supposed deeper truth of Theosophy as a system of belief—but rather to make the case for A. E.'s legitimacy as a theorist. More specifically, as indicated by the prominence of A. E.'s work as an intellectual across widely different areas of engagement—in his writing and other artistic endeavors as well as his work as an activist throughout the various cultural, political, and "Self-Help" movements of early twentieth-century Ireland—Theosophy enabled an innovative understanding of complexity and emergence operating *within* the historical context of the Revival itself. The esoteric principles which motivated A. E. offer a unique if neglected theorization of temporality which arguably was of consequential importance to the Revival in practical terms—but has long been subordinate to the teleological narrative that eventually became the foundation of a historical understanding of the period. Via the expansive spiritual and philosophical positions of Madame Blavatsky, A. E. held that all of the diverse types of particularity evident within the material world simultaneously exist beyond the immediate parameters of temporal and spatial perception as a unified, infinite, and eternal form of absolute Being. Consequently, the emergence of institutional, organizational, and representational frameworks could help bring about the realization of such an abstract condition of collective harmony as a political reality within the empirical limits defined by the historical specificity of time and place. A. E.'s attempt to unify Theosophical theory with revivalist practice offers a potential point of departure for a different structural understanding of the period. In *The Living Torch*, Gibbon's edited collection of excerpts from A. E.'s journalism and literary criticism, the section which gathers writing devoted to political and social issues is entitled "The Politics of Time and Eternity."[17] Variations on the phrase recur often in A. E.'s writing, and generally refer to what he regarded as the central problem he faced in his work as an artist, activist, and intellectual: the seemingly insurmountable problem of working simultaneously on behalf of *both* collective social and political progress in the material plane of existence *and* the greater personal apprehension of that which is knowable only in mystic terms beyond the limits of empirical perception. In order to grasp A. E.'s understanding of temporality and its ramifications, it is necessary to consider what he means by "Time" and "Eternity."

Blavatsky, Theosophy, and Ireland

The Dublin Lodge of the Theosophical Society emerged in April 1886 out of an earlier group called the Dublin Hermetic Society (a name A. E. would revive in 1904 for his own dissident Theosophical group after his break with the Lodge) which had a more broadly defined focus on occult esotericism in general. A. E. did not become a formal member of the Lodge for some time, but become increasingly drawn to Theosophy after personal correspondence from Madame

Blavatsky herself reassured him that unlike the original group it grew out of in Ireland, Theosophy was not primarily devoted to the study of Ritual Magic.[18] By late 1890 he officially belonged to the movement and until 1898 he played a primary role in what should very much be regarded as one of the fundamental intellectual institutions of the Revival.[19] During that time period—and in addition to a career as a clerk for a textile firm and the production of his first creative work as a painter and poet—he served in an administrative capacity within the Theosophical Society's board of governance and contributed to its key publications. More unusually given the time and place, he also lived in a communal house shared by the more prominent members of the Lodge in Dublin; there he participated in customary Theosophical practices like yoga, daily contemplative meditation, and the intensive study of Blavatsky's writing and various other sacred texts associated with Hinduism, Buddhism, and other forms of mysticism that she drew upon in her own writing.[20] In *The Candle of Vision* (1918), A. E.'s "spiritual autobiography" and guide to his understanding of Theosophical mysticism, he recollects that it was a period in which "I was at the time much more interested in the politics of eternity than in the politics of my own country, and would not have missed an hour of my passionate meditation on the spirit to have witnessed the most dramatic spectacle in any of our national movements."[21]

On one occasion in 1897, as a consequence of prolonged meditation in his shared room at the lodge, A. E. had a visionary experience which seemed different in both form and content than previous attempts to seek contemplative insight into standard Theosophical positions:

[m]y meditation was suddenly broken by a series of pictures which flashed before me with the swiftness of moving pictures in a theatre. They had no relation I could discover to the subject of my meditation, and were interpolated into it then perhaps, because in a tense state of concentration when the brain becomes luminous it is easier to bring to consciousness what has to be brought.[22]

The vision which follows consists of a series of ambiguous motifs with Irish connotations that A. E. understood through Blavatsky's doctrine of "the avatar" to indicate impending revolution:

> . . . I saw the whole of Ireland lit up from mountain to sea, spreading its rays to the heavens as in the vision which Brigid the seeress saw and told to Patrick. All I could make of the sequence was that some child of destiny, around whom the future of Ireland was to pivot, was born then or to be born, and that it was to be an avatar was symbolized by the descent of the first figure from the sky, and that before that high destiny was to be accomplished the power of empire was to be weakened, and there was to be one more tragic episode in Irish history. Whether this is truth or fantasy time alone can tell.[23]

A. E. appeared to believe in the literal truth of a coming divine incarnation of the spirit of national liberation ("I only know that I look everywhere in the face of youth, in the aspect of every new nobility, hoping before I die to recognize the broad browed avatar of my vision"), and by 1918, such recent events as the Easter Rising appeared to confirm the prophetic historical details suggested within a vision he claimed to have had more than twenty years earlier.[24]

Yet it seems that A. E. also understood the vision in allegorical terms in which the avatar signified the more practical goal of national sovereignty, a concept appropriate to a more rational framework defined by matters having to do with "the politics of my own country." While he never directly discusses it in *The Candle of Vision*, implicit behind A. E.'s mystical description of this particular vision is the subsequent shift which took place in his own focus as an intellectual around the time he purported to have had the experience, for it suggests that one might work in a practical sense toward the realization of political goals while also waiting for the arrival of the mystical avatar of national destiny. In 1897, A. E. would leave the communal life and contemplative focus of the Dublin Lodge behind and take a position as one of the primary organizers and activists working for the Cooperative movement. The following year, while under pressure from the leadership of the international organization with which the Dublin Lodge was aligned to renounce sociopolitical activism not directly tied to it, A. E. severed his ties with Theosophy as an organized movement. Importantly, A. E. did not suffer a crisis in faith regarding the original positions of Madame Blavatsky as his focus shifted to include more engaged forms of activism in addition to practices focused on solitary introspective contemplation.[25] The very formal structure of the vision A. E. claimed to have perceived ("a series of pictures which flashed before me with the swiftness of moving pictures in a theatre") reflects a fundamental understanding of Blavatsky's theorization of temporality. Although the distinction A. E. makes between "Time" and "Eternity" ultimately seeks to account for the difference between the phenomenal and the noumenal, within Blavatsky's systematic explanation of Theosophy they are simultaneous to each other and ultimately part of a greater unified whole both beyond *and* within temporality. The immediate synchronic moment does not necessarily reveal a full delineation of "Eternity," but the intimations which arrive from "Eternity" better prepare one to apprehend the complexity of the immediate moment. The vision A. E. remembers from 1897 presents a translation of this position into the historically specific context of the Revival. As a system of belief and basis for ethical practice, Theosophy attempted to explain the relationship between what A. E. refers to as "Time" and "Eternity" in order to unify theory and practice. For A. E., Blavatsky's theorization of Theosophy provided the basis for his movement between a theoretical commitment to "the Politics of Eternity" *beyond* rational and empirical proof and an engaged form of practice which responds to the immediate needs of "the Politics of Time" *within* the material plane of existence.

As one of the central reasons which obfuscates A. E.'s legitimacy as an intellectual, the critical recuperation of Theosophy for contemporary theoretical purposes presents even greater challenges than the reclamation of A. E.'s mystical writing. Ever since the foundation of the Theosophical Society by Madame Blavatsky, Henry Steel Olcott, and William Quan Judge in New York in 1875, the alternative spiritual movement has typically been regarded from a number of perspectives with disdain and as lacking credibility.[26] Blavatsky's three primary theoretical expositions of Theosophy—*Isis Unveiled* (1877), *The Key to Theosophy* (1889), and most significantly, *The Secret Doctrine: The Synthesis of Science, Religion, and Philosophy* (1888)—seek to unify *all* forms of mythological, religious, and esoteric belief into one vast system in which each presents fragments of different, culturally specific iterations of a larger universal truth. Drawing extensively on an archive of Buddhist and Hindu sacred texts that had only recently become available to Western scholars, Blavatsky subversively suggested that Judeo-Christian religious beliefs were only later expressions of a prior source of spirituality best apprehended in its original form in places like Tibet and Nepal that fell outside of European imperialist domination. Unlike many nineteenth-century orthodox religious positions *or* more esoteric movements such as Spiritualism or the various secretive societies devoted to Ritual Magic (many of which, incidentally, she *also* appropriated for her system) that defined themselves in opposition to positivism and rationalism, Blavatsky embraced contemporary scientific research in her elaboration of Theosophy. The work of Charles Darwin, recent discoveries in the field of organic chemistry, and innovative research regarding matter, energy, and electricity all have prominent positions within Blavatsky's writing. In each case, scientific advances supplement and confirm rather than refute the positions found in an older expansive conception of universal spirituality. One of Blavatsky's central positions held that none of these structures of belief, whether religious or scientific in origin, should be regarded as holding some form of absolute priority over the others. Importantly, Blavatsky never argued that Theosophy should be regarded as presenting a specifically defined alternative religion in itself (though later movements claiming descent from Blavatsky would come closer to this position; such insistence on the authority of doctrinal orthodoxy would eventually provide one reason for A. E's. movement away from organized Theosophy). To Blavatsky, the only type of real heresy was a dogmatic insistence that only one form of belief was valid at the expense of all others. Moreover, in its commitment to universal fraternity, racial, and gender equality, and in its opposition to political and social domination of any kind, the aims of Theosophy resonated with the emerging goals of such progressive movements as feminism, socialism, and anti-imperialism, and its early adherents often simultaneously participated in movements devoted to such causes.[27]

As a consequence of Blavatsky's larger project, more orthodox specialists and advocates of any number of the systems of belief and knowledge she appropriated—which ranged from the leaders of more conventional religions to academic scholars of "Oriental" languages and literature, from conventional biologists to political conservatives, from Marxists to self-described Rosicrucian magicians—found fault with the expansive nature of Theosophy, the credibility of her scholarship (including the charge that she probably plagiarized a number of her sources), and the cult of personality which developed around her. The supposed history of Madame Blavatsky's life both before and after the inception of Theosophy present some of the greatest difficulties in taking her ideas seriously. Her biography, as first recounted by her friend and early disciple A. P. Sinnett in *Incidents in the Life of Madame Blavatsky*, reads like an amalgamation of many of the clichés of nineteenth-century popular adventure fiction. Like the novels of Victorian politician and writer Edward Bulwer-Lytton, whose occult popular novels Blavatsky's mother translated into Russian and which appear to be the unattributed source of some of her more fantastical claims, such fiction probably *was* the point of origin for many of the incidents described in her biography rather than events which actually did occur in her life.[28] Blavatsky claimed that her discovery of Theosophy in general and the text of *The Secret Doctrine* in particular resulted from her capacity to telepathically communicate with several-hundred-year-old "Masters" (or "Mahatmas") who lived in a secret and remote monastery in Tibet. She asserted that she was given the mission of translating what had previously been "the secret doctrine" of Theosophical truth to humanity and that her writing was dictated to her psychically by the Masters themselves. Through their instruction, Blavatsky claimed to have learned the ancient (and hitherto unknown) language "Senzar," which enabled her to read, translate, and explicate the (also hitherto unknown) sacred text *The Book of Dzyan*—the foundational source of all forms of belief and the Theoscphical key to all of existence. When pressed for empirical proof of her capacity to communicate across the limits of time and space, Blavatsky produced letters purportedly written by the Masters which Sinnett then used as the basis for his books *The Occult World* and *Esoteric Buddhism* which helped popularize the movement.[29] "The Mahatma Letters," *The Book of Dzyan*, the language in which it was supposedly written—and even Blavatsky's claim to have ever traveled to Tibet in the first place—all appear to have been complete fabrications. An official investigation into Blavatsky and the Theosophical Society by Richard Hodgson of the British Society for Psychical Research in 1884 (and his exposure of the so-called "Coulomb Affair," in which disillusioned, estranged former members of the movement revealed what they claimed to be Blavatsky's fraudulent practices as a medium) determined that not only was she an imposter, but that many of her claims were plagiarized from other sources and that she relied upon a series of contrivances consistent with the less salubrious parlor-tricks of popular Spiritualism in order to establish the validity of Theosophy. Both Blavatsky's influence and the strength of the Theosophical Society continued to grow after the publication of the Hodgson Report in 1885 (and Blavatsky even presented some rather creative defenses against it in *The Secret Doctrine*). Yet the negative evaluation of its credibility in the Hodgson Report tainted Theosophy with a reputation for charlatanism from which it has never quite been able to completely free itself. After Blavatsky's death in 1891, the movement eventually broke apart into a number of different organizations which disparately regarded themselves as the sole adherents of Blavatsky's original vision and the movement gradually declined through the first half of the twentieth century. Almost one hundred and fifty years after the emergence of Theosophy, scholarship devoted to it tends to be split between a smaller esoteric fringe sympathetic to Blavatsky's fashioning of herself as an

irrefutable guru (various organized Theosophical movements continue to exist in the present day, if in much smaller numbers than
in its late-Victorian heyday), and a larger mainstream tradition in
which she is invariably presented as a scam-artist and author of an
elaborate and dubious hoax.

Theosophy is ripe for critical rediscovery.[30] Through its challenge
to standard and received assumptions about time, space, and causality, many artists found in Theosophy various suppositions which
became the basis for later Modernist formal experimentation. Blavatsky's influence is apparent in the writing of Yeats, D. H. Lawrence,
and H. D., in the painting of Wassily Kandinsky, Piet Mondrian,
and Nicholas Roerich, and in the musical compositions of Alexander
Scriabin, Henry Cowell, and Elisabeth Luytens among many, many
others who moved through the Theosophical Society at some point
in their lives. Blavatsky's writing enabled the conceptual possibility
of innovation in other interpretative modes of inquiry as well; such
disparate figures as Thomas Edison, William James, Albert Einstein,
Rudolph Steiner, Mohandas K. Gandhi, and C. G. Jung among others all credited exposure to Theosophy as part of the genealogy of
their own respective discoveries and positions. If one is willing to
look beyond some of its more fantastical details, certain aspects of
Blavatsky's writing rather strikingly anticipate much later theoretical
positions ranging from the intersectional nature of identity to Chaos
and Complexity Theory. Both a detailed exposition of Blavatsky's
explanation of Theosophy as a philosophical system and a larger reclamation of it as a crucially important, neglected aspect of modern
intellectual history are beyond the bounds of this essay. I do want to
suggest, however, that it is possible to concede the conceptual importance of what her work enabled without necessarily accepting the
literal truth of either Blavatsky's discredited claims about the reality
of the Masters who provided her with the "secret doctrine" or the
more fanciful positions her work describes (of which there are many).
Since A. E.'s understanding of the relationship between theory and
practice originated in the work of Madame Blavatsky, it is necessary
to briefly consider some of the primary positions formulated within

The Secret Doctrine, the foundational creed of the Dublin Lodge as well as the primary philosophical influence upon A. E.'s subsequent writing.[31]

Blavatsky proposes three fundamental positions about the universe as the theoretical basis for Theosophy in *The Secret Doctrine*, and the first asserts that from a cosmic perspective everything, whether of a phenomenal or noumenal nature, is part of some vast "Omnipresent, Eternal, Boundless, and Immutable PRINCIPLE on which all speculation is impossible, since it transcends the power of human conception and could only be dwarfed by any human expression and similitude. It is beyond the range and reach of thought."[32] Blavatsky's system depends upon the acceptance of an expansive concept of Totality which recurs within the history of philosophy from the ancient sacred texts of Hinduism to the more recent work of Hegel.[33] Just as a Hegelian philosophical perspective assumes an infinite form of Totality while conceding that it is impossible to comprehensively represent all of its details, the "Universal Root" (one of Blavatsky's terms for the Absolute "PRINCIPLE") lies beyond the capacity of representation to account for all of its qualities.[34] Yet one can begin to become aware of the Universal Root *not* through an understanding of the grand sum of what it includes, but rather through an acknowledgment of the separation into more particular concepts which appear beneath that condition of unified Absolute Being:

> [s]uch a state can only be symbolized; to describe it is impossible. Nor can it be symbolized except in negatives; for, since it is a state of Absoluteness *per se*, it can possess none of those attributes which serve us to describe objects in positive terms. Hence that state can only be suggested by the negatives of all those most abstract attributes which men feel rather than conceive, as the remotest limits attainable by their power of conception.[35]

Since the Absolute is too vast to comprehend, it can only be conceptualized as entailing that which exists beyond everything which *can* be understood in terms of particular qualities. Such a position acknowledges the differentiation between particularities, even if such distinctions are abolished at a higher level once they become unified within the Universal Root. Below the level of "the Absolute" are various cosmic planes of differentiation which descend to a distinction between Being and "Logos" (the capacity to represent Being in sensible terms), then between "Spirit" (that which is eternal) and that which takes material form as "Matter," and beyond that according to a principle of Identity ("Cosmic Ideation, MAHAT or Intelligence") which produces the logic which enables definitional classifications in regard to different qualities.[36] Successive planes of increasingly differentiated complexity continue to descend below the more unified levels of the Absolute above them until one reaches the boundaries of material existence, conditioned by the empirical limits of time, space, and individual subjectivity, in which all elements of the universe momentarily exist as arrangements of all possible particularities.

In support of this position, Blavatsky drew upon the duality of the Hindu concept of *Maya*, which she describes as "illusion; the cosmic power which renders phenomenal existence and the perceptions thereof possible."[37] The boundless plane of Infinite Eternity ("that alone which is eternal and changeless is called *reality*") is beyond perception framed by the limits of time, space, and matter; on the other hand, "all that which is subject to change through decay and differentiation and which therefore has a beginning and an end is regarded as *Maya*—illusion."[38] *Maya* isn't entirely illusory, since it provides the boundary of all which is knowable *within* the material world; instead, the illusion lies within the assumption that *only* that which can be apprehended beneath "the veil of *Maya*" accounts for *all* of existence. Since only the immediate physical plane is conditioned by the limits of *Maya*, almost all of existence occurs beyond it. All of the phenomena of the material world present the vast range of particularities of the Universal Root it is possible to encounter within the object-world; yet all such differences ultimately begin to unify beyond the limits of *Maya* as one ascends through multiple layers of infinite Being toward the Universal Root. As one of the determinative limits to human perception and consciousness within *Maya*, time is both real from an individual subjective perspective but also an illusion in regard to Eternity: "Time is only an illusion produced by the succession of our states of consciousness as we travel through eternal duration, and it does not exist where no consciousness exists in which the illusion can be produced; but 'lies asleep.'"[39] Temporal duration is "real" in that it defines the lived experience of human existence itself; but it is also an illusion which limits apprehension of the greater cosmic singularity of the Universal Root. For Blavatsky, the finite temporality of the material world is something different than timeless Eternity beyond it:

> The present is only a mathematical line which divides that part of eternal duration which we call the future, from that part which we call the past. Nothing on earth has real duration, for nothing remains without change—or the same—for the billionth part of a second; and the sensation we have of the actuality of the division of "time" known as the present, comes from the blurring of that momentary glimpse, or succession of glimpses, of things that our senses give us, as those things pass from the region of ideals which we call the future, to the region of memories that we name the past.[40]

Contrary to the assumptions of progressive teleology, initially time appears to flow backward within Blavatsky's theorization of temporality: the future has already occurred, and when one encounters it through the perceptual limits of the empirical world, individual consciousness classifies phenomena according to the familiar terms provided by memory. While this description better captures Blavatsky's understanding of the movement of time—and immediately indicates a vast difference from the progressive historicism which underlies so many historical narratives of the late nineteenth-century, both within the context of the Revival and beyond it—ultimately it too is only an illusion in regard to the singularity of the Universal Root beyond the material plane of existence. Since every particularity evident within empirical reality is part of a greater,

increasingly unified form of Being outside of time, the lived experience of temporality only disguises a larger cosmic simultaneity which
encompasses every facet of Spirit and Matter which exists, ever has
existed, or ever will exist. Since no particularity exists in a stable
or unchanging fashion, however, the material world is conditioned
by "the absolute universality of that law of periodicity, of flux and
reflux, of ebb and flow, which physical science has recorded in all
departments of nature," as Blavatsky asserts in her second fundamental proposition in *The Secret Doctrine*.[41] Moreover, an individual
human is not a unified monad unto itself—that is an illusion fostered
by subjective consciousness, another aspect of *Maya*—but rather is
comprised of a series of particularities which exist in unending, oscil-
lating relationship to each other for only a given moment. Just like
in A. E.'s description of visionary experience as a series of pictures
moving before him at great speed, an instance in time only reveals
the complexity of the relationship between the various particularities
which make up the self (or, beyond that, what philosophical traditions would regard under the category of Identity) for a fraction of
an instant. As Blavatsky explains,

> [t]he real person or thing does not consist solely of what is seen
> at any particular moment, but is composed of the sum of all its
> various and changing conditions from its appearance in the mate-
> rial form to its disappearance from the earth. It is these "sum-
> totals" that exist from eternity in the "future" and pass by degrees
> through matter, to exist for eternity in the "past."[42]

While Blavatsky's first proposition seeks to identify "Eternity" as a
cosmic condition of infinite unity beyond the limits of perception,
her second proposition attempts to delineate "Time" as comprised
of the seemingly endless flux of particularities within the empiri-
cally verifiable material world of lived existence. According to Blavatsky, the relationship between the Universal Root and the endless
flux of particularities within the material world is governed by what
she calls variously the "law of correspondences" or the "law of

analogy." This position presents a variation of the Hermetic doctrine defined by the axiom "as it is above, so it is below," which Blavatsky updated in the light of early atomic theory in order to argue that every aspect of the microcosm—from the smallest phenomenal particle of matter to the grandest noumenal mythologies which seek to explain existence—corresponds to the higher order of the macrocosm anchored by the primordial eternal unity of the Universal Root.[43] While every aspect of the microcosm is distinct in its particularity and such diversity should be celebrated, all of it is already unified as part of something larger the further one moves up the macrocosm toward Infinite Being.

This aspect of the belief system produces Blavatsky's third proposition, and it is in this final position one encounters the basis for what A. E. would later come to identify as "the politics of Time and Eternity." The practice of Theosophy depends on the need to discover "the fundamental identity of all Souls with the Over-Soul, the latter being itself an aspect of the Universal Root; and the obligatory pilgrimage for every Soul—a spark of the former—through the Cycle of Incarnation (or "Necessity") in accordance with Cyclic or Karmic law, during the whole term."[44] By "Cycle of Incarnation," Blavatsky refers to any specific period of individual life. Each particular lifetime

> presents momentarily to our senses a cross-section, as it were, of their total selves, as they pass through time and space (as matter) on their way from one eternity to another: and these two constitute that "duration" in which alone anything has true existence, were our senses but able to cognize it there.[45]

Such an understanding of Time both does *and* does not imply reincarnation. Blavatsky held that each version of the self who ever had or ever will exist was comprised of seven fundamental qualities.[46] Three of those qualities were eternal and described aspects of the self which persist beyond the material plane of existence in combination with other elements of the universe as one moved closer to the apprehension of the Universal Root; those three qualities reincarnate over several lifetimes. The other four qualities of a specific life form were specific to the material world conditioned by *Maya* and only existed in combination with the other qualities over a particular lifetime (though in Blavatsky's Heraclitian understanding of matter, these facets of ephemeral, biological life never disappear entirely from the material world, but reappear in different, recycled form over time). Every incarnation of life is unique and specific to a given time and place, but all seven aspects of that incarnation exist in a different ratio of combinations to each other across multiple lifetimes. Since chronological time is an illusion fostered by the limits of *Maya*, from a cosmic perspective one lives across several lifetimes simultaneously. Moreover, since those aspects of the Self which are eternal ultimately exist in unified combination with similar qualities of the Other beyond the limits of the material world, there is a profound symbiotic relationship between Self and Other beyond *Maya* despite their uniquely particular differences within the material world. The principle which holds all of these relationships together for Blavatsky—between Self and Other within a given lifetime, across different versions of the self through several lifetimes, and between that which exists above in eternal form and that which exists below in material form—is her variation of the Buddhist concept of Karma, which she defines as that which "neither punishes nor rewards, it is simply *the one* Universal LAW which guides unerringly, and so to say, blindly, all other laws productive of certain effects along the grooves of their respective causations."[47] Rather than serving as a fundamental determination which constructs the conditions of one's life in a beneficial or detrimental fashion according to one's actions in a past life—something impossible according to Blavatsky, since all lifetimes are ultimately simultaneous to each other beyond the limits of temporality—Karma identifies a universal current of energy which connects all instances of particularity into something larger and collective across time and space.

A commitment to Theosophy asserts that the "obligatory pilgrimage for every Soul" one undertakes in a given lifetime entails the renunciation of self-interest for the purpose of generating a harmonic form of Karma which unifies every aspect of existence. As a philosophical system, Theosophy begins with the recognition of the complexity of the material world, and seeks to align the various particularities within it—not to suppress such differences, but to celebrate and acknowledge them as unique instances of the sacred—in order to apprehend a greater organizational principle lurking behind it. If Karma provides the cosmic energy which links all particularities within the complexity of all existence, both the identification and generation of that process of unification bring about the emergence of something which has a profound impact upon the world. Ultimately, such efforts will evoke a coming interconnected collective "Golden Age" in which domination, inequality, and the various miseries of modernity no longer serve as the primary registers of human experience. While the "Golden Age" had not yet arrived from the specific temporal position in which Blavatsky revealed the "secret doctrine" and would not begin until far off in the future in her estimation, it is the endpoint of an evolutionary process which includes all of human (and even prehuman) history. Blavatsky's description of the "anthropogenesis" of previous and future cycles of the rise, decline, fall, and rebirth of various epochs of human civilization takes up the entire second volume of *The Secret Doctrine* and includes some of the stranger passages in all of her writing. However, such fanciful details should not necessarily diminish Blavatsky's larger point: from a Theosophical perspective the passage of time is in itself a perceptual limit imposed by the material plane of existence and all times are actually simultaneous to each other. In that regard, the "Golden Age" has already arrived even if it would not begin for thousands of years from the specific temporal standpoint of the late nineteenth century, and it was possible to evoke its qualities in the present through the production of positive energy. Theosophical practice works toward such a goal in a variety of ways. The comparative study of the links between all forms of knowledge—religious, scientific, historical, cultural, and more—presented ongoing research into "spiritual discernment" in order to align the particularities of each in the interest of delineating a more comprehensive awareness of an Infinite Totality ultimately beyond individual human perception. The practice of meditation as a form of "devotion" attempted to suppress the primacy of the material world in order to momentarily arrive at an awareness of insight—such as the various visions which A. E. felt he was susceptible to even before he discovered Theosophy and which he describes throughout his mystical writings and paintings—which originates beyond the limits of *Maya*. The solitary practice of meditation and scholarly research into the comparative links between all forms of knowledge were not enough to generate positive Karma, however, since they could lead to a quietist detachment from the world instead of a more active engagement with the consequences of negative Karma. As Blavatsky argues, "action must be performed, or the frame of things within which the individual can seek salvation will fall apart."[48] One could attempt to produce the realization of the karmic harmony Theosophy identifies with the "Golden Age" by working to ameliorate those unjust social, economic, and political conditions which characterize the objective reality of the modern world. As A. E. wrote in an article entitled "Concentration" published in the *Irish Theosophist* in 1893, these three central practices informed the mission of the Dublin Lodge:

> By uniting these three moods—action, devotion, and spiritual discernment—into one mood, and keeping it continuously alight, we are accompanying the movements of spirit to some extent. This harmonious action of all the qualities of our nature, for universal purposes without personal motive, is in *synchronous vibration* with that higher state . . . therefore we are at one with it.[49]

Blavatsky's propositions within *The Secret Doctrine* suggest a different understanding of what the Victorian concept of "self-help" meant within the historical context of the Revival. The causes most important to the Dublin Lodge (which included suffrage, pacifism, vegetarianism, anti-vivisection, temperance, the social purity movement, dress reform, and most especially an ongoing commitment to altruistic social work) were similar to progressive articulations of

Samuel Smiles's ideals of self-control and individual responsibility found elsewhere in the liberal reform movements of late nineteenth century Britain.[50] From a Theosophical perspective, however, "Self" was only a perceptual limit, and the Other who received the benefit of charity was only another incarnation of particularity which comprised a larger condition of unified Being alongside the Self beyond the material plane of existence. The goal of altruism from this perspective was not focused upon the reform of the personal character of the Other in order to encourage individual self-reliance, but rather toward a utopian unification between Self and Other which already existed beyond the limits of *Maya* in order to generate the karmic harmony typical of the "Golden Age." A. E.'s enthusiasm for altruism and social reform persisted beyond his participation in the Dublin Lodge, and Blavatsky's explanation of Theosophy helps contextualize later diverse commitments ranging from his ongoing mentorship of younger writers to his polemical support of the families of the Irish Transport and General Workers' Union in the Lockout of 1913. Yet the understanding of temporality he derived from Madame Blavatsky regarding the fundamental simultaneity of the past, present, and future led him into a more contentious area of national political engagement than the Dublin Lodge was willing to entertain, and finally became the primary focus of his work as an intellectual in the Revival. Ultimately, A. E.'s consideration of what generally goes by the name "tradition" from a standpoint qualified by the mystical politics of Time and Eternity raises the question of whether the word "revival" might be considered the best term to describe the period in the first place.

Simultaneity, Emergence, and National Sovereignty

The very word "revival" not only designates the specific period of Irish cultural history in which A. E. played a crucial role, but also implies a diachronic process in which something associated with the past—now lost over time as a consequence of the violence of colonization and modernization—reemerges in order to present the arrival of a different future. A. E.'s early expositions of Theosophy for an Irish audience trouble this relationship between periodization and teleology. "The Story of a Star," an early text published in the *Irish Theosophist* in 1894, indicates that even within the earliest years of the Revival A. E. held a quite different position to the progressive temporality of (re)emergence which eventually became the structural basis for a historical understanding of the period. Blurring the generic distinctions between prose-fiction (over a few sentences A. E. provides the slightest of frames to give it the appearance of a short story) and mystical allegory, "The Story of a Star" describes a visionary experience both inspired by and explanatory of Blavatsky's theorization of time. A. E. begins by describing how the ringing church-bells of a neighboring cathedral trigger "strange lapses into other worlds and times . . . changes from state to state" which ultimately present visionary sensations that produce an awareness of one of the key philosophical positions of Theosophy:

> I realized what is meant by the Indian philosophy of *Maya*. Truly my days were full of Mayas, and my work-a-day city life was no more real to me than one of those bright, brief glimpses of things long past. I talk of the past, and yet these moments taught me how false our ideas of time are. In the Ever-living yesterday, to-day and tomorrow are words of no meaning. I know I fell into what we call the past, and the things I counted as dead for ever were the things I had yet to endure. Out of the old age of earth I stepped into its childhood, and received once more the primal blessing of youth, ecstasy, and beauty. But these things are too vast to speak of, the words we use to-day cannot tell their story.[51]

A. E.'s stylistically arcane reflection implies that since everything which ever has or ever will exist is ultimately simultaneous to the present, one need not accept that immediate material conditions are permanent or unchangeable, or that the traces of the past have disappeared forever. But rather than develop these positions in rational terms—or even more clearly explain the meaning of *Maya*, which he doesn't refer to again—in the remainder of "The Story of a Star" A. E. instead presents a descriptive series of visions in which his consciousness travels to a distant location elsewhere in the universe to witness the birth of a new planet, the origins and development of its organic cycles of life, and finally the emergence and evolution of a "strange race" of sentient beings who surpass earthly humans in their knowledge and achievements. Throughout the vision, in which several thousands of years are compressed into a few instantaneous moments, A. E. describes the thrill of emergence ("Coincident with the appearance of these things I felt within myself, as if in harmonious movement, a sense of joyousness, an increase of self-consciousness: I felt full of gladness, youth, and the mystery of the new,") and understands the vision to be a prophecy of the future ("I felt that greater powers were about to appear, those who had thrown outwards this world and erected it as a palace in space.")[52] A. E. speaks to one of the alien life-forms, who makes it clear that all aspects of the vision present different facets of the Universal Root; moreover, everything within it had already taken place in the distant past even if it also predicts a far-off condition for humanity on earth:

> The end is creation, and creation is joy. The One awakens out of quiescence as we come forth, and knows itself in us; as we return we enter it in gladness, knowing ourselves. After long cycles the world you live in will become like ours; it will be poured forth and withdrawn; a mystic breath, a mirror to glass your being.[53]

The passage of time is something real within "The Story of a Star," whether in regard to the "work-day" experience of modernity which frames the text, the diachronic cycles of birth, development, and progress which seem to have taken place at some point in the distant past in some far corner of the universe on the planet glimpsed by A. E., or within the coming progression of time on earth which the vision forecasts. Yet time is also an illusion, and all of the elements of "The Story of a Star" exist beyond it as well as within it. A. E. is only able to perceive a larger infinite condition of Being in the first place because nonrational visionary experience provides a momentary apprehension of that which lies beyond the limits of *Maya*.

The meaning of "The Story of a Star" is extremely difficult to understand without a prior knowledge of Theosophy. Like much of A. E.'s writing, which takes Blavatsky's propositions as a theoretical foundation without bothering to explain them, the absence of conceptual clarification presents one of the primary obstacles to reading him and might indicate one of the reasons why a trajectory of critical history regarding his place within the Revival tends to emphasize his record of personal achievement at the expense of such elliptical, mystical speculation. Yet those historical accomplishments originate in the same series of philosophical commitments as the stylistic density and strangeness of his writing, and the recovery of what Gibbon described as the "illumination" necessary for understanding A. E. considerably clarifies these esoteric texts.[54] A. E.'s mystical writing demands further research into its source within the work of Madame Blavatsky, thus necessitating entry for his readers onto the path of "spiritual discernment" in search of further elucidation while also initiating them into one of the primary facets of the practice of Theosophy whether they are aware of it or not. "The Story of a Star" proposes an understanding of temporality which accepts it as an inevitable determination of perception, but also asserts the need to imagine a conceptual possibility beyond such limits in the interests of discovering a greater understanding of the complexity of the material word. From a vantage point beyond *Maya* but nevertheless accessible deep within our consciousness, every instance (or "thread") of particularity discernible in the object-world becomes part of a vast, unified fabric; yet because of the inevitable limits of *Maya*, such a condition can only be evoked in allegorical form rather than completely described:

> There is within us a little space through which all the threads of the universe are drawn; and surrounding that incomprehensible centre, the mind of man sometimes catches glimpses of things which are true only in those glimpses; when we record them the true has

vanished, and a shadowy story—such as this—alone remains. Yet, perhaps, the time is not altogether wasted in considering legends like these, for they reveal, though but in fantasy and symbol, a greatness we are heirs to, a destiny which is ours though it be yet far away.[55]

From A. E.'s Theosophical perspective, an awareness of the infinite complexity of eternity begins with the recognition of the cosmic simultaneity of all particularities even if they might not be immediately apparent in an empirical sense. Emergence does not indicate the inception of something new, but rather—like the birth and development of the planet he perceives in his vision—the recognition of the various processes of karmic unification between these particularities both within and beyond the limits of time and space according to a macrocosmic order defined by the primacy of the Universal Root. As A. E. suggests in his initial discussion of *Maya*, such a position cannot really be understood in a rational sense, but can be felt through visionary moments of intuition and awareness beyond the clarity of logic. While such intimations of esoteric insight are fleeting and ephemeral as lived experiences, one can reconstruct them in allegorical form through "fantasy and symbol." As the closing reflections of "The Story of a Star" suggest, imaginative representation itself could serve as a conceptual form of emergence by providing a framework for the documentation of the deeper insights of a Theosophical understanding of the universe. At this point early in his career as an intellectual, "The Story of the Star" appears to theorize and exemplify A. E.'s commitment to the apprehension of "the politics of Eternity" beyond the limits of temporality as a primarily aesthetic project.

By the late 1890s, A. E.'s visions seem to have changed to the extent that they now concerned the more pressing political needs of the time, as documented by his description of his sense of the impending arrival of a national avatar in *The Candle of Vision*. The practical experience of activism on behalf of organizations like the IAOS offered a more radical commitment to social and political justice than the devotion to altruism and rights-based activism identified with the

Dublin Lodge. More importantly, the Cooperative Movement and other organizations A. E. became affiliated with from this point on required the formation of collective institutions which could serve as frameworks *within* the material plane of existence for the karmic unification of simultaneous particularities. If A. E.'s claims about the aims of aesthetic representation in "The Story of a Star" sought to theorize a Theosophical concept of emergence in imaginative terms, his work as an activist presents a corresponding commitment in regard to the "politics of Time." National sovereignty—a matter which the Dublin Lodge appears to have been hesitant to directly engage with in the years leading up to A. E.'s departure from it—became a conceptual means for him to articulate that possibility of karmic unification.[56] As he wrote in an essay entitled "Nationality or Cosmopolitanism" (1899) in the aftermath of his break with the Dublin Lodge,

> [n]ationality was never so strong in Ireland as at the present time. It is beginning to be felt, less as a political movement than as a spiritual force. It seems to be gathering itself together, joining men who were hostile before, in a new intellectual fellowship: and if all these could unite on fundamentals, it would be possible in a generation to create a national ideal in Ireland, or rather to let that spirit incarnate fully which began among the ancient peoples, which has haunted the hearts and whispered a dim revelation of itself through the lips of the bards and peasant story tellers.[57]

Given the historical context of the Revival and A. E.'s deployment of some of its customary imagery, it is easy to overlook the larger mystical concept for the apparently cultural nationalist details. However, A. E.'s investment in nationality stems from its capacity to organize the unification of various types of particularity, whether between different positions evident within the immediate moment or between elements of the past, present, and future across the limits of temporality. Moreover, his identification with nationality as a "spiritual force" invokes the Theosophical "politics of Eternity" while also responding to the political needs of the time.

A. E.'s engagement with the Irish mythological tradition demonstrates the manner in which he subverted the customary imagery of more essentialist forms of cultural nationalism for Theosophical purposes. *The Candle of Vision*, which occasionally resembles a mystical reworking of the bildungsroman in its early sections due to its focus on the most important visionary epiphanies of his adolescence and young adulthood, begins with a prolonged description of what A. E. considered to be his first visionary intuition of that which exists beyond the limits of *Maya*. A. E. recalls a moment of emotional intensity while he walked through the Irish countryside as a teenager:

> Suddenly, I felt a fiery heart throb, and knew it was personal and intimate, and started with every sense dilated and intent, and turned inwards, and I heard first a music as of bells going away, away into that wondrous underland whither, as legend relates, the Danaan gods withdrew; and then the heart of the hills was open to me, and I knew that there was no hill for those who were there, and they were unconscious of the ponderous mountain piled above the palaces of light, and the winds were sparkling and diamond clear, yet full of colour as an opal, as they glittered through the valley, and I knew the Golden Age was all about me, and it was we who had been blind to it but that it had never passed away from the world.[58]

A. E.'s memory of the vision refers to the persistence of the Sídhe within the Irish landscape in imagery familiar from the poetry of Yeats or any number of other writers associated with the Revival. However, the intimation this mythological presence provides does not indicate the fundamental difference of ancient Celtic tradition from any other mythological tradition in the world, but rather evokes the utopian qualities of the harmonic unification of diverse particularities beyond the limits of temporal and spatial perception within Theosophical belief.

A. E.'s memory of his first visionary experience is described retrospectively through terms he would have been unaware of at the time since he would not acquire a deeper knowledge of either Irish mythology or Theosophy for roughly another decade. Like many prominent figures associated with the early years of the Revival, A. E.'s eventual discovery of Standish O'Grady's *History of Ireland: Heroic Period* would provide him with specific names and mythological personae through which to represent the otherness he perceived in his visions.[59] Yet his encounter with the writing of Madame Blavatsky at roughly the same time would provide a different framework for understanding what was typically classified as Irish tradition. From a Theosophical perspective, traces of the mythological past did not provide evidence of a uniquely Irish essence now lost but waiting to be recovered and revived in the present day; instead, it provided one aspect of Irish particularity which had never completely disappeared to begin with but persisted simultaneously in adjacency to the present beyond empirical perceptual limits. Moreover, while many of the linguistic details regarding names and places were specific to Ireland, ultimately the larger narrative patterns and divine entities found within Irish mythology corresponded to those of every other global cultural tradition. A. E. would develop this position in greater detail later in *The Candle of Vision* in a section entitled "Celtic Cosmogeny"; there, A. E. presents a creation myth with reference to various deities associated with the Tuatha Dé Danann.[60] While A. E.'s narrative merely appears to associate Irish names with the archetypes of *any* similar mythological foundation of belief found throughout the world rather than present actual historical research into ancient Irish literature, closer inspection reveals that the narrative reframes Blavatsky's theorization of the multiple planes of existence descending from Absolute Being: Lir is the local name for what is otherwise known as the Universal Root, Mananan and Dana refer to Spirit and Matter, and Angus Óg identifies the divine energy which binds them together. The fact that "Celtic Cosmogeny" was initially published in 1902 in Arthur Griffith's newspaper the *United Irishman* rather than a journal more specifically devoted to Theosophical or mystical concerns further indicates that A. E. deployed the imagery of a cultural nationalist understanding of tradition in order to connect it to a very different larger project.

To A. E., national particularity was *also* a condition framed by *Maya*. Just as temporality presents a real perceptual limit within a given round of incarnation but ultimately disguises an infinite form of Being lurking behind it, so too did spatiality. While various locations within the Irish countryside identify precise geographic locations within the material world, they also masked hidden portals to what A. E. refers to as the landscape of the "Many-Coloured Land" in which several orders of Being simultaneously coexist in relation to a given place.[61] From A. E.'s perspective, nationality had very little to do with race, blood, ethnicity, or any other categorical form of identity, but instead presented the intersection of one's momentary position in a given incarnation in respect to the specificity of historical time and geographical location. While categorical forms of identity were real within the limits of empirical reality, they only presented instances of particularity which contributed to but didn't essentially define one's individuality since one not only lived simultaneously across multiple times but also in numerous places.[62] One's individual personality encompassed a range of particularities which were at once local and global but momentarily unified by the incarnation of a given lifetime; consequently, the multiple inhabitants of a given place beyond the self alone required a collective organizational frame which could align them together in a larger process of unification. As this Theosophical understanding of the relation between Self and Other evolved into a political position for A. E. which sought to unify particularity with collectivity in order to evoke the karmic harmony of the "Golden Age," it proposed the need for a form of national sovereignty simultaneously cognizant of the local and the global. As he writes of his earlier motivations in the preface to *Imaginations and Reveries*, a collection of selected essays published after his achievements as an artist and activist had made him one of the most prominent and influential figures of the Revival,

[m]y conscience would not let me have peace unless I worked with other Irishmen at the reconstruction of Irish life. Birth in Ireland gave me a bias towards Irish nationalism, while the spirit which

inhabits my body told me the politics of eternity ought to be my only concern, and that all races equally with my own were children of the Great King.[63]

A. E.'s resolution to an apparent contradictory tension between a commitment to Irish nationalism and a spiritualist devotion to the "Great King" (which in this case does not refer to any earthly form of monarchy, but rather the Universal Root) was to recognize the fundamental unity between the two.

In the brief period between the Easter Rising and the end of World War I in late 1918, A. E. wrote two extended works which sought to unify his understanding of theory and practice in order to analyze the relationship between the "politics of Time" and the "politics of Eternity." *The National Being* (1916), written in the immediate aftermath of the Easter Rising, focuses on the former from a theoretical perspective motivated by the latter. It presents A. E.'s understanding of practice, and considers national specificity as a framework of emergence in regard to the immediate historical moment. The project of the "reconstruction of Irish life" provided the means to work with others in collective fashion toward the realization of the goal of aligning all of the particular traces of the past which had ever existed locally with the forms they took in a future which, from a Theosophical perspective, had already taken place. While the realization of national sovereignty and subsequent progressive development were immediate goals, such aims must be accompanied by a simultaneous commitment to the amelioration of worsening social conditions that so often accompanied processes of modernization. Furthermore, just as important to progress and the creation of an egalitarian social and political condition is the labor process itself, which contributes to the Theosophical aim of bringing together diverse individuals under a larger collective rubric:

[t]here is nothing more certain than that where men work alone or only with the aid of their families they are little higher than the animals. When they tend to unite civilization begins. Then arise

the towers, the temples, the cities, the achievements of the architect and the engineer. The earth is tapped of its arcane energies, the very air yields to us its mysterious powers. We control the etheric waves and send the message of our deeds across the ocean. Yet in the midst of these vast external manifestations of power, multitudes of men and women live in squalor, isolated in their labours, living in the slums of the cities; and this, if we examine it, comes about because the organization of human energies is not yet complete.[64]

In turn, a Theosophical focus on the global diversity which descends from the fundamental unity of the Universal Root inspires the project of the national "organization of human energies" so that development becomes a means to acknowledge the vast range of particularities which simultaneously exist within the material plane of existence and beyond the limits of time and place. *The Candle of Vision*, A. E.'s lengthiest consideration of Theosophy and esoteric matters, seeks to evoke a greater sense of the "politics of Eternity" while conceding that such aims are ultimately beyond the limits of human perception. In order to evoke that immensity, however, A. E. considers how various local particularities encountered within his own time simultaneously correspond and emerge into greater unified form beyond the limits of *Maya*. Both *The National Being* and *The Candle of Vision* supplement each other from the separate standpoints of the difference—but ultimate simultaneity—between Time and Eternity. Taken together, they present the primary justification for the critical recuperation of A. E. as a neglected theorist of the Revival.

Unfortunately, while *The National Being* and *The Candle of Vision* present the culmination of A. E.'s Theosophical intervention within the Revival and best delineate his contribution to a different structural understanding of that period, they also present a conclusion of sorts. The violence which began with the Easter Rising and continued through the Civil War and political consolidation of the Irish Free State made a profound impact on A. E.'s views regarding what he had previously hoped would be a period devoted to the collective development of an egalitarian Ireland. The possibility of evoking the harmonic karmic unification of the "Golden Age" became an increasingly remote possibility as the energy of the Revival dissipated into a bleaker condition of post-colonial statehood, as later extended prose fiction narratives like *The Interpreters* (1922) and *The Avatars* (1933) darkly indicate. Increasingly, A. E.'s political positions grew more conservative and closer to a Yeatsian insistence on the necessity of governance by an enlightened, intellectual elite.[65] Frustrated with the myopic and censorious qualities of the Irish Free State, A. E. would depart Ireland in 1933 for a period spent living in England and the United States before his death in 1935. Yet his eventual shift away from the radical possibilities offered by his translation of Theosophical positions into the context of the Revival should not diminish their importance for a different structural understanding of the period. More precisely, the significance of his adaptation of Madame Blavatsky's understanding of temporality as a point-of-departure for his attempt to unify theory and practice deserves wider critical recognition. As he suggests in a review of J. W. Dunne's *An Experiment with Time* written in the late 1920s which restates that position in succinct fashion, once one becomes aware of "an Everliving, in which past, present and future co-exist," then "all kinds of fantastic possibilities spring up in the imagination."[66] For A. E., the most fantastic possibility of all was the evocation of the utopian qualities lurking just beyond the limits of perception in which real and attainable political goals signaled movement toward the realization of an "Ever-living" karmic harmony which could unify the complex diversity of a seemingly infinite range of particularities. In practical terms, A. E.'s efforts to identify as many varieties of difference as possible within the veil of *Maya*, to organize possible terms of affiliation between them, and finally to construct the institutions which could develop the collective shared interest between such particularities constituted separate facets of the work-ethic he contributed to the Revival. This commitment serves as a consistent foundation for A. E.'s practical work across numerous areas of social and political engagement during the period and led him to embrace aspects of anarchism, socialism, and other forms of communalism as facets of organizational networks which sought to frame the simultaneous relationship between diversity and collectivity. While the importance of A. E.'s debt to such articulations of tangible radical political philosophies has been accounted for in more recent critical examinations of his role within the Revival, the centrality of A. E.'s commitment to mysticism and esotericism—not only as a symptom indicative of the historical moment in which he lived, but as the basis for a series of theoretical positions in their own right—needs greater recognition and clarification.[67] A. E.'s reiteration of Theosophical positions not only explains the motivation for his own writing and activism, but also suggests a theoretical model already at work within the historical context of the Revival which is aware of its complexity, processes of emergence, and the ultimate simultaneity of particularities otherwise obfuscated by the perceptual limits of temporality. Unlike teleological narratives of cultural history which take a linear and progressive form of temporality for granted or valorize the familiar tropes of supposed innovation, the mystical illumination provided by A. E.'s reading of Madame Blavatsky suggests that periods of cultural, social, and political transformation like the Revival do not occur as a consequence of a singular prior historical cause or through the heroic agency of the individual artist. One need not completely share A. E.'s devotion to Theosophy to concede the fantastic interpretative possibilities it enables for a different understanding of the period.

8

An Arts and Crafts Revival

Harry Clarke's Modernist Gaze

Kelly Sullivan

In 1914 the Civics Institute of Ireland announced a competition for a new plan for Dublin, aimed at confronting the city's notorious slums. Professor Patrick Abercrombie's winning entry appeared in 1922 as *Dublin of the Future*, with the planner and his team updating their original proposal to register the damages the city suffered during the 1916 Rising, the subsequent War of Independence, and the Civil War. The publication includes a frontispiece, "The Last Hour of the Night" (figure 1) by stained glass artist and illustrator Harry Clarke (1889–1931). This ominous black and white illustration suggests the postindependence state of major Dublin buildings—including the General Post Office, the Four Courts, and the Customs House—all envisioned in flames. On the right a Georgian tenement slum appears to disintegrate into the street. The illustration's central focus is a looming androgynous figure modeled on F. W. Murnau's *Nosferatu*, catwalking through Dublin with one hand on the tenements and the other stoking the fire, his flowing rags suggesting a flood of decay. Although the Dubliners in the image stroll past the destruction,

An earlier version of this chapter appeared as "Harry Clarke's Modernist Gaze" in *Éire-Ireland: An Interdisciplinary Journal of Irish Studies* 47, no. 3 and 4 (2012): 7–36, doi: 10.1353/eir.2012.0022. It is republished here with permission of the author and *Éire-Ireland*.

1. Harry Clarke, *The Last Hour of the Night* (1922), frontispiece to Patrick Abercrombie's *Dublin of the Future* (Civics Institute of Ireland), London: Hodder and Stoughton, 1922.

curiously immune to the violence and terror that preoccupy the illustrator, viewers cannot be so cavalier. Clarke's devil pointedly gazes out, fixing them with a cold, even derisive, stare, implying the viewer's modern Gothic complicity in the horrors of postrevolutionary Ireland's slum life.[1]

Clarke was a leading figure of the Irish Arts and Crafts movement, a group of artists and craftsmen and women working during a period roughly concurrent with the Irish Revival and the rise of International Modernism. Although influenced by English and North American Arts and Crafts activity, the Irish movement represented less a negative response to the mass production of modern industry and more a search for "modern vernacular expression" in a country experiencing both rural depopulation and urban poverty.[2] Nicola Gordon Bowe describes Irish Arts and Crafts in terms that might equally well apply to Harry Clarke's work:

> In Ireland, the movement was as much concerned with political, social and cultural ideology as the making of beautiful, functional, materially fitting objects and, in Dublin, with a passionate striving for individual, 'modern' visual expression based on glorious past achievement in craftsmanship, set against an urban backdrop of decay, unemployment and disease.[3]

As a visual corollary to the Irish Revival, the Arts and Crafts Movement similarly drew upon a tradition of Irish cultural heritage; and as in the Revival, artists also sought to express modern life by using but modifying a recognizable visual tradition.[4]

The poverty of tenement life in Dublin was familiar to Clarke, whose studios on North Frederick Street occupied a distinctly urban atmosphere. As prosperous city dwellers moved to southside suburbs like those of Rathgar and Terenure, the Georgian center of Dublin became a tenement catch basin for the rural poor migrating into the city. The most impoverished parts of the capital were in north-central Dublin, near Clarke's studios. Here the vast Georgian houses of North Great Georges Street and Mountjoy Square held as many as sixty or seventy tenants, and overcrowding, disease, and death rates in turn-of-the-century Dublin slums exceeded those of any other European city.[5] Such urban poverty, as well as the chaos of recent political upheaval, made life in this period insecure, even as nationalists strove to foster a sense of moral and cultural stability. A dark slum-urban Gothic—expressing itself in Clarke's imagery and finding its literary parallels in early twentieth-century Irish Modernism—remains largely hidden from historical record. Positioning his work in relation both to the Revival and to Modernism reveals an aesthetic attention to this overlooked aspect of early twentieth-century Irish life. Clarke's stained glass windows, like "The Last Hour of the Night," provide visual evidence of how an ominous modern Ireland generated such new Gothic cultural forms.

This essay explores Clarke's ecclesiastical stained glass work to reassess his oeuvre in the context of revisionary readings of early twentieth-century Irish culture and the Irish Revival. What did modern Ireland look like in the buildup to 1922, and how did artists and writers envision the future of the Free State? Until recently, interpretations of late nineteenth- and early twentieth-century cultural nationalism and revivalism generally ignored International Modernism, presumably in response to the conservative outlook of a nation state recently emerging from conflict. But in a landscape of revolution, civil war, and state building, did Ireland altogether bypass a modernist material culture? Recent scholarship suggests otherwise, reading the postcolonial nation-building project as sharing the same underpinnings as Modernism itself, even in a repressive and conservative Catholic state.[6] Although the postcolonial nationalism arising in the 1920s appeared antithetical in its values and characteristics to Modernism, the social and cultural conditions initiating revolution, civil war, and subsequent state formation were core sources for both. But whereas Modernism turned outward—to self-conscious experimentation and to a cosmopolitan outlook, as well as to a break from past forms and traditions—Irish political and cultural nationalism depended on an idealization of tradition, stability, and an inward-looking provincialism.[7] As the biographies of Ireland's great modernists James Joyce and Samuel Beckett are so often interpreted, one had to become an exile to become modern. A country that introduced censorship laws, upheld the value of family and female domesticity, and advocated a return to "traditional" Irish cultural practices seemingly provided little room for innovation and change. Likewise, the values and tenets of the Arts and Crafts movement in Ireland, which hinged on a search for Celtic symbolism, tradition, and continuity, appear complicit with a nationalistic idealization of the past; decorative arts in Ireland, by 1922, argues Bowe, "had become evocative instruments of national consciousness."[8] Artists working in this decorative tradition form a visual corollary to the literary Revival's search for cultural nationalist forms.

Yet an interest in traditional crafts and values did not necessarily produce artists with outlooks antithetical to change. The host of factors that led to International Modernism—catastrophe and chaos in postwar Europe, a revolt against Victorian values, technological innovation, mass warfare, women's and workers' liberation movements—overlap with the uncertainties and insecurities of a newly postcolonial nation. Thus, modern Ireland also experienced fracture, unrest, a dramatic split along political lines, new opportunities and freedoms for women, and technological and infrastructure innovations. As Luke Gibbons points out, to assess the existence and success of a specifically "Irish Modernism," we must shed rural/urban binaries and understand that the defining characteristics of that movement come not necessarily from subject matter but from the formal approach to themes.[9] Such a reevaluation of the characteristics of Modernism encourages the inclusion of cultural movements like Irish revivalism and Arts and Crafts within its purview.

A formal and aesthetic Modernism—particularly that of the late 1920s and 1930s—requires, in Terence Brown's words, "aesthetic self-consciousness or self-reflexiveness"; collage; "simultaneity, juxtaposition" or doubling; "paradox, ambiguity and uncertainty"; a certain amount of "dehumanization"; and some engagement with or troubled relationship to time.[10] Although considered by few cultural critics in reassessments of the period, these same modernist attributes can be found in the Free State's visual art and material culture, particularly in the work of Harry Clarke. Art historians acknowledge, in passing, Clarke's importance as a leading figure of the Irish Arts and Crafts movement, as a symbolist artist, a Beardsley-influenced illustrator, or as a stained glass craftsman; yet they generally avoid any sustained critical assessment, and outside of Ireland he remains largely unknown.[11] However, a fuller exploration of Clarke's innovative work within the culture and landscape of early twentieth-century Ireland establishes his role as a leading visual arts modernist, and as a central figure in revivalist visual culture.[12]

Arts and Crafts Glass: Terms and Techniques

Clarke remains relatively unknown outside Ireland in large part because his architecturally embedded stained glass windows are impossible to transport and exhibit in international settings.[13] And stained glass notoriously suffers in reproduction. Just as photographs and drawings of architecture or sculpture fail to capture the contexts and dimensions of such works, so too reproductions of stained glass—particularly in black and white print—inadequately convey the experience of viewing aesthetic artifacts designed to glitter and gain dimension as light filters through them. Yet an even more significant barrier to reading this oeuvre in a modernist context lies in its religious subject matter. Although Clarke designed and executed several major works on literary themes, most famously the *Geneva Window*, the majority of his windows were church commissions.[14] In creating such work, Clarke was limited in subject and, to some extent, in stylistic and symbolic experimentation. A 1925 article published in the *Illustrated Country Review*, based on "information supplied by Harry Clarke" to its author, suggests his frustration in working within the strict confines of his ecclesiastical commissions:

> The possibilities of glass are unbounded and if it were taken up by architects and others for domestic purposes Artists would not be hampered by tradition as they are in dealing with ecclesiastical

stained glass. The main support of the craft is obtained from the Church, but in all Church work there is some tradition or preconceived notion as to the appearance of each Saint or other object which is to be incorporated in the design required.[15]

Despite such thematic limitations—or arguably because of them—Clarke's work reaches a level of aesthetic innovation all the more striking for its traditional, even conservative, context. Indeed, much of the work emerging from the Irish Arts and Crafts movement, linked either to religious sites and ceremonies or to private interiors, remains little known and underanalyzed both for its aesthetic merits and in relation to a larger cultural landscape of revolution and change. Clarke himself expressed reservations about the possibility of creating worthwhile art in a conservative religious context; his letters reveal his ambivalence about the value and efficacy of Arts and Crafts work for Irish churches. He complained of the tasteless display of his windows in Saint Peter's Church, Phibsborough: "We *cannot* allow to any English Protestant how degraded is the taste of the Irish priests. If the rotten Arts + Crafts was worth a dam we might do something but it is not."[16] Yet his oeuvre attests to the value both of his individual talent and of the movement's cultural force within early twentieth-century Ireland. Although some priests and benefactors sought out Clarke and the Clarke Studios, suggesting support even within the religious community for significant new approaches to art, we know little about contemporary responses to the windows from parishioners.[17] With a few notable exceptions, however, critics seem to have sided with Clarke's frustrated response to the confines of his commissions and to his work within the Arts and Crafts movement as a whole. Thus, they praise his windows in passing and ignore the movement's influence on modern Ireland.[18] This essay argues for a critical reassessment both of Clarke's work and of the Arts and Crafts movement, in a period when the search for a vernacular tradition and the influence of Modernism intersect in unexpected and productive ways.[19]

The Irish Arts and Crafts movement encompassed not just the stained glass tradition in Ireland but also, among others, those of bookbinding, embroidery, lacemaking, woodworking, and metal and enamel work. Clarke's aesthetic form built on techniques developed over the course of centuries by master craftsmen. The medium of stained glass had reached its artistic pinnacle in medieval Europe, and Clarke argued that "practically no advance in technique has been made since the fifteenth century, with the exception of the more skilled application and manipulation of the medieval craft."[20] The revival of the form in Ireland was influenced by the philosophy of Christopher Whall, whom Bowe describes as "the father of English arts and crafts stained glass."[21] Advocating for stained glass work as an art, not just a craft, Whall became a key player in the English Arts and Crafts movement that sought to make beautiful, imaginative, and useful artifacts based on the idealization of tradition.[22] His protégé Alfred E. Child relocated to Dublin to teach at the Dublin Metropolitan School of Art where Clarke was a student and to run An Túr Gloine (the Tower of Glass), the stained glass studio operating under the direction of Sarah Purser.

Although the practice of making stained glass changed little over the centuries, its techniques require not only a skilled craftsman but also a talented artist. The fundamental physicality of this aesthetic object is best described by Whall in the opening of his seminal glass-revival text *Stained Glass Work* (1905): "You are to know that stained glass means pieces of coloured glasses put together with strips of lead into the form of windows; not a picture painted on glass with coloured paints."[23] The artist first creates a scale drawing of the window itself, and Clarke's cartoons or preparatory studies were brilliantly detailed, usually including a color scheme. Such drawings were then scaled up and worked into glass by Clarke or by craftsmen working under his supervision. The composition of most commissioned windows depends on openings provided by the church architecture, and each full window is divided into "lights," or individual openings surrounded by the building's stone frame. From his drawing, Clarke would trace the "lead lines" or "leading"—literally the shape of the lead with which the pieces of glass would be held in place. These lines become central to the overall effect of the window, clarifying and calling attention to particular sections of glass; depending on their placement they aid in flattening spaces or adding dimension.[24]

Drawing on a variety of techniques developed in the twelfth through sixteenth centuries, Clarke was particularly skilled in creating windows with rich and multilayered color, fine detail, and intricate design. He often used "flashed" glass, for which the glassmaker bonded a second color—usually something rich like Clarke's signature deep blue—to a clear or tinted sheet of molten glass. The artist could then obtain multilayered colors in one section of glass through "aciding," a process that requires removing levels of the flashed glass with hydrofluoric acid to reveal the color underneath. Clarke also employed "plating," a method he describes in a letter to his friend Thomas Bodkin as "doubling two pieces of glass. . . . [It] is quite a common device to get depth of color or to tone or change a color when a window has been finished."[25] Finally, Clarke used vitreous paints for details in faces, clothing, landscapes, and other fine points in the windows; these paints contained glass and metal oxides that fused onto the window when put through a kiln.[26]

The stained glass medium in which Clarke produced his finest work reached its aesthetic height in the twelfth to thirteenth centuries; not unexpectedly, then, recent analysis seeking to establish a tradition of Irish Modernism considers him "fundamentally anachronistic."[27] Such an assessment, nevertheless, acknowledges that he combines technical proficiency with a dizzying amalgamation of styles derived from Art Nouveau, Art Deco, Aubrey Beardsley, Edmund Dulac, and the Arts and Crafts movement, but all in a decidedly entrenched and conservative context and medium. Thus, Clarke has been variously linked to the medieval stained glass tradition in Europe, to the Pre-Raphaelites and the 1890s British Aesthetes, and to the innovations of Klimt and the Wiener Werkstätte.

Although his body of work evidences all of these influences, his windows transcend influence and anachronism; they are reshaped as something cohesive and new.[28] Through its deployment of skilled traditional craftwork, as well as modern allusion, juxtaposition, and compositional forms, Clarke's oeuvre offers a means of exploring the complex relationships within early twentieth-century Irish society during a period of religious conservatism under the stranglehold of a Catholic hierarchy. His stained glass windows evidence a richly complex modernist material culture in the Free State.

Engaging the Spectator: Clarke's Modernist Gaze

Clarke's glasswork serves as a bridge between Modernism and tradition. On the one hand, his windows embody the revivalist ideal of embracing an aesthetic that merges history and tradition with modern designs for a new, independent nation. But the work also registers the tension in bridging this gap. As in the work of Clarke's modernist contemporaries in the international art world, such tension manifests itself through temporal disjuncture; through fracture and collage; and in a deliberate self-consciousness about the engagement between viewer and subject and the misinterpretation inherent in this act of perception. The windows designed and executed between 1922 and 1930 display a keen imagination, a passion for color, and compositional approaches borrowed from examples Clarke viewed at Chartres and in cathedrals throughout England. The medieval stained glass he studied was principally narrative, as is most ecclesiastical art. Although his commissions generally required that he depict biblical scenes or honor particular saints through an array of religious symbols, his style and compositional choices make clear how he continually displaces viewers' expectations and creates a tension between a traditional narrative that relies on a closed system of interpretation based on predetermined symbolic values and a modernist temporal disjuncture. Norman Bryson defines the pre-Renaissance ethos that infuses most religious art:

> Since the overriding mandate of glass and mosaic is to present scrip-
> ture without further elaboration beyond that which is required to
> disseminate the pre-formed corpus of denotation . . . , there is no
> requirement that the text be articulated from the viewpoint of the
> individual craftsman or be received by an individuated spectator:
> just the reverse.[29]

It is precisely against this nonindividualistic, nontemporal *umwelt*
that Clarke's windows evidence his modernist preoccupations.
Instead of relaying information to a passive receptacle, they both
narrate to and self-consciously engage with audiences; his saints and
sinners both act in tableau and—often at key or discrete places—
gaze out at viewers, implicating them in the temporal duration of the
work itself and disrupting the formal divide between the image and
the physical space in which it is displayed.

Such temporal and perspectival disruption also relates to Modernism. In 1945 Joseph Frank's "Spatial Form and Modern Literature"
revolutionized the way that critics thought about spatiality in literary works. Frank argued that the modernist experiment represented
experience and coherence *spatially* rather than chronologically: that
it did away with sequential time and forced the reader to understand
images or psychological events or the units of poetry or literature as
"juxtaposed in space rather than unrolling in time."[30] Modern painters worked in inverse relation to their literary counterparts, but to
the same effect; artists like Matisse and Picasso stripped away perspective or toyed with it to produce works that flattened or distorted
expected representational dimension. But in both cases—the verbal
and the visual—the element of time becomes the experimental force.
Writers and painters of high Modernism strive to flatten, disrupt,
fragment, or even remove altogether chronological temporal figuration. Such a flattening or disruption of the temporal plane of a work
of art also heightens the awareness of its reception; the reader or
viewer becomes enmeshed in the timescape of the piece or recognizes
the juxtaposition of his or her time onto that of the text or work of
art. Thus, the division between viewer and object becomes troubled.

Clarke's most modernist windows reveal a preoccupation with the viewer-object divide, with perspective, and with the spatial presentation of time. As an artist working through a period of national identity reformation, Clarke drew on ancient Celtic design, symbolism, and story to depict Irish saints like Brendan, Dympna, and Gobnait in their regionally specific habitats. His work indeed links medieval Ireland to his contemporary moment—but it also projects into the future in startling ways. Many of his windows, and certainly the most artistically experimental of them, entangle the viewer within their temporal plane, juxtaposing symbolic narrative, the

2. Harry Clarke, *The Visitation* (1924), detail showing Mary and Elizabeth, Saints Peter and Paul Church, Balbriggan, Co. Dublin (photograph by Kelly Sullivan).

moment of the work's composition, and the contemporary moment of the viewing.

A striking example of Clarke's use of the "gaze" as a way of shifting the temporal plane of a work occurs in two exceptionally fine windows he designed and executed in 1924 for Saints Peter and Paul Church, Balbriggan, Co. Dublin. The two-light *The Visitation* depicts Mary visiting her cousin Elizabeth, with the two pregnant female figures dressed in deep hues against a largely light-colored background of foliage and medieval architecture (plate 1, displayed at the end of this chapter). In contrast to medieval windows that value overall balance and order in composition, *The Visitation* asymmetrically positions Elizabeth a step higher than Mary; nonetheless, the window creates a cohesive compositional whole even across the architectural division of the mullion, the slice of wall between the windows.[31] Mary approaches Elizabeth up a staircase and presents a pale blossom in her open palm. Elizabeth looms over the slightly lower woman, not only because she is placed a step higher than Mary in the window's composition, but also because she inclines her head forward and holds her hands in front of her (figure 2). Although these two figures communicate across two lights divided by the stone mullion, their connection is clear. Mary and Elizabeth appear to move toward each other and establish visual contact. The figural rendering of the narrative conveys the biblical example of Christ's divinity as Jesus blesses both Elizabeth and her unborn child.

The narrative of *The Visitation* occurs within the temporal bounds of the window's frame, just as medieval stained glass windows provide visual stories to educate parishioners. Yet a more subtle set of clues also enforces this intended message and finally compels the viewer to a different chronological end point. A profusion of vertical and horizontal lead lines as well as prominent "saddle bars"—horizontal metal shafts used to hold the window together—create a sense of flatness and pattern in a window featuring exceptionally sculptural faces and hands. Key angled lead lines thus give motion to the window, drawing the viewer's eye up and to the right from Mary to Elizabeth. These lines particularly emphasize and exactly demarcate an angled shaft of slightly pink-hued glass that connects Mary's hands to Elizabeth's, even across the vertical divide of the church wall itself. Clarke's use of leading in *The Visitation* represents a deliberately two-dimensional approach to his medium, one that both flattens space and creates temporal movement. Viewers connect Mary to Elizabeth, thereby completing the biblical story in which the two cousins embrace, and Elizabeth, feeling herself in the presence of the yet unborn Divine Savior, is filled with grace.

Clarke further complicates the viewer-object relationship in this window by allowing a figure within the work to gaze out of the window, disturbing the balance between subject and object and directly implicating the spectator in the temporal experience of the narrative. The compositional line that connects Mary to Elizabeth thus draws the viewer's eye beyond Elizabeth to her husband Zacharias, who stands looking over her shoulder. His body is obscured by his pregnant wife and by the blue geometric border of the window itself as he gazes out at the viewer with a pursed mouth and lowered brows (plate 2). Zacharias's compositional position at the culminating point of narrative movement represents both a recognition of, and challenge to, viewers. Staring as he does out of the narrative frame, he draws on the energy of the composition and compels it outward to the work's audience. And yet Clarke has not allowed this figure to break the careful balance of the window, for Zacharias is paired both in color and placement with the decoratively rendered maid standing at Mary's back (plate 1). Although the artist rarely cuts lead lines through the faces or heads of his figures, Zacharias's head covering includes two that neatly divide it into equal sections and flatten it into a two-dimensional plane.[32] This deliberately geometric and nonorganic use of leading makes the figure appear trapped within the glass even as he gazes out at us in acknowledgment of his predicament. As the culmination of narrative "movement" in the window, this figure brings Clarke's art into the present. Such a move shifts the work from the realm of symbolic narrative to a study of perception itself as Zacharias's gaze interrogates viewers, capturing them in the act of perceiving. This reversal of the viewer-viewed dichotomy presents, in David Lloyd's words, an "uncanny sensation of seeing one's own gaze given back from the figure in which it is suspended."[33]

In *The Visitation*, Clarke's compositional strategies and use of a figurative gaze draw viewers into the temporal experience of the glasswork, acknowledging both their somatic and spatial reality. The work testifies to Clarke's sense of the architectural site these windows occupy, for Zacharias's arresting stare accrues power as he looks down on viewers from a height. The two-light *The Assumption and the Coronation* (1925), one of eight windows Clarke created for Saint Mary's Catholic Church, Ballinrobe, Co. Mayo, offers another example of the artist's attention to spatial dynamics. Mary's flowing gown in the right light and her stiffly pointed toes in the left both lead the viewer's eye to a group of three disciples who watch her assent into heaven (figure 3). Positioned just above the viewers' heads, a gray-haired woman leans over the flower-strewn balcony and fixes us with her powerful stare. Clarke's use of leading and color makes the stylized flowers and the horizontal gray of the balcony stand out with three-dimensional clarity; thus, the woman seems to lean over those viewing the window from below. A thick horizontal lead line crosses just over the old woman's shoulders and appears to imprison her in the window itself from which she gazes unsettlingly at us (plate 3). By deliberately using the physics of architectural space, the artist creates a subtly threatening window that implicates the viewer in its temporal plane.

This attention to architectural siting points to a particular quality of Clarke's work: contextual permanence. Commissioned for both Catholic and Church of Ireland edifices, such windows were generally assured indefinite lifespans in their original locations. Unlike a work of art contained within a frame, and thereby "built to travel away from its maker and from its original context, carried by the frame into different times and places," Clarke's windows remain as permanent fixtures in the religious settings for which they were commissioned.[34] Yet paradoxically such permanence offers the artist the opportunity to experiment with a modernist juxtaposition of time and perspectival space; certain his windows would remain in

3. Harry Clarke, *The Assumption and Coronation* (1925), central panels, Saint Mary's Catholic Church, Ballinrobe, Co. Mayo (photograph by Kelly Sullivan).

situ, he could consider the audience of the future and self-consciously construct glass that layers symbolic narrative and the moment of the window's creation with the continuous present of the work's reception. The religious conservatism that marks modern Ireland therefore provided a stable platform from which Clarke experimented with subject-object relations and temporal perspective.[35]

The Widow's Son, situated in the north wall of Balbriggan, similarly reverses typical subject-object relations. Here a crowd of onlookers form a vertical line at the top of the central panel as they marvel at the widow's son, miraculously resurrected by Christ (plate 4). The figures' painted faces are sculptural, almost Pre-Raphaelite in their heightened realism, although the robes of Jesus and the widow's son are stiffly ornamental and flattened by regular lead lines. The rapt and sympathetic faces of the crowd draw the viewer's attention to the miracle at hand, yet one woman's face, half-obscured by a thick lead line, registers amazement at *us*, her viewers. Her surprised expression tells us that the real miracle is the act of perception itself, and Clarke self-consciously communicates to future viewers through her penetrating gaze. Perceived as a narrative and symbolic work based on Christian iconography, the window comfortably fits within a trajectory of previous influence. But if the viewer registers Clarke's signature use of the gaze, the relationship between subject and object shifts. The contemporary viewer—through the simultaneity of historical time and lived time Clarke implies—becomes, instead, drawn into the image, transformed from passive spectator to active participant in the work.

A Modernist Memento Mori: Clarke's Gothic Gaze

Just as Clarke drew on medieval compositional techniques to create strikingly modernist works of art, he also played with medieval themes of the macabre and grotesque in juxtaposition with the ethereal and beautiful. Both in stylistic execution and in theme, Clarke's darkest windows merge medieval Gothic architectural design and symbolism with modernist preoccupations—including doubling,

collage and juxtaposition, and the linking of psychological opposites.[36] Clarke grasped how Gothic architecture and art used systems
of measurement to create balance and harmony in forms that also displayed excess and asymmetry. For John Ruskin, a principal characteristic of Gothic architecture was its "naturalism": modeling drawn
from nature coupled with an equal sense of design. For Ruskin the
principle of balance and organic wholeness underlies Gothic work in
which the finest artists combine the grotesque with the beautiful, the
realistic with the imaginative, and the naturalistic with the rigidly
designed. Clarke recovers such Gothic tropes and juxtaposition in
work drawing on a modernist gaze to implicate viewers in this careful balance.[37]

The Dempsey Memorial Lancet of St. Maculind (1924), one of
Clarke's major Gothic windows, depicts the Irish Saint Maculind,
bishop of the abbey he founded in Lusk (figure 4).[38] As Maculind
looks out from the window, his position at the top of the long Gothic
lancet—an acutely pointed arch at the top of a thin window—directs
his soft gaze high over the heads of visitors to the ecclesiastical site.[39]
He benevolently encompasses his viewers en masse, fulfilling his role
as symbolic host of the church. Both artist and viewer become complicit in a symbolic exchange in which, in Bryson's formulation, "the
viewing subject is addressed liturgically, as a member of the faith,
and communally, as a generalised choric presence."[40]

In contrast, the lower section of the Saint Maculind lancet interrogates the viewer almost at eye level, introducing elements of dis-
cord. Here Clarke depicts the saint surrounded by his parishioners,
a motley bunch of the sinful, insane, and sick (plate 5). The composition drives upward from the kneeling worshippers at the bottom
of the light, two devout peasants dressed in patched rags and dirty
clothes, their faces rapt. At regular intervals faces appear around
the saint, including a madman at his left shoulder and a self-portrait
of Clarke himself, crouched in an act of devotion at his left flank.
Compositionally, the faces of the parishioners and the outstretched
arms of the saint create an almond-shaped vesica piscis, a form with
significance in Christian art (figure 5). Derived from the intersection

4a and 4b. Harry Clarke, *The Dempsey Memorial Lancet of St. Maculind* (1924), Saint MacCullin's Church, Lusk, Co. Dublin. Left: detail of Saint Maculind, upper panel (photographs by Kelly Sullivan).

of two circles, the vesica piscis serves as an element of measurement in medieval architecture, where such overlapping circles create the geometry of Gothic buildings. For these architects and artists, the shape represented harmony, in Jonathan Hale's words, "an emblem of unity achieved from duality."[41]

Most striking in this compositional arrangement are two inhuman figures positioned within the group of worshippers. At the saint's right hand and directly parallel to the appealing face of a red-haired girl sits a gnarled, bitter skull (plate 6). Viewed closely, he is not quite dead; his mouth snarls grotesquely, his nose is a half-open wound, pockmarks weep from his cheeks, and his eyes are sunk deep into his head. And yet this memento mori stares out with one eye firmly fixed on the viewer as his left eye rolls back into his head. This is no devoted parishioner of the bishop of Lusk but rather a reminder to future viewers that even in the world of bright light *et in arcadia ego*. Clarke's memento mori reflects traditional medieval stained glass work where figural representations of Death and the Last Judgment became popular just after, and probably as a result of, the fourteenth-century Black Death.[42] Here the skeletal figure plays a double role. His inclusion within the confines of the medieval vesica piscis invokes Ruskin's Gothic naturalism, uniting "terror and beauty."[43] But Clarke's figure also breaks the inclusive narrative space with a gaze that actively challenges contemporary viewers to understand his message of mortality. Rather than speaking to a communal, liturgical audience through a tableau enacted within the window—generally one in which Death interacts with other figures in the image—Clarke's modernist-inflected image of mortality interrogates and implicates viewers across the temporal and spatial divide.

Another grotesque, inhuman countenance contributes to the lancet's temporal and spatial play. Located in a vertical line directly below the skull and just outside the form of the vesica piscis, this second deformed face greets the spectator at eye level and arrests us with its direct and penetrating gaze (plate 7). The face is compositionally balanced by a young female figure, who likewise peers at viewers from behind the kneeling parishioner on the right of the

PRAY FOR THE SOULS
OF JOHN AND
CATHERINE DEMPSEY
OF GRACEDIEU

5. Vesica piscis overlaid on the lower panel of Harry Clarke's *St. Maculind* window, Saint MacCullin's Church, Lusk, Co. Dublin (photograph by Kelly Sullivan).

window. This set of two figures in turn balances the skull and the red-haired girl above, with all four participating in the window's pairings of the grotesque and the pleasing. The *St. Maculind* window openly draws on precedent, for medieval artists who created monumental works in glass were fascinated by the juxtaposition of the macabre and the beautiful. But Clarke's innovative use of composition and design, coupled with his modernist preoccupation with subject-object relations, charges his self-portrait and memento mori motifs with a modernist unease. The two sets of paired figures gazing out of the window delineate the corners of a rectangular shape that overlays the naturalistic vesica piscis; thus, Clarke juxtaposes the medieval Gothic composition based on a shape invoking nature with an inorganic rigidity—even a modernist abstraction. In so updating Gothic principles, he fashions a contemporary ecclesiastical work through temporal disruption. He combines traditional iconographic language with the chaotic historical moment of the work's creation and the present moment of the viewer's gaze—a very different sort of "unity achieved from duality."

This turn to the Gothic memento mori motif in a work completed just three years after Irish Independence suggests how fully Clarke shared his preoccupation with mortality with J. M. Synge, a key revivalist author he read and admired—and who, like him, was doomed to an early death.[44] Like Synge, Clarke creates versions of an opulent, pastoral Ireland that are filled, nevertheless, with reminders of death. In *The Aran Islands* the writer invokes the theme in the rural setting of Inishmaan, where an old woman discovers the skull of her long-dead mother while attending the funeral of a young man. Despite writing with a modernist anthropological focus, Synge narrates the scene with increasing agitation and even personal anguish. In his search for the "timeless" Irishness of an iconic West from which revivalists could forge a modern sense of nation, he found instead the skeletal hints of a universal mortality. On Aran he wrote he "could not help feeling that [he] was talking with men who were under a judgement of death."[45] Clarke's vision of Ireland emanates from the chaos and discontinuity of postrevolutionary urban Dublin burdened with poverty and disease, as well as with the death and destruction of the First World War and the Rising; his modernist works unite this slum-urban Gothic with Irish saints, Celtic iconography, and the symbols of a romanticized precolonial past. Both Synge and Clarke have a fundamentally antipastoral vision where malign forces disrupt and fracture any unified sense of the world.[46] Jean-Paul Riquelme argues that Gothic literature is "structurally and implicitly a negative version of pastoral," and that modernist Gothic literature relocates this antipastoral world to familiar places. By making the familiar ground of the Aran Islands or the Abbey of Lusk disturbing and bizarre, the Gothic aesthetic "invites us to see our own faces" within this portrayal of the macabre.[47]

Clarke's most surreptitiously shocking window, *The Last Judgement* (1930) for Saint Patrick's Church, Newport, Co. Mayo, was one of his final designs (figure 6). This work continues Clarke's innovations through the Gothic modernist trope of balancing opposites and creating doubles. The piece was commissioned when the artist was overworked and suffering from tuberculosis. Saint Patrick's Canon McDonald insisted that the work be entirely the artist's own, but although Clarke designed the cartoons for the full window, after much delay only one portion of the entire piece was finished under his supervision. He died of tuberculosis in 1931, and the completed work was installed a month later. Clarke's apocalyptic sense of composition and design contributes to a disturbing unity of opposites derived not only from the Last Judgment theme of the window itself but also from the increasingly angular and abstracted representation of movement in the right light, depicting the damned in their descent to hell. The detailed faces and bodies descending to hell include a self-portrait of the artist paired with a darkened visage, perhaps representing his anti-self. Both stare out at the viewer.

The Last Judgement is a carefully balanced, if stylistically asymmetrical, composition. Almost perfectly mirrored angels and saints are aligned to left and right of a central axis composed of the fold of Christ's red tunic, an angel's silver trumpet, and a thin emerald crucifix. The lower portions of the left and right lights, however, appear in

6. Harry Clarke, *The Last Judgement* (1930), Saint Patrick's Church, Newport, Co. Mayo (photograph by Kelly Sullivan).

abrupt and dynamic tension with such balance; the saved souls and angels of heaven work asymmetrically in contrast with the damned descending to hell. All compositional lines in this late work radiate from the central figure of the Art Deco Christ in the central light; but while the saved on the left direct their faces and outstretched hands toward him, turning the visual focus inward, the damned draw the viewer's focus down and to the right, out of the composition altogether. No border or design encases the window, and the bodies and faces of the damned elongate and become distorted as they disappear off the edge of the work. In contrast, the left light contains full figures of winged angels and souls, all neatly contained within the architectural confines of the window. An underlying sense of proportion and geometry in the work makes this asymmetrical descent to hell all the more disturbing; unlike the unity of macabre and beautiful in the *St. Maculind* lancet, here the damned fracture from the whole and quite literally descend out of the composition.

The profusion of elongated bodies in the lower right light invoke both Gothic and modernist effects. Derived from the artist's observation of the minutiae of the natural world, these grotesqueries descending into hell depict larvae, arms in *écorché*, monstrous cadaverous faces, and globular growths (plate 8). Austin Clarke reported Clarke's fascination with the shapes of nature:

> [He] told me excitedly that he had discovered a tank in the back garden of his lodgings, full of tiny wriggling monsters, some of them scarcely visible. He was exalted for he saw in these microscopic shapes new forms for experiment in art. He would develop in ornamental design these fantastic germ-shapes which had been almost hidden from the human eye for aeons.[48]

For Clarke, the natural world here becomes material for imaginative re-creation. As a representation of that world iterated to its most microscopic conclusion, *The Last Judgement* might even be aligned with the naturalism writers of the Counter-Revival developed in reaction to the revivalist search for traditional symbols—an alignment that also echoes Ruskin's definition of naturalism in Gothic architecture. Surely such naturalistic preoccupations—both in Clarke's last 1930 window and in key literary works of the period including Joyce's *Portrait of the Artist as a Young Man* (1916) and *Ulysses* (1922)—reflect a strand of Dublin slum-urban Gothic in which the individual's path through the social world, as in "The Last Hour of the Night" (figure 1), becomes grotesque and inhuman through modernist experimentation. Among these "wriggling monsters" that form the collage of semi-human bodies in *The Last Judgement*, the artist himself descends. Sliced at an oblique angle across the lower portion of the light, a green-colored self-portrait falls, upside down, into hell. Forming a mirror image of that descending figure, another face appears obscured by shadow; as in many of Clarke's modernist windows, both figures arrest the spectator with their penetrating gaze (plate 8). Doubled and reflecting each other, these visages invite comparison with the Gothic doppelgänger, and even with that doubling central to Yeats's idea of the self and anti-self—tropes Riquelme identifies as the Gothic legacy at work in Modernism.

Conclusion

Despite a recent upsurge in interest, Clarke's ecclesiastical windows remain distressingly understudied as major artistic achievements of a modern nation. They function as evidence of the complicated and rich cultural landscape of early twentieth-century Ireland—one simultaneously responding to both modern and traditional influence. Clarke created innovative work in stained glass, and his adaptations of medieval craftwork and Celtic symbolism have long marked him as an important symbolist artist and a leader of the Irish Arts and Crafts movement. But his oeuvre cannot be brushed over as simply "anachronistic" in its blend of 1890s Decadence, medieval grotesquerie, and religious symbolism. Instead, it might better be read in the context of a changing and revolutionary Ireland in conversation with avant-garde art movements across Europe. His work beckons viewers to step across a temporal divide and consider the complex roles of subject and object—and of viewer and viewed—in the modernist repertory. Reading his work this way further expands our sense of the urban and avant-garde in the Irish Revival.

Situated as they are in churches largely built for a rising Catholic middle class, these windows evidence the stirrings of modernist innovation even as nationalist Ireland sought traditional models upon which it might build a viable future. They exhibit meticulously skilled workmanship that draws upon medieval techniques; but as an innovative artist Clarke responds as well to fundamental historical changes in his own country and across Europe—leaving us with evidence of a richly modernist Irish culture in the 1920s, and the legacy of Irish revivalist work pushing beyond traditional boundaries.

Plate 1. Harry Clarke, *The Visitation* (1924), central panels, Saints Peter and Paul Church, Balbriggan, Co. Dublin (photograph by Kelly Sullivan).

Plate 2. Harry Clarke, *The Visitation* (1924), detail of Zacharias, Saints Peter and Paul Church, Balbriggan, Co. Dublin (photograph by Kelly Sullivan).

Plate 3. Harry Clarke, *The Assumption and Coronation* (1925), detail
of disciples, Saint Mary's Catholic Church, Ballinrobe, Co. Mayo (photograph by Kelly Sullivan).

Plate 4. Harry Clarke, *The Widow's Son* (1924), central panels, Saints Peter and Paul Church, Balbriggan, Co. Dublin (photograph by Kelly Sullivan).

PRAY FOR THE SOULS
OF JOHN AND 🕱🕮
CATHERINE DEMPSEY
OF GRACEDIEU 🕱🕮

Plate 5. Harry Clarke,
St. Maculind (1924), detail
of lower panel, Saint Mac-
Cullin's Church, Lusk, Co.
Dublin (photograph by
Kelly Sullivan).

Plate 6. Harry Clarke, *St. Maculind* (1924), detail of memento mori, Saint MacCullin's Church, Lusk, Co. Dublin (photograph by Kelly Sullivan).

Plate 7. Harry Clarke, *St. Maculind* (1924), detail, Saint MacCullin's Church, Lusk, Co. Dublin (photograph by Kelly Sullivan).

Plate 8. Harry Clarke, *The Last Judgement* (1930), detail showing self-portrait of the artist among the damned descending into hell, Saint Patrick's Church, Newport, Co. Mayo (photograph by Kelly Sullivan).

Part Five

Engendering Revivalism

Insight and Insurgency

Reviving the New Woman

Feminists, Revolutionaries, and Writers

Tina O'Toole

In his pioneering essay, "Queering the Irish Renaissance," Adrian Frazier explores the Revival from the perspective of cognate experiments in literary aestheticism, in which many well-known Irish authors were invested.[1] As part of this, describing the "strong current of male-male desire" in the coteries surrounding George Moore, W. B. Yeats, and Edward Martyn, among others, Frazier suggests an "erotics of literary influence" as an alternative framework within which to read these interactions and their representation in Irish culture. Frazier's scholarship reveals powerful counternarratives to the more traditional construction of the Revival, in which the movement is frequently depicted as a unified, nationalist (or narrow, heteronormative), and somehow *inevitable* cultural moment in the evolution of an independent Irish state. Extending the analysis Frazier begins here, more recent scholarship illuminates the extent to which an exploration of manliness, male homosocial relations, homoeroticism, and the male body were often a key focus of Irish cultural politics at the turn of the twentieth century.[2]

Unquestionably, these explorations have had a crucial effect on received ideas about the Revival, utterly transforming the way we think about and teach that period today, particularly in our understanding of the ways in which gender and sexual politics are inextricably linked with questions of national and cultural belonging during the Irish fin de siècle. However, sightings of women's lived experience and the female body (already missing from earlier scholarly accounts of the Revival) are rare enough in contemporary queer scholarship about this period. Much like Elizabeth O'Farrell in the famous "surrender shot" of the 1916 Rising, we sometimes catch a partial glimpse of her but, on the whole, she is difficult to discern.[3]

Focusing on the fiction of Rosamond Jacob (1888–1960), this essay sets out to reinscribe women's bodies, experience, sexualities, and fin de siècle feminist ideas at the heart of radical discourses in early twentieth-century Ireland. Reading Jacob's literary work, which extends the groundbreaking decadent writing of George Egerton (1859–1945) and her peers in the 1890s, it becomes clear that the radical impetus produced by Irish "new woman" writers was an important constituent of the discursive nexus that produced our revolutionary culture at the turn of the twentieth century. Nationalist women activists of the period are evidently much closer to the embodied and highly politicized female protagonists we encounter in Jacob's and Egerton's narratives, than to the more abstract, idealized, disembodied, and asexual feminine figures often held up as exemplars of Revival cultural production. In critically acclaimed and internationally best-selling fiction (that predates both *The Untill'd Field* and *Dubliners*) Egerton exposed the cultural stagnation and sectarian divisions of colonial Ireland, as I have discussed elsewhere.[4] Moreover, the transnational impetus of Egerton's work and her adherence to a diasporic Irish identity subvert the parochialism of later Revival texts and correspond closely with the lived experience of nomadic Irish revolutionaries from Anna Parnell and Hannah Lynch to Maud Gonne and Muriel McSwiney.[5]

Tracing these literary and ideological influences from decadent and new woman models into the writings of the revolutionary generation, I explore the complex webs of affiliation characterizing militant Irish women's activism and writing in early twentieth-century Ireland. Many nationalist activists were part of a generation of newly educated, empowered, and radical women in Ireland—scholars, educators, artists, and writers—who openly professed first-wave feminist ambitions and were engaged in public discourse and social activism of various kinds. Their intimate lives were no less conventional than that of their male peers; several were lesbian or bisexual, others were marriage resisters who refused to formalize long-term heterosexual relationships, while women like Alice Stopford Green, Kathleen Clarke, and others lived long and independent public lives after being widowed. While some women writers and cultural producers are included in mainstream accounts of the Revival discourse (in recent years, Eva Gore-Booth and Alice Milligan are among the chosen few), others are mentioned less frequently and rarely read or taught today (for instance, Rosamond Jacob, Dorothy Macardle, and Agnes O'Farrelly). Reinserting their work at the center of cultural nationalist experiments in the period, it seems to me, provides an opportunity to reassess the ideological constructions through which the cultural struggles of the period have subsequently been conceptualized.

The rise of the controversial new woman figure in 1890s Britain had important reverberations transnationally but her influence and the specifically Irish origins of this polemic have only recently been uncovered. As I discuss in *The Irish New Woman*,[6] the vital interaction of literary writing and Irish political culture at the turn of the twentieth century was key to the discursive nexus that produced the Irish new woman. New woman narratives might be described as the cultural wing of the first-wave feminist movement; these literary texts are often premised on a central character who, having her consciousness raised by feminist ideas, gains confidence in her ability to voice her rights and is ultimately willing to fight for them. Many authors associated (accurately or otherwise) with the new woman movement had Irish backgrounds, including George Egerton, Sarah Grand, L. T. Meade, Hannah Lynch, Katherine Cecil Thurston, E. L. Voynich, and Somerville and Ross, just to give a few examples.[7] The novelist and feminist campaigner Sarah Grand (born in Donaghadee, Co. Down) is a crucial figure in this feminist history of ideas; her fictional deployment of the new woman mounted a challenge no less radical than that of her fellow-activists involved in the campaigns for women's suffrage or for equal access to education and the professions.[8] By creating fictional feminists who prevailed against all odds, Grand's novels made way for readers to follow in the footsteps of their literary heroines; in other words, the imbrication of social activism and literary representation is part of this history.

Featuring erotically assertive women protagonists, George Egerton's literary experiments were instantly linked with emerging new woman discourses, although unlike Grand, she distanced herself absolutely from organized feminism. Egerton's name became practically synonymous with literary aestheticism when John Lane accepted her sexually bold first collection of short stories, *Keynotes*, for publication at the Bodley Head in 1893. When her story "A Lost Masterpiece" appeared in the scandalous first issue of the journal the *Yellow Book* the following year, the connection was sealed. Rapidly becoming one of the best-known and best-selling women writers of her generation, Egerton dissected the frustrations and opportunities presented to women in the swiftly changing social and cultural landscape of the period. In common with her new woman counterparts, embodiment is a central site of exploration in Egerton's fiction where class, gender, ethnicity, disability, malnutrition, pregnancy, and physiological responses to emotional states variously leave their marks on the bodies of her protagonists. Women in Egerton's short stories have clear views on sexual equality; they struggle autonomously with ethical issues; they take lovers, have unexpected pregnancies, and deal with the consequences; they worry about economic survival (and often, revealingly, about how to get on with their writing); ultimately, they find diverse ways to live their lives both in and outside heteronormative family situations. Egerton's outsider status enabled her to perceive "natural" social relations as part of an oppressive hegemony; her Irishness, her lack of a stable family background or class position, and her nomadic existence contributed to her dissident perspective of the social world. Ejected from polite (Catholic) Dublin society following her elopement with a married man when in her thirties, she later spent some years struggling as a single mother to raise her son while relying on her writing to make ends meet. Emerging from these lived experiences (following on from an adolescence steeped in poverty and near-destitution in Dublin), Egerton's fiction analyzes the social conventions that oppressed her and deconstructs them.

By rejecting what Katie Conrad terms the "passive and pure" representations of women privileged in many Irish Literary Revival texts, emerging feminist perspectives revealed in the writing of Egerton and her counterparts directly challenge received ideas of Irish women as silenced figures whose only available roles at the turn of the twentieth century were delimited by heteronormative and male-dominated family structures.[9] Elleke Boehmer, in her analysis of anti-colonial intelligentsias, highlights what she terms their "potentially productive in-betweenness;"[10] she describes members of such groups as "poised between the cultural traditions of home on the one hand and of their education on the other."[11] This description offers a productive way to approach Egerton's work and that of several other Irish women writers at the end of the nineteenth century. The early new woman novel *The Prince of the Glades* (1891), by Dublin writer Hannah Lynch (1859–1904), is an example of such "productive in-betweenness."[12] Lynch based her new woman protagonist on the life and character of her mentor, Anna Parnell, a member of the Protestant Anglo-Irish landowning class whose Irish nationalist activism set her in opposition to the interests of her caste. Parnell was leader of the Ladies' Land League, the first Irish nationalist organization to be directed and managed at all levels by women.[13] There are clear ideological links between Lynch's fictional new woman, Parnell's textual shaping of the Ladies' Land League in her journalism and public speeches, and the radical ideas emerging from first-wave feminist politics internationally (these connections were underpinned by close contacts between Parnell, Lynch, and well-known British feminist activists Helen Taylor and Jessie Craigen). While an agrarian uprising may seem an unlikely genesis for Irish feminist activism, Parnell's efforts to highlight women's abilities in the public sphere are testament to her belief that this was a moment with potential for social transformation.

While Hannah Lynch's novel is not that well-known today, one of the best-known novels of the period, *The Gadfly* (1897) by E. L. Voynich, has had a lasting reputation, particularly as a libretto. Translated into more than thirty languages, the novel sold over five million copies and was dramatized by G. B. Shaw, among others. *The Gadfly* foregrounds the Italian Risorgimento of the 1840s; it is suffused with character disguise and gender dissidence centering on a strong central female figure who is the leader of an activist cell of radical nationalists.[14] The novel's revolutionary plot was particularly popular in Russia where it was performed as an opera and filmed in 1955 with a score by Shostakovich. Voynich, the Cork-born daughter of mathematician George Boole and Mary Everest Boole (who was a scientist, philosopher, and educator), was personally involved in revolutionary politics relating to Russia. Her relationship with Wilfrid Wojnicz, a freedom fighter who had escaped from Siberia to London, began in 1890; the couple at first lived together in a free union, marrying only in 1902. That adherence to sexual and social liberty throughout Voynich's life and art recurs in the biographies of many Irish women of the period.[15]

Evidently, the work of radical women like Lynch and Voynich on the page and on the streets coincided with and drew on a turbulent time of anticolonial and class agitation at home and internationally, although neither were explicitly linked with the Revival. By contrast, for the Irish revolutionary generation who grew up in the period between the Land Wars of the 1880s and the 1916 Easter Rising, cultural nationalism offered women scope for participating in public life, whether political, intellectual, and/or creative. For instance, such a group in the Glens of Antrim combined aestheticism (characterized in this case by a deep interest in the ancient past, in rediscovering their local heritage and archaeology, and in a commitment to the recovery of the Irish language) with their adherence to the cause of Irish independence.[16] This coterie includes scholars, writers, and Irish language educators such as Úna Ní Fhaircheallaigh [Agnes O'Farrelly], Margaret Dobbs, Róis Ní Ógáin [Rose Young], Ada MacNeill, and Alice Stopford Green. Along with Alice Milligan and

Ethna Carbery, whose names are better known today, these women were active cultural and intellectual agents within the Revival ambit, and many of them were active members of the Gaelic League in the early years of the twentieth century. The 1904 Glens Feis organized by this group (whose legacy is remembered today because of the involvement of Roger Casement, a close friend and enthusiastic supporter of these women) might today be perceived as a "boutique festival" for revivalists, complete with arcane self-designed costumes, the celebration of ancient languages, customs, sports, arts and crafts, and nonheteronormative sexual identities. Sexual dissidence is intrinsic to their context, as soon becomes clear when we consider the range of gender and sexual identities represented among members of such radical coteries. This is underlined too in Adrian Frazier's treatment of masculinities during the Revival moment, as I've mentioned:

> [t]here is . . . a richness in the possibilities of masculinity during this period—when there were multiple forms of sexual practice (and non-practice) and shifting ways of acting out gender—before the emergent model of sexual identities (as hetero-, homo-, or bisexual) came into force in the early twentieth century, that makes our categorical identities inadequate: the more one studies the lives of certain particular authors, the more one concludes that the categories underdetermine the life studied; they fail in explanation and succeed in distortion.[17]

I will return to explore this point in more detail when addressing Rosamond Jacob's work.

As part of the centenary commemorations for the 1916 Easter Rising, those young Irish women who were on active service in 1916 began to be mentioned in the "official" national narrative. Yet, in the light of women's earlier involvement in Land League agitation, and Gillian McIntosh's work on the labor organizing of women mill-workers in Belfast in the same period,[18] it looks as though these women radicals were just the visible sign of happenings beneath the dominant surfaces of Irish culture in the late nineteenth century, subversive energies producing new resistance movements among women of different classes.[19] For a younger generation of Irish women coming to consciousness at the turn of the century, the decision to throw in their lot with the Irish national struggle is perfectly understandable. Simultaneously, however, some Irish feminist activists and writers maintained their Unionist affiliations; they saw no future for political radicalism in a Home Rule Ireland, and fought its advance as a threat to their feminist agenda. These include, for instance, Isabella Tod, Margaret Byers, and Mary Bulmer Hobson, as well as Edith Somerville and Martin Ross [Violet Martin].

Nor were such fears unfounded, as Irish nationalist feminists like Rosamond Jacob and Dorothy Macardle were to discover as the twentieth century wore on. Jacob's novel *The Troubled House* is testament to the imbrication of feminist and nationalist politics available to Irish women of the revolutionary generation, but its difficult publication history is indicative of the gradual curtailing of women's rights and their consequent invisibility in both the public sphere and cultural life of the emerging Irish Free State. Jacob finished the novel in the 1920s but could not find anyone willing to publish it; extracts were finally serialized by the *Irish Press* in 1936 but, according to her biographer, Jacob was horrified that they censored some passages.[20] The novel was finally issued by Dublin publishers Browne and Nolan, at her own expense, in 1938. This is despite the fact that she was an established writer by the early 1920s; moreover, her experience of publishing popular history in the same period, such as the very successful *The Rise of the United Irishmen* (1937), or the award-winning historical fiction *The Rebel's Wife* (1957), about Matilda Tone, suggests that *The Troubled House* provoked a very different reaction from publishers than her other work. The disjunct between the life world and political aspirations of *The Troubled House* and the mid-century hardships experienced by these two former members of Cumann na mBan, Jacob and Macardle, is revealing. Both contended with the increasingly limiting public space afforded to women in the Irish "Free" State; their persistent efforts to sustain themselves professionally as writers, to live independently of their families, and to have fulfilling intimate lives outside the narrow heteronormative expectations of the Catholic state in the 1930s and 1940s are revealing (moreover, their struggle anticipates the censorship, dismissal, and exile of a better-known generation of Irish women writers, such as Kate O'Brien, Elizabeth Bowen, and Maeve Brennan).

Born in 1888, Rosamond Jacob's formative years were spent in an atmosphere in which the writing of new women and literary aesthetes was extremely popular and widely diffused through British and Irish culture, and the Irish Literary Revival was happening on her doorstep; just as her later creative work is clearly influenced by this cultural radicalism, her career was heavily influenced by first-wave feminist activism and ideas. A life-long political activist, Jacob's commitment to social justice causes derives from her Quaker background and the community activism of the women in her family. Her aunt Hannah Harvey attended the Commons debates on suffrage in June 1884, four years before Jacob's birth;[21] with that background, it is unsurprising that Jacob would begin her writing career with pieces for the *Irish Citizen*, the Irish suffrage newspaper. Originally from Waterford city, Jacob divided her adult life between there and Dublin, contributing to Irish cultural nationalism in the early twentieth century as a member of the Gaelic League and of Inghinidhe na hEireann (founded and led by Maud Gonne), and attending plays produced by the Irish National Theatre Society. That rich cultural and political life characterizing turn-of-the-century Dublin emerges distinctly from the pages of *The Troubled House*, but this is not by any means an insular, self-contained world dominated by Irish separatist values. On the contrary, Jacob's incorporation of a wider world of Irish migrants and avant garde art movements opens up the world of the novel and defines a broad, transnational space for Irish identity in the twentieth century.

Her socialization is evident in Jacob's active participation in the Irish revolutionary movement as a founding member of the Waterford Sinn Féin branch in 1906 (along with her brother, Tom) and as a member of Cumann na mBan (the women's unit of the Irish Volunteers) and in her early political and historical writing. She also became a member of the Irish Women's Franchise League, having met one of its founders, Hannah Sheehy Skeffington, in 1913; according to one of Jacob's biographers, Damien Doyle, the two women became lifelong friends.[22] She went on to strike up a friendship with Madeleine ffrench-Mullen, and at her invitation began to write for *Bean na hEireann*, the newspaper of Inghinidhe na hEireann.[23] Ostensibly *The Troubled House*, which she began drafting in 1923, explores the apotheosis of Irish nationalist culture as Jacob experienced it in the previous decade; it centers on the experience of ordinary Dubliners caught up in the Anglo-Irish war, narrating a familiar Irish story of guerilla fighters on the run, an overbearing British army presence in the city, and the breakdown of everyday domestic life as the war rumbles on. However, by placing two visual artists, Nix and Josie, at the center of her novel, Jacob begins a conversation about "art for art's sake" and the place of the aesthetic in an independent Irish political landscape, while opening up a range of new sexual possibilities for its citizens. In this way, and by referencing the work of contemporary artists and art movements, Jacob's writing extended the avant garde experimentation of those literary aesthetes whose work influenced hers. I will argue that in so doing, Jacob represented in her fiction an intersectional counterculture plainly visible to her in the revolutionary 1920s, but one that scholars are only now beginning to perceive and recover.

Much of the action in Jacob's *The Troubled House* takes place in the home and studio of a new woman couple, Josephine Carroll and Narcissa Ogilvie (known to their friends as Josie and Nix), visual artists who live and work together in Dublin. Their friendship with the novel's narrator, Margaret Cullen (an older and more traditional figure) and her sons, one of whom is committed to the national struggle, creates a bridge between three important contemporary domains, the cultural avant garde, revolutionary politics, and the family home. The Cullen household is a synecdoche for the national family in early twentieth-century Ireland. James Cullen, the paterfamilias, represents the older generation; a lawyer and a constitutional nationalist or Home Ruler, he despises the "Fenians" and ejects his son, Liam, from the house when he discovers the latter has become involved in the military campaign.[24] At that, Liam loses his college place—his father having withdrawn payment of fees—and the boy joins the armed struggle. Meantime, Liam's older brother Theo is a pacifist, continually rowing with his brothers and mother about the futility of war, at one point remarking to his younger brother, Roddy: "I wish you were old enough to read Graham's book about the English conchies" [this reference is to a well-known book by John W. Graham, *War from a Quaker Point of View* (1915)].[25] In such passages, of course, Jacob deploys her own arguments in opposition to physical force; she came from a Quaker family in Waterford and was a self-described "pacifist Republican" who, according to her biographer Leann Lane, found it difficult to reconcile these oppositional values.[26] All the same, in a nod to her Irish Republican sympathies, the three Cullen boys in *The Troubled House* are named for Irish revolutionary heroes: Theo for Wolfe Tone, Liam for Liam Mellows,[27] a friend of Jacob's, and Roddy, the youngest son, is given Roger Casement's nickname.

Set during the Anglo-Irish war (referred to in Ireland as the Black and Tan War), *The Troubled House* shows the extent to which a normal everyday life in Dublin, even that of people not directly involved in the war, was impossible during that period; conventional, domestic scenes are continually interrupted by patrols, raids, the sound of gunfire, and random, often unprovoked, violence on the streets. "It's like having a gang of licensed burglars in the house, sometimes. Though burglars, after all, don't usually knock people around, or smash things out of pure spite . . . You've got to strip yourself of caring about *things* now, if you're not willing to lick the boots of the British."[28] Margaret Cullen is the "straight woman" of the text. On a visit from her son, Liam, by now on the run, she darns his clothing and criticizes his poor diet and housekeeping: "I reproached him with the state of his wardrobe, after all the pains I had taken, years ago, to teach him to sew and be independent of women."[29] On hearing an army raid come all too close to Liam's door, she promptly faints. That characterization gives Jacob plenty of scope for contrasting her life and ambition with that of the new woman who earns her living as a visual artist. Slightly appalled by her new friend's daring, Margaret asks "[do] you really sit on a campstool on the sidewalk, or have you access to the subconscious that forgets nothing? . . . And don't you ever get interfered with?"; to which Josie replies, "Yes, I get moved on by the police, and noticed by children; and once a man asked me what I meant by making maps of his house. I expect he still thinks he's marked for destruction."[30]

Despite these concerns about public opprobrium, Margaret is not a stock character; for one thing, she has independent means and determines to pay Liam's college fees herself in the face of her husband's obduracy. Moreover, that difference of opinion with her husband reflects their deeper political incompatibility; she has Republican sympathies. This, and the fact that the novel opens with her return to Ireland from a three-year stay with her sister in Australia, all suggest a somewhat more autonomous figure than the clichéd Irish mammy found elsewhere in Irish fiction. Her response to Nix Ogilvie's experiments in visual art is not to reject them outright, though she is honest in her response to that work, remarking on its aesthetic appeal:

> Quite a different style from Miss Carroll's; rough—nearly violent—with a queer notion of colour, and rather futurist sometimes, but the funny thing is they're never ugly; you feel that beauty is what interests her all the time. She seems to feel it some way that she can only express by that effect of violence—I can't explain.[31]

Moreover, Margaret's sneaking admiration for (and attraction to) the lifestyle of the two women artists "with their souls in their own work" is mentioned at several points in the novel, and underscored by this reflection on her way back from visiting them in their studios:

> It came into my mind, as I drew near the gate, what a queer thing it was that my life should spend itself thus, almost entirely in love and thought and anxiety over three men and a boy. Was I nothing

but a being relative to them, without real existence of my own? Each one of them led his own life, had his centre in his own soul, as a human creature should, but I had no purpose or driving force in myself; nothing that was independent of them. It seemed absurd, futile, unworthy . . . I could, at the most, influence them slightly by what I was, not by anything I tried to do . . . I thought all this intensely, but I knew that at present I could do nothing to free myself. My energy had all gone into one channel; I could not liberate enough of it to concentrate on any life of my own. But was it necessary for wives and mothers to be like that?[32]

All the same, when Nix turns her sexual attentions to Theo Cullen for a while, Margaret returns to type and becomes fiercely protective of her eldest son, seeing plainly that the formidable and sexually experienced older woman is merely toying with the "boy". She confides in Josie Carroll, who agrees with her that Theo needs saving from Nix, adding that the latter "can love a woman, but I doubt if she could ever love a man; she can't seem to get past the outside with them."[33] Discussing Jacob's own sheltered upbringing, Lane comments on her first interactions with Constance Markievicz and Helena Molony, which Jacob documents carefully in her diary. Jacob describes Molony thus: "She seems to regard men, as men, more as the relaxation of an idle hour than in any more serious light, does not appear to believe much in the love of a lifetime, but rather in one minor flame after another. She prefers women and Madame [Markievicz] prefers men."[34] The intersection of Jacob's experience and her literary fiction are fairly clear in this extract.

Following this exchange and earlier hints about the intimate lives of Josie and Nix, Jacob explores various ways in which the body may be performed and represented as a means to mobilize alternatives to the dominant culture, in terms of gender, sexual, and national dissidence. For instance, she subjects gender binaries to scrutiny, having Liam cross-dress on several occasions, ostensibly to evade capture and suspicion while on the run. The first time this theme crops up, his younger brother Roddy spots Liam on a tram, later describing the encounter to his mother: "At first I thought it must be a secret sister of ours that you'd been hiding somewhere. And when he saw me and started giving me the glad eye, I had to get up and go down inside the tram for fear I'd burst."[35] This kind of gender swap can be found in the new woman fiction of Egerton, Sarah Grand, and Katherine Cecil Thurston (as I explain in *The Irish New Woman*) but the open sexual ambiguity we find in this scene is not so common in their work. Many such episodes in *The Troubled House* are played for laughs and there is a definite appreciation of camp humor at work here. For instance, following Theo's escape from prison, he arrives at the Volunteer Army's safe house dressed in a Black and Tan uniform. In their relief at making this escape, the brothers indulge in some horseplay, with the cross-dressed Liam protesting, "Take your great coarse hands off me, you dastardly Black-and-Tan. How dare you assault a lady?"[36] In the midst of this pantomime, the boys are interrupted and called to order by their commanding officer, Kate Ryan. Ryan is described in gender-neutral terms as being "Very tall and slender, dressed in a shabby brown tweed costume and an old fold-up brown felt hat, she had a long, thin face, handsome and clearly cut, but cold in expression, with an obtrusively powerful chin."[37] Ryan reminds Margaret Cullen of Nix, we are told, a clear signal of her oddity in the text (moreover, she brings to mind real-life Cumann na mBan solider Margaret Skinnider).[38]

Within this specific context of subterfuge and disguise, such gender troubling goes unnoticed. However, the dominant culture reasserts itself in the form of Jim Carroll, who comes home early to find Liam secretly visiting Margaret. His response is damning, connecting Liam's gender dissidence with his political activities, "The sight of him giggling in those girl's clothes disgusts me. The fact is, I don't trust him, and neither would you if you could think calmly."[39] More to the point, Jacob demonstrates her awareness of the contingent nature of Liam's transgressiveness. At the end of the novel, when Nix and Liam discuss the disappearance of "his sister," Liam remarks, "after the things I told her about you she said she feared she was too old-fashioned to get on with you."[40] Here Jacob underlines the point that Nix is evidently the more radical of the two, when it comes to gender dissidence. Margaret Cullen makes this clear, too, in her description of Nix:

> For Nix, apart from her physical comeliness, seemed strangely lacking in the recognized attractions of womanhood to the male . . . Her most striking characteristic was ruthlessness, her only obvious virtues courage and honesty . . . Certainly she never flattered a man in any way, open or subtle. She took pleasure plainly enough in their society if they were attractive, but she often seemed to regard them as beings mentally inferior to herself. And she cared a hundred times more for her work than for any human relations.[41]

To return to Frazier's discussion of masculine performativity, his suggestion that the "multiple forms of sexual practice" in the period that render our "categorical identities inadequate" may just as well be applied to Nix's gender and sexual identity in this novel. Nix is clearly singled out as the "deviant" sign in *The Troubled House* but it is difficult to categorically confine her, or to apply identity tags from our own period to her. This is all the more obvious when one reads the novel in tandem with Jacob's unpublished novella "Nix and Theo," which details the sexual adventures of the two on a short holiday which they name a "honeymoon" in the Wicklow mountains. Nix is the dominant sexual partner throughout that episode, objectifying and feminizing Theo at various points, finally suggesting, "you're like a woman. That's why you'll never be a great painter." While a concentrated discussion of the novella is beyond the scope of this essay, it certainly bears further scrutiny in terms of Jacob's writing about sexuality. Ultimately, the function of Nix in *The Troubled House*, more than any specific identity or transgressiveness of her own, is the *potential* for fluidity, change, or difference she represents.

Jacob is very well aware of this potential, as is made clear in the wider resonance of Nix's art and lifestyle in *The Troubled House*. Margaret Cullen, left alone in the women's studio one afternoon, seizes the opportunity to riffle through their recent work. She dismisses Nix's experiments as "strange Cubist renderings of naked models—it was hard to tell if they were male or female—all oblongs and triangles. I saw in them nothing but meaningless ugliness."[42] This reference to Cubism and its reception in Dublin in the 1920s immediately introduces the work of a pioneering group of Irish artists including Mainie Jellett (1897–1944), Evie Hone (1894–1955), and Mary Swanzy (1882–1978). Having made specific reference to futurism and Cubism, given Jacob's enrollment in art classes at the Dublin Metropolitan School of Art in the 1920s, it is reasonable to assume that she attended their exhibitions and perhaps some of Jellett's public lectures in that period. When Mainie Jellett exhibited her first abstract Cubist paintings in her hometown in 1923, the Dublin art world responded in much the same way as Jacob's fictional protagonist, Margaret Cullen, does in the novel. Indeed, it is clear from the above passages that Jacob was familiar with the October 1923 *Irish Times* review of that exhibition, in which the reviewer states, "I fear that I did not in the least understand her two paintings. They are in squares, cubes, odd shapes, and clashing colours."[43] The critic goes on to say "[t]hey may, to the man who understands the most up-to-date modern art, mean something, but to me they presented an insoluble puzzle." As another well-known artist of the period, Paul Henry, observed in later life, "[i]t is difficult to realise how deep rooted was the ignorance and prejudice which existed at that time against any form of art which savoured, even remotely, of Modernism." [44] Where Jellett's work was concerned, the *Irish Times* continued to profess itself at a loss, categorizing her painting *Decoration* under the heading "Two Freak Pictures," which brings to mind fascist attacks on "degenerate" art in the following decade. Jacob gestures to this language when describing Nix's painting of Theo and Liam playing chess, which Margaret describes thus: "[t]he picture was in a half-finished state that added to its effect of freakish strangeness, and Nix's Cubist tendencies showed strongly."

Deriving from collage art of that period, Jellett's *Decoration* was inspired by the contemporary experiments of the teachers she had relocated to Paris to study with, André Lhote and Albert Gleizes, whose experiments revolutionized art in that period. To Irish audiences of the early 1920s, more accustomed at this high point of cultural nationalism to politically meaningful realist work, such abstractions may have seemed alienating and pointless. George Russell (A. E.), by then an enormously influential figure in art criticism and Irish cultural life, consistently dismissed Jellett's work, describing it as "sub-human" and as "aesthetic bacteria" in the pages of the *Irish Statesman*. This controversy has subsequently been characterized as a standoff between avant garde experimentalism and tradition, in which Russell occupies the latter position as the arch-conservative guarding the visual art establishment from the moderns. For instance, the curator of the 2018 EVA International (Ireland's biennial of contemporary art), Inti Guerrero, sums this up as such: "Russell—the establishment—rejecting a female artist through a very patronizing critique."[45] Such a construction of Russell's heated attacks on Jellett's avant garde work seems at odds with his social radicalism; biographer Nicholas Allen describes him as a man "fighting for a new Ireland of his own mind's eye."[46] Russell's virulent opposition to Jellett's work undermines his legacy as an enabling figure to younger male artists and writers during and after the Revival (which included praise for Jack B. Yeats's art), and his stand against censorship and the emerging conservative consensus of 1920s Ireland.[47] Perhaps, as Guerrero suggests, this signaled the likelihood that the Revival radicals had already become the establishment, protecting their insiders from a new generation, or from the merely "decorative" experiments of women artists.

Excavating Russell's staunch opposition to this abstract experimentalism, Riann Coulter suggests that Jellett's provenance may have provoked his ire more than anything else. Jellett came from a Dublin Protestant family with a Unionist tradition, and while her father was a solicitor rather than a member of the landed gentry (whose sudden death in 1936 left her in the role of family breadwinner), her privileged upbringing fostered an early commitment to her art practice, a luxury Russell could never himself afford despite his talent as a visual artist. Coulter suggests that Russell's "socialist concerns required that art be relevant beyond an artistic elite, his mysticism demanded that visions were translated for didactic purposes and his nationalism sought ways of connecting with Ireland, her people and her history."[48] As such, the issue here may not have been Jellett's break with tradition but rather, that in opting for abstraction, Russell heard a declaration of *non serviam* when it came to the public role of art in the new Irish state. Whatever the origins of his opposition, the effect was the same: radical women artists with the temerity to launch their modern work on an unsuspecting Irish public were not to be taken seriously. Indeed, Jacob's failure to make her mark with literary publishers in Ireland at the same time is consistent with this phenomenon.

While Russell's intemperate and persistent attacks were intended to ridicule Jellett's painting, his use of the term "aesthetic bacteria" may provide useful ways of thinking about her art and subsequent advocacy for it. Jellett was a serious student of her craft and of key avant garde interventions throughout her life, but perhaps more crucially, following in the footsteps of her tutor Gleizes, she believed firmly in the social mission of art.[49] As such, it was important for her to communicate that to her Irish audience. By 1923, unlike Swanzy, Roderic O'Connor, and many of her artist contemporaries, Jellett had returned home to live in Dublin where she planned to stay; at that point in her career she was influenced by and closely connected to key members of the Arts and Crafts movement in Ireland, including Susan and Elizabeth Yeats (who were among her early drawing tutors) and jewelry designer Mia Cranwill. Having made a crucial breakthrough on the international stage, her paintings exhibited in the important 1925 Paris exhibition *L'Art d'Aujourd'hui*, alongside that of Gleizes, Richard Delauney, and Fernand Léger, Jellett held her first solo exhibition at the Dublin Painters' Gallery in June of the same year.[50] In a landmark lecture to the Dublin Literary Society in 1926, she delivered a manifesto for Irish Cubism, positing modern art as a means to "make it new" and forge a specifically Irish tradition in the visual arts. Invoking the British art establishment, Jellett suggested that "when imitation is the chief aim of art the *creative power* dies."[51] Cubism, she argued, "far from renouncing nature, [could] give it new birth and new understanding."[52] As such, with ideas and influences from key art movements of the 1920s circulating like protective microscopic organisms through her paintings, public lectures, articles, and radio broadcasts, Jellett proposed the reinvigoration of Irish culture through Cubist experimentation.

By opening up a portal in her fiction to the contemporary visual art and educational program of Jellett and her peers, Jacob demonstrates a keen awareness of the potential offered by transnational modern art interventions, and perceived ways in which they might be mobilized in literary terms. Just as Jellett and her peers offer ways to deconstruct and reconfigure shape, form, and the power of the gaze, Jacob's fiction troubles received ideas about women's capacity, political ambition, and artistic production, particularly at this turbulent moment in Irish history. Clothing Nix in a Cubist garment is another way to make plain her identification with Jellett, Swanzy, and the French avant garde:

> I found Nix there, in a marvellous purple and yellow Cubist dressing-gown, laying the table. She looked very fascinating, with her shapely bare ankles, and the whiteness of her neck and breast gleaming against the strange purple garment, and the light shining from above on her cloud of bright brown hair.[53]

Transforming the artist into a Decadent installation, illuminated from above, produces her as spectacle, one that we are told "fascinates" the viewer. This moment in the novel is charged with literary aestheticism; that much-quoted line from *The Picture of Dorian Gray* comes to mind: "[o]ne should either be a work of art, or wear a work of art."[54] Moreover, by calling attention to the "strangeness" of this "shining" figure, Jacob invests her still life with an uncanny charge, again echoing Wilde's novel or perhaps the Gothic fiction of Jacob's comrade and housemate, Dorothy Macardle. The transformative power of art to liberate the individual thereby elevates Nix, transporting her out of the everyday realm into a supernatural or "freakish" zone, at least from the perspective of Margaret Cullen.

Margaret's inevitable response to this unsettling display of Cubist form, accompanied by shapely bare ankle and luminous breast, is to beat a hasty retreat. Earlier, in rejecting Nix's Cubist works, these "foreign" art forms, in favor of the more traditional and recognizably "Irish" work of Nix's housemate, Margaret turns to examine Josie's watercolors of the Dublin city streets. In doing so she comes upon a set of watercolor sketches of nude models by Josie:

> I went on placidly, comparing them in my mind with Miss Ogilvie's Cubist studies, much to the disadvantage of the latter, until—what was this? A study of Miss Ogilvie sitting in a rocking-chair without a shred of clothes on her. She was leaning back, with her hands clasped behind her head, watching the movements of a big black and white cat, that sat, licking himself, on the floor before her. How beautiful they both were! How the light slid along the woman's creamy skin and gleamed on the cat's silky fur! How like they were, in their strong, lithe gracefulness! I have said that Miss Ogilvie's face was not beautiful, but her naked form, portrayed here, gave me a shock of admiration as strong as I had felt at the sight of her diver [painting] . . . she sat there as if it were the most natural thing in the world to have no clothes on, and the grave inscrutable eyes and lips told that all her attention was centred on the cat at her feet . . . she was here looking at the cat's soul, or at least thinking of it. And feeling, I thought, sympathy with it.[55]

Margaret Cullen's attraction to Nix, an "admiration" similar to the one she had felt in response to the beautiful male body in the diving picture, provides the "shock" she experiences here. That shock deliberately provokes the reader to question the heteronormative assumptions we have made about Margaret Cullen. Moreover, given the preconceived ideas we tend to have about the repression of the body and the erotic in early-twentieth-century Irish culture, the effect of this expressive and lucid depiction of women's sexual intimacy and of same-sex attraction between women in 1920s Dublin is quite profound.

However, the radical sexual possibilities opened up at this transgressive moment are brought to sudden halt by a violent raid and subsequent murder. During their search for Liam, the Black and Tans systematically shred the women's paintings, and Nix's fury is unbounded. Her disavowal of the political turbulence raging all around the studio marks Nix out from every other character in the novel, all of whom—including Nix's partner, Josie—are deeply invested in the nationalist struggle. Without question, Nix is the most charismatic character in the novel, and the energy of her depiction clearly suggests an author deeply invested in this representation. For the highly politicized Jacob, whose first-hand experience of the War of Independence had nothing in common with that of Nix, this is an interesting disjunction. Jacob's best-selling biography of Matilda Tone, for instance, cuts a sharply different heroic figure but Nix sounds a dissonant note here; we might well ask why Jacob valorizes such an apolitical figure who is so clearly committed to her art above all else. Notwithstanding her proximity to leading figures in the contemporary Irish political establishment, as Doyle points out, by the early 1920s Jacob was beginning to distance herself from the political formations taking shape here. Quoting directly from her diary, he explains that by the time the first Irish Dáil met in 1919, Jacob had "lost a great deal of interest in it on account of there being no women in it and couldn't respect it very much either, for the same reason."[56]

Jacob's realization that the new state would never deliver on the radical political promise envisaged by her generation, particularly where women's roles and public representation were concerned, is reflected in her dismay at the Catholic conservatism of the new Irish Constitution. Suggesting that female aesthetes questioned the value and the limits of the expansion of women's roles at the turn of the twentieth century, Talia Schaffer argues that the key difference between female aesthetes and new women is that "where new woman novelists protested against existing laws, female aesthetes imagined an ideal woman."[57] While Jacob's activist life was evidently that of a

new woman, as part of a generation whose early lives had been suffused in and deeply marked by the national struggle, perhaps according to Schaffer's definition this novel marks a change of direction
for her; certainly, by the late 1920s she had begun to count the cost
of such intense political engagement. By allowing free rein to a protagonist in her post-war novel who is *permitted* to nurture her talent
and behave selfishly in the pursuit of her own art, Jacob is perhaps
projecting an idealized future for herself.

One aspect of this idealized future, perhaps, may be the capacity to create art that is transformative, transmuting the social and
political moment, providing catharsis. Margaret Cullen describes
the painting at the center of this novel, which Nix prizes as her best
work, as follows:

> Then she took away the beautiful diver and put before us another
> picture, taken, I saw, from a different pile. This showed a naked
> man, apparently dead; lying on bare ground. There was a long red
> wound in his side, and a dark stain on the earth under him. His
> face was contracted; his head twisted to one side, his attitude a
> strange mixture of stiffness and grace. A cold grey light showed up
> one side of his face and body. It was a horrible picture.[58]

While Margaret shies away from the naturalism of this painting
when she first sees it, it continually resurfaces in the novel, haunting
Margaret's dreams, and ruining Nix's relationship with her friends
when it is destroyed by the Black and Tans. In stark contrast to the
art we associate with the Irish revolutionary period, such as Seán
Keating's iconic "Men of the South" (1922) which idealizes physical
force nationalism, Nix's portrait is much closer to William Orpen's
"The Revolutionary" (c. 1902).[59] Orpen, who had been Keating's
tutor, represents the body of a young man, possibly a casualty of the
Cuban War of Independence 1895–98, just as Jacob describes it here.
It is an excruciation scene in the style of Mantegna's "Lamentation of
Christ" (c. 1480). By introducing an image like Orpen's evocation of
the dead soldier into her novel, Jacob gives the reader a representation

of the absolute cost of high political ideals and reinscribes the everyday violence committed by members of the revolutionary generation, the sacrifices they made during the armed struggle, as well as the sustained grief of everyone who lost family members during that period.

As such, Margaret Cullen, the spectator of this figure, is overwhelmed by what the painting represents, clearly anxious that this may yet be the fate of her own sons. She represents a generation of Irish mothers, partners, and sisters who watched their men go out to fight national and transnational wars in those years. Moreover, the novel's author had endured the relentless executions and deportations following the Easter Rising, and by 1923 she and her revolutionary comrades had survived two hard-fought and bloody wars at close quarters; Jacob's friend Liam Mellows was executed by Free State forces on December 8, 1922. This was a generation in mourning. *The Troubled House* brings the reader right into the middle of that experience, right down to the naming of the younger generation of Cullens in honor of men executed during different Irish wars. In her discussion of Althea Gyles's life and work, Kristin Mahoney describes the fin de siècle as a "moment when multiple utopian movements promised that a new era would come if enough individuals were simply willing to enter fully into the spirit of a cause and sacrifice themselves for the sake of a new age."[60] Jacob was not herself immune to this atmosphere, having sublimated her own career and a domestic future she ardently wished for in favor of a variety of political causes throughout the early twentieth century. Nonetheless, *The Troubled House* suggests an author who is wise to the damaging effects of the cult of self-sacrifice endemic to Irish nationalist culture in the period; for instance, Jacob's protagonist consistently worries about the immaturity of her younger sons, and the effect on them of early exposure to brutality and the compulsion to follow orders.

Taken as a whole, it becomes clear that this 1920s novel wrestles with the emotional aftereffects of revolutionary engagement at individual and community level. Moreover, Jacob quietly but consistently interrogates the propaganda deployed in favor of Irish nationalism, proposing pacifist readings and feminist standpoints as a means to unsettle elements of groupthink in the period. Nonetheless, just like the relationship between Mainie Jellett's painting *Decoration* and the Irish visual arts canon, *The Troubled House* is not entirely removed from the ideological underpinnings *or* the artistic strategies of the Revival moment. Despite the controversy it caused when first exhibited, Jellett's painting uses Cubist strategies to replicate well-known religious iconography, and her later works continually deployed images of the Madonna or refer to the west of Ireland, as in her painting *Achill Horses* (1939). This strategy placated the Irish artistic establishment such that by 1941 the *Irish Independent* could describe her as "one of our leading artists."[61] One might argue that Jellett's work makes a radical break with tradition only to be recuperated by an Irish national canon by this turn to familiar iconography. Similarly, as I've said, Nix's best-loved painting in *The Troubled House* may be read as an excruciation scene and, as such, it is not very far from the pietà imagery Susan Cannon Harris interrogates in her discussion of Revival drama:

> The sacrificial story that gets played out in nationalist Irish drama requires a male victim whose body can be more easily translated. It requires, also, a female counterpart—the mother/wife/lover who accepts the sacrifice and whose body can then fulfil the more "natural" role of transforming that death into a rebirth . . . [Such] representations of sex, gender, and sacrifice are the way they are because Catholic dogma and iconography have made Christ and the Virgin Mary the only culturally acceptable role models available to Irish men and women.[62]

With this in mind, Nix's role in relation to the body of the boy soldier, "a dark stain on the earth under him," as the Black and Tans put their knives to work in her studio, may be said to implicate her in the position of the Virgin Mary in this scene. Constructed in such a way, the novel's dénouement might lend itself to what Harris calls the "sacrificial spectacle" of Irish cultural nationalism.

However, such a tableau would first have to silence Nix, as she rages at the Black and Tans and then at Liam: "I wish to God they tore you into shreds before they touched my pictures—I wish you died of leprosy in the gutter before we let you in!"[63] This insistence on the importance of her practice and on the art objects she has created, above and beyond any claims made by the glorious nationalist cause (whether Irish or British), reject any adherence to communal or individual sacrifice in favor of the "greater good." This refusal to be conscripted to a social or political cause is, of course, synonymous with the core values of 1890s aestheticism. More crucially, to reinscribe Nix in the role of grieving Virgin Mother would be to radically misrepresent this protagonist's livid energy throughout the course of the novel, her social and sexual autonomy, as well as her childlessness and urgent refusal of a care-giving role in relation to Liam or his brother. Ultimately, to fix her in such a way is to ignore Jacob's enduring commitment to her own professional life as an active cultural producer, a commitment she clearly implicates Nix in too: "she cared a hundred times more for her work than for any human relations."[64]

As readers, we empathize with Nix when her canvas suffers the same fate as the violence wrought to the human body in her painting; in slow motion, as it were, we watch the repeated desecration of the boy's body as the painting is systematically shredded by the Black and Tans in an act of war. This empathy lends its own energy to the episode, connecting with Jacob's emotional investment in the importance of art, in its capacity to pass on to the coming generations the affective experience of those who died or were bereaved. Given the crucial role of the Revival in the years leading up to the war of independence, Jacob may be signaling the extent to which art had become symbolically nationalized in Ireland during that period; to acknowledge the importance of the arts in the Revival period was to truly know your country. However, as is evident from my discussion of Jellett's art vis-à-vis cultural nationalism above, a careful selectivity operated as to who (meaning: *which men*) might be permitted to represent the nation, or what form that might take, whether on canvas or on the page (meaning: *abstract art or fiction need not apply*). By repeatedly invoking avant-garde European experiments in the novel, Jacob signaled a clear intention to break out of the compressed poetics of the national into a wider sphere of art and human experience, and an understanding of the transformative power of art to effect this. By channeling cosmopolitan and aesthetic values, as represented by Jellett's work and by the 1890s aesthetic tradition that informs her writing, Jacob's novel seeks a breathing space, a counterculture, somewhere to explore alternatives to the mainstream; even, possibly, a way to protest or break out of the increasingly narrowing viewpoint of Irish nationalist hegemonies as the 1920s wore on.

However, despite the radical futures imagined at the end of *The Troubled House*, written at a time when Jacob and her contemporaries had won limited independence from Britain and began to call for redefinition of the Irish social contract, the two new states founded on the island of Ireland proved to be repressive and socially conservative. Over the course of the twentieth century, received ideas about the revolutionary period and the Revival were constrained and their radical proposals curtailed. Following two devastating civil wars on the island and the economic and cultural stagnation experienced in the newly liberated Irish Republic, the radical promise held out to *and by* Jacob's generation was lost. As a result, later Irish generations, including my own, inherited a confined and limiting national space, a narrow social and political world that defined itself by those it excluded, rather than by an expansive welcoming of difference and wider possibility. The writers discussed here, along with an entire revolutionary generation of feminist writers, literary aesthetes, and any number of radical activists, were rendered invisible by twentieth-century social and political hegemonies. At the end of the novel, when reflecting on his relationship with Nix, Theo tells his mother that none of his friends had liked her, "neither men nor women. They're all afraid of her . . . One man told me it was the sign of a lost soul to like her. He meant it too. Said she was an unsexed monster . . . They all say Nix is an unnatural woman. It's a poor compliment to nature if she is."[65] Our narrator, Margaret Cullen, is given the final lines of the novel, and her response is this: "She's a new sort of woman, that's all. There will probably be more like her, as time goes on."[66] Jacob was eventually proven right in this assertion, of course, but when writing these lines in the 1920s she cannot have realized that it would take another five decades or more for the necessary social and cultural movements to rise up again and agitate for the kind of change that would make this possible. Meantime, Jacob's radical new women protagonists and their "freak pictures" became submerged and disappeared from view, taking with them a significantly more complex and radical construction of the Revival and the Irish revolutionary period.

10

"All the Green World Is on Our Side"

Radical Suffragism and Ecofeminism
in the Writings of Eva Gore-Booth

Anne Fogarty

Eva Gore-Booth (1870–1926) was one of the outstanding Irish radical feminists of the twentieth century. She was distinctive in combining activism—as a suffragist, a pacifist, and a trade unionist—with the passionate pursuit of art. She has left behind a multi-faceted, but still little-known, legacy as poet, playwright, philosopher, and political thinker. Owing to her manifold allegiances and her variegated writing, the figure of Gore-Booth seems at once iconic, ungraspable, anomalous, and lost to historical contingency, and yet electrifyingly modern and of our moment. Born into a land-owning Ascendancy family, she moved from Ireland to Manchester to live and work with her life partner, Esther Roper, in 1897, severing her ties to the family estate in Lissadell, Co. Sligo. As a consequence, she is frequently seen as peripheral to the Irish Revival or treated as disengaged from its main concerns. Even though she traveled regularly between Ireland and England and was especially closely connected to her sister, Constance Markievicz, her geographical dislocation has impacted how she is apprehended and has led to a fragmented reception.[1]

The burden of this essay is that Gore-Booth created her work at once in the spirit of and at a critical distance from the Irish Revival as ordinarily conceived. The challenge she poses to its definitional boundaries unfolds on two chief planes: her insistence on the interconnectedness of the causes of feminism, nationalism, workers' rights, and suffragism, and her utopian representation of modes of human attachment and life forms as what Jane Bennett calls "vibrant materiality." The natural world that is the bedrock of her imagination is depicted as sharing and focalizing the energy suffusing all of organic existence both human and nonhuman. The radical impetus in her texts, as in the reformist politics in which she engaged, derived from an unwavering belief in the efficacy of group action and in the "agency of assemblages."[2] Additionally, writing the feminine, the achievement of independence for women, and the quest for spiritual enlightenment as well as material well-being were for her the essential objectives of the social and cultural revolution that she sought to effect in Britain and in Ireland.

Gore-Booth is an unsettling author because she decouples subjectivity from self-possession and urges nonproprietary ways of reflecting on principles of attachment and social bonds. Despite her involvement in numerous political organizations with decided and delimited agendas, a hallmark of her life and work was an ability to overhaul her beliefs and goals, to renegotiate ideas, and to test them out in a nondeterminative fashion. Her work is motivated by an imperative for change, an investment in the fluid, and the embrace of what Rosi Braidotti has termed the "nomadic," that is, the facility for inhabiting mobile and provisional states of Being and the relinquishment of any nostalgia for fixity.[3] As a convinced communitarian and adept rhetorician, she habitually strove to synthesize ideas and to counterbalance polar perspectives by taking on board and parrying with positions that were not her own. Reciprocity for her was an intellectual and affective mainstay that advanced rather than undermined the self and allowed a necessary immersion in the worldview of the Other. This ability to entertain countervailing views is especially evident in her personal and textual interrelationships with Constance Markievicz and Roger Casement, whose advocacy of physical force nationalism was seemingly diametrically opposed to her deep-seated belief in pacifism. Yet, it is in keeping with her political ethos to entertain and spar with points of view that diverged sharply from her own, while never ceding ground on fundamental values such as the maintenance of peace and the salving aspects of love in all its forms.

I will first briefly outline the chief facets of Gore-Booth's career as an activist, trade unionist, and feminist and then inspect some of the lynchpins of her thinking. I will then examine how her underappreciated plays—*The Buried Life of Deirdre* and *The Death of Fionavar*—and her collaborative reworking of her drama, *The Triumph of Maeve*, with her sister—illustrate and reflect upon the nature of her creative practices and the confluence among the different political causes that Gore-Booth pursued. Finally, the philosophical and ecofeminist underpinnings of Gore-Booth's poetry will be explored.

Gore-Booth's initiation into activism partly grew out of the reforming practices of her parents who were compassionate landlords, assisting their tenants during periods of famine and instituting rent reforms as advocated by the Land League. Gore-Booth's mother established a school of needlework to augment the income of the women on the family's estate at Lissadell, Co. Sligo. However, Gore-Booth's desire to alleviate poverty was also spurred by a deep-seated reaction against her privileged background and influenced by the numerous self-help initiatives that were launched in Ireland at the end of the nineteenth century aimed at boosting the drive toward political independence while improving living conditions and morale. She had close knowledge of the positive impact of the cooperative movement, as Josslyn, her brother, formed the Drumcliff Creamery Co-operative Agricultural and Dairy Society in 1895. And the *Irish Homestead*, the publication of the Irish Agricultural Organization Society, was one of the first venues in which she published her poetry.[4]

Above all, her revolutionary zeal was set aflame by her meeting with Esther Roper in the villa of the Scottish writer and minister, George MacDonald, in Bordighera, Italy, in 1896. As a result of this fateful, lifechanging encounter she set up a Sligo Branch of the Irish Women's Suffrage and Local Government Association in December 1896 with her siblings. As secretary, she spoke at its first meeting, eloquently pleading that women should be granted the vote to "have our interests protected and views represented" so that the state "may gain the services of a great many capable and intelligent citizens."[5] This conjoining of stances, combining the advocacy of women's difference and particular points of view with an argument insisting on their admission to the public sphere as equal agents and citizens, remains a characteristic hallmark of her flexible political thinking. In her hybrid philosophy, the quest for universal human rights is compatible with an espousal of feminist separatism.

Abandoning her rural, aristocratic background for industrialized Manchester in 1867, Gore-Booth pitched herself fully into public activism alongside Roper to achieve female enfranchisement and to improve working conditions for the industrial workers of the city. In contradistinction to the militant, middle-class suffragette movement spearheaded by Emmeline and Christabel Pankhurst, Jill Liddington and Jill Norris coined the term "radical suffragism" to describe the grass-roots, working-class initiatives in Manchester and neighboring cities that were driven by trade unionism and often aligned with Labour politics.[6] Largely dissociating themselves from party political ties, Roper and Gore-Booth played central roles in molding this radical suffragist activism with the particular purpose of politicizing and mobilizing the underpaid women working in the textile industry and of improving the conditions under which they worked. Gore-Booth orchestrated the foundation of dozens of unions for women workers and served as co-secretary of the Women's Trade Union Council before forming the umbrella organization, the Manchester and Salford Women's Trade and Labour Council, with Sarah Dickenson, in 1904.

Crucially, women's labor issues and the battle for female suffrage were for her intrinsically cross-connected and she was adamant that gaining the vote should not remain a middle class issue.[7] Critical of Emmeline Pankhurst's use of militant tactics and manipulation of the media, she broke with the Northern suffrage organization, setting up the national Industrial and Professional Women's Suffrage Society in 1905. The wide range of groups supported by Gore-Booth testifies to the latitude of her concerns and the extensiveness of the social reform at which she aimed politically, economically, and artistically. In 1899, she set up the Ancoats Elizabethan Society, an outreach educational group for women that concentrated on the study of drama, in an impoverished working-class district of Manchester. From 1907–8 she campaigned against protectionist measures aimed at barring women from working as barmaids and as gymnasts, circus workers, and music hall artists; she protested laws proposing to prevent florists' assistants working late at night; and in 1911 she agitated against measures designed to halt pit brow lasses from working in collieries, spending a week underground in order to prove that women could undertake strenuous labor such as tub-shoving.

With the advent of World War I, suffrage campaigns were largely suspended, and thereafter Gore-Booth, although continuing to fight for women's enfranchisement, devoted herself to the cause of pacifism and to battling against conscription, notwithstanding the hostility which such a stance provoked in a country engaged in war. She joined the League of Peace and Freedom in 1915; the transversal nature of her sympathies is evident in her support both of interned conscientious objectors whose trials she attended as a "watcher," or independent witness, and of imprisoned Germans who had been living in the United Kingdom. Thus gaining awareness of the adverse conditions in which inmates, including her sister Constance, were held in Irish and British prisons, she also fought for the improvement of the penal system and opposed the death penalty. In all of her involvements, she actively took part in street politics and was an indefatigable and persuasive speaker; she regularly addressed large suffragist gatherings, including the three thousand women demonstrating on behalf of the National Union of Women's Suffrage Societies, the so-called Mud March, in London on February 7, 1907, the largest protest of its kind in the period. In later life she spoke courageously about the religious aspects of nonresistance at a conference held at Caxton Hall, London in July 1915.

Uniting the causes that she supported was an unwavering belief in the emancipation of women and their right to recognition as citizens. Jane Rendall has contended that suffragism, far from being unitary, drew upon sundry discourses within liberal thinking.[8] Gore-Booth's political writings evince an even wider political ambit, as they sew together a complex patchwork of views; her arguments unite and interweave socialist, liberal, and radical feminist positions. Thus, while she deplores the "political subjection of women" in her 1904 essay "The Women's Suffrage Movement among Trade Unionists," she concedes that allowing women to work in jobs that exploit them is a necessity given "their terrible struggle with poverty."[9] In the same essay, her argument in support of enfranchisement hinges on the belief in the rights of the individual and on a philosophy of self-ownership; votes should be given, she contended, not to "houses and lodging" (that is, holders of property), but to "flesh and blood."[10] However, she also recognized that a socialist revolution was required to undo the corruption of the class system and "the incalculable harm" of the injustices done to women and that "political enfranchisement" was merely a step toward "industrial emancipation."[11]

Her political battles to improve the material conditions of women's lives, moreover, reinforced her conviction that feminist radicalism was a prerequisite for social change. In 1912, she joined the Aëthnic Union, a group founded by Thomas Baty that aimed at the abolition of all gender distinctions. Along with other members, she cofounded in 1916 an avant-garde journal, *Urania*, predicated on the principle, as announced in its first issue, that "sex was an accident and formed no essential part of an individual's nature."[12] The journal exposed how women were discriminated against on multiple fronts, but also daringly amassed articles from around the world on cross-dressers, transsexuals, and those who transgressed gender roles.[13] The title of the publication, as Tiernan has indicated, subtly but purposefully encoded its incendiary and progressive objectives.[14] The temple of Isis-Urania was the first federation of the Hermetic Order of the Golden Dawn, founded in 1888, a group devoted to the study of magic and esoteric philosophy.[15] Urania was the muse of astronomy and was also associated with universal love. Although inherently hierarchical, unlike the Free Masons and the Rosicrucians, the Order of the Golden Dawn allowed a female membership. Compounding the subversiveness of this publication, uranianism had the further meaning of same-sex love; a coinage from the mid-nineteenth century, it was popularized as a term by Edward Carpenter in *The Intermediate Sex*. Thus, while overtly questioning and upturning the false dichotomy between the sexes, *Urania* boldly opened up avenues for contemplating, unveiling, and celebrating queer love. Difference was at once questioned and tagged in radical new ways in the journal; a quest for equality went hand in hand with an affirmative and empowering queer vision of the world.

Given the habitual malleability and openness of Gore-Booth's evolving and fluctuating conceptualization of female identity and of political doctrines and modes of action, an affinity between her ideas and the deconstructive feminism of Catherine Malabou may be discerned. Malabou has contended that, to sidestep the "constant escape of deconstruction" which regularly downgrades and hypostatizes the feminine, feminist philosophy requires a notion of essence, but reconceived as transformability and plasticity.[16] She notes that plasticity, the ability of cells to modify and change, has latterly been identified as an intrinsic facet of biology and neuroscience. By analogy, she propounds a concept of ontic plasticity that acknowledges the existence and importance of difference while resisting the urge either to reify or to disincarnate it.[17] Femininity in the dramatic and lyrical worlds Gore-Booth invents is depicted in accord with what Malabou has styled "non-essential essentialism" and "ontological transformability."[18] Her texts persistently question the dominance of dualisms and expose their destructiveness, uncover the unsettling power of difference and its ability to undo fixity, and locate meaning in liminal spaces that yet hover between worlds and particularly trouble the divisions between the internal and the external.

"I have lived many lives": Feminist Ethics in *The Hidden Life of Deirdre* and *The Death of Fionovar*

Matthew Arnold pronounced that the "sensibility of the Celtic nature, its nervous exaltation, have something feminine in them," thus lauding but also stereotyping what he saw as the quintessential traits of Irish writing, at once vital but also dreamlike and effete.[19] Countering such views, W. B. Yeats proposed a more masculinist and robust interpretation of the important characteristics of Celtic folklore: it was "nearer to ancient chaos, every man's desire" than other forms of imagining.[20] The concerted attempt to locate and adapt the primal energies of Celtic mythology and to harness them for a nationalist reawakening was one of the central endeavors of the Irish Revival, but it was also a charged and contested activity. When George Russell praised Eva Gore-Booth for having slipped at last in her 1904 collection of poems, *The One and The Many*, into "the Celtic manner," declaring that such expression "ought to be natural" for her as a "West of Ireland woman," he unwittingly pinpointed several of the pitfalls of revivalism for the feminist artist and replicated Arnold's problematically gendered and racialized stance. In fact, many of the key women writers of the Revival were at pains to question the association of Celticism with conventional femininity and to produce probing representations of central mythological female figures, foremost amongst them Deirdre, Maeve, and Grainne.

The popular tableaux vivants staged from 1900 onward by the members of Inghinidhe na hEireann (the Daughters of Ireland), as Mary Trotter has outlined, created an innovative dramatic mode for re-envisaging symbolic depictions of mythic and historical figures, such as the Children of Lir, Brian Boru, and Maeve in their first performance in 1900.[21] The staging of George Russell's *Deirdre* and W. B. Yeats's *Cathleen Ni Houlihan* by actors from Inghinidhe na hEireann and other organizations under the direction of Frank J. and William Fay in April 1902 further testified to the resonance of these performances; they also provided the spark for the foundation of the Irish National Theatre Society in 1903. Yet, what ultimately became the Abbey Theatre in 1904, as Trotter and Cathy Leeney have contended, turned its back in large part on these feminist and alternative dramaturgical practices with their commingling of suffragist and nationalist radicalism and the populist tactics of street theater and spectacle that was among its early promptings.[22]

By contrast, Gore-Booth's drama feeds off the competing energies of revivalism, protest movements, and suffragism, weighing up and debating their often clashing objectives, focal points, and ethical priorities. Harnessing what Paige Reynolds has dubbed the "feminist theatricality" of Irish suffragist démarches, it also interrogates the themes of heroism, violence, female self-abnegation, and national identity represented in key works of the Literary Revival stage such as Yeats's *On Baile's Strand* (1904) and John Millington Synge's *The Playboy of the Western World* (1907).[23] Above all, from the vantage point of the suffragist ideal of female independence, Gore-Booth probed the protagonists of Irish mythological lore and entirely redisposed their stories. This revisionist intent is conspicuously to the fore in *Unseen Kings*, which was published in 1904 and first staged by Casimir Markievicz's Independent Theatre Company in the Abbey Theatre in January 1912. In a thoroughgoing dismantling of prominent redactions of the myth, it reorganized the story of Cuchulain to concentrate on the philosophical tussles of the female figures that surround him; Eineen the Sorrowful, his lover, Niamh, an eloquent prophetess, and the Stranger, the daughter of Cailtin whom he has slain. The warrior, as Cathy Leeney has observed, is transposed into a nonpatriarchal domain whose primary purpose is to explore "femininity in relation to itself."[24]

At the outset, Niamh tries to persuade Cuchulain to embrace peace and attend to "the deep silence of the inmost flame," but he is lured into a final battle with Queen Maeve which will end, as has been foretold, with his death.[25] The Stranger, seeking vengeance for the death of her father, assumes the guise of Niamh but reverses her soul-searching philosophy about the need to distinguish illusion from reality by appealing to his vanity and thus reawakening his thirst for combat. The death of Cuchulain, even though depicted as a cataclysm, is sidelined and elided; his beguilement by the Stranger is juxtaposed with and even superseded by her seduction of Niamh. The tragic demise of the epic hero is played down and precedence is given instead to debates between the women about truth, love, and desire, and the enunciation of Niamh's quest for some force that will "set the tranced spirit free."[26] The white fog that fills the stage space with "heavy fumes" at the end heralds the advent of the Stranger and the return of Niamh, and symbolizes the displacement of a war-torn world, scarred with the "graves of warriors," by a feminine domain whose wisdom and certainty have yet to be plumbed.[27] Yet, the play also blurs the polarities between inner and outer, peace and violence, truth and illusion, aggression and pacifism, female vision and male ideology. Even if Niamh survives in the aftermath of the death of Cuchulain, the way forward ultimately is unclear. The pressing need to decipher the demands of inner and hidden things is, however, underscored. Cuchulain has unquestioningly—and fatally—followed the unseen kings he saw as calling on him; Niamh by contrast urges paying more careful attention to the motions and claims of an interior feminine realm which yet is sited in the outer world.

The Hidden Life of Deirdre and *The Death of Fionovar*, plays that were never produced in Gore-Booth's lifetime, continue her reimagining of Irish myth, particularly her foregrounding of female agency. They radically replot the stories of Deirdre and Maeve, leading protagonists of the Ulster cycle, usually seen as tragically flawed heroines and problematic embodiments of female sovereignty, who set in motion unstoppable cycles of violence and revenge. *The Hidden Life of Deirdre* was published posthumously by Esther Roper in 1930, illustrated by an incomplete series of drawings on which Gore-Booth had been working prior to her death. She initially composed the play from 1908–12; she returned to it in the wake of the Easter Rising in 1916, when the philosophical issues it treated—pacifism, the recursive nature of violence, and polarized views of gender roles—acquired pressing resonance. *The Death of Fionovar* (1916) reframes the final acts of her drama *The Triumph of Maeve*, and was a cocreation with Constance Markievicz, who sketched a decorative border. It was designed to distract the latter from the rigors of months of incarceration in isolation in Kilmainham and Mountjoy prisons in Dublin and the possibility of execution for her involvement in the Easter Rising. It is, as a consequence, an urgently immediate but variegated reflection on the meaning of revolution, social change, and the ethics of armed engagement produced by these intimately connected sisters.

Anthony Roche has nicely observed that writing a version of the myth of Deirdre was something of a rite of passage for male playwrights in the Revival.[28] But each in different ways also struggled with this material. Eleanor Hull has noted how the "forceful, uncontrolled and barbaric" Deirdre in eleventh and twelfth century versions of the folktale was softened and gradually transformed into a "sobbing and fibbing" figure in seventeenth- and eighteenth-century redactions.[29] This troubling conception of a mythic figure who is at once fatally flawed, Other, and the quintessence of tragic femininity is at the core of the treatments of male writers. In George Russell's *Deirdre* performed in April 1902, the main protagonist declared herself "a priestess of tears" and sacrificed herself not just for the common good but offered herself as a Romantic template to an Ireland of the future where Naisi and she "will be a memory to sigh over."[30] Yeats's *Deirdre* hinges on the power struggle between an unyielding and merciless Conchubar and a defiant heroine who shockingly commits suicide in order to preserve her love for the murdered Naisi. But, as Ronald Schuchard has detailed, Yeats battled for several decades with the directors of successive productions of his play whom he felt miscast the chief role, failing as a result to capture its tragic sonority. John Millington Synge's *Deirdre of the Sorrows* remained unfinished at his death in 1909 and was completed posthumously by Yeats and Molly Allgood prior to being staged in the Abbey in 1910. Synge draws out the painful contradictions of Deirdre, who is at once capricious and vain, but dauntingly superhuman in her final acting out of her heroic role, announcing triumphantly that she "has put away sorrow like a shoe that is worn out and muddy."[31]

By contrast with all the existing translations and stage versions, Gore-Booth freely remolds the plot, entirely reconfiguring aspects of it. The Deirdre she envisages is analytical, free-spirited, independent, and resolute but, startlingly, she is also transgendered.[32] She confesses to Naisi that she "has lived many lives" and is a reincarnation of a former king who a thousand years ago killed the woman he loved for betraying him with another.[33] Deirdre's story hence over-arches the play temporally as she struggles to decide whether she has done enough to expiate her crime in the past; her internal struggle upstages and diminishes the importance of the conflict between Conor and Naisi for her love. In effect, her career preempts and enfolds elements of theirs. Even though in this rendering Deirdre carries a burden of immemorial guilt, she deviates from the template of the ill-fated victim enshrined in traditional versions of the myth. Rather, she is empowered, declaring to Conor, "I do not defy you. I am of those who do not defy, yet cannot obey," and placed centrally in the spotlight.[34] Furthermore, she stoutly resists the destiny of being "the bringer of sorrow and destruction to the land of Uladh" as predicted at the beginning of the play.[35]

But as well as inventing a heroine who overrides traditional gender divisions, Gore-Booth also accentuates the dualisms that divide her protagonists and cleave the world she depicts. She represents the clashes between Conor, Naisi, and Deirdre, not as constituents of a tragic love story or of a battle about male honor whose outcome is foreknown, but as a struggle between antithetical worldviews and belief systems: Conor and Naisi are devoted to Angus, "the possessive and exclusive passion of love, as the author explains in her "Introduction," while her heroine is a devotee of Mannanan who represents "the freedom and universality of loving."[36] In sum, she politicizes the well-known love story, transforming it into a drama about pacifism and the tension between the pursuit of female self-determination, and the dissolution of gendered polarities. Love and freedom are inextricably bound up with each other for Deirdre. She affirms that "[t]there is none that can conquer love. It is free to come and go, like the four winds of heaven."[37] Ultimately, the love that she describes has less to do with her subjective feelings for Naisi than with her conception of the self as a semiautonomous part of suprapersonal historical processes and her conviction that self-perpetuating cycles of violence can be halted. Conspicuously, this vision of love is emancipatory, open-ended, and ethically engaged; it is, moreover, couched in terms of elemental and cosmic images which were for Gore-Booth ciphers of the feminine.

Gore-Booth shifts the customary focus of this myth from the fate of the doomed lovers to the philosophical problems denominated and reflected on by Deirdre which she teases out with her interlocutors. Deirdre is not only proactive in this play, but also compellingly ratiocinative. The play pits her disputes with Conor and Naisi against her altercations with Lavarcam, a druidess, who is also her foster-mother. The exchanges between the two women consistently undercut the premises of the male-centered focus on conflict and ownership. Further, despite the seeming undeniability of the superordinate workings of fate underwriting male violence and possessiveness, the action of the play is ultimately driven by Deirdre and analyzed in terms determined by her. As Cathy Leeney astutely observes, she, in effect, acts as the work's dramaturge, inspecting, marshaling, and changing its motivating forces.[38] After she reveals her murderous crime as an "old, jealous king" in the past to Lavarcam, her foster-mother, the latter concludes that everything is dictated by the anger of the gods. Deirdre, despite having enunciated the gloomy view that there "is no one young and innocent anymore,"[39] flatly rejects such determinism and counters that it is the evil that people have wrought themselves that works itself out over time. Reincarnation for her betokens the possibility of renewal but also implicates her in the guilt of the past. She is impelled not by private grief as in customary accounts of her story but by a metaphysical sorrow triggered by the recognition that there "is no present . . . The past evermore becomes the future."[40] Naisi accuses her of being lost in hazy dreams, but she pointedly uncovers the precise nature of her musings, namely that she may be able to blot the past out by breaking with "the web of desire."[41]

Aesthetically, Gore-Booth's play eschews naturalist conventions, drawing instead on symbolist devices prevalent in the work of European writers such as Maurice Maeterlinck. This is especially evident in the scenography and the symbolic import of space in the text.

The three acts of the play take place outside Lavarcam's hut, in a refuge in Alban (Scotland) where Naisi and Deirdre have fled, and in a room at Emain, the palace of Conor. The human abodes are inset in natural scenes that harbor inscrutable forces which are sometimes inimical but often liberatory. Movements outdoors and underground especially concretize Deirdre's desire to rescript the world she lives in, redesign gendered identity, cut across male cycles of violence, and reorient the action. In act 1, although Naisi proposes escape to Scotland, it is Deirdre who leads the way to "a passage under the ground" which, despite being "very low and dark and long," will lead them to freedom and "the open country."[42] In act 3, she proposes they use the same dark passage to escape Conor. Reminiscent of Julia Kristeva's notion of the chora which is associated with the maternal body, an organic bedrock, and the "non-expressive totality" that precedes the acquisition of language in infancy, this dark, subterranean passageway in Gore-Booth's play serves as a ritualistic ingress to the domain of the Other; it leads suggestively to an occulted feminine sphere, which is never fully identified, yet wholly subtends the play.[43] It is into this space that Deirdre escapes at the end; she steps out into the darkness and is killed in lieu of Naisi. Unlike in other versions of this story, her death precedes his, thereby overshadowing it. Drawing on the alternative vision of a "soul [that] knows the truth," she dies to shield him and in this final heroism completely sidesteps the tragic arc that was portended for her.[44]

Moreover, her final gesture confounds gendered norms, commingling male bravado with female defiance. Indeed, Gore-Booth's repurposing of the Deirdre myth noticeably reorients the roles of all of the main protagonists; as well as being lovers and antagonists, they are all resituated in an entangled web of family connections and friendly alliances. Conor is viewed by Deirdre as a father and former protector, Naisi refers to his lover in transgendered terms as a "true guide, brave comrade and wise counsellor," while, above all, Lavarcam, the heroine's foster-mother, is depicted as an intimate confederate in the espousal of the universal love represented by Mannanan.[45] Even though Conor and Lavarcam make uneasy peace in the final moments, thereby endorsing the pacifist philosophy that Deirdre advanced, the overriding emotion at the close of the play is Lavarcam's grief for "her beloved, the white flower of the world."[46] Conspicuously, the ambiguously queer emotion of maternal and amatory mourning replaces the feminine sorrows traditionally associated with Deirdre. The play resoundingly redefines heroism as female and shows pacifism to be an irreducible aspect of the ethos of Deirdre, bearing out Leeney's claim that this play is "the most explicitly feminist vision in Irish theatre in the twentieth century."[47]

Grief for the death of a daughter, and disordered human connections that refuse neatly oppositional alignments, also give peculiar definition to the action of *The Death of Fionovar*. Contemporary reviews made much of the irony that Markievicz lent her name to a text preoccupied with pacifism.[48] In so doing, they failed to note its transactional nature, the points of intersection between the sisters' thought processes, the irresolution of the ending, and the plurality of frameworks in which it is embedded. In her introduction, Gore-Booth defends her right to interpret the myth of Maeve as she sees fit and in particular to reimagine her as an emblem of pacifism. However, the play represents the utopian ideal of peace itself as radically unsettling and leading to "terror and antipathy."[49] Revolutionary violence and pacifism are shown to share utopian impulses, while the abandonment of force foments social dissension rather than accord. The poems prefacing the play further indicate the torn nature of the sympathies informing it. An elegy, "To the Memory of the Dead," although it honors the executed 1916 leaders and her imprisoned sister, grants special mention to the pacifist Francis Sheehy-Skeffington murdered during the Rising, and contrarily wishes that the revolutionaries had "dreamed the gentler dream of Maeve."[50] However, a four-stanza poem about Maeve, "The Triumph of Maeve," depicts her warrior zeal and spirituality as irreducibly cross-connected, positing her simultaneously as a supernatural being, a role model for feminist action, and a generative feminine vitality inherent in the Sligo landscape:

I have seen Maeve of the Battles wandering over the hill,
And I know that the deed that is in my heart is her deed;
And my soul is blown about by the wild wind of her will,
For always the living must follow whither the dead would lead—
I have seen Maeve of the Battles wandering over the hill.[51]

Provocatively, Gore-Booth entirely transforms prevalent apprehensions of Maeve as warmongering and willful by tracking her retreat from warfare, her abdication, and her decision to pursue peace and freedom. It is notable too that her pursuit of conflict in the play is a result of female solidarity; she does battle in order to avenge the death of Deirdre, not because of rivalry with her husband Ailell over who possesses the most. The event that triggers Maeve's change of heart is the death of her daughter, Fionavar, who dies from pity when she visits the battlefield to gain acquaintance with her mother's work and is appalled by the carnage she sees there. This puzzlingly opaque allegory highlights the horror of war but also underlines the harrowing process of ushering in a new idealistic regime.[52] A grief-stricken Maeve, despite being victorious, has to deal with fractious subjects at the end of the play who bring their quarrels to her for adjudication, including a warrior who seeks recompense for the wife who has left him and an old man who desires vengeance for the death of his son. The songs of the bard Nera about the secret wisdom of Tirnanogue, the Celtic other world, beguile the queen but sow dissension among her subjects who ultimately kill the poet as they are not ready to countenance difference.

At the end of the play, leaving her society in "confusion and wild disorder," Maeve abandons her throne and heads for a place of "deep shadows" where she will find the way to her "own soul."[53] The journey outward into a pristine Irish landscape coincides with an inward turn and presages the recuperation of the feminine: "Since the world began / My soul was bound with many a secret bond / Unto the intimate will of the brown soil."[54] Moreover, the private and the communal are held to be in alignment. The other space to which

Maeve gravitates, "the hazel boughs / In Tirnanogue," is depicted as sublime, but also as having material consequence and reparative potential.[55] It is, in effect, a feminine counter-public sphere, a zone from which social transformation may emerge; it is counterpoised to the violent, murderous world that she leaves behind. Yet, no resolution is proffered. Thus, while the play indicates that renewal may be brought about by Maeve's abandonment of violence and militarism, it does not reach for closure or suggest that social divisions have been healed. The difficulty of insinuating utopian thinking into the polity over which Maeve ruled is challengingly held up as an intractable problem at the end. The quest for peace ironically has bred division.

Markievicz's decorative borders and images in part draw out the utopian dimensions of the plot through featuring pastoral and esoteric images such as entwined rose stems, a light-filled chalice, caterpillars and pupae, and a sun rising over a hill toward which a river directs its course. But in consonance with her sister's text, they also underline conflict and struggle: in particular, a depiction of wind-tossed birds flying over a tempestuous seascape recurrently punctuates the text. Markievicz's borders further allow space for dissonance since the repeated motifs of renewal and rebirth, while complementing Gore-Booth's pacifism, also hint at a counternarrative of the Rising, as Lauren Arrington has contended, as "transformative defeat."[56]

Malabou has argued that essence needs to be redefined as "change and metamorphosis."[57] Such an altered conception underlies *The Death of Fionovar*; the text ultimately overspills its boundaries and balks at any fixity, moving as it does between critique, forceful action, and idealism. The final leaves of the volume include a lyric, "Eineen's Song of Illusion," which returns to the mourning for the dead expressed in the preface.[58] A parting axiom adorning the last page on which an image of Pegasus is poised above a crescent moon declares that "The winged horse shall be harnessed to many ploughs and the aether vibrates to the rhythm of unseen light."[59] In this final iteration, a feminist philosophy of transformability has animated the text, draws together earth and air, and cross-configures the labor of practical politics and populist agitation (the "many ploughs") with the utopianism propelling, in divergent manners, both suffragism and revolutionary nationalism.

Poetry and the Political Ecology of the Feminine

In her unfinished autobiography, "The Inner Life of a Child," Gore-Booth describes how she communicated telepathically with an "old nurse" as a child, a facility she later drew on to converse mentally with Constance when she was in prison, thus underscoring the centrality of esoteric thinking in her worldview.[60] The child, Gore-Booth claimed, is close to the "ante-natal mystery" and can readily leap between the abstract and the physical.[61] Poetry for her is also capable of tapping into this inner power that breaches thresholds and brings matter and spirit together. The eight volumes of poetry that Gore-Booth published over the course of her lifetime gave ongoing expression to, but also fully dissected, this visionary function.[62] As her autobiography indicated, the boundary-crossing capacity of poetry is consequent on its ability to knit together "the flying dreams that whirl us through the inner spheres" and the affective impact of natural scenes apprehended in childhood: "there are sunsets one will never forget, blue skies that never fade, Atlantic breakers that are immortal in their opal arches of green water, flashing with unknown light."[63]

Searchingly represented symbolic landscapes peopled with preponderantly feminine allegorical figures, alive with vital energies, and rooted in the myth-endowed scenery surrounding her childhood home in Sligo are the mainstay of Gore-Booth's verse.[64] Borrowing a term from Seamus Heaney, Matthew Campbell has argued that late nineteenth-century Irish poetry is defined by being "through-other," due to its in-between state poised between British and Irish traditions, the sonic musicality of Gaelic poetry and the formal lineation and meters of Victorian verse.[65] The final section of this essay will argue that this condition of the through-other typifies the lyrics of Eva Gore-Booth which highlight mystic quests, states of process and metamorphic change, cross over and dissolve gender identities, and range across political differences. Her poetry, moreover, is hybrid in that it conjoins symbolist verse, aestheticism, Celtic Twilight lyricism, religious meditations, and esoteric and feminist imaginings. In constantly revisiting and sifting through pivotal images of twilight, wind, waves, the coastal and the estuarial, the sacred and the hidden, it repeatedly indexes and recalibrates metaphors that are crucial counters in her personal philosophy of an empowered and insurrectionary femininity. Additionally, the symbolic landscapes that she depicts combine the human and the nonhuman and rethink agency "across an ontologically heterogeneous field" in the mode advocated by Jane Bennett.[66] Nonessentialist views of femininity, nonbinary accounts of gender, and partisan invocations of queer love jostle against each other in her poems as they track the pathways between the material and the sublime, the flesh and the spirit.

In a pioneering essay, Emma Donoghue cogently observed that Gore-Booth lesbianizes and feminizes the forms and myths that she inherits.[67] Her poems abound in female presences and mythic figures, who are addressed as muses, counter-selves, and founts of power and vitality, and are regularly conceived of in unorthodox ways that confound determinate identities, sexualities, and plotlines. An early poem, "A Love Song," evokes a mutating beloved, "my lady of the Spring" and "my lady of the Hills" who is at once an organic, nonhuman, primal life force, a mystical energy, and the poet's alter ego:

> All the strength, and the hope, and the
>   gladness of living are hers,
> And her voice is the voice of the wind
>   In a forest of firs.[68]

The Other is often plural, unfixed, and gender-indeterminate in Gore-Booth's imaginings, even if also invariably linked with the feminine. Thus, in "A Song," the lyric I sides with the mischievousness and humility of a rippling river, variously seen as male and neutral, who is taunted by "clear-voiced Pleaids" and "white-armed Naiads."[69] The fluvial waters mingling with the "ocean of yesterday" is posited at the end of the text as a more enticing and satisfying image of completion than the sky inhabited by "love-sick maids."[70] Instead of couples, love-triads frequently form the basis of Gore-Booth's poems. In "The Vision of Niamh," the love between Niamh and Maeve is celebrated by the interposing voice of the speaker who describes how the latter "dwelt among the hazel trees alone / So that she might look into Niamh's eyes."[71] Yet in mediating their erotic passion she also casts aside its polarities and carries forward its revolutionary nature into the present:

> Ah, Niamh, still the starry lamp burns bright,
> I can see through the darkness of the grave,
> How long ago thy soul of starry light
> Was very dear to the brave soul of Maeve.[72]

A similar startling change of perspective occurs in "The Inner Egeria," which describes the love of the "Wise Nymph" Egeria for the Roman ruler Numa in its initial stanzas, but turns from the bounded nature of heterosexual love to the transhistorical, roving intensity of same-sex love:

> Though Rome be far as Nineveh
> From the dark road my feet must tread,
> Yet, do I meet her every day—
> Salt on my cheek her tears are shed.
>
> Nymph of the stream of life, she hides
> In that small sacred wood apart,
> Where the enchanted king abides,
> And the first flowers bloom in my heart.[73]

Lines of division between self and Other, past and present, and forms of sexual identity are blurred here; the vitality of this transgressive love appears, moreover, to derive as much from its irregular, triadic nature as from its queer intensity. Notably too, the continuing power and wisdom of the nymph are equated with organic growth and the irrepressibility of a female life force that inter-animates and cross-connects everything.

Likewise, an insurrectionary feminism that is ecologically rooted is emphatically proclaimed in the manifesto-like "Women's Rights" which not only transposes suffragism to the Sligo countryside but sees it as intrinsic to it:

> Down by Glencar Waterfall
> There's no winter left at all.
>
> Every little flower that blows
> Cold and darkness overthrows[74]

Winter, it emerges, reigns "where men in office sit."[75] The poem ends with a rallying cry that is not only predicated on female solidarity but also on mobilizing the boundary-breaching power of nature and parsing greenness not in the light of Irish nationalism but of an organic, reformist energy that unites rather than divides:

> Oh, whatever men may say
> Ours is the wide and open way.
>
> Oh, whatever men may dream
> We have the blue air and the stream.
>
> Men have got their towers and walls,
> We have cliffs and waterfalls.
>
> Oh, whatever men may do
> Ours is the gold air and the blue.
>
> Men have got their pomp and pride—
> All the green world is on our side.

Political and gendered partisanship are here rejected in favor of a vitalism that cuts across division and interlinks the human and the nonhuman. "The Thriftless Dreamer" similarly posits Psyche, "waited on by Powers Invisible," as an embodiment of an irresistible insurrectionary feminism embedded in the Irish landscape, "radiant in meadows green."[76] The more Psyche is vilified and ostracized, the greater her ambit grows; difference becomes an unassailable energy that draws spirit and matter together and nullifies the false distinctions of those ruling the world and dictating what is of value:

> For round her, driven from this dark world, wait
>   Mysterious powers and unseen ministers,
> And all the vailèd Angels at the Gate
>   Guard with their swords this thriftless dream of hers.[77]

Gore-Booth's best-known lyric, "The Little Waves of Breffny," also depends on breaking down divisions between a blusteringly sublime, masculinist landscape and a hidden, local, feminine one which refutes, revises, and enfolds it:

> A great storm from the ocean goes shouting o'er the hill,
> And there is glory in it and terror on the wind,
> But the haunted air of twilight is very strange and still,
> And the little winds of twilight are dearer to my mind.
>
> The great waves of the Atlantic sweep storming on their way,
> Shining green and silver with the hidden herring shoal,
> But the Little Waves of Breffny have drenched my heart in spray,
> And the Little Waves of Breffny go stumbling through my soul.[78]

The effect of the enlivening landscape of Breffny is to break down the opposition between masculinist violence and feminine affect, land-bound security and sea-adventures. As well as dismantling gender differences, the vitalizing force of this landscape also cuts across the outer and the inner, the human and the nonhuman. It is more tentative and inchoate, but promises to leave a more lasting legacy than the obliterating "great waves" that form the counterview of the maritime.

Fencing with political differences while reaching for the vibrancy of mutual vision also underlies Gore-Booth's poetry about Roger Casement. She attended his trial in May 1916; though she did not know him personally, the epigraph to her volume, *Broken Glory*, published in 1917, prominently commemorated the date of his execution: "In Memory of August 3rd, 1916."[79] In so doing, she conspicuously aligns Casement with her feminist poetics and philosophy; in a slight variant of the phrase "the voice of the wind," she had similarly construed the ecological power of nature and queer passion in "A Love Poem." A poem on the revolutionary and diplomat who was hung for treason, "Roger Casement" variously thinks of him as dead, living, and on the point of death and conceives of him as someone with the magnetic force of a border-crosser:

> I dream of the peace in his soul,
> And the early morning hush on the grave of a hero
> In the desolate prison yard.
>
> I dream of the death that he died,
> For the sake of God and Kathleen ni Houlighaun,
> Yea, for love and the Voice on the Wind.
>
> I dream of one who is dead.
> Above dreams that float and fall in the water
> A new star shines in my mind.[80]

The poem noticeably shifts between inner and outer views of Casement; he is at once a dying man, a dead body, and a hero, but is most lastingly incarnated as part of the constellation of energies that propel her philosophy. Not least of the differences absorbed and reflected on in the poem is Casement's belief in militarism and armed force. Indeed, some of the terminology employed, such as the reference to Kathleen ni Houlighaun, belongs more to the subject of the poem than to the author. The ecofeminist poetics of the text, however, are capable of allowing for and debating a stance at variance to the writer's own and yet finding common ground in overarching ideals, the generosity of queer love, and a shared radicalism. The many sides of Casement as a figure are acknowledged, but he is ultimately co-opted for and seen as allied to the doctrine of ontic transformability underlying Gore-Booth's vision as a whole.

Eva Gore-Booth centrally connects with and complicates many of the guiding tenets of the Irish Revival and Irish revolutionary nationalism. She has been unjustly sidelined and overlooked not only because all of her life as activist and social reformer took place in the United Kingdom and not in Ireland, but also because of the daunting unwieldiness and expansiveness of her achievements. Remarkably, she turned her back on her class heritage to campaign for working-class women in Manchester, yet her writing took inspiration from the Celtic mythologies disinterred and rethought by the authors of the Irish Literary Revival and the mystical poetics of the Celticism practiced by late nineteenth-century Irish writers, among them W. B. Yeats. She, in fact, remained true to the challenges of these preoc-cupations when others had abandoned them, but retooled them in order to inform her searching body of work. Having embraced suf-fragism and socialism as a young woman, she passionately believed in freedom and pacifism, but was an advocate above all for a radical feminist philosophy and a defiantly queer ethos which she developed with élan and exacting involvement over the course of her career. Greenness for her involved not simply the belief in national sover-eignty, but also a deep-seated engagement with the arcane but pri-mordial forces that link women with the natural world.

Even more than the other feminist revolutionaries involved in the Revival, such as Maud Gonne and Hannah Sheehy-Skeffington, she refused to decouple feminism from socialism and nationalism. Her queer politics is so far ahead of its time that we can only now begin to appreciate its radical cast. An exhibition by ninety-three women artists responding to Gore-Booth's life and work, displayed in the Hamilton Gallery, Sligo, and the Museum of Literature Ireland, in Dublin, 2019–20, bears out the compelling resonances between her thinking and artistry and those of contemporary practitioners.[81] Her readiness to advocate the feminine while arguing for a nonessential difference has points of contact with activist movements in the present and with the deconstructive feminism put forward by Catherine Malabou. Ontic plasticity and transformability are abiding aspects of Gore-Booth's aesthetic. The final stanza of "The Hidden Beauty," a poem which Esther Roper saw as her signature work, is bound together with the recurrent line, "I have found the Hidden Beauty where the river finds the sea," which summarizes her evolving quest as a feminist and the openness of her vision of the world and engagement with her friends and associates.[82] Estuaries are transition zones between river and maritime environments; they are also spaces in which differing ecologies meet and interact. Gore-Booth's metaphor of the estuarial aptly crystalizes the multi-facetedness, intellectual dexterity, and capillary mobility of her radical suffragist, ecofeminist philosophy, and aesthetic.

Part Six

The Biopolitics of the Revival

Toward the Easter Rising

11

Nursing the Revival

Patrick Pearse, Breastfeeding, and Sacrifice

A b b y   B e n d e r

Patrick Pearse's rhetorical and embodied articulation of blood sacrifice is perhaps his most resonant contribution to Irish revolutionary and revivalist discourse. Yet Pearse frequently invoked another bodily fluid that he saw as similarly regenerative of the community: a fluid with the same occult nourishment, passing down through Irish generations, imbuing them, mnemonically, with the same imagined identity as that conferred by their Irish blood. This chapter examines the circulation of that substance—breastmilk—and the ubiquitous image of the nursing mother as she (or at times, indeed, he) appears in Pearse's political writings, poems, stories, and plays. Pearse enlists breastfeeding as a revivalist trope that flows generationally and laterally across the community in both literal fostering traditions and metaphors of nurture, akin to the blood metaphors of being "racy of the soil."

But the breastfeeding mother in Ireland was not, as a preliminary reading of Pearse might suggest, a figure associated only with nurture, nature, and the domestic interior or cozy homestead. While Rousseauian discourse asserted a national ideal of maternity in which a nursing mother feeds her children and the nation as an unambiguous sign of generation and futurity, the Irish breastfeeding mother was (and is still) fraught by the history of colonial power, famine, and the role of the Church. This mother gives not just the good breast but the bad: her breast is not only withheld but shriveled and empty; she threatens contagion and infection; she herself is also vampirized and incontinent. The association of breastfeeding with death and danger was reinforced by Irish folklore; again and again, we find the breast-feeding mother at risk of being abducted by ungentle fairies to suckle their own fairy children.[1] And as Joyce wrote, Mother Ireland was the sow who eats her farrow; this image of the cannibalistic nursing mother—mother as site of death, rather than life—is implicit in Pearse's texts as well.

Nearly a decade after the blood sacrifice of the Rising, Seán Keating's 1925 painting "An Allegory" presented the ironies of the post-revolutionary scene, including the particular irony of the breast-feeding mother. The painting's title announces its symbolic significa-tion, and most criticism has presented the scene as self-evident: the failure of post-revolutionary Ireland, the inanity of Ireland's Civil War. The men in the painting dig the grave of the nation, or they connive and judge at the margins. The painter himself appears seated on the ground, gazing out with menacing disgust, admonishing us for our failure to read the scene, and perhaps, particularly, the nurs-ing mother. Indeed, no element of the allegory has seemed more obvi-ous than the mother nursing her infant: as Síghle Bhreathnach-Lynch has suggested, "viewers . . . would assume that the mother and child represent the suffering innocents in all wars and conflicts," or "be thought emblematic of Mother Ireland."[2] But Keating does not imply that the mother is a center that holds amid the fatal violence that surrounds her; rather, she is off-center, and she is not rooted to the knotty tree against which she leans, but is seemingly transient; her posture recalls the figure of the evicted peasant; for when would such a mother nurse her child outside the cozy homestead?[3] The baby is draped in white, indicating a hope for the yet-to-be-written future in a scene where all else shows a ruinous past; but the draped cloth, shroud-like, visually echoes the other draped object in the painting: the coffin. Keating means to show the nursing mother allied to cul-tural and political distress rather than natural order; it is a slant light cast on the Pearsian version.

Pearse and Keating offer some of the few visible nursing mothers of the Revival's literary/artistic production: beyond a handful of mentions in Synge, Gregory, and Joyce, these mothers' labor is hidden away. It is not surprising, therefore, that Pearse's literal and metaphoric nursing mothers have been doubly invisible: hidden both by the anxiety around (and virtual absence of) nursing mothers in other revivalist texts, but also by the scholarly focus on Pearse's much-analyzed fetish of the male, not female, body. Moreover, the iconic, much-reported image of the dead or dying famine mother's empty breast haunts the very practice of breastfeeding in Ireland (with its unaccountably low rates throughout the twentieth century and into the twenty-first), and this image also haunts and informs the ironic contradictions of Pearse's own symbolic system of sacrificial nationalism. As we will see, Pearse proposes nursing as an act of sacrifice: a trinity of figures—the Irish rebel martyr, Christ, and the nursing mother—all converge in their sacrifice to and sustenance of the nation, even as the giving of precious fluid now signifies not only the beginning, but the end of life.

As with Pearse's elevation of the bleeding male body as a figure of revolutionary sacrifice and revival, the nursing mother also exposes, and indeed clarifies, the central tension around the sacrificial narrative: that is, its ironic anti-natalism, its anti-futurity, its biological, generational nihilism. For the blood sacrifice of revolution that gives life to the nation also brings death to its future, and particularly to the young on the verge of their biologically procreative powers, most iconically in Yeats and Gregory's *Cathleen Ni Houlihan* and Pearse's own *The Singer*.[4] Pearse's revival of breastfeeding as metaphor of both the fostering (nurture of children) on one hand, and sacrificial revolution (the sacrifice of children) on the other, reflects the essential paradox of his narrative of blood sacrifice, its ironic contradictions. Observing the many instances of nursing in Pearse's works also opens up more fluid ways to think about the gendering of his revolutionary discourse, which has seemed focused on the young male body, but is perhaps equally centered on the mother's, and the (liminal) space between them.

In Ireland the lactating breast has historically been a polarized site, promising both cultural connections through ancient Gaelic fostering (including wet-nursing) traditions, but also threatening subversion and contagion. As Jules Law has suggested in his book *The Social Life of Fluids*, "wet-nursing . . . engaged the culture's most profound ambivalences and contradictions."[5] Law looks at Victorian and fin de siècle novels, including the Irish classics of *Dracula* and *Esther Waters*, as dramas "of leaky bodies and troubling circulations of bodily fluids that threaten to undermine the ostensibly benign economy of maternal milk."[6] In Ireland, the discourses around wet-nursing particularly involved concerns of cultural exchange: Katie Trumpener has suggested that, in Maria Edgeworth's switched-at-birth novel *Ennui*, the Irish wet nurse's body becomes a site of "transcultural tolerance" between the peasant and the Anglo-Irish elite.[7] And as Julie Kipp elaborates, "In nurturing and feeding her oppressors, the wet nurse cultivated dangerous sympathies in the ruling classes."[8] It was Spenser, most famously, who saw the Irish wet-nurse as an activist, hybridizing threat, one he described as a "dangerous infection" in *A View of the Present State of Ireland*:

> The child that sucketh the milk of the nurse must of necessity learn his first speech of her. . . . The smack of the first will always abide with him, and not only of the speech, but of the manners and conditions. . . . They moreover draw into themselves, together with their suck, even the nature and disposition of their nurses . . . so that the speech being Irish, the heart must needs be Irish.[9]

In both colonial and anticolonial discourse, then, the nursing woman—mother and wet-nurse—is a site and an emblem of cultural and political knowledge. But breasts—like the female body-cast-as-Irish-land more generally—were also vulnerable. In Aodhagán Ó Rathaille's seventeenth-century aisling that Pearse reprinted in his journal at St. Edna's school, the cultural value of the nursing mother is threatened by the foreign other:

Long though thou has been, O majestic, gentle-mannered Erin,
A fair nursing-mother with hospitality and true knowledge;
Henceforth shalt thou be an unwilling handmaid to every
    withered band,
While every foreign churl shall have sucked thy breasts.[10]

In Mother Ireland's breast resides either "true knowledge" or a "dangerous infection."

When Pearse adopts this lactating body, he reworks the figure of the nursing mother from a sign of potential infection, or colonial rape, or, as we will see in famine texts, loss, to one of renewal.

In the Irish Revival, the nurse as giver of language, as storyteller, was recast as grassroots cultural inheritance rather than demonized as infection. As Lady Gregory tells it in the introduction to her *Cuchulain*: "I have told the whole story in plain and simple words, in the same way my old nurse Mary Sheridan used to be telling stories from the Irish long ago, and I a child at Roxborough."[11] It is Irish language (and here, Irish syntax), Irish culture, and indeed, revolutionary sympathy that the nurse conveys to her nursling. Similarly, Ernie O'Malley takes up the trope as the opening motif in *On Another Man's Wound*: "Our nurse, nannie," he writes, "told my eldest brother and me stories and legends." These included, as with Gregory, stories of Cuchulain and other mythic figures, and "songs and ballads of the people and of the land."[12] There was folklore, too, fairies and leprechauns, and "In low and often stilly tones she told and retold ghost stories." She told and retold; telling stories, giving language, is like eating: never completed, always repeated. O'Malley's nurse, Mary Anne Jordan, figures repeatedly in his writing as the source of cultural knowledge, as well as revolutionary affiliation; his handwritten poem from about 1930 titled "Mary Anne" attests to her influence, or at least the literary troping of her influence. It begins, "Our Mary Anne would tell us tales / And sing old ballads now forgot / She'd take us over hills and dales / And sit us in a shady spot. / And she could sing a lullaby."[13]

In fact, the lullaby was often seen as the originary site of cultural transmission. The nurse is the first teacher, and the lullaby is her first text, consonant with the nursling's first food. In Spenser's description, and then, indeed, Gregory's and O'Malley's, the nurse gives the first sustenance: milk and language. Pearse, too, described a similar experience with an Irish-speaking "nurse," and as Fionntán de Brún writes, "The case of Pearse's Gaelic 'nursemaid' [his grandaunt, Margaret Brady] is strikingly similar to others in the history of Irish revivalism . . . where the particular influence of a nursemaid or domestic servant had helped inspire a revivalist career."[14] While there is no evidence that these nurses gave milk from their own breasts along with their speech and cultural knowledge, the association is always there for Pearse between mothers (and foster-mothers), milk, cultural and political identity, and place. As Pearse writes in "Robert Emmet and the Ireland of Today," the revolutionary has imbibed his Irishness through the breast, and thus is faithful to "the place where his mother bore him . . . the breast that gave him suck."[15] In "Lullaby of a Woman of the Mountain," the child is metonymized as the "Little soft mouth that my breast has known," and the lullaby's knowledge becomes the child's, who will, like a golden candle, "guide all wayfarers who walk this mountain."[16]

These first moments of feeding and teaching form the archetype for Pearse's own pedagogy: that of intimate fostering between teacher and pupil—an echo of ancient Gaelic fostering traditions. In his 1916 play *The Singer*, MacDara, the figure so clearly identified with Pearse himself as educator, author, and architect of the imminent Easter Rising, explains his relationship with his student/fosterling with the metaphor of the wet-nurse: "I gave to the little lad I taught the very flesh and blood and breath that were my life. I fed him on the milk of my kindness; I breathed into him my spirit."[17] It is also a eucharistic metaphor: MacDara feeds the boy on his milk, but also, like Christ, flesh, blood, breath, spirit. The breast, for Pearse, is a version of Christ-the-mother as well as Mary, and it nurtures beyond gender; it is male as well as female. Pearse's breast—both in the sense of the one that he writes about and the one he seems to wear prosthetically (like the white nightdress that transforms a boy into a priest in his story "The Priest") nurtures beyond biological reproduction, as the source of native language given by a parent or foster parent of either sex. In *The Singer*, the revolutionary MacDara is witnessed returning to his homeplace as "a man *breasting* Cnoc an Teachta," an image that doubly invokes the breast in its suggestion of MacDara's breast turned toward the mountain, and also the traditional association of the Irish landscape with the female body.[18] By invoking the male breast as the source of nurture, Pearse enacts a sort of imaginative queering of breastfeeding, and a queering of the trope of Mother Ireland itself.[19]

Pearse ventriloquizes both Mother Ireland and the human mother most memorably in his poems "Mise Eire" and "The Mother," and as Moynagh Sullivan has argued, Pearse's writings "explicitly express this desire to 'mother' the nation."[20] When MacDara then tells his own teacher, "You are like a poor mother who spends herself in nursing children who go away and never come back to her," he is also referring to his own role as tragic mother, and linking the two sacrificial revolutionary roles. In the moments before Maire's son MacDara will become, as she says, "a noble corpse," Maire recalls him, in anaphoric trinity, as her own sacrifice for the nation: "Soft hand that played at my breast, strong hand that will fall heavy on the Gall, brave hand that will break the yoke!"[21] Like his mother, MacDara himself ruminates on the sacrifice of the mother/teacher: "Sometimes I think that to be a woman and to serve and suffer as women do is to be the highest thing. Perhaps that is why I felt it proud and wondrous to be a teacher, for a teacher does that."[22]

Breastfeeding would seem to be an example of what de Brún describes as Pearse's "quest for intergenerational continuity";[23] but in fact, what Pearse creates is a closed circuit of mother and child, a dualism that reproduces itself in isolation: mother birthing child who nurses and then dies; tragic sacrifice and occult revival; a pieta that repeats itself infinitely, with the nation's teachers, revolutionaries, and indeed, mothers, giving milk and receiving blood in return. Motherhood (and its surrogates) and sacrifice are indeed so imbricated with breastfeeding for Pearse that in his story "The Mother," Maire's singular wish for a child is only ever articulated as the wish to breastfeed that child: to "feel its hand or its mouth at her breast.[24]" She pleads to the Virgin Mary, "I have a request of you. . . . A child drinking the milk of my breast."[25] The fulfillment of this wish, though, includes loss that is inevitable, for the mother's imitation of Christ ("she stuck thorns into her flesh in memory of the crown of thorns that went on the brow of the Saviour"[26]) anticipates her and her child's role in the national sacrifice, and the story ends with a recognition not only of a woman's great joy, but her great sorrow. In Pearse's poem of the same name, the mother accepts her sons' blood sacrifice: "I do not grudge them: Lord, I do not grudge / My two strong sons that I have seen go out / To break their strength and die, they and a few, / In bloody protest for a glorious thing."[27] The mother speaks of her suffering, and suggests the inevitability of a closed cycle, rather than a continuing one, for her children's deaths are as certain as their births: "We suffer in their coming and their going." Even the Proclamation is in line with this discourse of the child who never grows up: as Vincent Quinn notes, "'Mother Ireland' maintains the entire populace in a state of perpetual infancy—four of the Proclamation's six paragraphs identify Ireland's inhabitants as 'children'."[28] In Pearse's vision, then, both breastfeeding and revolution are idiosyncratic in that they denote not only the expression of a new beginning (a means to a future, a means to an end), but a literal end, an ever-revolving but closed cycle: a perpetual revival.

The movement between blood sacrifice and milk sacrifice is fluid, just as the fluids of the body have long been imagined with a biological parity: the blood of a woman becomes her breastmilk; the blood of a man, his semen. Pearse seems particularly to adopt medieval Christianity's literary and visual paralleling of the blood of Christ's wounds and the milk of Mary's breasts.[29] In recounting the story of how Robert Emmet's housekeeper Anne Devlin was interrogated about his location after Emmet's retreat to the mountains, Pearse describes her refusal to answer the soldiers' questions: "They swung her up to a cart and half-hanged her several times. . . . They pricked her breast with bayonets until the blood spurted out in their faces. . . . Not one word did they extract from that steadfast woman."[30] The image of Devlin, blood spurting from her breast, suggests not only Christ's wounds, but Christ as mother; Pearse's imitation of Christ, which as Valente has shown is suffused with a discourse of manliness, is also suffused with maternity.[31]

Re-gendering the image of Anne Devlin's spurting breast in *The Singer*, Pearse has Sighle, MacDara's foster-sister and ostensible love-interest, imagine the bodies of dead boys on the hillsides of Ireland, with "maybe a red wound in their white breasts, or on their white foreheads." Yeats and Gregory, whose play *Cathleen ni Houlihan* this line echoes, gave us red cheeks and pale cheeks, but Pearse's recasting of the life-force in the breast—pouring out blood instead of milk—disrupts our modes of thinking about gender in the revolutionary period in Ireland, replacing male sacrifice with sacrifice that is as maternal as it is masculine. It is not, moreover, solitary male life alone that is sacrificed, but the connection between parent and child: not only the mother and her biological (male) infant, but the foster-mother and her nursling, or the teacher and his student. To be sure, the child seems, in Pearse's vision, to be nearly always male, and the mother as nearly always female, but the binaries are also continually disrupted by the potentialities.

Ultimately, though, potential is short-lived in the teleology of blood sacrifice. The act of nursing, in Pearse's writings, also foregrounds the irony of blood sacrifice as an act of revival, for its literally life-giving act is made consonant with the wounded, lifeless breast.[32]

Scholars such as Eugene McNulty have suggested that it is exclusively "the *male* body as a site of a 'political theology' [that] becomes the explicit framing device for the action of his early work," and only in "the broken body of young manhood," does Pearse's work articulate the "postcolonial moment."[33] However, I want to suggest the seemingly inadmissible figure in Pearse's writing of the woman's body, the mother as more than witnessing mourner. In fact, the mother is the sacrifice too, and the young broken men with their perfected bodies are, in fact, constructed through the series of metonymies that I have been tracing—mother, breastmilk, blood—that link the mother directly with the sacrificial son.

The sovereignty myths of the Revival (including Pearse's *The Singer* and, above all, Yeats and Gregory's *Cathleen Ni Houlihan*), enact a substitution: a chaste blood sacrifice replaces the original story's plot of sexual intercourse between the prospective king and the old hag; the hag turns out to be Irish sovereignty, and is made young through the sexual act.[34] In the revivalist version, the blood of young men—rather than their semen—would be needed to nourish and regenerate the land.[35] Now let us remember that the sovereignty myth is a fertility myth, after all, one that condenses the procreative process into an archetype. And the repetitive, months-long process of infant feeding is structurally at odds with the magical transformation that national mythology and revolutionary rhetoric both require. The blood sacrifice that transforms the old queen into a young girl *stands in for*—that is, both replaces and also signifies—her more quotidian reproductive and child-feeding duties. In other words, the blood is not simply another form of semen: it is also the milk of the breastfeeding mother who generates the nation. And Pearse, whom we often think of as fetishizing male sacrifice, is in fact always reminding us of the mother's body: not merely as a symbol of Mother Ireland or a kind of realist corrective to that symbolism, but rather as a way to mediate between what Kiberd has called "the drive towards futurity" in Pearse, and the impossibility of a future for those who have spilled their blood in sacrifice.[36]

In her book *The Feminization of Famine*, Margaret Kelleher argues that "depictions of maternity . . . reproduce an ambivalence at the very heart of the maternal figure," particularly in famine texts. "The mother's milk," she writes, "is a central metaphor of the gift of life; her dry breast is thus one of the famine's deepest horrors, expressive of a primal fear, where 'the fountain of life' is now death-giving."[37] Kelleher marshals various examples of this particular trope of the empty breast, "the horror that the child's source of life has become the location of its death,"[38] including William Carleton's 1846 sketch in *The Black Prophet*:

> Lying close to her cold and shivering breast was an infant of about six months old, striving feebly, from time to time, to draw from that natural source of affection the sustenance which had been dried up by chilling misery and want.[39]

The profusion of such images in both visual and literary depictions creates a sense that the breast itself seems to be metonymically unwholesome, anxious, and diseased. The famine breast takes on the impoverishment of landscape, diet, and home, most famously described in Thomas Davis's "The State of the Irish Peasantry":

> Suckled by a breast that is supplied from unwholesome or insufficient food, and that is fevered with anxiety—reeking with the smoke of an almost chimneyless cabin—assailed by wind and rain when the weather rages—breathing, when it is calm, the exhalations of a rotten roof, of clay walls, and of manure, which gives his only chance of food—he is apt to perish in his infancy. Or he survives all this (happy if he have escaped from gnawing scrofula or familiar fever), and in the same cabin, with rags instead of his mother's breast, and lumpers instead of his mother's milk, he spends his childhood.[40]

The trope of the unnurturing breast of the famine mother also informs late nineteenth and twentieth century folklore attached to lactating mothers. As Angela Bourke writes, "Stories about babies taken away and replaced with changelings carry memories of real children whose appearance changed as they starved, making them look 'quaint' or 'wrinkled with care, so that appeared like aged persons.'"[41] The misery, described by Maud Gonne in her speech of "the famine of '48," included "women who have heard the last sigh of their children without being able to lessen their agony with one drop of milk."[42]

In fact, the empty, shriveled famine breast seems to haunt Pearse's nursing mothers, and serves perhaps as the originating nightmare of his fetish: one Pearse, in Freudian gesture, seems to be repressing and reenvisioning in his own fantasies of nursing, reanimating the famine breast in order to master the future.[43] Pearse literally brings the desiccated, empty breast, the "wrinkled paps," the shriveled, wizened infant, back to life: the skin is filled out again, smoothed over, and made "white" to emblematize the milk that makes this reanimation, this new breastfeeding, possible. As Pearse has Sighle in *The Singer* imagine these reanimated bodies, they are "so many young men, young men with straight, strong limbs, and smooth, white flesh, going out into great peril because a voice has called to them to right the wrong of the people."[44] Here, Pearse, by imagining "the milk of his kindness" nourishing the starved and wrinkled infants of Ireland, fills their bodies and smooths their skin. The whiteness that Pearse so often describes as the skin of the male sacrificed body is not just a sign of purity, but of milk—mothers' milk showing on their very skins.

When Sighle exclaims, "Oh, I would like to see the man that has set their hearts on fire with the breath of his voice!"[45] she too evokes the connection between breath, nursing, language, culture, and revolution. Michael Cronin, in line with a critical tradition that reads Sighle's description "of how physically desirable these men are" as suggestive of *Pearse's* longing for male bodies, rather than Sighle's, argues for "an insistent, discordant erotic undertone to that description—'their cheeks flushed and their red lips apart'" as a merging of political and sexual desire (rather than, as Roy Foster and others have suggested, its sublimation into political work).[46] Yet we might read this longing differently, in line with the many women of Pearse's plays and poems who long for a nursing child rather than a lover: the cheeks flushed and red lips apart are also the suckling lips of a nursing infant. In other words, the merging of sexual and political (and procreative) desire is also Sighle's (or Pearse-as-mother's): the desire of the woman for a child at her breast. Returning to the story "The Mother," we find that a year after her wish for a child to breastfeed, the mother is rewarded with "a child in her breast. There was that look on her that doesn't be on living soul but a mother when she feels the mouth of her firstborn at her nipple."[47] The mouth on the breast, at the nipple—an image Pearse uses so many times throughout these works—exemplifies the fluidity between mother and child, and like the kissing on the lips that we see so frequently in Pearse's writings, connects bodies even as it suggests the ultimate impossibility of a connected future. The centrality of breastfeeding in Pearse's writings creates mothers, foster-mothers, and teacher/revolutionaries who long to breastfeed, to revive what is withered, and then to suffer the inevitable loss of a sort of reverse vampirism.[48]

Vincent Quinn points out that Pearse, in his appropriation of Irish fostering traditions, "forgets foster-mothers almost as soon as he mentions them."[49] Certainly it is worth considering the argument that Pearse here appropriates the maternal role, or the procreative metaphor, simply to have it accrue to his discourse of manliness; Quinn's point that "Fosterage thus becomes a way of appropriating the only power that women wield in Pearse's imaginative universe" is apt. And yet, Pearse also suggests that the sacrifice *is* the foster-mother's, or the teacher's, or the mother's. In other words, Pearse's mode here is not simply appropriative; and it does more than reinforce the dominant ideologies of nationalist masculinity. At the very least, Pearse's attention to fluid bodies (and bodily fluids), his imagination of motherhood and cross-gender breastfeeding, tests our more rigid understandings of gender in his work. In light, today, of the repeal of the 8th amendment that required so many men to imagine women's bodily experience, perhaps we find that Pearse's cross-gender imaginings were, if not a model of possibility, an anticipation of it.

The breast is both symbolic and part of actual bodily practice (as David Lloyd has argued of the mouth).[50] So just as real Irish women have suffered the effects of their symbolization in the national imaginary—Mother Ireland, Erin—so too with the breast. Kelleher argues in *The Feminization of Famine* that Irish writers used maternal images to depoliticize famine, "separating the women's starvation from issues of legislative responsibility and political causation" and effectively suggesting that (like woman herself) famine is natural versus political.[51] Pearse's use of these images in their renewed form, where the breast is again full of the milk of nurture, culture, and eventually, revolution, suggests the repair of the "breakdown" that Kelleher sees in images of the famine nursing. Pearse's intent, however, is precisely the opposite of depoliticizing. Rather, if images of famine nursing depoliticize famine, their inverse function in Pearse's discourse is to naturalize revolution. And this queering of blood sacrifice, while it opens a new view on how gender functions in the Irish Revival, is still troubling.

Unlike Pearse's rhetoric of blood sacrifice, his focus on breastfeeding gained the practice no rhetorical purchase in what was, and remained until the past decade or so, an invisible, embarrassed, or shameful mode of infant feeding. Today, rates of breastfeeding remain lower in Ireland than in any other European country, almost anywhere in the world; at midcentury, Caitríona Clear suggests, breastfeeding had almost died out as the primary method of infant feeding.[52] By the early twentieth century, as Joyce's Stephen Dedalus observed, that poor old milkwoman, embodiment of the nation, had "old wrinkled paps," the milk she brought, "not hers." The suggestion that Mother Ireland no longer had milk of her own seems to have been not merely social or political, but presaging a shift in actual infant feeding practices. While Clear has proposed this shift as an act of women's empowerment, there is strong evidence too that, as Aoife Rickard notes, feelings of shame about the body "were instilled in the Irish people through the Catholic Church [so that] it comes as no surprise why rates of breast-feeding in Ireland are so low."[53]

On the postage stamp designed by Irish artist Robert Ballagh for the commemoration of Pearse's birthdate in 1979, it is fitting that the revolutionary's profile shares the space with a pair of breasts. In a stylized simplification of Delacroix's painting of revolutionary France, *Liberty Leading the People*, Ballagh has substituted the Irish tricolor for the French, but this seems less radical than the surprising nudity of the allegorical figure Liberty, whose breasts and nipples are notably asymmetrical, perhaps indicating their multidimensional, queered revolutionary energies. The stamp was mocked and reviled at the time as an "outrageous insult,"[54] and yet Liberty's half-undressed pose, bayonet and flag in hand, suggests nothing more strongly, in this context, than Pearse's MacDara at the end of *The Singer*. Tearing off his clothes as he walks forth into battle, here is a Christ who will redeem Ireland through his naked body—a body that can die for Ireland, but also nurse it; and in nursing, revive it.

12

Death before Disability

The Bioaesthetics of Blood Sacrifice

Joseph Valente

The imperialist discourse of stigma and stereotype, centered in the great European metropoles of the late 19th century, acquired an implicitly ableist cast with the emergence of the biopolitically infused racialism that Foucault anatomizes in texts like *Abnormal* and *Society Must Be Defended*.[1] As systems of social surveillance and control shifted from a disciplinary to a normative model, from a focus on disciplining individual bodies to regulating entire ethnobiological populations, the most pernicious ills were seen to be just that; ills, deviancies, debilities, and deficiencies of body or mind, which now served as explanatory ground for the time-honored *summum malum*, immorality or criminality.[2] The timing could not have been more fortuitous for the ideological self-fashioning of advanced Irish nationalism in its heroic, revivalist mode. The last great decolonizing push that eventuated in the Easter Rising coincided with the developmental moment of European biopower that was, in Foucault's words, "almost completely covered" by the discourses of degeneration,[3] many of which imputed this contagion to the contact of metropolitan peoples with the so-called lesser races of the colonial periphery.[4] As white subalterns, the Irish had reason to be anxious about being racially profiled as a source of degenerative contagion, all the more so as the supposedly endemic deficiencies of native Irish society were giving way, as a justification for continued British rule, to the supposedly intrinsic deviations of the Irish constitution from evolved, species-wide norms of self-governance: whether dispositional, affective, cognitive, or moral.[5] No less a notable than Lord Salisbury, the prime minister of the United Kingdom for most of the early revivalist period in Ireland (1885–1902), pronounced the Irish "no doubt the worst symptoms of the malady [of degeneracy]."[6] The Irish subject was being represented during this period as a proto-disabled and therefore naturally dependent subject.

At the same time, following the Act of Union, the Irish were also members, as well as inmates, of the United Kingdom and its empire, what I have elsewhere called metrocolonial subjects.[7] In accordance with this fissured geopolitical interpellation, many elites and opinion leaders in Ireland endorsed invidious principles subtending ethnonationalist supremacism, even as they contested the application of those notions to themselves. Phobic attitudes toward bodily difference and impairment were already present from the story of Nuada in the opening pages of the Fianna cycle, wherein we are told that by law any deformity or disability debars a man, in this case Nuada, from holding the scepter of kingship unless and until, as with Nuada, full bodily integrity is restored. The affirmative recycling of that foundational tale of Gaelic tribal rule (law/succession) in Lady Gregory's *Gods and Fighting Men* affords but one, especially ready instance of revivalist identification with authoritative norms of bodily form and function.[8]

From the start, the broad-based Irish Revival, which laid much of the ideological groundwork for the Easter Rising, advanced a decolonizing program that was powerfully invested in enforcing what Robert McRuer has termed "compulsory able-bodiedness."[9] Its first established organization, the Gaelic Athletic Association, proposed to renovate the Irish (male) physique as a step toward overthrowing its enervating condition and "demoralizing influence" of British rule,[10] and thereby rescuing Irishmen from the imposed enfeeblement of colonial peonage. Prominent patrons of the Gaelic Athletic Association spoke directly to the specter of degeneration that the new organization aimed to exercise. In the preface to the official *Gaelic*

Athletic Association Handbook, Archbishop Croke regrets that "national sports" were "held in dishonor" by "the degenerate dandies of the day," while Michael Davitt deplores "the degenerate gait and bearing of most of our young men" in the recent absence of "such games and pastimes as formerly gave to Irishmen the reputation of a soldier-like and self-reliant race."[11] Conversely, a series in the newspaper *Sinn Fein*, entitled "Athletic Ireland: Its Progress and Possibilities," shuddered at the "woeful tale" to be told "if the heart of the race, sinking under the weight of adversity, failed to feed the veins with invigorating blood" of the type the GAA competitions supplied.[12] As Irish sports historian W. F. Mandle observes, "In an era consciously and unconsciously affected by social Darwinism and eugenics, the Irish could not afford to let the case for the Celt go by default."[13]

The GAA was also, notoriously, a front and a recruiting vehicle for the Irish Republican Brotherhood, which shared the profound anxiety over ethnonational degeneracy that motivated the sporting revival. Indeed, the official organ of the Volunteers devoted two feature articles—"National Degeneration" and "How National Degenerates Are Made"—to the "colonial disease which is destroying [the Irishmen's] vitality."[14] It is no wonder that a Volunteer like Sean Mac Alla could write, in the same publication, "I have ever looked to the Gaelic Athletic Association as the first line of an Irish army."[15] Indeed the GAA also had a mythico-historical claim to being the "first line of the Irish army"; Cuchulain, nee Setanta, *became* Cuchulain—the archetypal Gaelic warrior, the Volunteer's model of blood sacrifice and the perfect physical specimen of Irish manhood—"by driving a hurling ball into the mouth of Culann's monstrous hound." Thus if Wellington could declare the battle of Waterloo to have been won on the playing fields of Eton, the Volunteers had reason to declare the Easter Rising to have begun on the playing fields of Emain Macha. In this regard, the GAA served as a bridge for the differently calibrated desires of the cultural and physical force nationalists to absolve the Irish body (politic) of any taint or suspicion of infirmity.

With the native Irish thus positioned as at once biopolitically suspect subalterns and as European exponents of biopolitically inflected racialism, it is no surprise that the Revival, and especially its most articulate manifestation, the Literary Revival, would regularly invoke only to ritually banish the specter of debility, disease, and declension—all manner, in sum, of dis-ability. Yeats's early Celtic twilight epic *The Wanderings of Oisin*, for example, allegorizes the extinction of the Gaelic warrior culture as the deterioration and decrepitude of the once stalwart, heroic body of the title character, now "bent and bald and blind."[16] In the schoolboy fictions of Patrick Pearse, such as *The Master* or *Isogan*, characters who have lapsed into defeat and demoralization find their renewal in the vision of vital, fetching, physically attractive, and above all healthy young lads. In Synge's mordant parody of his compatriots' propensity for ideological collusion with imperial biopower, *The Playboy of the Western World*, Christy Mahon's utterly bogus patricidal heroism keys his social and romantic advancement in part because it is identified, both tacitly at first and then explicitly, with the national imperative of race-improvement and even with folk-eugenics. One of the more memorable speeches in the play sees the father of Christy's intended, Pegeen Mike, overcome his fear of falling victim to patricide on just these terms.

> It's many would dread to bring your like into their house to end them maybe with a sudden end: but I'm a decent man of Ireland, and I'd liefer face the grave untimely and I seeing a score of grandsons growing up gallant little swearers by the name of God, than go peopling my bedside with puny weeds the like of what you'd breed, I'm thinking, out of Sean Keogh.[17]

Like the spokesmen for both the GAA and the Volunteers, Michael James Flaherty here takes on, however ironically, the perceived threat of national degeneration, which is to say he equates patriotism with racialized ableism, love of country with the eugenical management of romantic love and reproduction. To judge from these and like cases, the Revival's evident aim was to bring forth a new Ireland founded not just on the principle of "compulsory able-bodiedness," but on the symbolic conflation of able-bodiedness with all manner of redemptive possibility: social, political, racial, spiritual, and religious.

Revivalist Martyrology

At that border joining cultural and advanced nationalism, the GAA and the IRB, a new partnership emerged that clearly foreshadowed, if it did not actually foster, the events of Easter 1916: between a politicized aesthetic genre, modern sovereignty/aisling literature (Gregory and Yeats's *Cathleen Ni Houlihan*, Maud Gonne's *Dawn*, Lennox Robinson's *Patriots*, Pearse's *The Singer*), and the aestheticized political ethos of blood sacrifice that said genre represented, promoted and reenergized. From their shared anxiety over the real or reputed state of Irish embodiment, works elaborating this martyrological agenda compounded a new subspecies of revivalism that was strangely at odds in certain respects with the very concept of Revivalism itself. It might, in fact, be more accurate to designate these works *rehabilitationist*. A revival typically proposes to bring back something dead (or near dead) and gone; and of course much of the Revival—the Gaelic League, the manuscript translation of a Standish O'Grady or a Douglas Hyde, the folklore collections of Lady Gregory, etc.— exemplified this sort of recovery project. But in the revivalist canon prefiguring Easter 1916—the original poetry, drama, and narrative fiction of Gregory, Yeats, Synge, Plunkett, Pearse and MacDonagh— the presently living are given over to death in order to rehabilitate the Irish body politic, often imaged as *actual* infirm bodies.

Consider the archetypal modern sovereignty drama, Gregory and Yeats's *Cathleen Ni Houlihan*. Michael Gillane, pronounced "a fine strong man," goes off willingly to certain, militarily futile death to the effect of transforming a disabled old woman, broken of body and distrait of mind, into a "young girl" with the "walk of a queen."[18] That the woman, Cathleen, is the allegorical embodiment of Ireland poses a metonymical link between her impoverished political condition and her disordered biopolitical condition. In sacrificing his life to amend the first—to restore her "beautiful green fields"—Michael correlatively acts to remedy the second, to restore the stately vigor of her physical and mental frame. In Patrick Pearse's adaptation of the sovereignty drama, *The Singer*, the young "mountainy man," MacDara of the "strong hand," performs the same office for his mother, Maire, who, as a maternal hostess to the entire band of rebels, is also a figure of (Blessed) Mother Ireland. His avowed commitment to blood sacrifice arrests her slide from aged debility to a sleep portending death, and she proclaims her sudden revivification in terms that encapsulate the biopolitical transaction of, in Foucault's words, letting live and letting die. "My son MacDara is the Singer that has quickened the dead years and all the quiet dust . . . weave your winding sheets women, for there will be many a noble corpse to be waked before the new moon."[19] MacDara himself instances one of those rebel outlaws whom Lady Gregory's essay, "The Felons of Our Land," enshrines as salvaging Ireland's moral health by their fatal self-immolation.[20] Lastly, the speaker of Joseph Plunkett's aisling lyric, "The little black rose shall be red at last," enthusiastically expends his blood and his vitality to rejuvenate and rehabilitate an Irish rose, whose blight is emblematic not just of her national captivity and helplessness—by way of the allusion to James Clarence Mangan's "Roisin Dubh"—but her pathology and morbidity as well—by way of allusion to William Blake's "The Sick Rose."[21]

Each of these texts also directly analogizes the act of patriotic martyrdom to the passion of Christ.[22] Michael Gillane responds to the Poor Old Woman's summons, "If anyone would give me help, he must give me himself, he must give me all," a paraphrase of Christ's sentiments in Matthew 16:24.[23] MacDara explicitly identifies the salvational promise of his self-immolation to that of Christ: "One man can free a people as one Man redeemed the world."[24] Plunkett's penultimate line, "Praise God if this my blood fills the doom," echoes the phrase "This is my blood" from the Last Supper before Christ's crucifixion, linking directly the earthy life-giving properties of the former to the divine life-giving properties of the latter.[25] The repeated, seemingly unavoidable deployment of a Christological antitype in these works plainly aims to sublimate the secular quest of national martyrdom into a religious mission, thereby emphasizing its moral and spiritual aspects. But this favored antitype derives from a moment in the Christian narrative most particularly concerned with the death and resurrection of the body, with martyrological death *as* the resurrection of the body, and as such it also resonates the other way round, as a religious allegory of secular/national disability and rehabilitation.[26]

This reversibility of the religious and the secular, spiritual and biological, forms of regenerative martyrdom reaches an apex in the political writings, pedagogical programs, and stemwinding speeches of Patrick Pearse. On the one hand, Pearse decries the present generation of Irishmen in terms that speak to their failings not only of character but of constitution. Degraded by the material condition of slavery and by their own habituation to it, these base Irish have "lost their manhood," and have so lost their physical courage as to regard war and bloodshed at the "final horror."[27] They are not able to free themselves, he propounds, "because they are no longer fit for freedom," owing to the "terrible degradation they have reached."[28] "Guilty of a personal baseness" in "suffering themselves to be deprived of their manhood," that "greatest of indignities,"[29] they are no longer, by Pearse's lights, "in any real sense men at all."[30] Accordingly, in a clever turn on the Sovereignty myth popularized by Yeats in *Cathleen Ni Houlihan*, he likens the men of this generation more than once to an "old woman," aligning them with the disabled figure to be saved, the Shan von Vocht, rather than her stout saviors, as is their proper calling. Here again, ideals of embodiment dovetail with ideals of national identity and commitment, such that the colonial dependency of Ireland could indicate, in and by itself, a slough of collective degeneracy.

To combat this deficiency of "virtu," Pearse proposed to inculcate in his pupils at St. Enda's the "physical vigor" as well as the moral integrity necessary to follow both in the footsteps of the athlete/warrior,

Cuchulain, and in the way of the Cross; and to die ungrudgingly in the effort to redeem Ireland; i.e., not just to free the bodily politic from foreign rule, but in so freeing to relieve that body of its colonial debility, to make it once again "fit for freedom." The death of armed revolutionaries alone would prove redemptive not just of the bodily or spiritual reality of Ireland but of their mutual reflection in one another; what Lady Gregory, in whose footsteps Pearse unwittingly followed, framed as the "dignity" recovered by the fatal self-immolation of her "treason-felons."[31] Often delivered at the graves of noted Irish martyrs—Wolfe Tone, Robert Emmet, O'Donovan Rossa—Pearse's political oratory espoused just such a willingness to see the best, healthiest—yes, the fittest Irish blood, the blood of the new or coming generation—shed, and shed freely in order to remedy the corruption and degeneracy of established Irish manhood, the kind of corruption and degeneracy which, in the wider biopolitics of the Belle Epoque, was typically regarded as a blood-borne malady. If in the moral-spiritual register, Pearse might summarize his credo of blood-sacrifice as death before dishonor, that credo would, in the biopolitical register, read death before disability, disability *being* the dishonor, at once the effect of Irish political subordination and a chief cause of its continuation.

Thus, the conflation of national viability and autonomy with normative bodily strength and soundness, ethnic with somatic integrity, shaped not only the credo of blood sacrifice, its perceived stakes and consequences, but the parameters within which and the lines along which the act of martyrdom itself could be envisaged. Since the death embraced in patriotic song and story was not to count as the crowning impairment of Irish bodies but rather to function as a psychosymbolic shield against such impairment—i.e. the last line of defense of a normative, racialized dignity and somatic integrity— then the act of martyrdom would of ideological necessity be depicted as unravaged by the type of traumatic injury that would challenge or destroy that sound condition.

The chief obstacle to this perverse dynamic of purgation is that armed conflict, the scenario for nationalist martyrdom, deals not only the death to be embraced under this ethos, but the disability to be exorcised: from shattered limbs to lacerated organs to sensory impairment to post-traumatic stress disorder. Indeed, in the two years preceding the Easter Rising, the Great War had already demonstrated irrefutably the mutilating consequences of modern combat upon the "manhood" that Pearse was determined to cultivate. The solution to this apparent dilemma, however, was already built, had always been built, into the revivalist portrayal of blood sacrifice. It was to situate the martyr in the liminal space Lacan dubbed "between the two deaths,"[32] where a subject may decease symbolically, having met his "symbolic destiny," before expiring biologically, the latter estate being assured but not yet accomplished. The modern sovereignty drama and aisling verse tend to leave the hero at precisely that point, at which the symbolic death has been assured and thus accomplished while the material impact of death remains ever in abeyance and the threat of impairment is thus perpetually forestalled.

The template for this strategy was *Cathleen Ni Houlihan*. While the Old Woman proudly prognosticates slaughter for her devoted courtiers, she never limns their physical frame as being maimed or in any way degraded, as being marked by anything more severe than a change of complexion: "they that have red cheeks will have pale cheeks for my sake, and for all that, they will think they are well paid."[33] Michael Gillane himself "rushes" to meet his end offstage, leaving the impression of robust embodiment conserved in and by his inevitable extinction.[34] The consequent metamorphosis of Cathleen, the redemptive effect of Michael's heroism on the Irish body politic, comes at the expense of his life, which is already over symbolically, but not of the soundness or dynamism of his physique. The same is true of MacDara in *The Singer*. He passes through a crowd to pursue his doom, bursting with the force of his energy, a dead man walking impervious to debility.[35] The speakers in Sovereignty-related verse—Plunkett's "The Spark" and "The little black rose shall be free at last," MacDonagh's "On a Patriot Poet," Pearse's "Renunciation"—likewise predecease symbolically their continued expression of vigorous sexuality, joie de vivre, dogged principle, etc. Like the sovereignty heroes, they are still lives, or *nature morte*, given clean deaths that protect their frames from the slightest damage.

Upon opening St. Enda's, Pearse had a dream that encapsulates this pristine because always postponed martyrdom in the poetics of advanced nationalism. He observes a boy standing at the scaffold, beautiful in aspect, still, abiding an execution that remains in the offing.

> I saw a pupil of mine, one of our boys at St. Enda's, standing alone upon a platform above a mighty sea of people, and I understood that he was about to die there for some august cause, Ireland's or another. He looked extraordinarily proud and joyous, lifting his head with a smile almost of amusement. I remember noticing his bare white throat and the hair on his forehead stirred by the wind, just as I had often noticed them on the football field. I felt an inexplicable exhilaration as I looked on him . . . [36]

Thus lovingly elaborated by Pearse, this boy, like Gillane earlier, and MacDara later, represents an Irish ideal, at once irredentist, aesthetic, and biopolitical. It is not just that by his act, his blood sacrifice, he would redeem the nation, rendering it fit to be free; rather, in his martyrdom, endlessly deferred, his *being* stands as the frozen image of such fitness in every sense: the perfection of youthful masculine health and able-bodiedness in the advent of its voluntary self-immolation.

In *The Singer*, Pearse goes a step further. He manages to depict the youthful heroes of his revolutionary dream as being protected from bodily trauma in their projected material as well as spiritual death. Reversing the aisling scenario, he locates the only portrait of the slain Irish warriors in the dream-vision of a young maiden of Ireland, Sighle, the sweetheart of MacDara: "I see them with their cheeks flushed and their red lips apart. And then they will lie very still upon the hillside—so still and white, with no red on their cheeks, but maybe a red wound in their white breasts, or on their white foreheads."[37] With their composed, insistently white bodies, "dabbled

with blood," the rebels look like the subjects of pre-Raphaelite portraiture, where the sexuality and mortality so often commingle,
rather than the broken victims of battle slaughter.[38]

In her article, "Thinking of Her as Ireland," Elizabeth Cullingford remarks that the revivalist adaptation of the sovereignty myth
turned on the substitution of death for sex and the blood for semen.[39]
But the pre-Raphaelite tonalities of Sighle's extraordinary vision
reveal a counter-truth characteristic of modern sovereignty literature
generally: in insulating martyrdom from its disabling and disfiguring
effects, in situating the martyr between the two deaths, this genre
eroticizes him in his ordained demise. While the figuration of Ireland
as a maiden queen might have given her menfolk an unconscious,
heteroerotic stake in the country's freedom, as Luke Gibbons has
contended,[40] the sovereignty sees the erotic energy of both the characters and the audience redound back upon the male body of the
martyr.

The most decisive site of desire in *Cathleen Ni Houlihan* is not
the transformed Sovereignty hag, witnessed only by the marginal
boy, Patrick, but rather Michael himself, who in breaking off his
engagement to Delia has transformed himself into the proverbial lost
object, the site of desire as lack. MacDara bears an enhanced version
of the same status. As the vagrant singer, he is an object of longing
for friends and family from the outset of the play. Upon his return
home, he simultaneously tells Sighle of his love for her and announces
that he must withhold their first (and only) kiss in deference to the
mission of blood-sacrifice he has accepted, thereby turning himself into a lost object of amorous desire as well. Finally, MacDara
announces his martyrdom by likening himself to Christ crucified and
strips off his garments as he goes to meet his fate. In thus calling
attention to his deshabille, doomed but well-proportioned body as
an imitatio Christi, he plainly evokes the intensely homoerotic iconography of the savior characteristic of devotional poets like Herbert
and Crashaw and their descendants in the 19th century medieval
revival, of which Pearse's chivalric discourse is an offshoot.[41] The
key to this devotional homoeroticism of Christ, no less than his Irish

successors in blood sacrifice, is a submission to suffering and death that nevertheless leaves the body thus submitted miraculously intact. Whereas the representation of the Irish martyrs to be detains them "between the two deaths," before the material distress of the body becomes legible, the iconography of Christ sacrificed suspends Him between material death and His "symbolic destiny" of resurrection, an interval in which His body has somehow survived the insult of Crucifixion with but token, non-disfiguring, non-disabling wounds, the stigmata. In this respect Sighle's vision of the revolutionary dead in *The Singer* as merely "dabbled with blood" lends their imitatio Christi a certain pre-posthumous exactitude, which MacDara's self-eroticizing geste can be seen to iterate.

By contrast, Joseph Plunkett's allegory in "The Little Black Rose" does proceed along broadly heteronormative lines, with an emphasis on fulfillment rather than frustration. But even here, Plunkett is concerned to rate the martyr's death profoundly enabling, and to do so he tropes the act of martyrdom as virility in action; his orgasmic fertilization of the rose ("When at last the blood overleaps the final barrier") displays a species of sexual heroism that likewise renders the death itself, rather than the maiden "to die for," the center of sexual desirability and investment in the poem.[42]

Although, and perhaps because, "The little black rose" most clearly adheres to Cullingford's formula for sovereignty literature, it also most clearly illustrates that death does not in fact supplant sex in this work, it becomes itself sexualized; the speaker's blood does not supersede semen, it becomes semen. As Freud observed by the end of *Beyond the Pleasure Principle*, Thanatos could never simply replace Eros, for the two drives are deeply symbiotic, their respective aims subject to the deflecting operations of one another.[43] What Thanatos can do is to queer Eros, specifically by introducing a recursive twist, in which any given object choice serves less as the end sought than as a negative point of mediation for the jouissance, what Pearse called the "exhilaration," of the subject's possible extinction. In the case of the sovereignty, the introduction of Thanatos queers the heteroerotic romance that Luke Gibbons discerns in the sacrificial relationship of martyr to female persona of Ireland. To assert the indefeasible able-bodiedness of Irish manhood, sovereignty literature fetishes the intact grace of its martyrs, even unto death, training the thanatotic stirrings of all the players—author, audience, fellows—upon the male bodies exposed to death. It thereby incites an eroticism that refuses or exceeds the homo/hetero binary. While this eroticism is queer in its own right, however, in the sense of standing athwart the mandates of gender selectivity, it is squarely propped, as my essay will have shown, on a zealous nationalist compliance with dominant biopolitical imperatives, with the disqualification and indeed the forcible erasure of disability.

Revisionist Martyrology

One might assume that the precarious framing of blood-sacrifice could not have survived the fusillade of real bullets and their mutilating effects on real bodies. For hundreds that Easter week, death came in a far less pristine fashion than the authors cited here preferred to imagine; and for thousands wounding, maiming, and disability became as present a fact of their lives as they were absent in the fictions of sovereignty. But the most prominent leaders of the Rising and signers of the *Proclamation of the Irish Republic*, Plunkett and Pearse, attained the clean martyrdom they sought and were permitted to remain physically unmarred, even unto death, in the popular Imaginary. By electing to execute these men privately, behind the walls of Kilmainham Prison, the British unthinkingly did them the favor of situating them yet again "between the two deaths," albeit with the poles reversed. The real-life Volunteers had suffered real, material death as the army notices each day in early May pronounced. But they were left symbolically undead, their profiles still hygienically intact and able-bodied in the public minds' eye, all the readier to be resurrected, as they had promised, in the immediate future of national and Republican resistance.

Yeats's famous poem "Easter, 1916," effected just such a resurrection in the aesthetic register. In specific, Yeats's figuration of the dead rebels as a sleeping child can be seen to invoke precisely this sort of ultra-hygienic strain of martyrological portraiture.

> To murmur name upon name,
> As a mother names her child
> When sleep at last has come
> On limbs that had run wild.
> What is it but nightfall?
> No, no, not night but death[44]

To be sure, the closing retraction—"No, no . . . ."—stages Yeats's refusal to succumb to the temptation to aestheticize martyred death, as engendered and endorsed in the doctrine of blood sacrifice. But even as he acknowledges in order to forestall the politicized, eulogistic reflex of dressing mortality in soothing metaphor (nightfall), even as he sees through the aestheticization of death, he is far less vigilant or circumspect when it comes to mobilizing death *as* a mode of aestheticization. That is to say, even as Yeats nullifies, and makes a show of nullifying, his metaphorical equation of death and nightfall, he leaves (all the more securely) in place the sleeping child of great if dormant energy and vigorous if bestilled limbs as an image of the martyrs to be hallowed. Perhaps this figure is meant to intimate a youthful death, of the kind the Easter Volunteers suffered, but it also adumbrates a death that preserves undisturbed the health and vitality of its subject, or, to take matters further, a death whose sanitized cast actually serves to invoke healthy and vital embodiment as a sacrificial ideal.

While the laundered iconography of blood sacrifice took shape in advance of Easter 1916, Yeats's "Easter, 1916," was composed in the immediate aftermath of the event, which not only saw dozens of rebels and hundreds of civilians die, but saw thousands wounded, debilitated, or disabled, and all suffer physical impairment to one degree or another, a shattering of those metaphorical "limbs." To figure the martyrs and by extension their enterprise in terms of a physically hale and dynamic child at rest is, at minimum, to airbrush the disabling of Irish bodies that transpired in the Rising, to engage in a kind of aesthetic cryogenics, solidifying the frozen perfection of the iconic patriot's physique in the Revivalist fillips to revolution.

Is there a substantive distinction to be drawn between the proleptic exclusion of likely physical trauma and disability in the literary summons to blood sacrifice and Yeats's retrospective elision of the traumatic effects of its enactment? Yes, in at least one important sense. The forecast of a martyrdom free of Irish physical harm, disfigurement, and mutilation was designed to serve revivalist nationalism directly, a central tenet of which, that blood sacrifice will renovate the Irish race on normative bio- as well as geo-political lines, would be viscerally undercut by images of prospective martyrs broken or maimed. Once the event occurs, widespread bodily insult becomes an irrefutable fact, which must, for cognate reasons, be excluded for the collective archive of ideological evidence. Yeats's poem serves this purpose, by establishing a through line to the aesthetic memorials already fashioned in anticipation of the event, a through line between pre-hoc and post-hoc commemoration, between the before and after photos of revolutionary zeal, between Pearse's smiling lad and Yeats's dozing child.

In thus carrying forward the Revival's Imaginary of blood sacrifice, its enabling meconnaissance of undefiled martyrdom, Yeats also brings to the surface its ableist corollary. He evokes the profound, if unconscious, linkage that obtains between Pearse's defining credo of Irish revolutionary "manhood," that "bloodshed" must not be "regarded" as the "final horror," and its necessarily hidden predicate, that disability, unregarded, held that place instead.

Notes

Bibliography

Contributor Biographies

Index

Notes

Introduction

1. W. B. Yeats, *Autobiographies* (New York: Scribner, 1999), 410–11.

2. See, for example, Gregory Castle, *Modernism and the Celtic Revival* (New York: Cambridge Univ. Press, 2001).

3. See, for example, Betsey Taylor FitzSimon and James H. Murphy, eds., *The Irish Revival Reappraised* (Dublin: Four Courts Press, 2004); Anne Fogarty, ed., *Irish University Review* 34, no. 1 (2004) special Lady Gregory issue.

4. See, for example, Karen Steele, *Women, Press and Politics during the Irish Revival* (Syracuse: Syracuse Univ. Press, 2007) and Fionntán de Brún, *Belfast and the Irish Language* (Dublin: Four Courts Press, 2006).

5. P. J. Mathews, *Revival: The Abbey Theatre, Sinn Fein, the Gaelic League and the Co-operative Movement* (Cork: Cork Univ. Press, 2003).

6. Sinead Mattar, *Primitivism, Science, and the Irish Revival* (Oxford: Oxford Univ. Press) 2004; Abby Bender, *Israelites in Erin: Exodus, Revolution and the Irish Revival* (Syracuse, NY: Syracuse Univ. Press, 2015).

7. FitzSimon and Murphy, *The Irish Revival Reappraised*, 13.

8. For an introduction to complexity theory see Melanie Mitchell, *Complexity: A Guided Tour* (Oxford: Oxford Univ. Press, 2009); Neil Johnson, *Simply Complexity: A Clear Guide to Complexity Theory*, (London: One World, 2007); and M. Mitchell Waldrop, *Complexity: The Emerging Science at the Edge of Order and Chaos* (New York: Simon and Schuster, 1992).

9. Johnson, *Simply Complexity*, 8.

10. Johnson, *Simply Complexity*, 25–27.

11. Mitchell, *Complexity: A Guided Tour*, 236.

12. Mitchell, *Complexity: A Guided Tour*, 238.

1. The Celtic Literary Society

1. Founded in Dublin in 1845 with a view of cultivating and more widely diffusing a knowledge of the language, history, antiquities, bardic remains, etc., of Ireland.

2. Paul Ricoeur, "Life: A Story in Search of a Narrator," in *Facts and Values*, ed. M. C. Doeser and J. N. Kraay (Dordrecht: Martinus Nijhoff, 1986).

3. Matthew Kelly, " . . . and William Rooney Spoke in Irish," *History Ireland* 15, no. 1 (Jan/Feb 2007).

4. "Basically a front for the IRB." See Brian Maye, *Arthur Griffith* (Dublin: Griffith College Publications, 1997), 94–95.

5. See Brian Ó Conchubhair, "William Rooney: The Celtic Literary Society and the Gaelic League?" in *Proceedings of the Harvard Celtic Colloquium*, vol. 38, ed. Celeste Andrews, Heather Newton, Shannon Parker, and Elizabeth Gipson (Harvard: Harvard Univ. Press, 2018), 144–72.

6. See, for example, Máirtín Ó Murchú, *Cumann Buan-Choimeádta Na Gaeilge: Tús an Athréimnithe* (Dublin: Cois Life Teoranta, 2001); Philip O'Leary, *The Prose Literature of the Gaelic Revival, 1881–1921: Ideology and Innovation* (University Park, PA: Pennsylvania State Univ. Press, 1994); Timothy G. McMahon, *Grand Opportunity: The Gaelic Revival and Irish Society, 1893–1910* (Syracuse, NY: Syracuse Univ. Press, 2008); Ríona Nic Congáil, *Úna Ní Fhaircheallaigh agus an Fhís Utóipeach Ghaelach* (Dublin: Arlen House, 2011); Brian Ó Conchubhair, *Fin de Siècle na Gaeilge: Darwin, an Athbheochan agus Smaointeoireacht na hEorpa* (Indreabhán: An Clóchomhar, 2009); Brian Ó Conchubhair, "The Apotheosis of the Vernacular: Language, Dialects and the Irish Revival," in *Irish Literature in Transition, 1880–1940*, vol 4, ed. Marjorie Howes (Cambridge: Cambridge Univ. Press, 2020), 21–38; Brian Ó Conchubhair, "The Irish Language Revival 1876–1922," *Oxford History of Ireland,* Vol. 4., ed. Thomas Bartlett (Oxford: Oxford Univ. Press, 2018), 198–222; Brian Ó Conchubhair, "Capturing the Trenches of Language: World War One, the Irish Language and the Gaelic League," *Modernist Cultures* 13, no. 3 (2018): 382–98.

7. The intent here is not to propose a radical rereading of the Revival, but to examine the complexity and nuances involved in the Gaelic League's origins and how the existence of a largely unstudied rival organization molded and shaped the Gaelic League and by extension, a central part of the wider Irish Revival. While recent scholarship has detailed the relationship between the Gaelic League and other organizations (the GAA, the Co-Operative Society, the Abbey Theatre), the Celtic Literary Society remains largely forgotten and unexamined.

8. T. P. O'Neill, *Irish Press*, Sept. 6, 1967, 8.

9. Nelson Ó Ceallaigh Ritschel, "William Rooney," *History Ireland* 15, no. 2 (Mar/Apr. 2007): 8.

10. Frank Shovlin, "Who Was Father Conroy?: James Joyce, William Rooney, and 'The Priest of Adergool,'" *James Joyce Quarterly* 47, no. 2 (Winter 2010): 257.

11. Connolly suggests Sept. 29, 1873, while Bradley suggests Oct. 20, 1873.

12. See Matthew Kelly, http://www.generalmichaelcollins.com/life-times/1905 -founding-sinn-fein/william-rooney-sinn-fein/.

13. While several sources list Mabbot Street, Ó Conaire states that Rooney's birthplace was 23 Leinster Avenue, North Strand.

14. Tomas S. Cuff, "The 40th Anniversary of the Death of William Rooney Occurs in This Month," *Irish Press*, May 17, 1941, 2.

15. David Connolly, "'The Real Founder of Sinn Féin': William Rooney (Liam Ó Maolruanaidh), 1873–1901," Jun. 1, 2017, http://www.anphoblacht.com/contents /26896. Pádraic Óg Ó Conaire, in *Liam Ó Maolruanaidh 1897–1901* (Dublin: Clódhanna Teo., 1975, reprinted from the *Capuchin Annual*), suggest the family originated in Mayo, hence Rooney's attraction for the country and frequent trips there.

16. Participated in the 1916 Rising in St. Stephen's Green. See Ó Conaire, *Liam Ó Maolruanaidh*, 7.

17. Also participated in the 1916 Rising in Finglas. See Ó Conaire, *Liam Ó Maolruanaidh*, 7.

18. Patrick Bradley, "William Rooney—A Sketch of His Career," *Poems and Ballads: William Rooney* (Dublin: *The United Irishman*, 17 Fownes Street, n.d.).

19. Bradley, "William Rooney—A Sketch," xiv.

20. Connolly, "'The Real Founder of Sinn Féin.'"

21. Ó Conaire, *Liam Ó Maolruanaidh*, 4.

22. Ó Conaire, *Liam Ó Maolruanaidh*, 3.

23. Ó Conaire, *Liam Ó Maolruanaidh*, 9. Rooney apparently worked at Wallis's carriers for the post office. See J. J. O'Kelly ("Sceilig"), Bureau of Military History, Witness Statement 384, 4–5.

24. Nollaig Mac Congáil, "*Weekly Freeman* agus Irish Fireside Club ag Cothú an Náisiúnachais agus an Ghaelachais. Bealach na hÓige?" *Seanchas Ardmhacha: Journal of the Armagh Diocesan Historical Society*, 21, no. 2, and 22, no. 1, (2007/2008): 278–318.

25. Ríona Nic Congáil, "'Fiction, Amusement, Instruction': The Irish Fireside Club and the Educational Ideology of the Gaelic League," *Éire-Ireland* 44, no. 1 and 2 (2009): 91–117.

26. Nic Congáil, "'Fiction, Amusement, Instruction,'" 91–117.

27. Ó Conaire, *Liam Ó Maolruanaidh*, 5.

28. Nic Congáil, "'Fiction, Amusement, Instruction,'" 104. See also Ríona Nic Congáil, *An Óige agus an Athbheochan* (Dublin: Cló Léann na Gaeilge, 2022), 15.

29. Bradley, "William Rooney—A Sketch," xvi.

30. Bradley, "William Rooney—A Sketch," xvii. The style here is typical of Bradley's tone when lauding his wife's former intended.

31. Bradley, "William Rooney—A Sketch," xviii

32. Bradley, "William Rooney—A Sketch," xviii–xix.

33. Bradley, "William Rooney—A Sketch," xxiii.

34. Bradley, "William Rooney—A Sketch," xxiv. See also John Turpin, "1798, 1898 and the Political Implications of Sheppard's Monuments." *History Ireland* 6, no. 2 (1998): 44–48; www.jstor.org/stable/27724561.

35. See Senia Pašeta, "1798 in 1898: The Politics of Commemoration," *Irish Review* 22 (Summer 1998): 46–53.

36. Established in Belfast in January 1896 by Alice Milligan ("Iris Olkyrn") and Anna Johnson ("Ethna Carberry").

37. Ó Conaire, *Liam Ó Maolruanaidh*, 6. See Owen McGee, *Arthur Griffith* (Dublin: Merrion Press, 2015), 40; see also Seán Ó Luing, *Art Ó Gríofa* (Dublin: Sáirséal agus Dill, 1953), 53–55. Rooney is often named as the *United Irishman*'s joint editor.

38. Andrew Murphy, *Ireland, Reading and Cultural Nationalism, 1790– 1930: Bringing the Nation to Book* (Cambridge: Cambridge Univ. Press, 2018).

39. As a railway employee, he traveled for free on weekends.

40. Bradley claims that two regional newspapers offered him positions as editor but he refused. Bradley, "William Rooney—A Sketch," xxxiii.

41. "Deirtear go raibh lámh agus focal idir í féin agus Liam Ó Maolruanaidh a d'éag ar 6 Bealtaine 1901. Is inspéise gur tugadh Craobh Fhear na Muintire ar chraobh den Chonradh i gConga (*An Claidheamh Soluis*, 2 Bealtaine 1903)— bhí 'Fear na Muintire' ar cheann d'ainmneacha cleite Uí Mhaolruanaidh. Bhí sí ina ball den Choiste Gnó i 1902 agus 1904 nuair nach raibh ach beirt bhan eile ina mbaill: Úna Ní Fhaircheallaigh agus Máire Ní Aodáin. Tuairiscíodh (idem 30 Aibreán 1904) go raibh sí ag moltóireacht ag Feis Shligigh. Bhí éirithe as an gCoiste Gnó aici toisc, b'fhéidir, go raibh sí imithe abhaile go Conga. Phós sí Pádraig Ó Brolcháin, duine de chairde móra Uí Mhaolruanaidh, ann 30 Meitheamh 1904. Art Ó Gríofa a sheas le Pádraig. Bhí seachtar mac acu agus is le Gaeilge a thóg siad iad." https://www.ainm.ie/Bio.aspx?ID=699.

42. Ó Conaire, *Liam Ó Maolruanaidh*, 12.

43. Letter to Lady Gregory May 21, 1901, in *Lady Gregory Collected Letters*, vol. 3, ed. John Kelly and Ronald Schuchard (Oxford: Oxford Univ. Press, 1994), 72.

44. Carleton Younger, *Arthur Griffith* (Dublin: Gill and Macmillan, 1981), 21.

45. Ó Conaire, *Liam Ó Maolruanaidh*, 13.

46. *Southern Star*, May 11, 1901, 5; *Freeman's Journal*, Sept. 18, 1901. In a similar vein, the *Freeman's Journal* grieved that "the death of William Rooney in the dawn of his manhood deprived the society of its bravest labourer. While his hand held the helm we knew all was safe, but now that we are to know him no more, that we are never to hear his voice again urging us to be confident of the

future, it behooves us all to persevere more determinedly in the work to which he devoted his life is to be carried to fruition." See Colum Kenny, "An Introduction to the Use of Pen Names in Griffith's Publications," *Remembering Arthur Griffith: Cut and Paste 2020* (Dublin: Printwell, Design Ltd.) 5–6.

47. See James Joyce, *Occasional, Critical, and Political Writing*, ed. with an Introduction and Notes by Kevin Barry (Oxford: Oxford Univ. Press, 2000).

48. Ó Luing, *Art Ó Gríofa*, 98.

49. "Our first encounter with Father Conroy in Joyce's writing comes in the early pages of 'The Dead' where, as Gabriel Conroy's brother, he is mentioned in order to illustrate their mother's upwardly mobile and snobbish nature." Shovlin, "Who Was Father Conroy," 257.

50. Ó Conaire states that he was heavily involved in the production of *Eblana*, the Leinster Literary Society's magazine. See *Liam Ó Maolruanaidh*, 9.

51. For details of the Leinster Literary Society's final meeting, see McGee, *Arthur Griffith*, 18. M. Seery and J. Boland, two IRB leaders, managed this premises. See McGee, *Arthur Griffith*, 396n31.

52. Joseph Edmundson Masterson, writing in the *Irish Press* (Sept. 7, 1935, 8) argues that the Society initially met at his residence, 15 Sinnott Place, until another premises was procured.

53. Ó Luing, *Art Ó Gríofa*, 31.

54. Seamus MacManus, Bureau of Military History, Witness Statement S0283, 173.

55. *Western People*, July 10, 1971, 18.

56. *Freeman's Journal*, Sept. 25, 1893, 6. Also present at the meeting were John O'Leary, Joseph T. Doyle, James Murphy, John H. M. Derby, T. Thompson, James Ryan, John Clogg, John Doran, Wm Valentine, T. Wilson, T. P. Fox, John Nolan, Kevin O'Toole, Thomas Tallon, P. O'Nally, J. A. Meyrick, and John A. Whelan.

57. *Flag of Ireland*, Oct. 14, 1893, 7. Suppressed on more than one occasion, this publication appeared as *Insuppressible, Suppressed United Ireland*, and later as *United Ireland*.

58. *Freeman's Journal*, Sept. 25, 1893, 6. Vice president Joseph T. Doyle; treasurer, Mr. William Fanning; secretary, Mr. John E. Whelan; librarian, Mr. John Clogg; and Messers Murphy, Graham, Ryan, and Doran as committee.

59. *Freeman's Journal*, Sept. 25, 1893. McGee contends, "The disgruntled Griffith and his cousin Edward Whelan would not join Rooney's Celtic for some time, however. Instead, they took the opportunity to become members of the executive of the Young Ireland League (YIL), which was a far more influential body that campaigned for changes in the Irish educational system." See McGee, *Arthur Griffith*, 18.

60. Maye, *Arthur Griffith*, 15.

61. *Freeman's Journal*, Oct. 4, 1893, 5.

62. *The Revival of Irish Literature: Addresses by Sir Charles Gavan Duffy, K. C. M. G., Dr. George Sigerson, and Dr. Douglas Hyde* (London: T. Fisher Unwin, MDCCCXCIV).

63. " . . . the first Irish national society which accepted women as members on the same terms as men . . . From the beginning, women sat on its Branch Committees and Executive." See Jennie Wyse Power in *The Voice of Ireland*, ed. W. G. Fitzgerald (Dublin: Virtue, 1924), 158.

64. Brian Ó Conchubhair, "Capturing the Trenches of Language: World War One, the Irish Language and the Gaelic League," *Modernist Cultures* 13, no. 3, 382–98.

65. *Freeman's Journal*, Dec. 27, 1895; 5.

66. *Scientific and Learned Societies of Great Britain: A Handbook Compiled from Official Sources* (London: Allen and Unwin, 1901).

67. *Societies of Great Britain Handbook*.

68. *Freeman's Journal*, Sept. 12, 1900. The choir leader was a man named Lawless according to Henry C. Phibbs. See Bureau of Military History, Witness Statement 0848, 3–4.

69. *Freeman's Journal*, Sept. 12, 1900.

70. *Freeman's Journal*, Sept. 12, 1900.

71. Bradley, "William Rooney—A Sketch," xxv. Nonetheless, the impact of politics on the Leinster Literary Society was not forgotten. The Celtic Literary Society, according to McGee, "wisely resolved not to allow contemporary party politics to be discussed at its meetings." See McGee, *Arthur Griffith*, 18.

72. See Kelly, http://www.generalmichaelcollins.com/life-times/1905-founding -sinn-fein/william-rooney-sinn-fein/.

73. *Freeman's Journal*, May 26, 1896, 4.

74. Ó Conaire, *Liam Ó Maolruanaidh*, 9.

75. McGee, *Arthur Griffith*, 63.

76. Kelly, "Rooney Spoke in Irish."

77. Kelly, "Rooney Spoke in Irish."

78. Bradley, "William Rooney—A Sketch," xxvi.

79. See the *Monthly Review* 17 (1904): 128.

80. The *Nation*, Mar. 13, 1897, 13.

81. *Freeman's Journal*, Nov. 13, 1893, 6, and *Freeman's Journal*, Nov. 7, 1893, 2.

82. *Freeman's Journal*, Nov. 13, 1893, 6.

83. Maud Gonne MacBride, *The Autobiography of Maud Gonne: A Servant of the Queen*, eds. A. Norman Jeffares and Anna MacBride White (1938. Reprint,

Chicago: Univ. of Chicago Press, 1995), 94. For more on women in Cumann na nGaedheal, see J. MacPherson, *Women and the Irish Nation: Gender, Culture and Irish Identity, 1890–1914* (New York: Springer, 2012). She had attempted to join the Celtic Literary Society who "produced a Manuscript Journal *An Seanachie* which I found very interesting. I was so delighted with the Club and its activities that I told the secretary I wanted to become a member. He looked embarrassed. Willie Rooney was called to explain, as politely as he could, that the rules of the Club excluded women from membership."

84. *Freeman's Journal*, Nov. 13, 1893, 6.

85. *Freeman's Journal*, Dec. 13, 1893, 6.

86. *Freeman's Journal*, Apr. 4, 1894, 7.

87. *Freeman's Journal*, Jan. 28, 1896, 3.

88. M. J. Kelly, *The Fenian Ideal and Irish Nationalism, 1882–1916* (Woodbridge, Suffock: The Boydell Press, 2006), 10.

89. Patrick Nally (1868–1911) lived with his parents at 56 Eccles Street, Dublin. A founding member of Cumann na bPíobairí in February 1900, he published *An Modh Réidh, leis an nGaedhilge do mhúnadh* (An Cló-Chumann, 1904), 71 pages, the first textbook to use the direct method in Irish. He edited *An Gadaí Dubh Ó Dubháin*, which tale he sourced from Máire Ní Chillín. Micheál Ó Maoláin claimed Nally was the first person to teach Irish in Dublin as a living language. Nally was a cousin of Patrick William Nally (1857–91), a member of the Supreme Council of the Irish Republican Brotherhood, who was imprisoned in 1881 and died in prison in 1891. See Pádraig Ó Baoighill, *Nally as Maigh Eo* (Dublin: Coiscéim, 1998), 347–52. See also Ó Luing, *Art Ó Gríofa*, 32. Regarding *An Modh Réidh*, the preface explained its aim as follows: "Seo leabhar ar shlighe nua chun na Gaedhilge a mhúineadh. Tá ana-chuid suime á chur i múinteóireacht an Gaedhilge le déidheannaighe; táthar ag aighneas is ag díospóireacht go héachtach i dtaobh na ceiste seo. Ní héan droch-chomhartha é sin mar taispeánann go bhfuilimíd dáríribh chun na Gaedhilge a leathadh ar fuid na tíre go léir agus gur mhaith linn fios d'fhagháil ar ar gcuma b'fhearr chuige. Ná síltar go mbeidh éin cheann díobh ag déanamh cumhangthais ar an gceann eile. Beidh slighe a ndóthain dóibh go léir ann. Leabhairín ana-thairbheach is eadh an leabhairín seo an Mhodh Réidh. Ní labhartar éin-nídh ó thosach bárra leis na scoláirí acht Gaedhilg. Ní bhíd i bhfad ag foghluim ar an gcuma so nuair bhíonn a gcluasa oilte go leór ar fhuaim na teangan, agus as cuma dhóibhcad do bhuailfidh umpa as soin amach. Do réir deallraimh, is deacair rudaí simplidhe a sholáthar chun tosnughadh ar theangaidh ar an gcuma so. Bheidh cuid de na habairtibh go crapathe agus go haindeis i n-indeóin díchill duine. Tá rudaí crapaithe san leabhairín seo; acht ní fhágann soin é gan bheith n-a áise mhaith chun na Gaedhilge a mhúineadh acht é chur i láimh dhuine go bhfuil a fhios aige cad do bhaineann

316 Notes to Pages 27–30

le múinteóireacht. Is iad muinntir An Cló-Chumainn a chuir i gcló é, agus go deimhin ní holc a chuireadar chuige."

90. Ó Conaire, *Liam Ó Maolruanaidh*, 9. He also claims that Nally wrote a textbook similar to O'Growney's text, but this may be a reference to the folktale the Celtic Literary Society published. When Nally was ill, the antisemitic "Sceilig" (J. J. O'Kelly; future president of the Gaelic League, 1919–23; Minister of Education, 1921–22; Minister of Irish, 1920–21 in the Free State) taught the class. See Bureau of Military History, Witness Statement 384, 6.

91. *Freeman's Journal*, Nov. 5, 1894, 4.

92. "Irish Language Congress Committee," *Freeman's Journal*, Feb. 16, 1894, 4. See also *Report of the Proceedings of the Congress Held in Dublin on the 15, 16 and 17th of August, 1882 by the Society for the Preservation of the Irish Language, to consider the present position of the Irish Language as a Vernacular, and how its use might be prompted.*

93. See Ó Luing, *Art Ó Gríofa*, 30–32.

94. See Kelly, *The Fenian Ideal*, 103.

95. *Freeman's Journal*, Mar. 28, 1894, 2.

96. *Freeman's Journal*, Mar. 28, 1894, 2.

97. *Freeman's Journal*, June 11, 1894, 4.

98. *Freeman's Journal*, Nov. 21, 1894, 8.

99. *Freeman's Journal*, Dec. 22, 1894, 4.

100. *Freeman's Journal*, Nov. 11, 1895, 7.

101. *Freeman's Journal*, Sept. 18, 1901. Now the site of the Gate Hotel.

102. The text featured as a prescribed examination text for Scholarship Examination in 1907 as described in the *Annual General Report of the Department*, vol. 6, parts 1905–6.

103. See Ó Luing, *Art Ó Gríofa*, 33.

104. Among the founding members of the Cork Celtic Literary Society were Terence MacSwiney, Tomás MacCurtain, Seán O'Hegarty, and Daniel Corkery. See http://www.corkarchives.ie/media/U271web.pdf. The *Irish Independent* refers to David O'Conor as a member of the Cork Celtic Literary Society, who later in 1906 founded Sinn Féin in Cork. "Under the late Arthur Griffith, he was Foreign Editor of the *Sinn Fein Daily*, in 1909. Later he returned to Germany as Managing Editor of the *German Export Review*, and while there, he contributed many informative industrial articles to the Irish newspapers. On the outbreak of the War he went to America and was appointed national organiser of the Friends of Freedom for the United States during the visit of President de Valera to that country. Returning to Ireland in 1922 he was arrested and kept for six months in Cork prison. On his release he went again to Germany, where he received an important post in the

German Foreign Office." He returned to Ireland shortly before his death in 1934. See the *Irish Independent*, May 8, 1934, 9. For Fr. Kavanagh's role in the Cork Celtic Literary Society, see McGee, *Arthur Griffith*, 48–49.

105. *Freeman's Journal*, Sept. 12, 1900.

106. Major John MacBride (1868–1916) was a CLS member. In 1900, when Michael Davitt resigned his Mayo seat in the British House of Commons in protest at the Boer War, Arthur Griffith nominated John MacBride as a by-election candidate. The play, published in 1908 by Sealy, Bryers, and Waker (Middle Abbey Street, Dublin), notes the National Players' Society in Dublin staged the play in Samhain (November) 1907 as well as the Catholic Young Men's Society, Dundalk, in February 1908 and the Celtic Literary Society, Castlebar, in February 1908.

107. *Freeman's Journal*, Sept. 12, 1900.

108. *Freeman's Journal*, Sept. 12, 1900.

109. *Freeman's Journal*, Sept. 12, 1900, 22–23.

110. Younger, *Arthur Griffith*, 20.

111. Younger, *Arthur Griffith*, 20.

112. *Freeman's Journal*, Sept. 18, 1901.

113. Bureau of Military History 1913–21. Witness Liam de Roiste No. 2 Janemount, Sunday's Well, Cork. Identity. Member, Coiste Gnotha, Gaelic League. Member, Dáil Éireann, 1918–23. File No Form BSM2. Part 1, page 4, Military Archives, Ireland.

114. *Freeman's Journal*, Sept. 18, 1901.

115. *Irish Examiner*, Apr. 23, 1902; 6. Described as "Irisleabhar míosamhail chun cabharughadh leis an ndream athá a d'iaraidh Éire dhéanamh Gaedhealach."

116. *Southern Star*, July 4, 1903, 7.

117. *Freeman's Journal*, Oct. 24, 1904.

118. Griffith published "The Resurrection of Hungary: A Parallel for Ireland" in the *United Irishman* in 1904. See Cormac O'Hanrahan, "1917 Sinn Féin Convention (Day 1)," in *Remembering Arthur Griffith: Cut and Paste* (Dublin: Printwell, Design Ltd., 2020), 11–18.

119. See O'Hanrahan, "1917 Sinn Féin Convention," 11–18.

120. Ricoeur, "Life: A Story."

121. MacPherson, *Women and the Irish Nation*, 127–29. Working-class women appear conspicuously absent from both organizations.

122. Phibbs, Witness Statement 0848, 4–5.

123. Richard J. Finneran and George Mills Harper, eds., *The Collected Works of W. B. Yeats*, vol. II: *The Plays* (Simon and Schuster, 2010), 834.

124. See Timothy G. McMahon, "Douglas Hyde and the Politics of the Gaelic League in 1914," *Éire-Ireland* 53, no. 1 (2018): 29–47.

125. A. W. Frank, *The Wounded Storyteller: Body, Illness, and Ethics* (Chicago: Univ. of Chicago Press, 1985), 98.

126. Murphy, *Ireland, Reading and Cultural Nationalism*, 123–39.

2. Revival, Remediation, and the Irish Media Habitus

1. Sir Charles Gavan Duffy, "The Revival of Irish Literature," in *The Revival of Irish Literature: Addresses by Sir Charles Gavan Duffy, K. C. M. G., Dr. George Sigerson, and Dr. Douglas Hyde* (London: Fisher Unwin, 1894), 59. Subsequent references to this edition will be made in the notes as *Revival of Irish Literature*.

2. See, for example, P. J. Mathews, *Revival: The Abbey Theatre, Sinn Féin, the Gaelic League and the Co-operative Movement* (Cork: Cork Univ. Press, 2003); Karen Steele, *Women, Press and Politics* during the Irish Literary Revival (Syracuse, NY: Syracuse Univ. Press, 2007); and Catherine Morris, *Alice Milligan and the Irish Cultural Revival* (Dublin: Four Courts, 2012).

3. Pierre Bourdieu, *In Other Words: Essays towards a Reflexive Sociology*, trans. Matthew Adamson (Stanford: Stanford Univ. Press, 1990), 12.

4. Pierre Bourdieu, *The Logic of Practice*, trans. Richard Nice (Stanford: Stanford Univ. Press, 1990). 53.

5. Bourdieu, *Logic of Practice*, 57.

6. Pierre Bourdieu, *The Rules of Art: Genesis and Structure in the Literary Field*, trans. Susan Emanuel (Cambridge: Polity Press, 1996), 51; my emph. Bourdieu relates that "writers and artists" in the late nineteenth century "know that an article in *La Presse* or *La Figaro* creates a reputation and opens a future" (53).

7. See Pierre Bourdieu, "The Forms of Capital," in *Handbook of Theory and Research for the Sociology of Education*, ed. John G. Richardson (New York: Greenwood Press, 1986), 241–58. "Because the social conditions of its transmission and acquisition are more disguised than those of economic capital, [cultural capital] is predisposed to function as symbolic capital, i.e., to be unrecognized as capital and recognized as legitimate competence, as authority exerting an effect of (mis)recognition" (245).

8. Remediate, backformation from remediation, from Fr. *remediare*, remedy; *remedial*, curing, relieving; from L. *remediatis*, healing, curing; from L. *remedium*, remedy. Etymonline—Online Etymology Dictionary, https://www.etymonline.com/.

9. On the concept of the media habitus in journalism, see Glen Whelan, "Appropriat(e)ing Wavelength: On Bourdieu's *On Television*," *ephemera* 2, no. 2 (2002): 131–48. For a more recent application of the idea, see Zizi Papacharissi

and Emily Easton's concept of the social media habitus: "a set of dispositions that emerge out of the social architecture of social media and *frame but also constantly invite the remediation of agency*"; "In the Habitus of the New: Structure, Agency, and the Social Media Habitus," in *A Companion to New Media Dynamics*, eds. John Hartley, Jean Burgess, and Axel Bruns (Malden, MA: Wiley-Blackwell, 2013), 172; my emph.

10. Ronan McDonald, "Internal Others: Cultural Debate and Counter-Revival," in *A History of Irish Modernism*, eds. Gregory Castle and Patrick Bixby (Cambridge: Cambridge Univ. Press, 2019), 96.

11. D. P. Moran, *The Philosophy of Irish Ireland*, 2nd ed. (Dublin: James Duffy and Co., 1905), 77. Subsequent references to this edition will be cited in the notes as *PII*.

12. For further discussion of the concept of classical Bildung, see Gregory Castle, *Reading the Modernist Bildungsroman* (Gainesville: Univ. Press of Florida, 2006), especially the introduction and chapter 1.

13. Wilhelm von Humboldt, *The Limits of State Action*, ed. J. W. Barrow (1850. Reprint, Cambridge: Cambridge Univ. Press, 1969), 16; Moran, *PII*, 70; Patrick Pearse, "From the Prospectus of Scoil Éanna," in *A Significant Irish Educationalist: The Educational Writings of P. H. Pearse*, ed. Séamas Ó Buachalla (Dublin: Mercier Press, 1980), 317. Subsequent references to Ó Buachalla's text will be cited in the notes as *SIE*.

14. Slavoj Žižek, in *The Sublime Object of Ideology* (London: Verso, 1989), writes that "dialectics is for Hegel a systematic notation of the failure" of all attempts at "progressive overcoming" (6).

15. Frantz Fanon, *The Wretched of the Earth*, trans. Richard Philcox (New York: Grove Press, 2004), 200.

16. Anjali Prabhu, "Eros in Infinity and Totality: A Reading of Levinas and Fanon," *Levinas Studies* 7 (2012): 140, 132.

17. Prabhu, "Eros in Infinity and Totality," 142; my emph.

18. James Joyce, *Ulysses* (1934. Reset and corrected 1961. Reprint, New York: Vintage-Random, 1990), 331.

19. Moran, *PII*, 37.

20. On the "non-modern," see Lloyd, *Ireland after History* (Notre Dame: Univ. of Notre Dame Press, 1999), chap. 2, "Nationalisms against the State"; on the "ghostly," see Cheah, *Spectral Nationality: Passages of Freedom from Kant to Postcolonial Literatures of Liberation* (New York: Columbia Univ. Press, 2003), 200–208, 246–47.

21. Cheah, Spectral Nationality, 137.

22. Cheah, *Spectral Nationality*, 246; see also 129ff.

23. Slavoj Žižek, *Tarrying with the Negative: Kant, Hegel, and the Critique of Ideology* (Durham: Duke Univ. Press, 1993), 237, 202.

24. On the failure of personal Bildung in colonial and postcolonial locations, see Jed Esty, *Unseasonable Youth: Modernism, Colonialism and the Fiction of Development* (Oxford: Oxford Univ. Press, 2012).

25. Albert Memmi, in *The Colonizer and the Colonized*, trans. Howard Greenfeld, expanded edition (Boston: Beacon Press, 1991), notes that "[t]he most serious blow suffered by the colonized is being removed from history and from the community" (91).

26. On this feminist front in the press, see Steele, *Women, Press and Politics*.

27. Moran, *PII*, 85, 93. See also 97.

28. Nancy J. Curtin, "'A Nation of Abortive Men': Gendered Citizenship and Early Irish Republicanism," in *Reclaiming Gender*, ed. Marilyn Cohen and Nancy J. Curtin (New York: St. Martin's Press, 1999) 35, 37. For an in-depth discussion of manliness and manhood in the Revival era, see Joseph Valente, *The Myth of Manliness in Irish National Culture, 1880–1922* (Urbana: Univ. of Illinois Press, 2011).

29. Bourdieu, *Logic of Practice*, 54.

30. Bourdieu, *Logic of Practice*, 53–54; see also 69.

31. Slobodanka Vladiv-Glover and Gerald Frederic, "Pierre Bourdieu's *Habitus*: A Critique in the Context of C. S. Peirce's Belief as Habit," in *Practising Theory: Pierre Bourdieu and the Field of Cultural Production*, eds. Jeff Browitt and Brian Nelson (Newark: Univ. of Delaware Press, 2004), 32.

32. Bourdieu, *Logic of Practice*, 53.

33. Vladiv-Glover and Frederic, "Pierre Bourdieu's *Habitus*," 32–33.

34. Michel de Certeau, *The Practice of Everyday Life*, trans. Steven Rendall (Berkeley: Univ. of California Press, 1984), 39, 36. On Bourdieu's influence on de Certeau, see Jeremy Ahearne, *Michel de Certeau: Interpretation and Its Other* (Cambridge: Polity Press, 1995), part III, "Strategies and Tactics."

35. Ahearne, *Michel de Certeau*, 39.

36. de Certeau, Practice of Everyday Life, 117.

37. Cheryl Herr, *Joyce's Anatomy of Culture* (Urbana: Univ. of Illinois Press, 1986), 75.

38. Steele, in *Women, Press, and Politics*, distinguishes between "the two dominant national dailies, the *Freeman's Journal* and the *Irish Independent*, both of which advocated a constitutional nationalist policy of achieving Home Rule through the British Parliament," and "advanced nationalist journals [that] focused on transforming Ireland through cultural and revolutionary means instead" (2). She associates the latter with the Irish-Ireland movement.

39. Mark Hampton, *Visions of the Press in Britain, 1850–1950* (Urbana: Univ. of Illinois Press, 2004), 108.

40. Steele, *Women, Press, and Politics*, 86. Steele quotes from Gonne's "Irish Press," published in *United Irishman*, Feb. 7, 1903. See also Gonne's "The National Education of Children," *United Irishman*, Aug. 23, 1902.

41. Cheah, *Spectral Nationality*, 362.

42. Cheah, *Spectral Nationality*, 11.

43. On the institutions of Revival, see Clare Hutton, "Joyce and the Institutions of Revivalism," *Irish University Review* 33, no. 1 (Spring–Summer 2003): 117–32.

44. Christopher Morash, *A History of the Media in Ireland* (Cambridge: Cambridge Univ. Press, 2010), 3.

45. Benedict Anderson, Imagined Communities: Reflections on the Origin and Spread of Nationalism (London: Verso, 1991).

46. On social drama, see Victor Turner, *From Ritual to Theatre: The Human Seriousness of Play* (New York City: Performing Arts Journal Publications, 1982), 61–87.

47. On the regional and religious distinctions among the interlocutors in "Scylla and Charybdis," see Hutton, "Joyce and Institutions of Revivalism"; on Shakespeare, see Patrick McGee, *Paperspace: Style as Ideology in Joyce's* Ulysses (Lincoln: Univ. of Nebraska Press, 1988), 37–68.

48. See Tom Standage, *The Victorian Internet: The Remarkable Story of the Telegraph and the Nineteenth Century's On-Line Pioneers* (New York: Berkley Books, 1998).

49. Mathews, *Revival*, 2.

50. Space limitations alone prevent me from considering writers like Stephen Gwynn, Arthur Clery, and Arthur Griffith.

51. Moran, Preface to the second edition, *PII*.

52. Moran, *PII*, 2.

53. Moran, *PII*, 2.

54. Moran, *PII*, 66.

55. Moran, *PII*, 70. As Michael Valdez Moses writes, Moran's text is "a democratic experiment-in-living in which many idiosyncratic versions of Irishness compete in the marketplace of ideas." Moses, "Irish Modernist Imaginaries," in *The Cambridge Companion to Irish Modernism*, ed. Joe Cleary (Cambridge: Cambridge Univ. Press, 2014), 193–220.

56. Moran, *PII*, 19.

57. Moran, *PII*, 37.

58. Douglas Hyde, "The Necessity for De-Anglicising Ireland," in *Revival of Irish Literature*, 127–28.

59. Patrick Pearse, *Three Lectures on Gaelic Topics* (Dublin: M. H. Gill, 1898).

60. Pearse, *Three Lectures*, 5.

61. Lacan, in "The Instance of the Letter in the Unconscious," introduces his written text by "situating it between writing and speech—it will be halfway between the two." He adds that it will require a "tightening up" that will "leave the reader no other way out than the way in, which I prefer to be difficult." See *Écrits: A Selection*, trans. Bruce Fink (New York: Norton, 2002), 138.

62. Pearse, *Three Lectures*, 33.

63. Pearse, *Three Lectures*, 51.

64. Pearse, *Three Lectures*, 5–6.

65. Pearse, *Three Lectures*, 29.

66. Pearse, *Three Lectures*, 12.

67. Pearse, *Three Lectures*, 57.

68. Pearse, *Three Lectures*, 31.

69. Pearse, *Three Lectures*, 38–39.

70. Pearse, *Three Lectures*, 39, 45.

71. Pearse, *Three Lectures*, 50–51. Pearse's appeal for a "pure, good, healthy, natural literature" finds a telling resonance in Max Nordau's *Degeneration* (New York: D. Appleton, 1895), a work contemporaneous with Moran's lectures that condemned Nietzschean nihilism as well as Wildean aestheticism.

72. Pearse, *Three Lectures*, 52, 54.

73. Pearse, *Three Lectures*, 55.

74. Pearse, *Three Lectures*, 58; my emph.

75. See Moran, *PII*, 37ff. "The '98 and '48 movements, the Fenians and Parnellite agitation, were Pale movements in their essence, even when they were most fiercely rebellious" (38).

76. Pearse, *Three Lectures*, 57–58.

77. Pearse, "The Murder Machine," in *SIE*, 372.

78. Pearse, "The Murder Machine," in *SIE*, 378. Pearse, "Education under Home Rule," in *SIE*, 355.

79. Pearse, "The Murder Machine," in *SIE*, 377. On fostering, see Pearse, "Irish Education," in *SIE*, 359.

80. Pearse, "Education under Home Rule," in *SIE*, 354. Pearse speaks of "two characteristics" of ancient Irish education: "first, freedom for the individual; and, secondly, an adequate inspiration. Without these two things you cannot have education, no matter how you may elaborate educational machinery, no matter how you may multiply educational programmes." Pearse, "Irish Education," 363.

81. Pearse, "From the Prospectus of Scoil Éanna," in *SIE*, 317; cf. Humboldt's plan for Prussian children: "every type of mind would find its appropriate place, and no decision on a vocation would have to be taken until, in his general development, the individual was ready for it" (quoted in Paul R. Sweet, *Wilhelm von*

Humboldt: A Biography, vol. 2: 1808–1835 (Columbus: Ohio State Univ. Press, 1980), 42.

82. Pearse, "Education under Home Rule," in *SIE*, 354. On Pearse's interest in Montessori, see "Irish Education," in *SIE*, 362–63. Pearse wrote extensively on Belgium and bilingual education; see *SIE* 24–34, 254–310.

83. Synge's *Playboy*, understood as social drama, is a stellar example of this opening up; see my *Modernism and the Celtic Revival* (Cambridge: Cambridge Univ. Press, 2001), chapter 2.

84. Pearse, *Three Lectures*, 55.

85. Duffy, "Revival," 20–21.

86. Duffy, "Revival," 13, 16.

87. Duffy, "Revival," 47.

88. As reported in *United Ireland*, Aug. 13, 1892. Cited in *The Collected Letters of W. B. Yeats*, vol. 1: 1865–1895, eds. John Kelly and Eric Domville (Oxford: Clarendon Press, 1986), 312n7.

89. Duffy, "Revival," 20–21.

90. Duffy already had considerable experience. In the late 1840s and early 1850s, while editor of the *Nation*, he ran the Library of Ireland book series which published, among other things, Duffy's *The Ballad Poetry of Ireland* (1845); see Charles Gavan Duffy, *My Life in Two Hemispheres*, vol. 1 (1898. Reprint, Shannon: Irish Univ. Press, 1969), 129–36, 169–70.

91. Yeats, *Letters*, 313n3. Others were less sanguine. Edward Garnett, editor and reader at T. Fisher Unwin, asked Yeats to work with T. W. Rolleston to limit Duffy's actual influence: "Dont [sic] let loose the dogs of war against a Duffy Dictatorship when it could be turned into a Duffy Figureheadship" (Yeats, *Letters*, 350n).

92. W. B. Yeats, *Uncollected Prose,* vol. 1: 1886–1896, ed. John P. Frayne (New York: Columbia Univ. Press, 1970), 241–42.

93. Yeats, *Uncollected Prose*, 208.

94. Yeats, *Uncollected Prose*, 223

95. Yeats, *Letters*, 312n7.

96. Yeats, *Letters*, 349, editor's note.

97. Yeats, *Letters*, 398. A decade later, Yeats writes of having contended with Duffy "over what seemed to me a too narrow definition of Irish interests." See "*Samhain*: 1904—First Principles," in *The Irish Dramatic Movement*, vol. 8, *The Collected Works of W. B. Yeats*, eds. Mary FitzGerald and Richard J. Finneran (New York: Scribner, 2003), 63.

98. John Eglinton, W. B. Yeats, A. E. [George Russell], and William Larminie, *Literary Ideals in Ireland* (London: T. F. Unwin, 1899).

99. Eglinton et al., *Literary Ideals*, unsigned editors' note.

100. Don Gifford and Robert J. Seidman note of the *Daily Express* that "its announced policy involved 'the development of industrial enterprises' and a reconciliation of 'rights and impulses of Irish nationality with the demands and obligations of imperial dominions.'" See Don Gifford and Robert J. Seidman, Ulysses *Annotated*, 2nd ed (Berkeley: Univ. of California Press, 1989), 134. Declan Kiberd, in *Irish Classics* (London: Granta, 2000), notes that the "major debates of the literary revival were conducted in the pages of the *Daily Express* and *United Irishman*" (464).

101. The imprimatur of the pamphlet reads, "Published by T. Fisher Unwin, London And at the *Daily Express* Office Dublin." As for the latest trends, in 1905, Unwin published several books by Vernon Lee and one by H. B. Thompson called *Mental Traits of Sex: Experimental Investigation of Normal Mind in Men and Women.*

102. Joyce, *Ulysses*, 125; Joyce, "The Dead," in *Dubliners: Authoritative Text, Contexts, Criticism*, ed. Margot Norris (New York: Norton, 2006), 163.

103. Hutton, "Joyce and Institutions of Revivalism," 118.

104. Yeats, "A Note on National Drama," in Eglinton et al., *Literary Ideals*, 19.

105. Eglinton, "National Drama and Contemporary Life," in Eglinton et al., *Literary Ideals*, 24.

106. Eglinton, "Mr. Yeats and Popular Poetry," in Eglinton et al., *Literary Ideals*, 42; my emph.

107. Yeats's more considered view of the issues raised by Eglinton can be found in Yeats, "*Samhain*: 1904," 53ff.

108. In "Truth and Lies in a Nonmoral Sense," Nietzsche argues for a concept of truth grounded in metaphor, that is to say, a concept of truth as "good deception." Friedrich Nietzsche, "Truth and Lies in a Nonmoral Sense," in *Philosophy and Truth: Selections from Nietzsche's Notebooks of the Early 1870*, ed. and trans. Daniel Breazeale (Atlantic Highlands, NJ: Humanities Press, 1979), 90.

109. Lady Augusta Gregory, trans. and ed. *Cuchulain of Muirthemne: The Story of the Men of the Red Branch of Ulster* (London: John Murray, 1903).

110. In *Ulysses*, Joyce deflates some of the Literary Revival's highhandedness by invoking the distinction that Yeats and Gregory enjoy when he has Buck Mulligan upbraid Stephen Dedalus for not giving *Cuchulain at Muirthemne* a good review: "Couldn't you do the Yeats touch?" (216).

111. Valente, in *Myth of Manliness*, discusses the late nineteenth century resurgence of interest in Cuchulain, including Standish O'Grady's *History of Ireland* and Eleanor Hull's *Cuchulain* (see 140–48). The "invention of Cuchulain" involved a kind of purposeful ambivalence, for "Cuchulain had to emerge not only as an individual man, against otherwise interchangeable warriors or tribesmen, but also as a manly individual, someone who channels the ferocity expected of the

elite warrior into a strenuous discipline and dutifullness, born of an allegience to an agonistic code of honor" (142).

112. Eglinton et al., "Editor's Note," *Literary Ideals*, 5.

113. James Joyce, *Letters*, vol. 2, ed. Richard Ellmann (New York: Viking Press, 1966). 134.

114. de Certeau, *Practice of Everyday Life*, 38.

115. Yeats in Eglinton et al., *Literary Ideals*, 18–19.

3. Yeats, Gregory, and the Revival's Print Cultures

1. Andrew Brooker and Peter Thacker, "General Introduction," in *The Oxford Critical and Cultural History of Modernist Magazines* (Oxford: Oxford Univ. Press, 2009), 5.

2. See, for some examples, Mark Morrison, *The Public Face of Modernism: Little Magazines, Audiences, and Reception 1905–1920* (Madison: Univ. of Wisconsin Press, 2001); Karen Steele, *Women, Press and Politics during the Irish Revival* (Syracuse, NY: Syracuse Univ. Press, 2007); George Bornstein, *Material Modernism: The Politics of the Page* (Cambridge: Cambridge Univ. Press, 2001).

3. Yug Mohit Chaudhry, *Yeats, the Irish Literary Revival and the Politics of Print* (Cork: Cork Univ. Press, 2001), 43.

4. Alan Grossman comments in passing that he thinks they "represent the anxiety for authenticity which haunted him throughout his life" and that their function is to place the poems in relation to "a more than temporary truth." Alan Grossman, *Poetic Knowledge in the Early Yeats: A Study of* The Wind among the Reeds (Charlottesville: Univ. Press of Virginia, 1969), 79, 80. See also Steven Putzel, *Reconstructing Yeats*: The Secret Rose *and* The Wind among the Reeds (Dublin: Gill and Macmillan, 1986).

5. One exception was this note: "It is probable that only students of the magical tradition will understand me when I say that 'Michael Robartes' is fire reflected in water, and that Hanrahan is fire blown by the wind, and that Aedh . . . is fire burning by itself." W. B. Yeats, *The Wind among the Reeds* (London: Elkin Mathews, 1899), 73.

6. Dublin *Daily Express*, April 22, 1899, 3.

7. The *Speaker*, April 29, 1899, 499.

8. R. F. Foster, *W. B. Yeats: A Life, Vol I: The Apprentice Mage 1865–1914* (Oxford: Oxford Univ. Press, 1997), 217.

9. *The Collected Letters of W. B. Yeats*, online version https://www.nlx .com/collections/130. "Francis Thompson thought the 'clumsy expedient of explanatory notes created "wanton difficulty"' . . . Richard Le Gallienne was bored by Irish mythology, [which was] 'too remote, too provincial, too grotesque' . . .

Arthur Symons . . . feared . . . the notes would not 'do quite all that is needed' in familiarizing readers with Irish tradition."

10. Foster, *Yeats: A Life*, 214.

11. Fiona MacLeod, "A Group of Celtic Writers," *The Fortnightly Review* LXV (January to June 1899): 43.

12. "The Valley of the Black Pig," "He Gives His Beloved Certain Rhymes," "The Binding of the Hair," "The Unappeasable Host," "He Bids His Beloved Be at Peace," "He Reproves the Curlew," "To His Heart, Bidding it Have no Fear," "The Secret Rose," "He Remembers Forgotten Beauty," and "The Travail of Passion."

13. See Joseph Valente, "Nation for Art's Sake: Aestheticist Afterwords in Yeats's Irish Revival," in *Yeats and Afterwords*, ed. Marjorie Howes and Joseph Valente (Notre Dame: Univ. of Notre Dame Press, 2014), 100–26.

14. Laurel Brake, "Aestheticism and Decadence: *The Yellow Book* (1894–97), *The Chameleon* (1894), and *The Savoy* (1896)", in *The Oxford Critical and Cultural History of Modernist Magazines*, ed. Peter Brooker and Andrew Thacker (Oxford: Oxford Univ. Press, 2009), 94.

15. Stanley Weintraub, ed., *The Savoy: Nineties Experiment* (University Park: Penn State Univ. Press, 1966), xv.

16. Weintraub, *The Savoy*, xxxii.

17. *The Autobiography of William Butler Yeats* (New York: Macmillan, 1965), 219.

18. Augusta Gregory, "The Felons of Our Land," *Cornhill Magazine*, May 1900, 622–34; W. B. Yeats, "What is 'Popular Poetry'?" *Cornhill Magazine*, March 1902, 344–49.

19. Barbara Quinn Schmidt, "The *Cornhill Magazine*: Celebrating Success," *Victorian Periodicals Review* 32, no. 3 (1999): 203.

20. Andrew Maunder, "'Discourses of Distinction': The Reception of the *Cornhill Magazine* 1859–60," *Victorian Periodicals Review* 32, no. 3 (1999): 241.

21. Maunder, "'Discourses of Distinction,'" 241.

22. Lady Grove, "Social Solecisms," *Cornhill Magazine*, March 1902, 350–57.

23. Andrew Lang and 'X,' A Working Man, "The Reading Public," *Cornhill Magazine*, December 1901, 783–95.

24. Foster, *Yeats: A Life*, 255.

4. Ourselves (Transnationally) Alone

1. Christopher Morash, *A History of the Media in Ireland* (Cambridge, UK: Cambridge Univ. Press, 2010), 115.

2. R. F. Foster, *Vivid Faces: The Revolutionary Generation in Ireland 1890–1923* (New York: Norton, 2014), 146.

3. Caroline Levine, *Forms: Whole, Rhythm, Hierarchy, Network* (Princeton: Princeton Univ. Press, 2017), 113.

4. See *Victorian Periodicals Review*, Special Issue: Victorian Networks and the Periodical Press 42, no. 2 (Summer 2011).

5. Laurel Brake, "'Time's Turbulence': Mapping Journalism Networks," *Victorian Periodicals Review*, Special Issue: Victorian Networks and the Periodical Press 42, no. 2 (Summer 2011): 117.

6. Alexis Easley, "Introduction to Special Issue: Victorian Networks and the Periodical Press," *Victorian Periodicals Review*, Special Issue: Victorian Networks and the Periodical Press 42, no. 2 (Summer 2011): 112.

7. Lucy McDiarmid, "Stalking Yeats: The Celebrity System of Revivalist Dublin," in *Synge and Edwardian Ireland*, ed. Brian Cliff and Nicholas Green (Oxford: Oxford Univ. Press, 2012), 36.

8. Foster, *Vivid Faces*, 8.

9. Foster, *Vivid Faces*, 9.

10. The "Napolean of Fleet Street," the Dublin-born Alfred Harmsworth, later Viscount Northcliffe (1865–1922) was one of the most successful newspaper magnates of his day; his mastery of daily journalism found its most pure expression in the *Daily Mail*, which he founded in 1896. An editor for the *Northern Echo*, *Pall Mall Gazette*, and *Review of Reviews*, W. T. Stead (1849–1912) was the exemplary practioner and theorist of "new journalism." which was distinguished by sensational and investigative journalism.

11. Brake, "'Time's Turbulence,'" 121.

12. Foster, *Vivid Faces*, 2.

13. Levine, *Forms*, 115.

14. Amanda Tucker and Moira E. Casey, eds., *Where Motley Is Worn: Transnational Irish Literatures* (Cork: Cork Univ. Press, 2014), 2.

15. Françoise Lionnet and Shu-mei Shih, "Introduction: Thinking through the Minor, Transnationally," in *Minor Transnationalism* (Durham: Duke Univ. Press, 2005), 8.

16. Padraic Colum, *Ourselves Alone! The Story of Arthur Griffith and the Origin of the Irish Free State* (New York: Crown Press, 1959), 32. Hyde's final verse translates thus: "It is time for every fool to have knowledge that there is no watch cry worth any heed but one—Sinn Féin amhain—Ourselves Alone!"

17. *Shan Van Vocht*, April 3, 1899, 68.

18. Virginia Glandon, *Arthur Griffith and the Advanced Nationalist Press, 1900–1922* (New York: Peter Lang, 1985), 12.

19. Glandon, *Arthur Griffith*, 12; Karen Steele, *Women, Press, and Politics during the Irish Revival* (Syracuse, NY: Syracuse Univ. Press, 2007), 64–67.

20. F. S. L. Lyons, *Ireland since the Famine* (London: Weidenfeld and Nicolson, 1971), 248; Owen McGee, *Arthur Griffith* (Dublin: Merrion Press, 2015), 54.

21. McGee, *Arthur Griffith*, 55.

22. McGee, *Arthur Griffith*, 55.

23. Colum, *Ourselves Alone!*, 16–18.

24. Among Griffith's most consistent pseudonyms were Cuguan, Shanganagh, Ier, Lugh, Rathcoole, Mise, Nationalist, Old Fogey, and Mafosta. Colum, *Ourselves Alone!*, 18.

25. Quoted in Colum, *Ourselves Alone!*, 19.

26. Glandon, *Arthur Griffith*, 13.

27. Foster, *Vivid Faces*, 154.

28. Lyons, *Ireland since the Famine*, 248.

29. *United Irishman*, March 4, 1899, 2.

30. Ciara Meehan, "'The Prose of Logic and of Score': Arthur Griffth and *Sinn Féin*, 1906–1914," in *Irish Journalism before Independence: More a Disease Than a Profession*, ed. Kevin Rafter (Manchester: Manchester Univ. Press, 2011), 188.

31. Glandon, *Arthur Griffith*, 15.

32. *United Irishman*, Nov. 25, 1900, 2.

33. Glandon, *Arthur Griffith*, 15.

34. *United Irishman*, Mar. 11, 1899, 2; Mar. 26, 1899, 3.

35. *United Irishman*, Mar. 11, 1899, 2; Mar. 26, 1899, 3.

36. Foster, *Vivid Faces*, 151.

37. Lionnet and Shih, "Thinking through the Minor," 7.

38. Glandon, *Arthur Griffith*, 18; Seamus Deane, ed., *The Field Day Anthology of Irish Writing*, vol. 2 (Derry: Field Day Publications, 1991), 371.

39. Colum, *Ourselves Alone!*, 62.

40. Foster, *Vivid Faces*, 155.

41. Lyons, *Ireland since the Famine*, 250; Foster, *Vivid Faces*, 158; Felix M. Larkin, "Arthur Griffith and the *Freeman's Journal*," in *Irish Journalism before Independence: More a Disease Than a Profession*, ed. Kevin Rafter (Manchester: Manchester Univ. Press, 2011), 174; Colum Kenny, "'An Extraordinarily Clever Journalist': Arthur Griffith's Editorships, 1899–1919," in *Periodicals and Journalism in Twentieth-Century Ireland: Writing against the Grain*, ed. Mark O'Brien and Felix Larkin (Dublin: Four Courts Press, 2014), 20.

42. By 1908, Griffith's *Sinn Féin* was quoting Christabel Pankhurst in its columns. See "The Woman Suffragists and the Irish Parliamentarians," *Sinn Féin*, Sept 5, 1908, 2.

43. Lyons, *Ireland since the Famine*, 251.

44. Lyons, *Ireland since the Famine*, 251; Glandon, *Arthur Griffith*, 16.

45. Patrick Maume, "The *Irish Independent* and Empire, 1891–1919," in *Newspapers and Empire in Ireland and Britain: Reporting the British Empire, c. 1857–1921*, ed. Simon Potter (Dublin: Four Courts, 2004), 127.

46. *Sinn Féin*, Sept. 13, 1913.

47. Patrick Maume, "William Martin Murphy," in *Dictionary of Irish Biography*, ed. James McGuire and James Quinn (Cambridge: Cambridge Univ. Press, 2009), accessed online Dec. 10, 2015; Thomas J. Morrissey, *William Martin Murphy* (Dundalk: Dundalgan Press, 1997), 31. At the death of his father, when he was eighteen, Murphy inherited a sawmilling and building business worth £4,000, a fortune at the time; Padraig Yeates, "The Life and Career of William Martin Murphy," in *Independent Newspapers: A History*, ed. Mark O'Brien and Kevin Rafter (Dublin: Four Courts Press, 2012), 16.

48. Maume, "William Martin Murphy."

49. Kevin Rafter, "Profits, Politics, and Personal Position: The Role of the Proprietor," in *Independent Newspapers: A History*, ed. Mark O'Brien and Kevin Rafter (Dublin: Fourt Courts Press, 2012), 195. Murphy claimed that he planned to invest £50,000 to relaunch the *Independent* ("The Story of a Newspaper," *Independent*, Jan. 2, 1909, 4). By 1910, it was making a profit (Maume, "William Martin Murphy"). Felix Larkin notes that daily circulation rose from an initial 25,000 to 100,000 by 1915. Felix Larkin, "No Longer a Political Side Show: T. R. Harrington and the 'New' Irish Independent, 1905–31," in *Independent Newspapers: A History*, ed. Mark O'Brien and Kevin Rafter (Dublin: Four Courts Press, 2012), 30.

50. Maume, "William Martin Murphy."

51. Maume, "The *Irish Independent* and Empire," 127. According to Maume, the *Independent* was making £15,000 a year by 1915 and £40,000 a year by 1919 when Murphy died, 129.

52. Morrissey, *William Martin Murphy*, 23.

53. Maume, "The *Irish Independent* and Empire," 129; Colum Kenny, "Tom Grehan: Advertising Pioneer and Newspaper Man," in *Independent Newspapers: A History*, ed. Mark O'Brien and Kevin Rafter (Dublin: Four Courts Press, 2012).

54. Brian Feeney, *Sinn Féin: A Hundred Turbulent Years* (Dublin: O'Brien Press, 2002), 19.

55. Larkin, "Arthur Griffith," 179.

56. *Irish Independent*, Jan. 2, 1905.

57. Quoted in Larkin, "No Longer a Political Side Show," 33.

58. Larkin, "No Longer a Political Side Show," 34.

59. Maume, "The *Irish Independent* and Empire," 129.

60. *Irish Independent*, Jan. 2, 1905, 4.

61. Aoife Uí Fhaoláin, "Language Revival and Conflicting Identities in the *Irish Independent*," *Irish Studies Review* 22, no. 1 (2014), 65.

62. Maume, "The *Irish Independent* and Empire," 129–34.

63. Maume, "The *Irish Independent* and Empire," 138.

64. Maume, "The *Irish Independent* and Empire," 136.

65. Maume, "The *Irish Independent* and Empire," 127.

66. Maume, "The *Irish Independent* and Empire," 141.

67. Uí Fhaoláin, "Language Revival," 71.

68. Uí Fhaoláin, "Language Revival," 73–74.

69. *Irish Independent*, Apr. 27, 1905, 4; Feb. 15, 1905, 4.

70. Maume, "The *Irish Independent* and Empire," 135.

71. Miglena Ivanova, "Dublin 1907," *Encyclopedia of World's Fairs and Expositions*, ed. John E. Findling and Kimberly D. Pelle (Jefferson, NC: McFarland and Company, 2008), 190.

72. *Irish Independent*, May 1, 1907, 4.

73. Maume, "The *Irish Independent* and Empire," 136.

74. Declan Kiberd, *Inventing Ireland* (Cambridge, MA: Harvard Univ. Press, 1993), 255.

75. Howes, Marjorie, and Joseph Valente, eds. *Yeats and Afterwords* (Notre Dame: Notre Dame Univ. Press, 2014), 3.

5. School Stories

1. W. B. Yeats, "Dramatis Personae, 1896–1902," in *The Autobiography of William Butler Yeats* (New York: Collier Books, 1965), 293.

2. Yeats, "Dramatis Personae, 1896–1902," 294.

3. Yeats, "Dramatis Personae, 1896–1902," 294.

4. As Frazier argues, "Yeats wrote long after events, and with the aim of detraction." Adrian Frazier, "'I No Longer Underrate Him': The Question of Moore's Value," in *George Moore: Artistic Visions and Literary Worlds*, ed. Mary Pierse (Newcastle, Cambridge Scholars Press, 2006), 4. Contemporary reviews of Moore's *The Untilled Field* support Frazier's argument. See, for instance, "The Untilled Field," *English Review* (December 1914), which claims that "these stories reveal a new character in Moore—sentiment and a depth of feeling which astonish" and concludes that "in what is called style he has no rival" (124).

5. Ernest Boyd, *Ireland's Literary Renaissance* (Dublin and London: Maunsel & Company, Ltd., 1916), 374.

6. Boyd, *Ireland's Literary Renaissance*, 388.

7. In his words, "The realistic work of George Moore, James Joyce, Brinsley MacNamara, and others might tempt us to distinguish an Irish Literary Renaissance

from the Irish Literary Revival. By the former (which more accurately might be termed a 'naissance') I would mean the tremendous release of literary energy in Ireland around the turn of the century, whatever its direction and ideology; to the Renaissance Moore and Joyce contributed hugely. By the Irish Literary Revival, I would mean the work of those who sought to employ literature in a resuscitation of elder Irish values and culture that they hoped would transform the reality of the Ireland they inhabited." John Wilson Foster, *Fictions of the Irish Literary Revival: A Changeling Art* (Syracuse, NY: Syracuse Univ. Press, 1987), xvi. Also, see Rónán McDonald, who claims that the Irish Revival rejects "empiricism, realism, and linear temporality" in "Irish Revival and Modernism" in *The Cambridge Companion to Irish Modernism*, ed. Joe Cleary (Cambridge: Cambridge Univ. Press, 2014), 52.

8. Although Cleary uses the term "naturalism," he notes that "the distinction between realism and naturalism has never been fully clear, and the two terms are often used interchangeably" in *Outrageous Fortune: Capital and Culture in Modern Ireland* (Dublin: Field Day Publications, 2007), 112. I refer to Moore's fiction as realist because I think it best captures the range of his writing. However, it is important to note that Moore's realism also adopts and adapts elements of naturalism.

9. Cleary, *Outrageous Fortune*, 131.

10. Clare Hutton, "Joyce and the Institutions of Revivalism," *Irish University Review* 33, no. 1 (Spring–Summer, 2003): 118. Other scholars also note how the Revival works through institutions. As P. J. Mathews argues, "W. B. Yeats, Lady Gregory, George Moore and Edward Martyn were not only artists but also the 'arts planners' and 'arts administrators' of their day." P. J. Mathews, *Revival: The Abbey Theatre, Sinn Féin, the Gaelic League and the Co-operative Movement* (Cork: Cork Univ. Press, 2003), 10. Also see Andrew Kuhn who shows how revivalist institutions endure in "'Make a Letter like a Monument': Remnants of Modernist Literary Institutions in Ireland," in *Modernist Afterlives in Irish Literature and Culture*, ed. Paige Reynolds (New York: Anthem Press, 2016), 93–94.

11. Roderick Ferguson, *The Reorder of Things: The University and Its Pedagogies of Minority of Difference* (Minneapolis: Univ. of Minnesota Press, 2012), 18.

12. Ferguson, *The Reorder of Things*, 7.

13. David Lloyd takes this argument a step further indicating that the literature of the Revival, itself, functioned as an institution: "For the Irish tradition of cultural nationalism, literature has always had a primary productive role, both in providing the national institutions that stood in for the political institutions yet to be, and in forming citizens in anticipation of the founding of the state for which they were to be the citizens." *Anomalous States: Irish Writing and the Post-Colonial Moment* (Durham: Duke Univ. Press, 1993), 69.

14. In Ferguson's words: "We may call this incorporation of modes of difference and the calculus that seeks to determine the properties and functions of those modes *as a will to institutionality*. The will to institutionality not only absorbs institutions and modern subjects; it is itself a mode of subjection as well." "Administering Sexuality; or, The Will to Institutionality," *Radical History Review* (Winter 2008): 163.

15. Adrian Frazier, *George Moore, 1852–1933* (New Haven: Yale Univ. Press, 2000), 95.

16. Frazier, *George Moore*, 273.

17. Declan Kiberd, "George Moore's Gaelic Lawn Party," in *The Irish Writer and the World* (Cambridge: Cambridge Univ. Press, 2005): 97–8.

18. "Manifesto," *The Academy* (Apr. 13, 1901): 320.

19. George Moore, *Hail and Farewell: Ave, Salve, and Vale*, ed. Richard Allen Cave (Gerrards Cross: Colin Smythe Ltd., 1985), 77.

20. John Wilson Foster makes one version of this argument, saying: "I should have suspected that Moore's defection from the Irish Revival was probably hastened by his prior achievements in realism." *Irish Novels 1890–1940: New Bearings in Culture and Fiction* (Oxford: Oxford Univ. Press, 2008), 9–10.

21. Moore, *Hail and Farewell*, 559.

22. In his words: "This is why I have said so many times that naturalism is not a school, as it is not embodied in the genius of one man, nor the ravings of a group of men, as was romanticism; that it consists simply in the application of the experimental method to the study of nature of man." Émile Zola, *The Experimental Novel, and Other Essays*, trans. Belle M. Sherman (New York: Cassell Pub. Co, 1893), 44.

23. Zola, *Experimental Novel*, 44.

24. George Moore, "My Impressions of Zola," *The English Illustrated Magazine* (Feb. 1894): 480.

25. Moore, "My Impressions of Zola," 481. According to Simon Joyce in "Impressionism, Naturalism, Symbolism: Trajectories of Anglo-Irish Fiction at the Fin de Siècle," *Modernism/modernity* 21, no. 3 (2014), this "fugitive contradictory thinking" expresses how Moore experiments with impressionism as well as naturalism (795). Fugitivity also captures Moore's relationship to institutions: he always flees from them.

26. For instance, Moore calls Hardy "a village schoolmaster." Geraint Goodwin, *Conversations with George Moore* (London: Ernest Benn Limited, 1929), 47.

27. George Moore, *Literature at Nurse, or Circulating Morals: A Polemic on Victorian Censorship*, ed. Pierre Coustillas (Hassocks: The Harvester Press Limited, 1976), 19.

28. Goodwin, *Conversations with George Moore*, 87.

29. Moore, *Hail and Farewell*, 143. John Eglinton says this within the book, but Moore reflects on the phrase, suggesting that this is one of the reasons why the language is necessary (while also comparing Eglinton to a schoolmaster).

30. W. B. Yeats, "The Trembling of the Veil," in *The Autobiography of William Butler Yeats* (New York: Collier Books, 1965), 154.

31. Moore, "Preface," in *The Untilled Field*, ed. Richard Allen Cave (Gerrards Cross: Colin Smythe Limited, 2000), xxxii.

32. Gregory, "Editor's Note," in *Ideals in Ireland*, ed. Lady Gregory (London: At the Unicorn, 1901), 9.

33. Douglas Hyde, "What Ireland Is Asking For," in *Ideals in Ireland*, ed. Lady Gregory, 55.

34. P. H. Pearse, *The Murder Machine* (Dublin: Whelan & Son, 1916), 6. See, for instance, D. P. Moran's "The Battle of Two Civilizations," in *Ideals in Ireland*, ed. Lady Gregory, which argues that "If an Irishman received a higher English education, and lost touch with Irish aspirations, he practically became an Englishman" (31). Yeats's "A Postscript" in *Ideals in Ireland*, ed. Lady Gregory, argues that the energy of the Revival "would show their education its sterility" (106).

35. Maude Gonne, "Our Irish Children," in *Maud Gonne's Irish Nationalist Writings: 1895–1946*, ed. Karen Steele (Dublin: Irish Academic Press, 2004), 152.

36. Yeats, "Trembling of the Veil," 112.

37. Maude Gonne MacBride, *The Autobiography of Maud Gonne: A Servant of the Queen*, ed. A. Norman Jeffares and Anna MacBride White (Chicago: Univ. of Chicago Press, 1994), 19.

38. W. B. Yeats, "Irish National Literature: Contemporary Prose Writers," *The Bookman* (Aug. 1895): 140.

39. Lady Augusta Gregory, *Our Irish Theatre: A Chapter of Autobiography* (New York: G. P. Putnam's Sons, 1913), 8–9.

40. As Gregory Castle argues in "Irish Revivalism: Critical Trends and New Directions," *Literature Compass* 8, no. 5 (2011), while many revivalist institutions are "minor"—grounded in negative critique—"Synge's plays, together with the dramatic productions of Yeats and Gregory, got Irish audiences involved in the process and made possible the creation of a *major* literature, even a foundational one" (293).

41. Edna Longley, *Yeats and Modern Poetry* (Cambridge: Cambridge Univ. Press, 2013), 28.

42. Moore, *Hail and Farewell*, 343.

43. As Pádraigín Riggs argues: "In spite of the obvious need, in 1902, both for reading material in Irish and for contemporary literary models in the language, the critical response to *An t-Úr-Ghort* was not enthusiastic. Because the viability of Irish as a modern literary medium was a matter of controversy at the time, the reviewers focused on the language of the stories at the expense of the subject

matter." Riggs, "*An T-Úr-Ghort* and *The Untilled Field*," in *George Moore: Artistic Visions and Literary Worlds*, ed. Mary Pierse (Newcastle: Cambridge Scholars Press, 2006), 131.

44. As I have already discussed, Joe Cleary offers one version of this argument. Also see Terry Eagleton, *Heathcliff and the Great Hunger* (London: Verso, 1995), 223.

45. David Lloyd, for instance, argues that realism is a form of subject-production—it assimilates individuals into normative social narratives. *Anomalous States*, 134.

46. Anna Kornbluh, "The Realist Blueprint," *The Henry James Review* 36, no. 3 (Fall 2015): 199. For Kornbluh, realism's affinity with architecture makes it utopic rather than referential or normative. In her words, "Realism's exploration of the city, governmentally, labor, and law affirms *that there is* institution but does not inherently affirm any particular institution or form thereof" (209).

47. Robert Welch, "Moore's Way Back: *The Untilled Field* and *The Lake*," in *The Way Back: George Moore's* The Untilled Field *and* The Lake, ed. Robert Welch (Totowa, New Jersey: Barnes & Noble Books, 1982), 39.

48. George Moore, *The Untilled Field* (London: T. Fisher Unwin, 1903), 203. Hereafter cited parenthetically in the text.

49. Alison Harvey suggests that Irish realism's focus on "minor figures" distinguishes these novels from their Victorian counterparts in "Irish Aestheticism in Fin-de-Siècle Women's Writing: Art, Realism, and the Nation," *Modernism/modernity* 21, no. 3 (September 2014): 808.

50. In the 1931 edition, Moore combines "In the Clay" and "The Way Back" into a new story, "Fugitives." This story begins with Father McCabe's architectural visions and more clearly articulates his debt as it describes him "as the propounder of a scheme for the revival of Irish Romanesque." In *Untilled Field*, ed. Cave, 180.

51. See for instance, a 1903 review that claims that Moore "seems to have lost faith in the possibility of the much-heralded Celtic renaissance"; "The Untilled Field," *The Bookman* (June 1903): 110.

52. Moore reimagines the Grania myth in a 1901 play that he wrote with W. B. Yeats, *Diarmuid and Grania*. Critical accounts of this play tend to suggest, as Maureen Waters does in "Lady Gregory's 'Grania': A Feminist Voice," *Irish University Review* 25, no. 1 (Spring–Summer 1995), that "Grania remains a time-worn cypher, beautiful and unfathomable" in their play (15). Alice Milligan also reimagines the myth in *Last Feast of the Fianna* (1900), as does Lady Gregory in *Grania* (1910). In turn, Emily Lawless names her protagonist Grania in her New Woman novel, *Grania: The Story of an Island* (1892).

53. As Maureen Waters and Cathy Leeney suggest, although the Grania story focuses on the triangular relationship between Grania, Finn, and Diarmuid, it can

also be a feminist story. See Cathy Leeney, "The New Woman in a New Ireland?: 'Grania' after Naturalism," *Irish University Review* 34, no. 1 (Spring–Summer, 2004): 163–64.

54. In future editions, Moore separated this long story into four stories, "Some Parishioners," "Patchwork," "The Wedding Feast," and "The Window."

55. Heather Ingman in *A History of the Irish Short Story* (Cambridge: Cambridge Univ. Press, 2009) suggests that "the lack of unity in *The Untilled Field* is both thematic and stylistic" (89).

6. An Ordinary Revival

1. John Wilson Foster, *Fictions of the Irish Literary Revival: A Changeling Art* (Syracuse, NY: Syracuse Univ. Press, 1987), xi.

2. Foster, *Fictions of the Revival*, xii.

3. See, for example, Clare Hutton on print practices, P. J. Mathews on "self-help" institutions, Aoife McGrath on dance, Paige Reynolds on spectacle, Karen Steele on the advanced nationalist press. Representative scholarship appears in Margaret Kelleher, ed. *Irish University Review: Special Issue, New Perspectives on the Irish Literary Revival* 33, no. 1 (Spring/Summer 2003). Other critics have introduced new literary forms to our discussions of the Revival, such as Tina O'Toole and Heather Edwards on New Woman novels, while others have underscored the importance of previously marginalized figures in single author studies, such as Nicholas Allen's study of George Russell, Elaine Sisson's of Patrick Pearse, or Catherine Morris's of Alice Milligan. For an overview of women's writing across this period, see Paige Reynolds, "Prose, Drama, and Poetry, 1891–1920," *A History of Modern Irish Women's Literature*, eds. Heather Ingman and Clíona Ó Gallchoir (Cambridge: Cambridge Univ. Press, 2018), 131–48.

4. W. B. Yeats, ed. *Representative Irish Tales* (1891. Reprint, Dublin: Colin Smythe, 1979).

5. George Russell (A. E.), "Introduction," *New Songs* (Dublin: O'Donoghue & Co, 1904), 5.

6. Margaret Kelleher, "*The Cabinet of Irish Literature*: A Historical Perspective on Irish Anthologies," *Éire-Ireland* 38, no. 3–4 (2003): 68–89.

7. Horatio Sheafe Krans, *Yeats and the Irish Literary Revival* (New York: McClure, Phillips, and Co., 1904), 3. https://babel.hathitrust.org/cgi/pt?id=coo.31 924013576594&view=1up&seq=21. Accessed September 12, 2015.

8. Antoinette Quinn, introduction, "Ireland/Herland: Women and Literary Nationalism," in *The Field Day Anthology of Irish Writing: Irish Women Writers and Tradition*, vol. 5, ed. Angela Bourke et al. (New York: New York Univ. Press, 2002), 900.

9. For a study of this novel, see Claire Connolly, "Counting on the Past: Yeats and Irish Romanticism," *European Romantic Review* 28, no. 4 (2017): 473–87.

10. See for example Donna Potts, "Irish Poetry and the Modernist Canon: A Reappraisal of the Poetry of Katharine Tynan," in *Border Crossings: Irish Women Writers and Nationalism*, ed. Kathryn Kirkpatrick (Tuscaloosa: Univ. of Alabama Press, 2000), 79–99, and essays in Deirdre Toomey, ed. *Yeats and Women* (Basingstoke: Palgrave Macmillan, 1997).

11. W. B. Yeats, preface, *Representative Tales of Ireland*, in *W. B. Yeats Prefaces and Introductions*, ed. William H. O'Donnell (Basingstoke: Palgrave Macmillan, 1988), 57. See Rosa Mulholland, "Wanted: An Irish Novelist," *Irish Monthly* 19 (1891): 368–69.

12. W. B. Yeats, "Irish National Literature, Contemporary Prose Writers: Mr. O'Grady, Miss Lawless, Miss Barlow, and the Folk-lorists," *The Bookman* 7–8 (Aug. 1895): 139.

13. Hannah Freed-Thall, *Spoiled Distinctions: Aesthetics and the Ordinary in French Modernism* (Oxford: Oxford Univ. Press, 2015), 4.

14. Michel de Certeau, *The Practice of Everyday Life*, trans. Steven F. Rendell (Berkeley: Univ. of California Press, 1984); Henri Lefebvre, *Everyday Life in the Modern World*, trans. Sacha Rabinovitch (1968. Reprint, New Brunswick, NJ: Transaction Publishers, 1984).

15. Tina O'Toole, *The Irish New Woman* (Basingstoke: Palgrave Macmillan, 2013), 9.

16. Joseph Valente, *The Myth of Manliness in Irish Nationalist Culture, 1880–1922* (Urbana: Univ. of Illinois Press, 2011).

17. Liesl Olson, *Modernism and the Ordinary* (Oxford: Oxford Univ. Press, 2009).

18. Aurelia Annat, "Class, Nation, Gender, and Self: Katharine Tynan and the Construction of Political Identities, 1880–1930," in *Politics, Society, and the Middle Class in Modern Ireland*, ed. Fintan Lane (Houndmills: Palgrave Macmillan, 2010), 201.

19. Potts, "Irish Poetry and the Modernist Canon," 80–81.

20. Katharine Tynan, *Twenty-Five Years: Reminiscences* (London: Smith, Elder and Co, 1913), 273.

21. W. B. Yeats, "The Celtic Element in Literature," *Ideas of Good and Evil* (London: A. H. Bullen, 1903), 270–95, 280.

22. Michael Sheringham, *Everyday Life: Theories and Practices from Surrealism to the Present* (Oxford: Oxford Univ. Press, 2009), 21.

23. W. P. Ryan, *The Irish Literary Revival: Its History, Pioneers and Possibilities* (London: Ward and Downey, 1894), 146. https://catalog.hathitrust.org/Record/001371167.

24. W. B. Yeats, *The Letters of W. B. Yeats*, ed. Allan Wade (London: R. Harte Davis, 1954), 248.

25. W. B. Yeats, "Irish National Literature, IV: A List of the Best Irish Books," in *The Collected Works of W. B. Yeats, vol. 9: Early Articles and Reviews*, ed. John P. Frayne and Madeline Marchaterre (New York: Scribner, 2004), 273.

26. Antares Skorpios (Jane Barlow), *History of a World of Immortals without a God: Translated from an Unpublished Manuscript in the Library of a Continental University* (Dublin: William McGee, 1891), 159. Subsequent references parenthetical. This first edition of the novel, used for this study, has been made available on Internet Archive: https://archive.org/details/historyofworldof000barl/page/n5/mode/2up. The authorship sometimes has been attributed to Barlow's father, James William Barlow, as in Jack Fennell, "James William Barlow," *The Green Book: Writings on Irish Gothic, Supernatural and Fantastic Literature* 18 (Samhain 2021), 29–36. Or to both James and Jane Barlow, as in Jack Fennell, "The Machine in the (Holy) Ghost: Anti-Scientific Literature, Genre Fiction, and Irish Modernism, 1890–1940," *Irish Modernisms: Gaps, Conjectures, Possibilities*, eds. Paul Fagan, John Greaney, and Tamara Radak (New York: Bloomsbury, 2021), 185–96. However, the presentation copy given originally to the American book collector James Carleton Young, and subsequently owned by John Quinn, has an inscription that describes the novel as "a small work which has the advantage of Rarity (only twenty copies being in existence)" signed by Jane Barlow as "the Author, Antares Skorpios." See *The Library of John Quinn, Part One (A–C)* (New York: The Anderson Galleries, 1923), 27.

27. Amy Boesky, *Founding Fictions: Utopia in Early Modern England* (Athens: Univ. of Georgia Press, 1997), 10.

28. Sinéad Garrigan Mattar, *Primitivism, Science, and the Irish Revival* (Oxford: Oxford Univ. Press, 2004), 19. See also Kathryn Conrad, Coílín Parsons, Julie McCormick Weng, eds., *Science, Technology, and Irish Modernism* (Syracuse, NY: Syracuse Univ. Press, 2019).

29. Rosa Mulholland, *Father Tim* (London: Sands and Co., 1910), 71. Subsequent references parenthetical. The first edition of the novel used for this study is available at HathiTrust Digital Library: https://catalog.hathitrust.org/Record/009954705.

30. Suzanne Clark, *Sentimental Modernism: Women Writers and the Revolution of the Word* (Bloomington: Indiana Univ. Press, 1991).

31. Ben Highmore, *Ordinary Lives: Studies in the Everyday* (New York: Routledge, 2011).

32. Katharine Tynan, *Memories* (London: E. Nash and Grayson, 1924), 296.

33. Maurice Blanchot, *The Infinite Conversation*, 1969, trans. and foreword Susan Hanson (Minneapolis: Univ. of Minnesota Press, 1993), 239.

7. "The Politics of Time and Eternity"

1. This does not mean that there have not been attempts to reinterpret A. E.'s significance in recent years. In the wake of the archival turn in Irish Studies which has motivated the critical recuperation of neglected figures associated with the Revival, the work of A. E. has not been an exception. See in particular Nicholas Allen's book-length study *George Russell (A. E.) and the New Ireland, 1905–1930* (Dublin: Four Courts Press, 2003), which provides a perceptive overview of the evolution of A. E.'s writing in relation to his changing political positions throughout his life. My account of the historical details of A. E.'s life draws heavily upon Allen's excellent research. See also Joseph Lennon, *Irish Orientalism: A Literary and Intellectual History* (Syracuse, NY: Syracuse Univ. Press, 2004), 290–97, which focuses on A. E.'s interests in Hinduism and Buddhism as well as his influence on other mystically inclined writers like James Cousins and James Stephens; Michael McAteer, *Standish O'Grady, AE, and Yeats: History, Politics, Culture* (Dublin: Irish Academic Press, 2002), 104–25; the essays of Leeann Lane—both McAteer and Lane focus on A. E.'s practical political activism and writing on behalf of Plunkett's Co-operative Movement; and Frances Flanagan, *Remembering the Irish Revolution: Dissent, Culture and Nationalism in the Irish Free State* (Oxford: Oxford Univ. Press, 2015), 121–62, which tracks A. E.'s memorialization of the Easter Rising and subsequent disillusionment with the political conservativism of the Irish Free State through the 1920s.

2. Yeats's historical account of the Revival is rooted in his neo-Platonic esotericism and recurs throughout his later writing, but is perhaps best crystalized in "The Irish Dramatic Movement," his 1923 acceptance speech for the Nobel Prize for literature; see *Autobiographies* (New York: Scribner, 1999), 410–18. His assertion that the cultural activity of the Revival presented a teleological anticipation of a distinct national political identity was not unique to Yeats alone within early historical accounts of the period; it also presents one of the underlying foundations to Ernest Boyd, *Ireland's Literary Renaissance* (Dublin: Maunsel and Co., 1916, 7–9.

3. On the critique of the ahistorical qualities of Yeats's periodization of the Revival, see R. F. Foster, "Thinking from Hand to Mouth: Anglo-Irish Literature, Gaelic Nationalism and Irish Politics in the 1890s" in *Paddy and Mr. Punch: Connections in Irish and English History* (London: Penguin Books, 1995), 262–80; for the larger claim about the Revival as an event which supersedes the limits of Yeats's cultural focus, see in particular P. J. Mathews, *Revival: The Abbey Theatre, Sinn Féin, the Gaelic League and the Co-operative Movement* (Cork: Cork Univ. Press, 2003), 6–12, 146–48.

4. George William Russell, *Imaginations and Reveries*, 2nd ed. (Dublin: Maunsel and Roberts, 1921), 115.

5. See Allen's book in particular, which presents a comprehensive account of A. E.'s work as an intellectual in regard to a more historically expansive understanding of the Revival.

6. Boyd, *Ireland's Literary Renaissance*, 238. Unlike the works which follow, Boyd does consider the aesthetic qualities of A. E.'s poetry in addition to registering his personal achievements as activist and mentor—and rather surprisingly (at least from a contemporary perspective) suggests that ultimately someday A. E. might be considered a more significant poet than Yeats. See 219–20.

7. George Moore, *Hail and Farewell: Ave, Salve, and Vale*, ed. Richard Allen Cave (Gerrards Cross: Colin Smythe Ltd., 1976), 577–87.

8. Yeats, *Autobiographies*, 196. On the history of the tangled friendship between Yeats and A. E. and the influence they had upon each other's work, see Peter Kuch, *Yeats and A. E.: The Antagonism that Unites Dear Friends* (Gerrards Cross: Colin Smythe Ltd., 1986).

9. See W.B. Yeats, *A Vision: The Original 1925 Version* (New York: Scribner, 2008), 86–89.

10. John Eglinton, *A Memoir of A. E.: George William Russell* (London: Macmillan, 1937) and Monk Gibbon, "A. E.," in Gibbon, ed. *The Living Torch: A. E.* (London: Macmillan, 1937), 3–81. *The Living Torch* collects a wide selection of excerpts from A. E.'s literary, political, and economic journalism, but none of his literary works.

11. As Joseph Lennon argues of A. E. and the similarly neglected James Cousins, "to read the poetry of a writer like Cousins or A. E. according to a modern or postmodern aesthetic can seem painful because the reader's criteria conflict and share few of the assumptions and hopes of the author." Lennon, *Irish Orientalism*, 377.

12. Yeats, *Autobiographies*, 200. Yeats's critique rests not only on his perception of what he considers A. E.'s debt to his own style, but moreover that the artistic ideal of the "Unity of Being" lay beyond his grasp due to an inability to distinguish between self and "Mask" in a manner that was typical of the "Conditional Man."

13. Gibbon, "A. E.," 51, 53.

14. Gibbon, "A. E.," 50–51.

15. Gibbon, "A. E.," 59.

16. These are the positions apparent in the work of, respectively, Selina Guinness, "'Protestant Magic' Reappraised: Evangelicalism, Dissent, and Theosophy," *Irish University Review* 33, no. 1 (2003), 14–27; Lennon; McAteer; and Allen.

17. Gibbon, *The Living Torch*, 181–230.

18. The correspondence is included in *Descent of the Gods*. See Raghavan Iyer and Nandini Iyer, eds., *The Descent of the Gods: The Mystical Writings of G. W. Russell—A. E.: Part Three of the Collected Works* (Gerrards Cross: Colin

Smythe Ltd., 1988), 653–57. A. E.'s anxieties appear to be a consequence of Yeats's involvement in the movement. Yeats had persuaded Blavatsky to found a secretive inner Esoteric Section of the Theosophical Society devoted to the study of more occult areas of study; A. E. regarded this focus as potentially dangerous since it could lead to a blasphemous emphasis on individual self-empowerment rather than toward collective and egalitarian forms of spirituality. Yeats would eventually leave the Theosophical Society precisely because of his failed attempt to control the Esoteric Section, and would soon find a more appropriate venue for his aspirations in the Hermetic Order of the Golden Dawn. A. E.'s very first independent publication of any sort was a pamphlet that dates from 1894 titled *To the Fellows of the Theosophical Society* which declared allegiance to the American section of the Theosophical Society led by William Quan Judge against the more powerful organization based in Adyar, India, led by Annie Besant and Henry Steel Olcott in the schism which occurred after the death of Blavatsky; see Iyer and Iyer, *Descent of the Gods*, 659–64. Judge, an Irish immigrant to New York who held a simultaneous commitment to the utopian socialism of Edward Bellamy as well as to Theosophy, served as the most important influence upon A. E.'s thought after Blavatsky and would prove to be an inspirational figure to some of the more politically radical forms of the movement which would later appear in the United States. See Paul Eli Ivey, *Radiance from Halcyon: A Utopian Experiment in Religion and Science* (Minneapolis: Univ. of Minnesota Press, 2013), 21–32.

19. For a brief history of the formation and various figures associated with the Dublin Lodge, see Guinness, "'Protestant Magic.'"

20. See Guinness, "'Protestant Magic,'" 19, 26; Allen, *George Russell*, 17–18.

21. Iyer and Iyer, *Descent of the Gods*, 127.

22. Iyer and Iyer, *Descent of the Gods*, 127.

23. Iyer and Iyer, *Descent of the Gods*. Blavatsky defines "avatar" as "Divine Incarnation. The descent of a god or some exalted Being who has progressed into the body of a simple mortal" in *The Theosophical Glossary* (Los Angeles: Theosophical Publishing House, 1918), 41. For a thorough historical contextualization of the circumstances of the moment in which A. E. originally had the vision and in which he chose to describe it more than twenty years later in *The Candle of Vision*, see Iyer and Iyer, *Descent of the Gods*, 94–96.

24. Iyer and Iyer, *Descent of the Gods*, 128.

25. Eglinton confirms A. E.'s ongoing philosophical commitment to Blavatsky despite his formal break with Theosophy as an organized movement, and suggests that it even distantly provided an echo of his personal background in dissenting forms of Protestantism: "This meant no loss of faith in Theosophy, but a natural and common-sense claim for freedom. Theosophy may be said to have repeated, on a small scale, the early history of the Christian faith, in which, when the Founder

had passed, the retention of His power and doctrine was claimed more and more exclusively by the Church. For A. E. the Society was nothing, apart from its inspired founders. In other words, he was a Protestant Theosophist." See Eglinton, *A Memoir of A. E.*, 52.

26. For a scholarly overview of Theosophy that is respectful of its key tenets and seeks to place it within a longer two-thousand-year-old history of occult and esoteric tradition, see Nicholas Goodrick-Clarke, *The Western Esoteric Traditions: A Historical Introduction* (Oxford: Oxford Univ. Press, 2008), 211–28. See also Goodrick-Clarke, *Helena Blavatsky* (Berkeley: North Atlantic Books, 2004). My discussion of Theosophy as a systematic form of belief is heavily indebted to Goodrick-Clarke. As far as the more common representation of Blavatsky as a scam-artist goes—an assumption which runs through both academic and popular histories of Theosophy—Peter Washington's *Madame Blavatsky's Baboon: A History of the Mystics, Mediums, and Misfits Who Brought Spiritualism to America* (New York: Shocken, 1995) is a representative example.

27. As Blavatsky wrote of the "objects" of the movement, "they are three, and have been so from the beginning. 1. To form the nucleus of a Universal Brotherhood of Humanity, without distinction of race, colour, or creed. 2. To promote the study of Aryan scriptures and other Scriptures, of the World's religions and sciences, and to vindicate the importance of old Asiatic literature, namely, of the Brahmanical, Buddhist, and Zoroastrian philosophies. 3. To investigate the hidden mysteries of Nature under every aspect possible, and the psychic and spiritual powers latent in man especially." See Blavatsky, *The Key to Theosophy*, 39. The term "Aryan"—as well as Blavatsky's use of the term "root race" in her periodization of the cyclic history of human civilization in *The Secret Doctrine*—has led to the ultimately inaccurate charge that Theosophy is consistent with and anticipates Eurocentric esoteric racism. Helena Petrovna Blavatsky, *The Secret Doctrine: Vol. I* (London: The Theosophical Publishing House Ltd., 1888). To be clear, Blavatsky's use of the term "Aryan" refers to what would now be classified in the terms of comparative linguistics to mean "Indo-Iranian" and has no connection to the Northern European, "Nordic" associations the Comte Arthur de Gobineau and Houston Stewart Chamberlain sought to associate it with in the same time period. "Root Race" refers to the general condition of humanity within a given period or epoch rather than to a biological construction of race as it was understood in the late-nineteenth century. While Blavatsky's attempt to construct a universal narrative of the cycles of *all* human civilization which incorporated and claimed to go beyond all recorded history, beliefs found within comparative religions and mythologies, global languages, *and* Darwinian theories of biological evolution in the second volume of *The Secret Doctrine* includes late-nineteenth century anthropological assumptions regarding different populations throughout the world that are clearly

racist in contemporary terms, Blavatsky's understanding of racial difference sought to abolish the hierarchical nature of such positions in order to make the claim for universal human equality between all races (and indeed between all specific categorical identities in general). Blavatsky, *The Secret Doctrine*.

28. A. P. Sinnett, *Incidents in the Life of Madame Blavatsky* (London: George Redway, 1886).

29. Sinnett's books about Theosophy were the initial inspirations for the Dublin Theosophical Society after the nineteen-year-old Yeats received them as a gift from his aunt and made them available to his classmates Charles Johnston, Charles Weekes, and A. E.; see R. F. Foster, *W. B. Yeats: A Life, Vol I: The Apprentice Mage 1865–1914* (Oxford: Oxford Univ. Press, 1997), 45–47. Yeats would play a key role in the Theosophical Society both in Dublin and London until his departure from the movement after a series of disputes with Blavatsky in late 1890. See Foster, *Yeats: A Life*, 102–4. The letters purportedly written by the Masters to Sinnett—conspicuously, most of which were written in Blavatsky's handwriting— were eventually also published; see A. Trevor Barker, ed. *The Mahatma Letters to A. P. Sinnett*, 2nd ed. (Pasadena: Theosophical Univ. Press, 1926).

30. The recent work of Gauri Viswanathan presents one strong indication that such a rediscovery is already underway. While Viswanathan has produced significant research on Theosophy since the 1990s, recent publications have focused especially on the theoretically innovative qualities of Blavatsky's writing. See in particular Gauri Viswanathan, "In Search of Madame Blavatsky: Reading the Exoteric, Retrieving the Esoteric," *Representations* 141 (2018): 67–94 and "Conversion and the Idea of the Secret," *Nineteenth-Century Literature* 73, no. 2 (2018): 161–86.

31. See Guinness, "'Protestant Magic,'" 7.

32. Blavatsky, *The Secret Doctrine*, 14.

33. "The ABSOLUTE: the *Parabrahm* of the Vedantins or the one Reality, SAT, which is, as Hegel says, both Absolute Being and Non-Being." Blavatsky, *The Secret Doctrine*, 16.

34. Writing from a position motivated by a defense against Poststructuralist charges of universalism, Fredric Jameson places emphasis upon a comprehensive understanding of the concept: "Totality is not available for representation, any more than it is accessible in the form of some ultimate truth (or form of Absolute Spirit)." See Fredric Jameson, *The Political Unconscious* (Ithaca: Cornell Univ. Press, 1981), 55.

35. Blavatsky, *The Secret Doctrine*, 21.

36. Blavatsky, *The Secret Doctrine*, 16.

37. Blavatsky, *The Theosophical Glossary*, 195.

38. Blavatsky, *The Theosophical Glossary*, 195–96.

39. Blavatsky, *The Secret Doctrine*, 37.

40. Blavatsky, *The Secret Doctrine*, 37.

41. Blavatsky, *The Secret Doctrine*, 17.

42. Blavatsky, *The Secret Doctrine*, 37.

43. Blavatsky, *The Secret Doctrine*, 542. On the Western history of the doctrine of "as above, so below," which Goodrick-Clarke traces to Plotinus's Neoplatonic absorption of Alexandrian Hermeticism in the 3rd Century and which reappears in virtually every esoteric belief system since then, see Goodrick-Clarke, *The Western Esoteric Traditions*, 8–10, 18–23.

44. Blavatsky, *The Secret Doctrine*, 17.

45. Blavatsky, *The Secret Doctrine*, 37.

46. For a concise overview regarding Blavatsky's understanding of the septenary division of human incarnation, see Goodrick-Clarke, *The Western Esoteric Traditions*, 220–23.

47. Blavatsky, *The Theosophical Glossary*, 161.

48. Blavatsky, *The Secret Doctrine*, 44.

49. Iyer and Iyer, *Descent of the Gods*, 457.

50. On the social movements specifically supported by the Dublin Lodge, see Guinness, "'Protestant Magic,'" 18.

51. Iyer and Iyer, *Descent of the Gods*, 472.

52. Iyer and Iyer, *Descent of the Gods*, 474.

53. Iyer and Iyer, *Descent of the Gods*.

54. Gibbon, *The Living Torch*, 59.

55. Iyer and Iyer, *Descent of the Gods*, 475.

56. On the Dublin Lodge's reluctance to engage with the "national question," see Guinness, "'Protestant Magic,'" 18.

57. Russell, *Imaginations and Reveries*,4–5.

58. Iyer and Iyer, *Descent of the Gods*, 86.

59. On A. E.'s discovery and lifelong enthusiasm for O'Grady, see Allen, *George Russell*, 15–21.

60. Iyer and Iyer, *Descent of the Gods*, 154–63.

61. Iyer and Iyer, *Descent of the Gods*, 95–99.

62. In a letter to Yeats written in 1897, A. E. takes this position to (unintentionally?) comic length by expressing his anxiety that his recently published collection of poetry *The Earth Breath* might not be received very well by critics due to its inability to recreate the stereotypical qualities of the "Celtic temperament," a designation which doesn't suit him very well due to the global diversity of his other incarnations on earth: "I am afraid it would be a futile task to try consciously for the Celtic traditional feeling. A certain spirit of it I have, but I am not Celt inside, not for many lives. I remember vividly old America and Chaldea, and sometimes as

a mountain beyond lesser heights I get glimpses of the Dedanaan days but they lie behind tradition and history . . ." Alan Denson, ed., *Letters from A. E.* (London: Abelard-Schuman, 1961), 20.

63. Russell, *Imaginations and Reveries*, vii.

64. George William Russell, *The National Being* (Dublin: Maunsel and Company, 1916), 172–73.

65. For an extended discussion of A. E.'s growing disillusionment with post-revolutionary Ireland and move toward a more politically conservative position, see Flanagan, *Remembering the Irish Revolution*, 121–62; on the relationship between that shift and the more experimental qualities of works like *The Interpreters* and *The Avatars*, see Allen, *George Russell*, 116–43.

66. Gibbon, *The Living Torch*, 131, 132.

67. For an extensive delineation of A. E.'s interest in political radicalism, see Allen, *George Russell*, in particular.

8. An Arts and Crafts Revival

1. For an extended postcolonial reading of this frontispiece and of the city plan, see Andrew Kincaid's *Postcolonial Dublin: Imperial Legacies and the Built Environment* (Minneapolis: Univ. of Minnesota Press, 2006), 1–57. For more on *Dublin of the Future* in relation to James Joyce and to Irish literature, see Liam Lanigan's *James Joyce, Urban Planning, and Irish Modernism* (New York: Palgrave, 2014). For more on state formation and the rhetoric of the Gothic in Ireland, and for a related reading of this Clarke frontispiece, see Caoilfhionn Ní Bheacháin's "Seeing Ghosts: Gothic Discourses and State Formation," *Éire-Ireland* 47, no. 3 and 4 (2012): 37–63.

2. Nicola Gordon Bowe, "The Arts and Crafts Movement in Ireland." *Antiques* 142, no. 6 (Dec. 1992), 865.

3. Nicola Gordon Bowe and Elizabeth Cumming, *The Arts and Crafts Movement in Dublin and Edinburgh: 1885–1925* (Dublin: Irish Academic Press, 1998),77.

4. See Vera Kreilkamp's introduction to Kreilkamp, ed. *The Arts and Crafts Movement: Making It Irish* (Boston: McMullen Museum of Art, Boston College, 2016), as well as my "Modernist Heresies: Irish Visual Culture and the Arts and Crafts Movement" in *The Edinburgh Companion to Irish Modernism*, ed. (2021), 234–51.

5. Kevin Corrigan Kearns, *Georgian Dublin: Ireland's Imperiled Architectural Heritage* (London: David and Charles, 1983), 46–47.

6. For recent work on Modernism in Ireland, see in particular Maud Ellman, Siân White, and Vicky Mahaffy, eds., *The Edinburgh Companion to Irish*

Modernism (Edinburgh: Edinburgh Univ. Press, 2021); Nicholas Allen, *Modernism, Ireland, and Civil War* (Cambridge: Cambridge Univ. Press, 2009); Edwina Keown and Carol Taaffe, eds. *Irish Modernism: Origins, Contexts, Publics* (Bern, Switzerland: Peter Lang, 2010); Emer Nolan, "Modernism and the Irish Revival," in *The Cambridge Companion to Modern Irish Culture*, ed. Claire Connolly and Joe Cleary (Cambridge: Cambridge Univ. Press, 2004), 157–72; and Enrique Juncosa and Christina Kennedy, eds. *The Moderns* (Dublin: Irish Museum of Modern Art, 2011). Allen notably includes analysis of the visual art of Jack B. Yeats in *Modernism, Ireland, and Civil War*. The 2011 Irish Museum of Modern Art's *The Moderns* exhibition and companion catalog, edited by Juncosa and Kennedy, provides sustained reassessment of Modernism in relation to Ireland's visual arts and architecture. Michael Levenson's *Modernism* (New Haven, CT: Yale Univ. Press, 2011) offers a provocative new perspective on the international movement as it relates to seemingly peripheral aesthetic schools such as Symbolism, Naturalism, Surrealism, and Expressionism.

7. Terence Brown, "Ireland, Modernism, and the 1930s," in *Modernism and Ireland: The Poetry of the 1930s*, ed. Patricia Coughlan and Alex Davis (Cork: Cork Univ. Press, 1995), 27.

8. Bowe, "Arts and Crafts Movement," 866.

9. Luke Gibbons, "Peripheral Visions: Revisiting Irish Modernism," in *The Moderns*, ed. Enrique Juncosa and Christine Kennedy (Dublin: Irish Museum of Modern Art, 2011), 96. See also John Wilson Foster, "Irish Modernism," in *Colonial Consequences: Essays in Irish Literature and Culture* (Dublin: Lilliput Press, 1991), 44–59.

10. Brown, "Ireland, Modernism, and the 1930s," 31.

11. Nicola Gordon Bowe's biography of Clarke provides an important study of his work. See Bowe, *The Life and Work of Harry Clarke* (Blackrock, Dublin: Irish Academic Press, 1989) and Bowe, *Harry Clarke: His Graphic Art* (Dublin: Dolmen Press, 1984). See also Nicola Gordon Bowe, David Caron, and Michael Wynne, *Gazetteer of Irish Stained Glass* (Dublin: Irish Academic Press, 1988) and James White and Michael Wynne, *Irish Stained Glass* (Dublin: Gill and Son, 1963). Dorothy Walker limits her analysis of Clarke's work to a comparison with Evie Hone, Wilhelmina Geddes, and Michael Healy, concluding that Clarke "did more for religious art in his lifetime than any other artist, even if his achievement is less serious, in artistic terms, than that of Evie Hone." Dorothy Walker, *Modern Art in Ireland* (Dublin: The Lilliput Press, 1997), 30. S. B. Kennedy's *Irish Art and Modernism 1880–1950* (Belfast: Institute of Irish Studies, Queens University, 1991) mentions Clarke only in passing; and the recent catalogue *The Moderns*, ed. Enrique Juncosa and Christine Kennedy, published in conjunction with the Irish Museum of Modern Art's exhibition of the same name, considers Clarke "certainly

not modernist." The catalogue, however, lists him alongside other artists who have been included in the exhibit (in his case, in relation to his illustrations) because they "also have contributed to modern Ireland" (*The Moderns*, 6).

Since the first publication of this essay, there has been interest in stained glass work in Ireland and in Harry Clarke's work in particular. Three major publications are of particular note: the collection of essays *Harry Clarke and Artistic Visions of the New Irish State*, edited by Angela Griffith, Marguerite Helmers, and Róisín Kennedy (Irish Academic Press, 2018); Nicola Gordon Bowe's magisterial *Wilhelmina Geddes, Life and Work* (Four Courts Press, 2015); and most recently Irish Academic Press's revised new edition of the *Gazetteer of Irish Stained Glass* edited by Nicola Gordon Bowe, David Caron, and Michael Wynne (Dublin: Irish Academic Press, 2021), updated with beautiful photographs and new entries.

12. Adrian Frazier's "Harry Clarke and the Material Culture of Modern Ireland," *Textual Practice* 16, no. 2 (2002): 303–21, marks one instance of sustained interest in Clarke's influence on the material culture of Ireland. Frazier uses the Ballinrobe windows as example and writes that "[t]hose windows signify an Ireland in which vernacular cultural forms are reverenced while giving personal expression to a widely humanistic and modern sensibility, an adaptation that one finds, for instance, in modern Irish poetry," 319.

13. Clarke produced more than one hundred sixty windows, mostly for ecclesiastical commissions. His work can be found in Ireland, England, Scotland, Australia, and the United States. Lucy Costigan and Michael Cullen's *Strangest Genius: The Stained Glass of Harry Clarke* (Dublin: The History Press Ireland, 2010), provides a lavishly illustrated catalogue of the artist's glasswork.

14. This window was commissioned by the Free State government as Ireland's contribution to the League of Nations building in Geneva, Switzerland. When the government failed to display the window, Clarke's widow bought it back for the same price her husband was paid for the commission. The *Geneva Window* is now on display at the Wolfsonian Museum in Miami, Florida.

15. Quoted in Bowe, *Life and Work of Harry Clarke*, 241.

16. Harry Clarke to Thomas Bodkin, June 11, 1920. Harry Clarke Papers MS39202/A: Correspondence, 1.i (xxxi), National Library of Ireland.

17. Clarke typically exhibited his windows in his studio before installing them in churches or other locations, and often these studio exhibitions, open to the public, garnered praise in newspaper reviews and elsewhere. It was on the strength of his exhibition of five windows made for the Honan Chapel, his first major commission, that Clarke was commissioned to produce six more for that church. This early success helped cement his career and also suggests his work was greatly appreciated for its intensity, originality, and skillful execution. See Bowe, *Life and Work of*

Harry Clarke, 88. But a full study of his reception among ecclesiastical commissioners awaits further research.

18. Nicola Gordon Bowe remains both the foremost scholar of the Irish Arts and Crafts movement and Clarke's biographer. For her work on Clarke, see Bowe, *Harry Clarke: The Life and Work*, rev. and updated ed. (Dublin, Ireland: History Press Ireland, 2012) and Bowe, *Harry Clarke: His Graphic Art*. See also Bowe, Caron, and Wynne, eds. *Gazetteer of Irish Stained Glass*, and White and Wynne, *Irish Stained Glass*. See also Costigan and Cullen, *Strangest Genius*. For assessment of the Arts and Crafts Movement in Ireland with reference to Clarke, see Bowe and Cumming, *Arts and Crafts Movement*; Bowe, "Arts and Crafts Movement;" Bowe, "The Arts and Crafts Society of Ireland (1894–1925) with Particular Reference to Harry Clarke," *Journal of the Decorative Arts Society* 9 (1985): 29–40; see also Janice Helland, *British and Irish Home Arts and Industries: 1880–1914* (Dublin: Irish Academic Press, 2007).

19. For an overview of the Irish Revival in relation to modernism, see Nolan, "Modernism and the Irish Revival."

20. Quoted in Bowe, *Life and Work of Harry Clarke*, 242.

21. Bowe, "Arts and Crafts Movement," 872.

22. Bowe succinctly summarizes Arts and Crafts ideals in "Arts and Crafts Movement," 865.

23. J. A. Whall, *Stained Glass Work: A Text-book for Students and Workers in Glass* (New York: D. Appleton and Co., 1905), 29.

24. In *Life and Work of Harry Clarke*, Bowe observes that "one of the most important lessons he learned [in 1914] was to enhance each piece of glass by the lead line which surrounded it," 33. She also notes that although the grooved strips of lead used to hold each piece of glass are technically known as "calmes," she will refer to them as "lead lines," 33n33. I follow her choice in this article, using the terms "lead lines" and "leading" interchangeably.

25. Harry Clarke to Thomas Bodkin, Nov. 3, 1918. Harry Clarke Papers, MS39202.

26. Costigan and Cullen, *Strangest Genius*, 46. For more on Clarke's stained glass techniques, see Costigan and Cullen, *Strangest Genius*, 41–48, and Bowe, *Life and Work of Harry Clarke*, appendix 1; for information on stained glass production at the turn of the century, see Whall, *Stained Glass Work*.

27. Robert O'Byrne, "Irish Modernism: The Early Decades," in *The Moderns,* ed. Enrique Juncosa and Christine Kennedy (Dublin: Irish Museum of Modern Art, 2011), 13.

28. For a particularly thoughtful analysis of Clarke's Honan Chapel windows in relation to art history, see Bowe, *Life and Work of Harry Clarke*, 43–68.

29. Norman Bryson, *Vision and Painting: The Logic of the Gaze* (Yale: Yale Univ. Press, 1983), 96.

30. Joseph Frank, "Spatial Form in Modern Literature: An Essay in Two Parts." *The Sewanee Review* 53, no. 2 (Spring 1945), 227.

31. This compositional arrangement is echoed in the side windows of the chancel of Saints Peter and Paul Church, four of which were made in 1937 by the Harry Clarke Studios (White and Wynne, *Irish Stained Glass*, 25). The Studios continued to produce stained glass until 1973.

32. In *Life and Work of Harry Clarke*, Bowe points out that this is a practice Clarke learns from medieval scholars, and he uses it to notable effect in his Saint Gobnait window in the Honan Chapel, 58.

33. David Lloyd, "The Gaze Is a Thing: Beckett's *Film* and Bram Van Velde," in *The Moderns*, ed. Enrique Juncosa and Christine Kennedy, 122. Lloyd uses these words to describe the effect of the "gaze" in the work of Modernist Bram Van Velde and links this visual shift in subject-object relations to Beckett's *Film*.

34. Mieke Bal and Norman Bryson, "Introduction: Art and Intersubjectivity," *Looking In: The Art of Viewing* (Amsterdam: G+B Arts, 2001), 3.

35. Peter Cormack argues, in *Arts and Crafts Stained Glass* (New Haven: Yale Univ. Press, 2015), that many artists turned to stained glass work precisely to reach a broad public audience.

36. See Jim Hansen, *Terror in Irish Modernism: The Gothic Tradition from Burke to Beckett*. (Albany: SUNY Press, 2009), 1–26; for more on the literary Gothic legacy in Modernism, see Andrew Smith and Jeff Wallace, "Introduction: Gothic Modernisms: History, Culture and Aesthetics," in *Gothic Modernisms*, ed. Andrew Smith and Jeff Wallace (New York: Palgrave, 2001), 1–10, and John Paul Riquelme, "Toward a History of Gothic and Modernism: Dark Modernity from Bram Stoker to Samuel Beckett." *Modern Fiction Studies* 46, no. 3 (Fall 2000): 585–605.

37. See John Ruskin, *The Stones of Venice*, vol. 2 (1853; Project Gutenberg 2009); www.gutenberg.org/etext/30755, 165–213.

38. Costigan and Cullen, *Strangest Genius*, 159.

39. The shape of this lancet window also subtly references the round tower that formed a part of St. Maculind's original church, now a visitor's site maintained by the Office of Public Works. Part of the Gothic references Clarke incorporates in this window may indicate he knew the Abbey's history of constant pillaging and devastation.

40. Bryson, *Vision and Painting*, 96.

41. Jonathan Hale, *The Old Way of Seeing* (New York: Houghton Mifflin, 1994),77, 76–86.

42. For more information on the inclusion of memento mori in British medieval stained glass, see Emma Jane Wells, "Henry Williams and the 'Ymage of Deth'

Roundel, Stanford-on-Avon, Northamptonshire." *Vidimus* 40 (May 2010) Panel of the Month (ISSN 1752–0741, accessed Aug. 30, 2012).

43. Ruskin, *Stones of Venice*, 197. The primacy of the vesica piscis, a shape based on that of an organic form—for example, a leaf or fish or almond—supports Ruskin's assertion that the principles governing Gothic architecture derive from a study of vegetation; thus, the tenet of "naturalism" in Gothic art emerges directly from nature, 206–7.

44. Harry Clarke died of tuberculosis in 1931, at age forty-one. A grueling work schedule and contact with toxic chemicals used in stained glass production may have contributed to a life of ill health and to his early death. Synge suffered from Hodgkin's disease and died in 1909, at thirty-seven.

45. J. M. Synge, *The Aran Islands*, ed. Tim Robinson (1907, Reprint London: Penguin, 1992), 114.

46. See W. J. McCormack, "Irish Gothic and After," in *The Field Day Anthology of Irish Writing*, vol. 2, ed. Seamus Deane (Derry: Field Day Publications, 1991) on Irish Gothic writing of the twentieth century, including that by Synge, Yeats, and Bowen, 846–54.

47. Riquelme, "Toward a History of Gothic and Modernism," 587.

48. Austin Clarke, *A Penny in the Clouds* (1960), quoted in Bowe, *Life and Work of Harry Clarke*, 264.

9. Reviving the New Woman

1. Adrian Frazier, "Queering the Irish Renaissance: The Masculinities of Moore, Martyn, and Yeats," in *Gender and Sexuality in Modern Ireland*, ed. Antony Bradley and Maryann Gialanella Valiulis (Amherst: Univ. of Massachusetts Press, 1997), 8–38.

2. See for instance Susan Cannon Harris, *Irish Drama and the Other Revolutions: Playwrights, Sexual Politics, and the International Left, 1892–1964* (Edinburgh, Edinburgh Univ. Press, 2017); Joseph Valente, *The Myth of Manliness in Irish National Culture, 1880–1922* (Urbana: Univ. of Illinois Press, 2010); Patrick Mullen, *The Poor Bugger's Tool: Irish Modernism, Queer Labor, and Postcolonial History* (Oxford: Oxford Univ. Press, 2012).

3. Elizabeth O'Farrell, a nurse and member of Cumann na mBan, is perhaps best-known today for the controversy surrounding the "airbrushing" of her image from the photograph taken at the end of the 1916 Easter Rising; only the hem of her dress and her feet are visible in the photograph taken of Pearse delivering the surrender to Brigadier General William Lowe.

4. See Tina O'Toole, "The New Woman *Flâneuse* or Streetwalker? George Egerton's Urban Aestheticism," in *Reconnecting Aestheticism and Modernism:*

Continuities, Revisions, Speculations, ed. Bénédicte Coste, Catherine Delyfer, and Christine Reynier (London: Routledge, 2017), 19–30.

5. See Tina O'Toole, "George Egerton's Translocational Subjects," *Modernism/modernity* 21, no. 3 (September 2014): 827–42.

6. Tina O'Toole, *The Irish New Woman* (Basingstoke: Palgrave Macmillan, 2013).

7. For a survey account of the main authors involved in Irish new woman writing, see Tina O'Toole, "The (Irish) New Woman: Political, Literary, and Sexual Experiments," in *The History of British Women's Writing*, vol. 7, ed. Holly Laird (London: Palgrave Macmillan, 2016), 23–34.

8. See Sarah Grand, "The New Aspect of the Woman Question," *North American Review* 158 (1894): 270–76.

9. Kathryn C. Conrad, *Locked in the Family Cell: Gender, Sexuality and Political Agency in Irish National Discourse* (Wisconsin: Univ. of Wisconsin Press, 2004), 11.

10. Elleke Boehmer, *Colonial and Postcolonial Literature: Migrant Metaphors* (Oxford: Oxford Univ. Press, 2005), 21.

11. Boehmer, *Colonial and Postcolonial Literature*, 21.

12. Hannah Lynch was born in Dublin; her father was a member of the Fenian movement. As is evident from her semiautobiographical *Autobiography of a Child* (Edinburgh and London: William Blackwood; New York: Dodd, Mead and Company, 1899; published in *Blackwood's Magazine* 164–65, 1898–99), she attended a Catholic convent boarding school in England before working as a governess in mainland Europe. She traveled widely and earned a living predominantly through her literary writing, translations, and journalism; she was Paris correspondent for the *Academy*, for instance. For further information on Lynch, see the entry in the Oxford *Dictionary of National Biography* by Faith Binckes; see also Faith Binckes and Kathryn S. Laing, "A Vagabond's Scrutiny: Hannah Lynch in Europe," in *Irish Women Writers: New Critical Perspectives*, ed. Elke D'hoker, Raphael Ingelbien, and Hedwig Schwall (Bern: Peter Lang, 2010), 111–32; and Faith Binckes and Kathryn S. Laing, *Hannah Lynch 1859–1904: Irish Writer, Cosmopolitan, New Woman* (Cork: Cork Univ. Press, 2019).

13. Mobilized in 1880 as a result of the proscription of the Land League and imprisonment of Parnell's brother, Home Rule politician Charles Stewart Parnell.

14. E. L. Voynich, *The Gadfly* (1897, Reprint London: Mayflower, 1973).

15. It is rumored that her 1895 affair with Sidney Reilly, a Russian-born British secret service agent, and their voyage to Florence together provided inspiration for *The Gadfly*.

16. For a deeper and more nuanced exploration of the synergies and dissonances between aestheticism and revivalist culture, see Joseph Valente, "Nation for Art's Sake:

Aestheticist Afterwords in Yeats's Irish Revival," in *Yeats and Afterwords*, ed. Marjorie Howes and Joseph Valente (Indiana: Univ. of Notre Dame Press, 2014), 100–126.

17. Frazier, "Queering the Irish Renaissance," 11.

18. Gillian McIntosh, "Providing an Alternative to the Public House: The Irish Temperance League and the Creation of the First Coffee Chain in Belfast in the 1870s." Unpublished report for the Irish Temperance League (2012).

19. McIntosh, "Providing an Alternative," 26.

20. Leeann Lane, *Rosamond Jacob: Third Person Singular* (Dublin: Univ. College Dublin Press, 2010), 172, 194.

21. Rosamond Jacob papers, National Library of Ireland, MS 33,133/1–5.

22. Damien Doyle, "Rosamond Jacob (1888–1960)," in *Female Activists: Irish Women and Change 1900–1960*, ed. Mary Cullen and Maria Luddy (Dublin: Woodford Press, 2001), 173.

23. Lane, *Rosamond Jacob*, 50.

24. Interestingly, Jacob's mother Henrietta was a constitutional nationalist and Redmondite, while her children were Sinn Féin members. See Lane, *Rosamond Jacob*, 43, for further detail on the Jacob family's political affiliations.

25. Rosamond Jacob, *The Troubled House* (Dublin: Brown and Nolan, 1938), 144.

26. Lane, *Rosamond Jacob*, 171.

27. The hero of Jacob's earlier novel, *Callaghan*, was based on Mellows, who was a family friend; a member of the Fianna in his youth, Mellows was a founding member of the Irish Volunteers and became a member of the IRB in 1912. See R. F. Foster, *Modern Ireland* (London: Penguin, 1989), 511.

28. Jacob, *The Troubled House*, 34.

29. Jacob, *The Troubled House*, 44.

30. Jacob, *The Troubled House*, 51.

31. Jacob, *The Troubled House*, 52.

32. Jacob, *The Troubled House*, 91.

33. Jacob, *The Troubled House*, 107. Describing Helena Molony, Jacob writes, "She seems to regard men, as men, more as the relaxation of an idle hour than in any serious light, does not appear to believe much in the one love of a lifetime, but rather in one minor flame after another. She prefers women" (Aug. 4, 1911, diary entry from RJD Ms., quoted in Lane, *Rosamond Jacob*, 21).

34. Lane, *Rosamond Jacob*, 64.

35. Jacob, *The Troubled House*, 198.

36. Jacob, *The Troubled House*, 218.

37. Jacob, *The Troubled House*, 203.

38. Skinnider is remembered today as the only woman to be wounded in action during the 1916 Rising; cross-dressed, she worked as a scout and also took

up position as a sniper on the roof of the College of Surgeons that week, having smuggled bomb-making equipment into the country from Scotland in the run-up to Easter week.

39. Jacob, *The Troubled House*, 239.

40. Jacob, *The Troubled House*, 263.

41. Jacob, *The Troubled House*, 185–86.

42. Jacob, *The Troubled House*, 60.

43. Quoted in Bruce Arnold, *Mainie Jellett and the Modern Movement in Ireland* (New Haven: Yale Univ. Press, 1992), 79–80.

44. Quoted in *Paul Henry, Further Reminiscences*, ed. Edward Hickey (Belfast: Blackstaff Press, 1973), 65.

45. Quoted in Sarah Bochicchio, "The Female Painter Whose Modern Art Shocked Ireland," https://www.artsy.net/article/artsy-editorial-female-painter-modern-art-shocked-ireland.

46. Nicholas Allen, *George Russell (A. E.) and the New Ireland, 1905–1930* (Dublin: Four Courts Press, 2004), 60.

47. See Allen, *George Russell*.

48. Riann Coulter, "Translating Modernism: Mainie Jellett, Ireland, and the Search for a Modernist Language," *Apollo*, 164, no. 535 (September 2006), 100.

49. Coulter underlines the public works, such as mural projects, Gleizes undertook as part of his commitment to the social role of an artist (104).

50. Arnold, *Mainie Jellett*, 91.

51. Arnold, *Mainie Jellett*, 93.

52. Arnold, *Mainie Jellett*, 94.

53. Jacob, *The Troubled House*, 115.

54. Oscar Wilde, *The Picture of Dorian Gray* (New York: Norton, 2006), 42.

55. Jacob, *The Troubled House*, 63–64.

56. Doyle, *Rosamond Jacob*, 176.

57. Talia Schaffer, *The Forgotten Female Aesthetes: Literary Culture in Late-Victorian England* (Charlottesville: Univ. of Virginia Press), 25.

58. Jacob, *The Troubled House*, 60–61.

59. Given the small scale of the visual arts community in Dublin, and Orpen's close association with the art school Jacob attended (although he was no longer teaching there by the time she enrolled), she may well have seen this painting and/or heard it discussed while at the Dublin Metropolitan School of Art.

60. Kristin Mahoney, *Literature and the Politics of Post-Victorian Decadence* (Cambridge: Cambridge Univ. Press, 2015), 120.

61. Coulter, "Translating Modernism," 109.

62. Harris, *Irish Drama*, 4.

63. Jacob, *The Troubled House*, 158.

64. Jacob, *The Troubled House*, 186.

65. Jacob, *The Troubled House*, 270.

66. Jacob, *The Troubled House*, 271.

10. "All the Green World Is on Our Side"

1. Recent expanded accounts of the Revival have tended to neglect or frag-ment her output. Thus, Gore-Booth is not considered in *The Irish Revival Reap-praised*, ed. Betsey Taylor Fitzsimon and James H. Murphy (Dublin: Four Courts Press, 2004), while R. F. Foster in *Vivid Faces: The Revolutionary Generation in Ireland 1890–1923* (London: Penguin, 2014), touches on her only cursorily in con-nection with Constance Markievicz. *Handbook of the Irish Revival: An Anthology of Irish Cultural and Political Writings, 1891–1922*, ed. by Declan Kiberd and P. J. Mathews (Dublin: Abbey Theatre Press, 2015), includes a single poem, "Women's Rights," a text that inscribes feminist politics into the Irish landscape and co-opts Celticism for radical social change, rather than a more representative range of work. In *The Field Day Anthology of Irish Writing*, vol. 4 and 5, ed. Angela Bourke et al (Cork: Cork Univ. Press, 2002), her work does appear under several rubrics, captur-ing the diversity of her writing but also pointing up its disparateness and the divided constituencies it addresses. Politically, Gore-Booth proves even more elusive and resistant to categorization. Because she was not a member of Irish political groups, Louise Ryan omits her in her investigations of how Irish women won the vote; Ryan, *Winning the Vote for Women: The Irish Citizen Newspaper and the Suffrage Movement in Ireland* (Dublin: Four Courts Press, 2018). She is also, on similar grounds, excluded from Senia Pašeta's study of Irish women nationalists; Pašeta, *Irish Nationalist Women, 1900–1918* (Cambridge: Cambridge Univ. Press, 2013), and, more surprisingly, from her exploration of the links between British suffrage and Irish feminism; Pašeta, *Suffrage and Citizenship in Ireland, 1912–18* (London: Institute of Historical Research, 2019). Eavan Boland, on the other hand, lists her in a rollcall of Irish suffragettes in her poem, "Our Future Will Become the Past of Other Women," a text commissioned in 2018 to mark the centenary of women gaining the vote in Ireland (*Irish Times*, Dec. 10, 2018, 11–12). But the feminist aims she pursued of equality, social justice, and enfranchisement frequently fell out-side of or ruptured the determining frameworks of Irish nationalism, thus making her connections to the Revival difficult to discern. Biographical explorations of Eva Gore-Booth have been even more bedeviled than attempts to situate her culturally and politically. The most enduring but troubling recollection was put forward by W. B. Yeats in his elegy, "In Memory of Eva Gore-Booth and Con Markiewicz" which loftily dismisses Gore-Booth's dreams as "some vague utopia" and chillingly sees her ageing body as a moral retribution for her wrong-headed politics; Yeats,

The Poems, ed. by Daniel Albright (London: Everyman, 1990). Gifford Lewis's *Eva Gore-Booth and Esther Roper: A Biography* (London: Pandora, 1988) refuted the view of Gore-Booth as a directionless visionary. But she tacitly endorsed the Yeatsian assumption that Markievicz and Gore-Booth embodied opposing qualities, the proactive energy of the former contrasting with the complaisant passivity of the latter. More damagingly, she tendentiously argued that the relationship between Roper and Gore-Booth was platonic and not sexual, thereby pruriently censoring an aspect of their relationship and denying the historical reality of lesbian lives. Emma Donoghue and Sonja Tiernan have roundly contested Lewis's stance and argued that Gore-Booth's lesbianism was both an incontestable aspect of her identity and an integral component of her political and literary works. See Donoghue, "'How Could I Fear and Hold Thee by the Hand': The Poetry of Eva Gore-Booth," in *Sex, Nation, and Dissent in Irish Writing*, ed. Éibhear Walshe (Cork: Cork Univ. Press, 1997), 16–42, and Tiernan, "Challenging Presumptions of Heterosexuality: Eva Gore-Booth: A Biographical Case Study," *Historical Reflections/Réflexions Historiques* 37, no. 2 (2011), 58–71. The queering of Gore-Booth has enabled an increasing recognition of her radicalism; Tiernan's epochal research project, *Eva Gore-Booth: An Image of Such Politics* (Manchester: Manchester Univ. Press, 2012) has made Gore-Booth comprehensively available to contemporary readers, highlighting her indefatigable endeavors as a social reformer and drawing out the imbrication of her art and political thinking. Her pioneering biography, which revealingly mined the family papers held in the Public Record Office in Belfast, raised Gore-Booth, as Deirdre Toomey has observed, from "a brief footnote in history" and also brought home her manifold political involvements, nonconformism, unflagging energy, and friendships with other avant-garde writers, including Dorothy Macardle and Katherine Cecil Thurston; Toomey, "'Both Beautiful, One a Gazelle': An Essay Reviewing Sonja Tiernan, *Eva Gore-Booth, An Image of Such Politics* and Lauren Arrington, *Revolutionary Lives: Constance and Casimir Markievicz*," in *Yeats's Legacies: Yeats Annual No. 21*, ed. Warwick Gould (London: Open Book Publishers, 2018), 545. Additionally, Tiernan has edited Gore-Booth's hitherto-unknown suffrage play *Fiametta*, produced the first modern compilation of her poems, and assembled a selection of her political writings, thereby bringing home the multiplicity of her interventions.

2. Jane Bennett, *Vibrant Matter* (Durham: Duke Univ. Press, 2010), 21–38.

3. Rosi Braidotti, *Nomadic Subjects: Embodiment and Sexual Difference in Contemporary Feminist Theory*, 2nd ed. (New York: Columbia Univ. Press, 2011), 57.

4. See P. J. Mathews, *Revival: The Abbey Theatre, Sinn Féin, the Gaelic League and the Co-operative Movement* (Cork: Cork Univ. Press, 2003), 5–34, for

a discussion of the self-help ethos that straddled the cultural, social, and political spheres in late nineteenth- and early twentieth-century Ireland.

5. "The Women's Suffrage Movement: Meeting at Drumcliffe," *Sligo Champion*, Dec. 26, 1896, 8, www.irishnewspapersarchive.com/. Accessed Apr. 14, 2020.

6. Jill Liddington and Jill Norris, *One Hand Tied behind Us: The Rise of the Women's Suffrage Movement* (London: Virago, 1978), 15.

7. For the varied underpinnings of suffragism see Blanca Ritschel Rodriguez-Ruiz and Ruth Rubio-Marín, "Introduction: Transition to Modernity: The Achievement of Female Suffrage and Women's Citizenship," in *The Struggle for Female Suffrage in Europe: Voting to Become Citizens*, ed. Blanca Rodriguez-Ruiz and Ruth Rubio-Marín (Leiden: Brill, 2012), 1–46; and Carole Pateman, "Three Questions about Womanhood Suffrage," in *Suffrage and Beyond: International Feminist Perspectives*, ed. Caroline Daley and Melanie Nolan (Auckland: Auckland Univ. Press, 1994), 331–48.

8. Jane Rendall, "Citizenship, Culture and Civilisation: The Languages of British Suffragists, 1866–1874," in *Suffrage and Beyond: International Feminist Perspectives*, ed. Caroline Daley and Melanie Nolan (Auckland: Auckland Univ. Press, 1994), 127–50.

9. Eva Gore-Booth, *The Political Writings of Eva Gore-Booth*, ed. Sonja Tiernan (Manchester: Manchester Univ. Press, 2015), 61.

10. Gore-Booth, *Political Writings*, 57.

11. Gore-Booth, *Political Writings*, 55.

12. Tiernan, *Gore-Booth: Such Politics*, 224.

13. For an analysis of *Urania*, see Sonja Tiernan, "Tabloid Sensationalism or Revolutionary Feminism?: The First Wave Feminist Movement in an Irish Women's Periodical," *Irish Communications Review* 12, no. 1 (2010), 74–87.

14. Tiernan, "Tabloid Sensationalism," 225.

15. On the ideals of the Hermetic Order of the Golden Dawn, dedicated to esoteric wisdom, of which W. B. Yeats was a member, see George Mills Harper, *Yeats's Golden Dawn* (London: Macmillan, 1974), 1–13.

16. Catherine Malabou, *Changing Difference: The Feminine and the Question of Philosophy*, trans. Carolyn Shread (Cambridge: Polity, 2011), 120.

17. Malabou, *Changing Difference*, 34.

18. Malabou, *Changing Difference*, 38.

19. Matthew Arnold, *On the Study of Celtic Literature* (London: Smith Elder, 1981), 82.

20. W. B. Yeats, "The Celtic Element in Literature," in *Essays and Introductions* (London: Papermac, 1989), 178.

356   Notes to Pages 257–63

21. Mary Trotter, *Ireland's National Theaters: Political Performance and the Origins of the Irish Dramatic Movement* (Syracuse, NY: Syracuse Univ. Press, 2001), 73–100.

22. See Trotter, *Ireland's National Theaters*, 73–100, and Cathy Leeney, "Women and Irish Theatre before 1960," in *The Oxford Handbook of Modern Irish Theatre*, ed. Nicholas Grene and Chris Morash (Oxford: Oxford Univ. Press, 2016), 396–97.

23. Paige Reynolds, *Modernism, Drama, and the Audience for Irish Spectacle* (Cambridge: Cambridge Univ. Press, 2007), 77.

24. Cathy Leeney, *Irish Women Playwrights, 1900–1939: Gender and Violence on Stage* (London: Peter Lang, 2010), 70.

25. Eva Gore-Booth, *The Plays of Eva Gore-Booth*, ed. Frederick S. Lapisardi. (San Francisco: Edwin Mellen, 1991), 5.

26. Gore-Booth, *Plays*, 21.

27. Gore-Booth, *Plays*, 21.

28. Anthony Roche, *The Irish Dramatic Revival, 1899–1939* (London: Bloomsbury Methuen Drama, 2015), 40.

29. Eleanor Hull, "The Story of Deirdre in Its Bearing on the Social Development of the Folktale," *Folklore* 15, no. 1 (1904), 26.

30. George Russell (A. E.), *Deirdre: A Legend in Three Acts* (Chicago: DePaul Univ. Press, 1970), 19, 18–19. See Anthony Coleman, "A. E.'s Deirdre and the Fays," *Notes and Queries* 26, no. 4, 1979, 326–28.

31. J. M. Synge, *The Complete Plays* (London: Methuen Drama, 1963), 272.

32. For analyses of *Deirdre*, see Shonagh Hill, *Women and Embodied Mythmaking in Irish Theatre* (Cambridge: Cambridge Univ. Press, 2019), 206–83, and Leeney, *Irish Women Playwrights*, 86–95.

33. Gore-Booth, *Plays*, 209.

34. Gore-Booth, *Plays*, 163.

35. Gore-Booth, *Plays*, 158.

36. Gore-Booth, *Plays*, 152.

37. Gore-Booth, *Plays*, 163.

38. Leeney, *Irish Women Playwrights*, 89.

39. Gore-Booth, *Plays*, 166.

40. Gore-Booth, *Plays*, 176–77.

41. Gore-Booth, *Plays*, 178.

42. Gore-Booth, *Plays*, 171, 172.

43. Julia Kristeva, *Revolution in Poetic Language,* trans. by Margaret Waller (New York: Columbia Univ. Press, 1984), 93.

44. Gore-Booth, *Plays*, 212.

45. Gore-Booth, *Plays*, 187.

46. Gore-Booth, *Plays*, 215.

47. Leeney, *Irish Women Playwrights*, 94.

48. For discussion of this play see Hill, *Women and Embodied Mythmaking*, 59–63 and Maureen O'Connor, "Eva Gore-Booth's Queer Art of War," in *Women Writing War: Ireland 1880–1922*, ed. Tina O'Toole and Muireann O'Cinnéide (Dublin: Univ. College Dublin Press, 2016), 85–102.

49. Gore-Booth, Eva. *The Death of Fionovar: From the* Triumph of Maeve, illustrated by Constance Gore-Booth (London: Erskine Macdonald, 1916), 13.

50. Gore-Booth, *Death of Fionovar*, 9.

51. Gore-Booth, *Death of Fionovar*, 18.

52. See Marian Eide, "Maeve's Legacy: Constance Markievicz, Eva Gore-Booth and the Easter Rising," *Éire-Ireland* 51, no. 3–4 (Winter 2016), 80–103, who suggests that the death of Fionovar also captures Gore-Booth's conflicted feelings about her sister's political beliefs.

53. Gore-Booth, *Death of Fionovar*, 81, 77, 76.

54. Gore-Booth, *Death of Fionovar*, 79.

55. Gore-Booth, *Death of Fionovar*, 81.

56. Lauren Arrington, *Revolutionary Lives: Constance and Casimir Markievicz* (Princeton: Princeton Univ. Press, 2016), 152.

57. Malabou, *Changing Difference*, 121.

58. Gore-Booth, *Death of Fionovar*, 83–84.

59. Gore-Booth, *Death of Fionovar*, 87.

60. Eva Gore-Booth, *Poems of Eva Gore-Booth: Complete Edition*, ed. Esther Roper (London: Longmans Green, 1929), 55.

61. Gore-Booth, *Poems*, 59.

62. For a discussion of Gore-Booth's poetry see Sonja Tiernan's Introduction in Eva Gore-Booth, *Eva Gore Booth: Collected Poems* (Dublin: Arlen House, 2018), 13–59.

63. Gore-Booth, *Poems*, 56.

64. For an account of ecofeminist dimensions of her work, see Maureen O'Connor, "Vegetable Love: The Syncretic Nation in the Writings of Margaret Cousins and Eva Gore-Booth," *Journal of Irish Studies* XXVIII (2013), 18–33.

65. Matthew Campbell, *Irish Poetry under the Union, 1801–1924* (New York: Cambridge Univ. Press, 2014), 18–20.

66. Bennett, *Vibrant Matter*, 23.

67. Donoghue, "'How Could I Fear,'" 16–42.

68. Gore-Booth, *Poems*, 106.

69. Gore-Booth, *Poems*, 122.

70. Gore-Booth, *Poems*, 122.

71. Gore-Booth, *Poems*, 498.

72. Gore-Booth, *Poems*, 498.

73. Gore-Booth, *Poems*, 481.

74. Gore-Booth, *Poems*, 409.

75. Gore-Booth, *Poems*, 409.

76. Gore-Booth, *Poems*, 407.

77. Gore-Booth, *Poems*, 408.

78. Gore-Booth, *Poems*, 244.

79. Gore-Booth, *Poems*, 506.

80. Gore-Booth, *Poems*, 511.

81. See https://hamiltongallery.ie/eva-gorebooth-exhibition, accessed May 2020.

82. Gore-Booth, *Poems*, 548.

11. Nursing the Revival

1. See, for example, "The Fairy Nurse," in *Legendary Fictions of the Irish Celts, Collected and Narrated by Patrick Kennedy* (London: Macmillan and Co., 1891). Kennedy explains the popularity of the legend, and that "It is only natural in the social condition of the fairies that they should steal human children, and also nurses to give suck to their own puny offspring" (100).

2. Síghle Bhreathnach-Lynch, "Crossing the Rubicon: Sean Keating's *An Allegory*," *New Hibernia Review* 12, no. 2 (January 2008): 120–26, 123.

3. The mother, nursing in the open (only Travelers did this, says the conventional wisdom), is shadowed by the Big House which stands accusingly in the background, as if she may be a wet-nurse to the Ascendancy nursling—a common scenario in which the nurse's own baby was then denied breastmilk (and so "sacrificed"). On the sacrifice of the wet-nurse's child, see Jules Law, *The Social Life of Fluids: Blood, Milk, and Water in the Victorian Novel* (Ithaca: Cornell Univ. Press, 2010), 127–45.

4. As Joseph Valente writes, "both *Cathleen* and *The Singer* lay particular stress upon this exclusionary dynamic by having the commitment to blood sacrifice directly interrupt or preclude a prospective marital commitment." See "The Mother of All Sovereignty" in *The Myth of Manliness in Irish National Culture, 1880–1922* (Urbana-Champaign: Univ. of Illinois Press, 2011), 97.

5. Law, *Social Life of Fluids*, 11.

6. Law, *Social Life of Fluids*, 128.

7. Katie Trumpener, *Bardic Nationalism: The Romantic Novel and the British Empire* (Princeton: Princeton Univ. Press, 1997), 128–57. Quoted in Julie Kipp, *Romanticism, Maternity, and the Body Politic* (Cambridge: Cambridge Univ. Press, 2003), 98.

8. Kipp, *Romanticism, Maternity*, 99.

9. Edmund Spenser, *A View of the Present State of Ireland*, ed. W. L. Renwick (Oxford: Clarendon Press, 1970), 68.

10. Aodhagán Ó Rathaille, "An Heroic Poet," in *An Macaomh*, edited by P. H. Pearse (Rathfarnham: St. Enda's, 1913), 187.

11. Lady Gregory, trans. and ed., *Cuchulain of Muirthemne: The Story of the Men of the Red Branch of Ulster* (London: John Murray, 1903), vi.

12. Ernie O'Malley, *On Another Man's Wound: A Personal History of Ireland's War of Independence* (Boulder: Roberts Rinehart, 1999), 11.

13. Ernie O'Malley, Archives of Irish America, Tamiment Library, NYU. Permission to quote from poem granted by Cormac O'Malley.

14. Fionntán de Brún, "Temporality and Irish Revivalism: Past, Present, and Becoming," *New Hibernia Review* 17, no. 4 (Winter/Geimhreadh, 2013), 44.

15. Padraic H. Pearse, *Collected Works of Padraic H. Pearse: Political Writings and Speeches* (Dublin: Phoenix, 1924), 48.

16. Padraic H. Pearse, *Collected Works of Padraic H. Pearse: Plays, Stories, Poems* (Dublin: Phoenix, 1917), 311. Lady Gregory's translation, held in the Berg Collection of the NYPL and published in 2016, is more direct: "O little mouth that sucks at my breast / It is Mary herself will kiss you on your road." Lady Gregory, "What Was Their Utopia?" *International Yeats Studies* 1, no. 1 (2016).

17. Pearse, *Plays, Stories, Poems*, 31.

18. Pearse, *Plays, Stories, Poems*, 15.

19. See Fiona Giles, "'Relational, and Strange': A Preliminary Foray into a Project to Queer Breastfeeding." *Australian Feminist Studies*, 19, no. 45 (Nov. 2004), 301–14. See also Edith Frampton on Queering breastfeeding.

20. Moynagh Sullivan, "The Treachery of Wetness: Irish Studies, Seamus Heaney and the Politics of Parturition," *Irish Studies Review* 13, no. 4 (2005), 465n56.

21. Pearse, *Plays, Stories, Poems*, 42.

22. Pearse, *Plays, Stories, Poems*, 31.

23. de Brún, "Temporality and Irish Revivalism," 43.

24. Pearse, *Plays, Stories, Poems*, 132.

25. Pearse, *Plays, Stories, Poems*, 134.

26. Pearse, *Plays, Stories, Poems*, 132.

27. Pearse, *Plays, Stories, Poems*, 333.

28. Vincent Quinn, "Fostering the Nation: Patrick Pearse and Pedagogy," *New Formations* 42 (Winter 2001), 82.

29. See Caroline Walker Bynum, especially the chapter "Woman as Body and as Food" in *Holy Feast and Holy Fast: The Religious Significance of Food to Medieval Women* (Berkeley: Univ. of California Press, 1987), 271, 272.

30. Pearse, *Political Writings and Speeches*, 50.

31. Valente, *Myth of Manliness*, 104–5.

32. As Valente puts it, "The mutually renovative effects of blood sacrifice are set in countervailing juxtaposition to the doubtful material-political consequences of the practice," *Myth of Manliness*, 102.

33. Eugene McNulty, "Waiting for the Exceptional: Pearse's Drama and the Space between Law and Law," in *Patrick Pearse and the Theatre: Mac Piarais agus an Téatar*, ed. Eugene McNulty and Róisín Ní Ghairbhí (Dublin: Four Courts Press, 2017), 89, 92, my emphasis.

34. See Valente: "The heroic self-immolation of blood sacrifice replaces the act of sexual congress as a means of attaining Sovereignty and inducing the Old Woman's transformation," *Myth of Manliness*, 96.

35. Valente, *Myth of Manliness*, 97.

36. Declan Kiberd, "Patrick Pearse: Irish Modernist," in *The Life and Afterlife of P. H. Pearse*, ed. Roisin Higgins and Regina Uí Chollatáin (Dublin: Irish Academic Press, 2009), 65.

37. Margaret Kelleher, *The Feminization of Famine: Expressions of the Inexpressible?* (Durham: Duke Univ. Press, 1997), 29. As Kelleher argues throughout the book, "Depictions of the dry-breasted mother unable to feed her child, of a woman unable to bury her child, or a mother torn between the competing claims of her children, or of a child suckling the breast of its dead mother occur not only throughout present-day accounts but also embody the worst consequences of famine in literary and historical texts" (2).

38. Kelleher, *Feminization of Famine*, 37.

39. Quoted in Kelleher, *The Feminization of Famine*, 36.

40. Thomas Davis, "The State of the Irish Peasantry," in *Literary and Historical Essays* (Dublin: James Duffy, 1854), 204–5.

41. Quoted in Angela Bourke, *Voices Underfoot: Memory, Forgetting, and Oral Verbal Art* (Cork: Cork Univ. Press, 2016), 32. Emma Donoghue's recent novel *The Wonder* (New York: Little, Brown, and Co., 2016), evokes the withered, desiccated famine child for whom breastmilk is a sort of contagion.

42. Quoted in Kelleher, *Feminization of Famine*, 112.

43. Maud Ellmann, *The Hunger Artists* (Cambridge: Harvard Univ. Press, 1993). "Freud argues that victims of trauma repeat their terrors in their actions and dreams in order to become the masters, rather than the victims, of their past. By starving themselves voluntarily, the Irish hunger strikers of this century may still be trying to defeat the bloodsuckers and to overcome the nightmare of their history" (11). Perhaps Ellmann's theory also accords to the fraught state of Irish breastfeeding practice throughout the twentieth and twenty-first centuries.

44. Pearse, *Plays, Stories, Poems*, 10.

45. Pearse, *Plays, Stories, Poems*, 10.

46. Michael Cronin, "'To Right the Wrong of the People': Vulnerability and Revolutionary Desire in Patrick Pearse's Drama," in *Patrick Pearse and the Theatre: Mac Piarais agus an Téatar*, ed. Eugene McNulty and Róisín Ní Ghairbhí (Dublin: Four Courts Press, 2017), 114. Cronin observes, "The longing that is evoked, or called forth, by bodies (specifically male bodies) merges with that longing that is evoked, or called forth, by utopian visions of a transformed future" (112).

47. Pearse, *Plays, Stories, Poems*, 134–35.

48. As Valente writes of blood in *Dracula*, we might read breastmilk as a "master signifier" whereby "the material substance itself animates and authorizes the entire range of its figurative meanings," including the potential threat of passing along degeneration through the axes of both "descent and contagion." Here, though, rather than degeneration, the contagion is the narrative of blood sacrifice itself. Joseph Valente, "Stoker's Vampire and the Vicissitudes of Biopower," in Bram Stoker, *Dracula*, ed. John Paul Riquelme (Boston: Beford/St. Martin's, 2nd edition, 2012), 649–50; 652.

49. Quinn, "Fostering the Nation," 74–75; 80.

50. David Lloyd, *Irish Culture and Colonial Modernity 1800–2000: The Transformation of Oral Space* (Cambridge: Cambridge Univ. Press, 2011), 2.

51. Kelleher, *Feminization of Famine*, 39; 228–29.

52. Caitríona Clear, *Women of the House: Women's Household Work in Ireland 1922–1961: Discourses, Experiences, and Memories* (Dublin: Irish Academic Press, 2000), 129.

53. Aoife Rickard, "The Shame of Breast-Feeding? An Aspect of Irish Culture in Historical Perspective." *PaGes: Postgraduate Research in Progress* (Vol. 4, 1997), Accessed at http://www.ucd.ie/pages/97/contents4.html. I discussed the biopolitics of Irish breastfeeding in relation to shame at the Ireland in Psychoanalysis 2: Irish Shame Conference at the University of Buffalo in September 2018.

54. Brian Crowley discusses the controversy around the stamp, noting that "one correspondent to the letters page of the *Irish Independent* objected to the stamp as 'an outrageous insult' to Pearse" by using "the most pagan of symbols." Brian Crowley, "Pearse's Profile: The Making of an Icon," in *Making 1916: Material and Visual Culture of the Easter Rising*, ed. Lisa Godson and Joanna Brück (Liverpool: Liverpool Univ. Press, 2015), 131. For the complete letter, see Shauna Gilligan, "Image of a Patriot: The Popular and Scholarly Portrayal of Patrick Pearse, 1916-1991", unpublished master's thesis, University of California, Davis, 1993, 83. Maureen Murphy recalls a punning joke at the time: "Erin gan Bragh": "gan" meaning "without" in Irish. I am grateful to Lucy McDiarmid for encouraging a closer look at this controversy and sharing Dr. Murphy's personal recollection.

12. Death before Disability

1. Michel Foucault, *Abnormal: Lectures at the College De France* (New York: Picador, 2003); Michel Foucault, *Society Must Be Defended* (New York: Picador, 2003).

2. Foucault, *Society Must Be Defended*, 241–56.

3. Michel Foucault, *Ethics: Subjectivity and Truth* (New York: New Press, 1997), 51.

4. Nancy Stepan, "Biology and Degeneration: Race and Proper Places," in *Degeneration: The Darker Side of Progress*, ed. J. Edward Chamberlain and Sander L. Gilman (New York: Columbia Univ. Press, 1985), 97–120.

5. See L. P. Curtis, *Anglo-Saxons and Celts* (Bridgeport: Univ. of Bridgeport Press, 1968). See my *The Myth of Manliness in Irish National Culture, 1880–1922* (Urbana: Univ. of Illinois Press, 2011), 11–21.

6. Lord Salisbury, "Disintegration," in *Lord Salisbury on Politics: A Selection from His Articles in the Quarterly Review (1860–1883)*, ed. Paul Smith (Cambridge: Cambridge Univ. Press, 1977), 343.

7. Lord Salisbury, "Disintegration," 12.

8. Lady Augusta Gregory, *Gods and Fighting Men* (London: John Murray, 1910), 5–15.

9. Robert McRuer, *Crip Theory: Cultural Signs of Queerness and Disability* (New York: New York Univ. Press, 2006), 9.

10. *United Ireland*, Dec. 20, 1884, 2.

11. *The Gaelic Athletic Association* (Dublin: A and E Cashell, 1884), viii–ix.

12. Survival, in "Athletic Ireland: Its Progress and Possibilities," *Sinn Fein* Jan. 25, 1908, 1.

13. W. F. Mandle, *The Gaelic Athletic Association and Irish Nationalist Politics, 1884–1924* (Dublin: Gill and MacMillan, 1987), 154.

14. A. Newman, "National Degeneration," *Irish Volunteer*, Nov. 7, 1914, 1–2. See also A. Newman, "How National Degenerates Are Made," *Irish Volunteer*, Nov. 14, 1914, 9–10.

15. Sean Mac Alla, "The GAA and the Volunteers," *Irish Volunteer*, Apr. 25, 1914, 11.

16. W. B. Yeats, *The Collected Poems of W. B. Yeats* (New York: Simon and Schuster, 1989), 355.

17. John M. Synge, *The Playboy of the Western World*, in *Collected Plays and Poems and the Aran Islands* (London: J. M. Dent, 1996), 159.

18. For Cathleen's mental state see Marion Quirici, "*Cathleen Ni Houlihan* and the Disability Aesthetics of Irish National Culture," *Eire-Ireland* 50, no. 3–4 (Fall/Winter 2015): 74–93.

19. Patrick Pearse, *Poems/Stories/Plays* (Dublin: Talbot, 1916), 42.

20. Lady Augusta Gregory, "The Felons of Our Land," *Cornhill Magazine*, May 1900, 622–34.

21. Joseph Mary Plunkett, "The little black rose will be red at last," in *The 1916 Poets*, ed. Desmond Ryan (Dublin: Gill and MacMillan, 1995), 160.

22. In so doing, they initiated a gradual sea change in the sectarian politics of physical force nationalism. The Catholic Church had always stoutly opposed the violent sallies of advanced nationalism, as is exemplified by Bishop Moriarty's famous observation "that eternity is not long enough nor hell hot enough to punish these [Fenian] miscreants." But as Revivalist Martyrology increasingly borrowed from the liturgical rhetoric of Catholicism, culminating in Patrick Pearse's devotional radicalism, the Church lapsed into an arguably consensual silence on the morality of revolution. See Liz Curtis, *The Cause of Ireland: From the United Irishmen to Partition* (Dublin: Colour Books, 1994), 71.

23. W. B. Yeats, *Cathleen Ni Houlihan*, in *The Collected Plays of W. B. Yeats* (New York: MacMillan, 1934), 55.

24. Pearse, *Poems/Stories/Plays*, 44.

25. Plunkett, *The 1916 Poets*, 160.

26. It should be noted that the ableism characteristic of Revival biopolitics is not without its own Biblical sanction, under the rubric of what we might call moral degeneration. Throughout the Christian Testament, physical disabilities like blindness, paralysis, leprosy, lameness, etc., and cognitive/psychosocial disabilities going by the name of "possession" were seen to be the embodied manifestations and effects of sin, evil, or demonic forces, the outward sign of a spiritual corruption for which the victim was to be blamed as well as pitied. Accordingly, Jesus's ministry in curing disability, evidence of his divine provenance, often required the repentance and ensuing absolution of the sufferer.

27. Patrick Pearse, *Collected Works of Padraic Pearse: Political Writings and Speeches* (London: Maunsel and Roberts, 1922), 99, 163.

28. Pearse, *Political Writings and Speeches*, 195.

29. Pearse, *Political Writings and Speeches*, 97, 154.

30. Pearse, *Political Writings and Speeches*, 194, 203.

31. Gregory, "Felons," 622–34.

32. Slavoj Žîzêk, *The Sublime Object of Ideology* (London: Verso, 1989), 135.

33. Yeats, *Collected Plays*, 56.

34. If one were to do a film adaptation of the play, Michael's last moments might be freeze-framed to emphasize the spiritual uplift that his commitment to self-immolation produces while eliding the somatic effects of the sacrifice itself. Think, for example, of the ending to *Butch Cassidy and the Sundance Kid*.

35. Pearse, *Poems/Stories/Plays*, 44.

36. Patrick Pearse, "By Way of Comment," *An Macaomh* 11, no. 2 (May 1913): 6.

37. Pearse, *Poems/Stories/Plays*, 9.

38. Pearse, *Poems/Stories/Plays*, 9.

39. Elizabeth Cullingford, "Thinking of Her . . . as Ireland: Yeats, Pearse and Heaney," *Textual Practice* 4 (1990): 11.

40. Luke Gibbons, *Transformations in Irish Culture* (Notre Dame: Notre Dame Univ. Press, 1996), 20–22.

41. For the homoerotics of Christ's body in devotional poetry, see Richard Rambuss, *Closet Devotions* (Durham: Duke Univ. Press), 1998.

42. Plunkett, *The 1916 Poets*, 160.

43. Sigmund Freud, *Beyond the Pleasure Principle* (New York: Norton, 1961), 56–58.

44. Yeats, *Collected Poems*, 181.

Bibliography

Abercrombie, Patrick. *Dublin of the Future*, vol. 1: Publications of the Civics Institute of Ireland. London: Hodder and Staughton, 1922.

Ahearne, Jeremy. *Michel de Certeau: Interpretation and Its Other.* Cambridge: Polity Press, 1995.

Allen, Nicholas. *George Russell (A. E.) and the New Ireland, 1905–1930.* Dublin: Four Courts Press, 2003.

Allen, Nicholas. *Modernism, Ireland and Civil War.* Cambridge: Cambridge Univ. Press, 2009.

Anderson, Benedict. *Imagined Communities: Reflections on the Origin and Spread of Nationalism.* London: Verso, 1991.

Annat, Aurelia. "Class, Nation, Gender, and Self: Katharine Tynan and the Construction of Political Identities, 1880–1930." In *Politics, Society, and the Middle Class in Modern Ireland*, edited by Fintan Lane, 194–211. Houndmills: Palgrave Macmillan, 2010.

Annual General Report of the Department, vol. 6: parts 1905–6.

Arnold, Bruce. *Mainie Jellett and the Modern Movement in Ireland.* New Haven: Yale Univ. Press, 1992.

Arnold, Matthew. *On the Study of Celtic Literature.* London: Smith Elder, 1981.

Arrington, Lauren. *Revolutionary Lives: Constance and Casimir Markievicz.* Princeton: Princeton Univ. Press, 2016.

Bal, Mieke, and Norman Bryson. "Introduction: Art and Intersubjectivity." *Looking In: The Art of Viewing.* Amsterdam: G+B Arts, 2001. 1–40.

Barker, A. Trevor, ed. *The Mahatma Letters to A. P. Sinnett.* Pasadena: Theosophical Publishing House, 1926.

Barker, A. Trevor, ed. *The Mahatma Letters to A. P. Sinnett.* 2nd ed. Pasadena: Theosophical Publishing House, 1926.

Bender, Abby. *Israelites in Erin: Exodus, Revolution and the Irish Revival.* Syracuse, NY: Syracuse Univ. Press, 2015.

Bennett, Jane. *Vibrant Matter.* Durham: Duke Univ. Press, 2010.

Bhreathnach-Lynch, Síghle. "Crossing the Rubicon: Sean Keating's *An Allegory.*" *New Hibernia Review* 12, no. 2 (Jan. 2008): 120–26.

Binckes, Faith, and Kathryn S. Laing. "A Vagabond's Scrutiny: Hannah Lynch in Europe." In *Irish Women Writers: New Critical Perspectives*, edited by Elke D'hoker, Raphael Ingelbien, and Hedwig Schwall, 111–32. Bern: Peter Lang, 2010.

Binckes, Faith, and Kathryn S. Laing. *Hannah Lynch 1859–1904: Irish Writer, Cosmopolitan, New Woman.* Cork: Cork Univ. Press, 2019.

Blanchot, Maurice. *The Infinite Conversation.* Translated and foreword by Susan Hanson. Minneapolis: Univ. of Minnesota Press, 1993.

Blavatsky, Helena Petrovna. *The Key to Theosophy.* London: The Theosophical Publishing House Ltd., 1889.

Blavatsky, Helena Petrovna. *The Secret Doctrine: Vol. I.* London: The Theosophical Publishing House Ltd., 1888.

Blavatsky, Helena Petrovna. *The Theosophical Glossary.* Los Angeles: Theosophical Publishing House, 1918.

Bochicchio, Sarah. "The Female Painter Whose Modern Art Shocked Ireland," Apr. 18, 2018. https://www.artsy.net/article/artsy-editorial-female-painter-modern-art-shocked-ireland.

Boehmer, Elleke. *Colonial and Postcolonial Literature: Migrant Metaphors.* Oxford: Oxford Univ. Press, 2005.

Boesky, Amy. *Founding Fictions: Utopia in Early Modern England.* Athens: Univ. of Georgia Press, 1997.

Boland, Eavan. "Our Future Will Become the Past of Other Women." Illustrated by Paula McGloin. *Irish Times*, Dec. 10, 2018, 11–12.

Bornstein, George. *Material Modernism: The Politics of the Page.* Cambridge: Cambridge Univ. Press, 2001.

Bourdieu, Pierre. *In Other Words: Essays towards a Reflexive Sociology.* Translated by Matthew Adamson. Stanford: Stanford Univ. Press, 1990.

Bourdieu, Pierre. *The Logic of Practice.* Translated by Richard Nice. Stanford: Stanford Univ. Press, 1990.

Bourdieu, Pierre. *The Rules of Art: Genesis and Structure in the Literary Field.* Translated by Susan Emanuel. Cambridge: Polity Press, 1996.

Bourdieu, Pierre. "The Forms of Capital." In *Handbook of Theory and Research for the Sociology of Education*, edited by John G. Richardson, 241–58. New York: Greenwood Press, 1986.

Bourke, Angela. *Voices Underfoot: Memory, Forgetting, and Oral Verbal Art*. Cork: Cork Univ. Press, 2016.

Bowe, Nicola Gordon. "The Arts and Crafts Movement in Ireland." *Antiques* 142, no. 6 (Dec. 1992): 864–75.

Bowe, Nicola Gordon. "The Arts and Crafts Society of Ireland (1894–1925) with Particular Reference to Harry Clarke." *The Journal of the Decorative Arts Society* 9 (1985): 29–40.

Bowe, Nicola Gordon. *Harry Clarke: His Graphic Art*. Dublin: Dolmen Press, 1984.

Bowe, Nicola Gordon. *Harry Clarke: The Life and Work*. Revised and updated ed. Dublin, Ireland: History Press Ireland. 2012.

Bowe, Nicola Gordon. *The Life and Work of Harry Clarke*. Blackrock, Dublin: Irish Academic Press, 1989.

Bowe, Nicola Gordon. *Wilhelmina Geddes, Life and Work*. Four Courts Press, 2015.

Bowe, Nicola Gordon, and Elizabeth Cumming. *The Arts and Crafts Movement in Dublin and Edinburgh: 1885–1925*. Dublin: Irish Academic Press, 1998.

Bowe, Nicola Gordon, David Caron, and Michael Wynne. *Gazetteer of Irish Stained Glass*. Dublin: Irish Academic Press, 1988.

Bowe, Nicola Gordon, David Caron, and Michael Wynne. *Gazetteer of Irish Stained Glass*. Dublin: Irish Academic Press, 2021.

Boyd, Ernest. *Ireland's Literary Renaissance*. Dublin: Maunsel and Company, Ltd., 1916.

Bradley, Patrick. "William Rooney—A Sketch of His Career." In *Poems and Ballads: William Rooney*. Dublin: The United Irishman, 17 Fownes Street, n.d.

Braidotti, Rosi. *Nomadic Subjects: Embodiment and Sexual Difference in Contemporary Feminist Theory*. 2nd ed. New York: Columbia Univ. Press, 2011.

Brake, Laurel. "Aestheticism and Decadence: *The Yellow Book* (1894–97), *The Chameleon* (1894), and *The Savoy* (1896)." In *The Oxford Critical and Cultural History of Modernist Magazines*, edited by Peter Brooker and Andrew Thacker. Oxford: Oxford Univ. Press, 2009.

Brake, Laurel. "'Time's Turbulence': Mapping Journalism Networks." *Victorian Periodicals Review*, Special Issue: Victorian Networks and the Periodical Press 42, no. 2 (Summer 2011): 115–27.

Brooker, Andrew, and Peter Thacker. "General Introduction." In *The Oxford Critical and Cultural History of Modernist Magazines*. Oxford: Oxford Univ. Press, 2009.

Brown, Terence. "Ireland, Modernism, and the 1930s." In *Modernism and Ireland: The Poetry of the 1930s*, edited by Patricia Coughlan and Alex Davis, 24–42. Cork: Cork Univ. Press, 1995.

Bryson, Norman. *Vision and Painting: The Logic of The Gaze*. New Haven: Yale Univ. Press, 1983.

Burke, Mary. "'Disremembrance': Joyce and Irish Protestant Institutions." *Éire-Ireland* 55, no. 1 (Spring/Summer 2020).

Bynum, Caroline Walker. *Holy Feast and Holy Fast: The Religious Significance of Food to Medieval Women*. Berkeley: Univ. of California Press, 1987.

Campbell, Matthew. *Irish Poetry under the Union, 1801–1924*. New York: Cambridge Univ. Press, 2014.

Carpenter, Edward. *The Intermediate Sex: A Study of Some Transitional Types of Men and Women*. London: George Allen and Unwin, 1908.

Castle, Gregory. "Irish Revivalism: Critical Trends and New Directions." *Literature Compass* 8, no. 5 (2011): 291–303.

Castle, Gregory. *Modernism and the Celtic Revival*. New York: Cambridge Univ. Press, 2001.

Castle, Gregory. *Reading the Modernist Bildungsroman*. Gainesville: Univ. Press of Florida, 2006.

Chaudhry, Yug Mohit. *Yeats, the Irish Literary Revival and the Politics of Print*. Cork: Cork Univ. Press, 2001.

Cheah, Pheng. *Spectral Nationality: Passages of Freedom from Kant to Postcolonial Literatures of Liberation*. New York: Columbia Univ. Press, 2003.

Clark, Suzanne. *Sentimental Modernism: Women Writers and the Revolution of the Word*. Bloomington: Indiana Univ. Press, 1991.

Clarke, Harry. Papers. National Library of Ireland, MS39202.

Clear, Caitríona. *Women of the House: Women's Household Work in Ireland 1922–1961: Discourses, Experiences, and Memories*. Dublin: Irish Academic Press, 2000.

Cleary, Joe. *Outrageous Fortune: Capital and Culture in Modern Ireland.* Dublin: Field Day Publications, 2007.

Coleman, Anthony. "A. E.'s Deirdre and the Fays." *Notes and Queries 26,* no. 4 (1979): 326–28.

Colum, Padraig. *Ourselves Alone! The Story of Arthur Griffith and the Origin of the Irish Free State.* New York: Crown Press, 1959.

Connolly, Claire. "Counting on the Past: Yeats and Irish Romanticism." *European Romantic Review* 28, no. 4 (2017): 473–87.

Connolly, David. "'The Real Founder of Sinn Féin': William Rooney (Liam Ó Maolruanaidh), 1873–1901." Jun. 1, 2017. http://www.anphoblacht .com/contents/26896.

Conrad, Kathryn C. *Locked in the Family Cell: Gender, Sexuality and Political Agency in Irish National Discourse.* Madison: Univ. of Wisconsin Press, 2004.

Conrad, Kathryn, Coílín Parsons, and Julie McCormick Weng, eds. *Science, Technology, and Irish Modernism.* Syracuse, NY: Syracuse Univ. Press, 2019.

Copjec, Joan. "Vampires, Breast-Feeding, and Anxiety." *October* 58 (1991).

Cormack, Peter. *Arts and Crafts Stained Glass.* New Haven: Yale Univ. Press, 2015.

Costigan, Lucy, and Michael Cullen. *Strangest Genius: The Stained Glass of Harry Clarke.* Dublin: The History Press Ireland, 2010.

Coulter, Riann. "Translating Modernism: Mainie Jellett, Ireland, and the Search for a Modernist Language." *Apollo,* 164, no. 535 (September 2006).

Cronin, Michael. "'To Right the Wrong of the People': Vulnerability and Revolutionary Desire in Patrick Pearse's Drama." In *Patrick Pearse and the Theatre: Mac Piarais agus an Téatar,* edited by Eugene McNulty and Róisín Ní Ghairbhí, 110–25. Dublin: Four Courts Press, 2017.

Crowley, Brian. "Pearse's Profile: The Making of an Icon." In *Making 1916: Material and Visual Culture of the Easter Rising,* edited by Lisa Godson and Joanna Brück. Liverpool: Liverpool Univ. Press, 2015.

Cuff, Tomas S. "The 40th Anniversary of the Death of William Rooney Occurs in This Month." *Irish Press* (May 17, 1941).

Cullingford, Elizabeth. "Thinking of Her . . . as Ireland: Yeats, Pearse and Heaney." *Textual Practice* 4 (1990): 11.

Curtin, Nancy J. "'A Nation of Abortive Men': Gendered Citizenship and Early Irish Republicanism." In *Reclaiming Gender: Transgressive Identities in Modern Ireland*, edited by Marilyn Cohen and Nancy J. Curtin, 33–52. New York: St. Martin's Press, 1999.

Curtis, L. P. *Anglo-Saxons and Celts*. Bridgeport: Univ. of Bridgeport Press, 1968.

Curtis, Liz. *The Cause of Ireland: From the United Irishmen to Partition*. Dublin: Colour Books, 1994.

Davis, Thomas. "The State of the Irish Peasantry." In *Literary and Historical Essays*. Dublin: James Duffy, 1854.

Deane, Seamus, ed. *The Field Day Anthology of Irish Writing*, vol. 2. Derry: Field Day Publications, 1991.

de Brún, Fionntán. *Belfast and the Irish Language*. Dublin: Four Courts Press, 2006.

de Brún, Fionntán. "Temporality and Irish Revivalism: Past, Present, and Becoming." *New Hibernia Review* 17, no. 4 (Winter/Geimhreadh, 2013).

de Certeau, Michel. *The Practice of Everyday Life*. Translated by Steven Rendall. Berkeley: Univ. of California Press, 1984.

Delay, Cara. "Women, Childbirth Customs, and Authority in Ireland, 1850–1930." *Lilith* 21 (Jan. 2015).

Denson, Alan, ed. *Letters from A. E.* London: Abelard-Schuman, 1961.

De Waal, Ariane. "Performing the 'Ultimate Private Act' in Public: The Biopolitics of Breastfeeding in London." *Journal for the Study of British Cultures* 23, no. 2 (2016).

Donoghue, Emma. "'How Could I Fear and Hold Thee by the Hand': The Poetry of Eva Gore-Booth". In *Sex, Nation, and Dissent in Irish Writing*, edited by Éibhear Walshe, 16–42. Cork: Cork Univ. Press, 1997.

Donoghue, Emma. *The Wonder*. New York: Little, Brown, and Co., 2016.

Doyle, Damien. "Rosamond Jacob (1888–1960)." In *Female Activists: Irish Women and Change 1900–1960*, edited by Mary Cullen and Maria Luddy. Dublin: Woodford Press, 2001.

Duffy, Sir Charles Gavan. *My Life in Two Hemispheres*, vol. 1. 1898. Reprint, Shannon: Irish Univ. Press, 1969.

Duffy, Sir Charles Gavan. "The Revival of Irish Literature." In *The Revival of Irish Literature: Addresses by Sir Charles Gavan Duffy, K. C. M. G., Dr. George Sigerson, and Dr. Douglas Hyde*. London: Fisher Unwin, 1894. 9–59.

Duffy, Sir Charles Gavan, Dr. George Sigerson, and Dr. Douglas Hyde. *The Revival of Irish Literature: Addresses by Sir Charles Gavan Duffy, K. C. M. G., Dr. George Sigerson, and Dr. Douglas Hyde.* London: T. Fisher Unwin, MDCCCXCIV.

Eagleton, Terry. *Heathcliff and the Great Hunger.* London: Verso, 1995.

Easley, Alexis. "Introduction to Special Issue: Victorian Networks and the Periodical Press." *Victorian Periodicals Review*, Special Issue: Victorian Networks and the Periodical Press 42, no. 2 (Summer 2011): 111–14.

Egerton, George. "A Lost Masterpiece." *The Yellow Book*, no. 1 (1894): 189–96.

Eglinton, John. *A Memoir of A. E.: George William Russell.* London: Macmillan, 1937.

Eglinton, John, W. B. Yeats, Æ [George Russell], and William Larminie. *Literary Ideals in Ireland.* London: T. F. Unwin, 1899.

Eide, Marian. "Maeve's Legacy: Constance Markievicz, Eva Gore-Booth and the Easter Rising." *Éire-Ireland* 51, no. 3–4 (Winter 2016): 80–103.

Ellmann, Maud, Siân White, and Vicky Mahaffy, eds. *The Edinburgh Companion to Irish Modernism.* Edinburgh: Edinburgh University Press, 2021.

Ellmann, Maud. *The Hunger Artists.* Cambridge, MA: Harvard Univ. Press, 1993.

Enright, Anne. *Making Babies: Stumbling into Motherhood* (New York: Norton, 2013).

Esty, Jed. *Unseasonable Youth: Modernism, Colonialism and the Fiction of Development.* Oxford: Oxford Univ. Press, 2012.

Etymonline—Online Etymology Dictionary. https://www.etymonline.com/.

Fanon, Frantz. *The Wretched of the Earth.* Translated by Richard Philcox. New York: Grove Press, 2004.

Feeney, Brian. *Sinn Féin: A Hundred Turbulent Years.* Dublin: O'Brien Press, 2002.

Fennell, Jack. "James William Barlow." *The Green Book: Writings on Irish Gothic, Supernatural and Fantastic Literature* 18 (Samhain 2021): 29–36.

Fennell, Jack. "The Machine in the (Holy) Ghost: Anti-Scientific Literature, Genre Fiction, and Irish Modernism, 1890–1940." In *Irish Modernisms: Gaps, Conjectures, Possibilities*, edited by Paul Fagan, John Greaney, and Tamara Radak, 185–96. New York: Bloomsbury, 2021.

Ferguson, Roderick A. "Administering Sexuality; or, The Will to Institutionality." *Radical History Review* (Winter 2008): 158–69.

Ferguson, Roderick A. *The Reorder of Things: The University and Its Pedagogies of Minority of Difference.* Minneapolis: Univ. of Minnesota Press, 2012.

Finneran, Richard J., and George Mills Harper, eds. *The Collected Works of W. B. Yeats*, vol. II: *The Plays.* New York: Simon and Schuster, 2010.

FitzSimon, Betsey Taylor, and James Murphy, eds. *The Irish Revival Reappraised.* Dublin: Four Courts Press, 2004.

Flanagan, Frances. *Remembering the Irish Revolution: Dissent, Culture, and Nationalism in the Irish Free State.* Oxford: Oxford Univ. Press, 2015.

Fogarty, Anne, ed. *Irish University Review* 34, no. 1 (2004).

Ford, Ford Madox. "John Galsworthy and George Moore." *The English Review* (Aug. 1933): 130–42.

Foster, John Wilson. *Fictions of the Irish Literary Revival: A Changeling Art.* Syracuse, NY: Syracuse Univ. Press, 1987.

Foster, John Wilson. "Irish Modernism." In *Colonial Consequences: Essays in Irish Literature and Culture.* Dublin: Lilliput Press, 1991. 44–59.

Foster, John Wilson. *Irish Novels 1890–1940: New Bearings in Culture and Fiction.* Oxford: Oxford Univ. Press, 2008.

Foster, R. F. *Paddy and Mr. Punch: Connections in Irish and English History.* London: Penguin Books, 1995.

Foster, R. F. *Vivid Faces: The Revolutionary Generation in Ireland 1890–1923.* London: Penguin Books, 2014.

Foster, R. F. *Vivid Faces: The Revolutionary Generation in Ireland 1890–1923.* New York: Norton, 2014.

Foster, R. F. *W. B. Yeats: A Life, Vol I: The Apprentice Mage 1865–1914.* Oxford: Oxford Univ. Press, 1997.

Foucault, Michel. *Abnormal: Lectures at the College De France.* New York: Picador, 2003.

Foucault, Michel. *Ethics: Subjectivity and Truth.* New York: New Press, 1997.

Foucault, Michel. *Society Must Be Defended.* New York: Picador, 2003.

Frank, A. W. *The Wounded Storyteller: Body, Illness, and Ethics.* Chicago: Univ. of Chicago Press, 1985.

Frank, Joseph. "Spatial Form in Modern Literature: An Essay in Two Parts." *The Sewanee Review* 53, no. 2 (Spring 1945): 221–40.

Frazier, Adrian. *George Moore, 1852–1933.* New Haven: Yale Univ. Press, 2000.

Frazier, Adrian. "Harry Clarke and the Material Culture of Modern Ireland." *Textual Practice* 16, no. 2 (2002): 303–21.

Frazier, Adrian. "'I No Longer Underrate Him': The Question of Moore's Value." In *George Moore: Artistic Visions and Literary Worlds*, edited by Mary Pierse. Newcastle, Cambridge Scholars Press, 2006. 2–11.

Frazier, Acrian. "Queering the Irish Renaissance: The Masculinities of Moore, Martyn, and Yeats." In *Gender and Sexuality in Modern Ireland*, edited by Antony Bradley and Maryann Gialanella Valiulis, 8–38. Amherst, Mass.: Univ. of Massachusetts Press, 1997.

Freud, Sigmund. *Beyond the Pleasure Principle.* New York: Norton, 1961.

The Gaelic Athletic Association. Dublin: A and E Cashell, 1884.

Gibbon, Monk. "A. E." In *The Living Torch: A. E.*, edited by Monk Gibbon, 3–81. London: Macmillan, 1937.

Gibbons, Luke. "Peripheral Visions: Revisiting Irish Modernism." In *The Moderns*, edited by Enrique Juncosa and Christine Kennedy, 88–101. Dublin: Irish Museum of Modern Art, 2011.

Gibbons, Luke. *Transformations in Irish Culture.* Notre Dame: Notre Dame Univ. Press, 1996.

Gifford, Don, and Robert J. Seidman. Ulysses *Annotated.* 2nd ed. Berkeley: Univ. of California Press, 1989.

Giles, Fiona. "'Relational, and Strange': A Preliminary Foray into a Project to Queer Breastfeeding." *Australian Feminist Studies* 19, no. 45 (Nov. 2004): 301–14.

Gilligan, Shauna. "Image of a Patriot: The Popular and Scholarly Portrayal of Patrick Pearse, 1916–1991." Unpublished master's thesis, University of California, Davis, 1993.

Glandon, Virginia. *Arthur Griffith and the Advanced Nationalist Press, 1900–1922.* New York: Peter Lang, 1985.

Golightly, Karen B. "Lady Gregory's Deirdre: Self-Censorship or Skilled Editing?" *New Hibernia Review* 11, no. 1 (2007): 117–26.

Gonne, Maud. "The National Education of Children." *United Irishman.* Aug. 23, 1902. 6.

Gonne, Maude. "Our Irish Children." In *Maud Gonne's Irish Nationalist Writings: 1895–1946*, edited by Karen Steele, 151–52. Dublin: Irish Academic Press, 2004.

Goodrick-Clarke, Nicholas. *Helena Blavatsky*. Berkeley: North Atlantic Books, 2004.

Goodrick-Clarke, Nicholas. *The Western Esoteric Tradition: A Historical Introduction*. Oxford: Oxford Univ. Press, 2008.

Goodwin, Geraint. *Conversations with George Moore*. London: Ernest Benn Limited, 1929.

Gore-Booth, Eva. *The Death of Fionovar: From the* Triumph of Maeve, illustrated by Constance Gore-Booth (Countess Markievicz). London: Erskine Macdonald, 1916.

Gore-Booth, Eva. *Eva Gore-Booth: Collected Poems*. Edited by Sonja Tiernan. Dublin: Arlen House, 2018.

Gore-Booth, Eva. *Fiametta*. Edited by Sonja Tiernan. Lewiston: Edwin Mellen, 2010.

Gore-Booth, Eva. *The Plays of Eva Gore-Booth*. Edited by Frederick S. Lapisardi. San Francisco: Edwin Mellen, 1991.

Gore-Booth, Eva. "*Poems* (1929)." In *The Field Day Anthology of Irish Writing: Volume IV: Irish Women's Writing and Traditions*, edited by Angela Bourke, Siobhán Kilfeather, Maria Luddy, Margaret Mac Curtain, Gerardine Meaney, Máirín Ní Dhonnchadha, Mary O'Dowd, and Clair Wills, 1107–9. Cork: Cork Univ. Press in association with Field Day, 2002.

Gore-Booth, Eva. "*Poems* (1929)." In *The Field Day Anthology of Irish Writing: Volume V: Irish Women's Writing and Traditions*, edited by Angela Bourke, Siobhán Kilfeather, Maria Luddy, Margaret Mac Curtain, Gerardine Meaney, Máirín Ní Dhonnchadha, Mary O'Dowd, and Clair Wills, 918–20. Cork: Cork Univ. Press in association with Field Day, 2002.

Gore-Booth, Eva. *Poems of Eva Gore-Booth: Complete Edition*. Edited by Esther Roper. London: Longmans Green, 1929.

Gore-Booth, Eva. *The Political Writings of Eva Gore-Booth*. Edited by Sonja Tiernan. Manchester: Manchester Univ. Press, 2015.

Gore-Booth, Eva. "A Psychological and Poetic Approach to the Study of Christ in the Fourth Gospel." In *The Field Day Anthology of Irish Writing: Volume IV: Irish Women's Writing and Traditions*, edited by

Angela Bourke, Siobhán Kilfeather, Maria Luddy, Margaret Mac Curtain, Gerardine Meaney, Máirín Ní Dhonnchadha, Mary O'Dowd, and Clair Wills, 659–63. Cork: Cork Univ. Press in association with Field Day, 2002.

Grand, Sarah. "The New Aspect of the Woman Question." *North American Review* 158 (1894): 270–76.

Gregory, Lady Augusta. *The Collected Plays II: Tragedies and Tragic Comedies*. Edited by Ann Saddlemyer. Gerrards Cross: Colin Smythe, 1979.

Gregory, Lady Augusta, trans. and ed. *Cuchulain of Muirthemne: The Story of the Men of the Red Branch of Ulster*. London: John Murray, 1903.

Gregory, Lady Augusta. "The Felons of Our Land." *Cornhill Magazine*, May 1900, 622–34.

Gregory, Lady Augusta. *Gods and Fighting Men*. London: John Murray, 1910.

Gregory, Lady Augusta, ed. *Ideals in Ireland*. London: At the Unicorn, 1901.

Gregory, Lady Augusta. *Lady Gregory Collected Letters*, vol. 3. Edited by John Kelly and Ronald Schuchard. Oxford: Oxford Univ. Press, 1994.

Gregory, Lady Augusta. *Our Irish Theatre: A Chapter of Autobiography*. New York: G. P. Putnam's Sons, 1913.

Gregory, Lady Augusta. "What Was Their Utopia?" *International Yeats Studies* 1, no. 1 (2016).

Griffith, Angela, Marguerite Helmers, and Róisín Kennedy, eds. *Harry Clarke and Artistic Visions of the New Irish State*. Irish Academic Press, 2018.

Grossman, Alan. *Poetic Knowledge in the Early Yeats: A Study of* The Wind among the Reeds. Charlottesville: Univ. Press of Virginia, 1969.

Guinness, Selina. "'Protestant Magic' Reappraised: Evangelicalism, Dissent and Theosophy." *Irish University Review* 33, no. 1 (2003), 14–27.

Hale, Jonathan. *The Old Way of Seeing*. New York: Houghton Mifflin, 1994.

Hampton, Mark. *Visions of the Press in Britain, 1850–1950*. Urbana: Univ. of Illinois Press, 2004.

Hansen, Jim. *Terror in Irish Modernism: The Gothic Tradition from Burke to Beckett*. Albany: SUNY Press, 2009.

Harper, George Mills. *Yeats's Golden Dawn*. London: Macmillan, 1974.

Harris, Susan Cannon. *Irish Drama and the Other Revolutions: Sexual Politics and the International Left, 1892–1964*. Edinburgh: Edinburgh Univ. Press, 2017.

Harvey, Alison. "Irish Aestheticism in Fin-de-Siècle Women's Writing: Art, Realism, and the Nation." *Modernism/modernity* 21, no. 3 (Sept. 2014): 805–26.

Helland, Janice. *British and Irish Home Arts and Industries: 1880–1914*. Dublin: Irish Academic Press, 2007.

Herr, Cheryl. *Joyce's Anatomy of Culture*. Urbana: Univ. of Illinois Press, 1986.

Hickey, Edward, ed. *Paul Henry, Further Reminiscences*. Belfast: Blackstaff Press, 1973.

Highmore, Ben. *Ordinary Lives: Studies in the Everyday*. New York: Routledge, 2011.

Hill, Shonagh. *Women and Embodied Mythmaking in Irish Theatre*. Cambridge: Cambridge Univ. Press, 2019.

Hogan, Caelainn. *Republic of Shame: Stories from Ireland's Institutions for "Fallen Women."* New York: Penguin, 2020.

Hull, Eleanor, "The Story of Deirdre in Its Bearing on the Social Development of the Folktale." *Folklore* 15, no. 1 (1904): 24–39.

Humboldt, Wilhelm von. *The Limits of State Action*. Edited by J. W. Barrow. 1850. Reprint, Cambridge: Cambridge Univ. Press, 1969.

Hutton, Clare. "Joyce and the Institutions of Revivalism." *Irish University Review* 33, no. 1 (Spring–Summer 2003): 117–32.

Hyde, Douglas. "The Necessity for De-Anglicising Ireland." In *The Revival of Irish Literature: Addresses by Sir Charles Gavan Duffy, K. C. M. G., Dr. George Sigerson, and Dr. Douglas Hyde*. London: Fisher Unwin, 1894. 115–61.

Ingman, Heather. *A History of the Irish Short Story*. Cambridge: Cambridge Univ. Press, 2009.

"Irish Language Congress Committee." *Freeman's Journal*, Feb. 16, 1894, 4.

Ivanova, Miglena. "Dublin 1907." In *Encyclopedia of World's Fairs and Expositions*, edited by John E. Findling and Kimberly D. Pelle, 190–92. Jefferson, NC: McFarland and Company, 2008.

Ivey, Paul Eli. *Radiance from Halcyon: A Utopian Experiment in Religion and Science*. Minneapolis: Univ. of Minnesota Press, 2013.

Iyer, Raghavan, and Nandini Iyer, eds. *The Descent of the Gods: The Mystical Writings of G. W. Russell—A. E.: Part Three of the Collected Works.* Gerrards Cross: Colin Smythe Ltd., 1988.

Jacob, Rosamond. Private papers, National Library of Ireland. MS 33,133/1–5.

Jacob, Rosamond. *The Troubled House.* Dublin: Browne and Nolan, 1938.

Jameson, Fredric. *The Political Unconscious.* Ithaca: Cornell Univ. Press, 1981.

Johnson, Neil. *Simply Complexity: A Clear Guide to Complexity Theory.* London: One World, 2007.

Joyce, James. *The Critical Writings.* Edited by Ellsworth Mason and Richard Ellmann. Cornell Univ. Press, 1989.

Joyce, James. *Letters,* vol. 2. Edited by Richard Ellmann. New York: Viking Press, 1966.

Joyce, James. *Occasional, Critical, and Political Writing.* Edited with an Introduction and Notes by Kevin Barry. Oxford: Oxford Univ. Press, 2000.

Joyce, James. *Selected Letters of James Joyce.* Edited by Richard Ellmann. New York: Viking Press, 1975.

Joyce, James. *Ulysses.* 1934. Reset and corrected 1961. Reprint, New York: Vintage-Random, 1990.

Joyce, James. *Ulysses.* Paris: Shakespeare and Co., 1922.

Joyce, Simon. "Impressionism, Naturalism, Symbolism: Trajectories of Anglo-Irish Fiction at the Fin de Siècle." *Modernism/modernity* 21, no. 3 (2014): 787–803.

Juncosa, Enrique, and Christina Kennedy, eds. *The Moderns.* Dublin: Irish Museum of Modern Art, 2011.

Kearns, Kevin Corrigan. *Georgian Dublin: Ireland's Imperiled Architectural Heritage.* London: David and Charles, 1983.

Kelleher, Margaret. "*The Cabinet of Irish Literature*: A Historical Perspective on Irish Anthologies." *Éire-Ireland* 38, no. 3–4 (2003): 68–89.

Kelleher, Margaret. *The Feminization of Famine: Expressions of the Inexpressible?* Durham: Duke Univ. Press, 1997.

Kelleher, Margaret, ed. *Irish University Review: Special Issue, New Perspectives on the Irish Literary Revival* 33, no. 1 (Spring/Summer 2003).

Kelly, M. J. *The Fenian Ideal and Irish Nationalism, 1882–1916.* Woodbridge, Suffock: The Boydell Press, 2006.

Kelly, Matthew. " . . . and William Rooney Spoke in Irish." *History Ireland* 15, no. 1 (Jan/Feb 2007).

Kelly, Matthew. http://www.generalmichaelcollins.com/life-times/1905 –founding-sinn-fein/william-rooney-sinn-fein/.

Kennedy, Patrick. *Legendary Fictions of the Irish Celts, Collected and Narrated by Patrick Kennedy*. London: Macmillan and Co., 1891.

Kennedy, S. B. *Irish Art and Modernism, 1880–1950*. Belfast: Institute of Irish Studies, Queens University, 1991.

Kenny, Colum. "'An Extraordinarily Clever Journalist': Arthur Griffith's Editorships, 1899–1919." In *Periodicals and Journalism in Twentieth-Century Ireland: Writing against the Grain*, edited by Mark O'Brien and Felix Larkin, 16–30. Dublin: Four Courts Press, 2014.

Kenny, Colum. "An Introduction to the Use of Pen Names in Griffith's Publications." In *Remembering Arthur Griffith: Cut and Paste*, edited by Cormac O'Hanrahan, 5–6. Dublin: Printwell Design Ltd., 2020.

Kenny, Colum. "Tom Grehan: Advertising Pioneer and Newspaper Man." In *Independent Newspapers: A History*, edited by Mark O'Brien and Kevin Rafter. Dublin: Four Courts Press, 2012. 52–66.

Keown, Edwina, and Carol Taaffe, eds. *Irish Modernism: Origins, Contexts, Publics*. Bern, Switzerland: Peter Lang, 2010.

Kiberd, Declan. "George Moore's Gaelic Lawn Party." In *The Irish Writer and the World* (Cambridge: Cambridge Univ. Press, 2005): 91–104.

Kiberd, Declan. *Inventing Ireland*. Cambridge, MA: Harvard Univ. Press, 1993.

Kiberd, Declan. *Irish Classics*. London: Granta, 2000.

Kiberd, Declan. "Patrick Pearse: Irish Modernist." In *The Life and Afterlife of P. H. Pearse*, edited by Roisin Higgins and Regina Uí Chollatáin, 65–80. Dublin: Irish Academic Press, 2009.

Kiberd, Declan, and P. J. Mathews, eds. *Handbook of the Irish Revival: An Anthology of Irish Cultural and Political Writings, 1891–1922*. Dublin: Abbey Theatre Press, 2015.

Kincaid, Andrew. *Postcolonial Dublin: Imperial Legacies and the Built Environment*. Minneapolis: Univ. of Minnesota Press, 2006.

Kipp, Julie. *Romanticism, Maternity, and the Body Politic*. Cambridge: Cambridge Univ. Press, 2003.

Kornbluh, Anna. "The Realist Blueprint." *The Henry James Review* 36, no. 3 (Fall 2015): 199–211.

Krans, Horatio Sheafe. *Yeats and the Irish Literary Revival*. New York: McClure, Phillips, and Co., 1904.

Kreilkamp, Vera, ed. *The Arts and Crafts Movement: Making It Irish*. Boston: McMullen Museum of Art, Boston College, 2016.

Kristeva, Julia, *Revolution in Poetic Language*. Translated by Margaret Waller. New York: Columbia Univ. Press, 1984.

Kuch, Peter. *Yeats and A. E.: The Antagonism that Unites Dear Friends*. Gerrards Cross: Colin Smythe Ltd., 1986.

Kuhn, Andrew. "'Make a Letter like a Monument': Remnants of Modernist Literary Institutions in Ireland." In *Modernist Afterlives in Irish Literature and Culture*, edited by Paige Reynolds, 93–110. New York: Anthem Press, 2016.

Lacan, Jacques. "The Instance of the Letter in the Unconscious." In *Écrits: A Selection*, translated by Bruce Fink. New York: Norton, 2002. 412–41.

"Lady Grove." "Social Solecisms." *Cornhill Magazine*. March 1902.

Lane, Leann. "Female Emigration and the Co-operative Movement in the Writings of George Russell." *New Hibernia Review* 4, no. 8 (2004), 84–100.

Lane, Leann. "George Russell and James Stephens: Class and Cultural Discourse, Dublin 1913." In *A Capital in Conflict: Dublin 1913*, edited by Francis Devine, 333–52. Dublin: Four Courts Press, 2013.

Lane, Leann. "'It Is in the Cottages and Farmers' Houses That the Nation Is Born': A. E.'s *The Irish Homestead* and the Cultural Revival." *Irish University Review* 8, no. 4 (2003), 165–81.

Lane, Leann. *Rosamond Jacob: Third Person Singular*. Dublin: University College Dublin Press, 2008.

Lane, Leann. "'There Are Compensations in the Congested Districts for Their Poverty': A. E. and the Idealized Peasant of the Agricultural Cooperative Movement." In *The Irish Revival Reappraised,* edited by Betsey Taylor Fitzpatrick and James H. Murphy, 33–48. Dublin: Four Courts Press, 2004.

Lang, Andrew, and 'X,' A Working Man. "The Reading Public." *Cornhill Magazine*. December 1901.

Lanigan, Liam. *James Joyce, Urban Planning, and Irish Modernism*. New York: Palgrave, 2014.

Larkin, Felix M. "Arthur Griffith and the *Freeman's Journal*." In *Irish Journalism before Independence: More a Disease Than a Profession,* edited by Kevin Rafter, 173–85. Manchester: Manchester Univ. Press, 2011.

Larkin, Felix M. "No Longer a Political Side Show: T. R. Harrington and the 'New' Irish Independent, 1905–31." In *Independent Newspapers: A History*, edited by Mark O'Brien and Kevin Rafter, 26–38. Dublin: Four Courts Press, 2012.

Law, Jules. *The Social Life of Fluids: Blood, Milk, and Water in the Victorian Novel*. Ithaca: Cornell Univ. Press, 2010.

Leeney, Cathy. *Irish Women Playwrights, 1900–1939: Gender and Violence on Stage*. Oxford: Peter Lang, 2010.

Leeney, Cathy. "The New Woman in a New Ireland?: 'Grania' after Naturalism." *Irish University Review* 34, no. 1 (Spring–Summer, 2004): 157–70.

Leeney, Cathy. "Women and Irish Theatre before 1960." In *The Oxford Handbook of Modern Irish Theatre*, edited by Nicholas Grene and Chris Morash, 394–422. Oxford: Oxford Univ. Press, 2016.

Lefebvre, Henri. *Everyday Life in the Modern World*. Translated by Sacha Rabinovitch. 1968. Reprint, New Brunswick, NJ: Transaction Publishers, 1984.

Lennon, Joseph. *Irish Orientalism: A Literary and Intellectual History*. Syracuse, NY: Syracuse Univ. Press, 2004.

Levenson, Michael. *Modernism*. New Haven, CT: Yale Univ. Press, 2011.

Levine, Caroline. *Forms: Whole, Rhythm, Hierarchy, Network*. Princeton: Princeton Univ. Press, 2017.

Lewis, Gifford. *Eva Gore-Booth and Esther Roper: A Biography*. London: Pandora, 1988.

The Library of John Quinn, Part One (A–C). New York: The Anderson Galleries, 1923.

Liddington, Jill, and Jill Norris. *One Hand Tied behind Us: The Rise of the Women's Suffrage Movement*. London: Virago, 1978.

Lionnet, Françoise, Shu-mei Shih, and Suzanne Gearhart, eds. *Minor Transnationalism*. Durham, NC: Duke Univ. Press, 2005.

Lloyd, David. *Anomalous States: Irish Writing and the Post-Colonial Moment*. Durham: Duke Univ. Press, 1993.

Lloyd, David. "The Gaze Is a Thing: Beckett's *Film* and Bram Van Velde." In *The Moderns*, edited by Enrique Juncosa and Christine Kennedy, 116–27. Dublin: Irish Museum of Modern Art, 2011.

Lloyd, David. *Ireland after History*. Notre Dame: Univ. of Notre Dame Press, 1999.

Lloyd, David. *Irish Culture and Colonial Modernity 1800–2000: The Transformation of Oral Space*. Cambridge: Cambridge Univ. Press, 2011.

Longley, Edna. *Yeats and Modern Poetry*. Cambridge: Cambridge Univ. Press, 2013.

Lynch, Hannah. *Autobiography of a Child*. Edinburgh and London: William Blackwood; New York: Dodd, Mead and Company, 1899. Published in *Blackwood's Magazine* 164–65, 1898–99.

Lynch, Hannah. *The Prince of the Glades*. London: Methuen, 1891.

Lyons, F. S. L. *Ireland since the Famine*. London: Weidenfeld and Nicolson, 1971.

MacBride, Maud Gonne. *The Autobiography of Maud Gonne: A Servant of the Queen*. Edited by A. Norman Jeffares and Anna MacBride White. 1938. Reprint, Chicago: Univ. of Chicago Press, 1994.

Mac Congáil, Nollaig. "*Weekly Freeman* agus Irish Fireside Club ag Cothú an Náisiúnachais agus an Ghaelachais. Bealach na hÓige?" *Seanchas Ardmhacha: Journal of the Armagh Diocesan Historical Society* 21, no. 2, and 22, no. 1 (2007/2008): 278–318.

MacLeod, Fiona. "A Group of Celtic Writers," *The Fortnightly Review* LXV (January to June 1899).

MacManus, Seamus. Bureau of Military History. Witness Statement S0283.

MacPherson, J. *Women and the Irish Nation: Gender, Culture and Irish Identity, 1890–1914*. New York: Springer, 2012.

Mahoney, Kristin. *Literature and the Politics of Post-Victorian Decadence*. Cambridge: Cambridge Univ. Press, 2015.

Malabou, Catherine. *Changing Difference: The Feminine and the Question of Philosophy*. Translated by Carolyn Shread. London: Polity, 2011.

Mandle, W. F. *The Gaelic Athletic Association and Irish Nationalist Politics, 1884–1924*. Dublin: Gill and MacMillan, 1987.

"Manifesto." *The Academy* (Apr. 13, 1901): 320–21.

Masterson, Joseph Edmundson. *Irish Press* (Sept. 7, 1935).

Mathews, P. J. *Revival: The Abbey Theatre, Sinn Fein, the Gaelic League and the Co-operative Movement*. Cork: Cork Univ. Press, 2003.

Mattar, Sinead Garrigan. *Primitivism, Science, and the Irish Revival*. Oxford: Oxford Univ. Press, 2004.

Maume, Patrick. "The *Irish Independent* and Empire, 1891–1919." In *Newspapers and Empire in Ireland and Britain: Reporting the British Empire, c. 1857–1921*, edited by Simon Potter, 124–42. Dublin: Four Courts, 2004.

Maume, Patrick. "William Martin Murphy." In *Dictionary of Irish Biography*, edited by James McGuire and James Quinn. Cambridge, UK: Cambridge Univ. Press, 2009. https://www.dib.ie/biography/murphy-william-martin-a6106.

Maunder, Andrew. "'Discourses of Distinction': The Reception of the *Cornhill* Magazine 1859–60." *Victorian Periodicals Review* 32, no. 3 (1999).

Maye, Brian. *Arthur Griffith*. Dublin: Griffith College Publications, 1997.

McAteer, Michael. *Standish O'Grady, AE, and Yeats: History, Politics, Culture*. Dublin: Irish Academic Press, 2002.

McAuliffe, Mary. *Margaret Skinnider*. Dublin: University College Dublin Press, 2020.

McCormack, W. J. "Irish Gothic and After." In *The Field Day Anthology of Irish Writing*, vol. 2, edited by Seamus Deane, 831–54. Derry: Field Day Publications, 1991.

McDiarmid, Lucy. "Stalking Yeats: The Celebrity System of Revivalist Dublin." In *Synge and Edwardian Ireland*, edited by Brian Cliff and Nicholas Green, 34–44. Oxford: Oxford Univ. Press, 2012.

McDonald, Rónán. "Internal Others: Cultural Debate and Counter-Revival." In *A History of Irish Modernism*, edited by Gregory Castle and Patrick Bixby, 91–107. Cambridge: Cambridge Univ. Press, 2019.

McDonald, Rónán. "Irish Revival and Modernism." In *The Cambridge Companion to Irish Modernism*, edited by Joe Cleary, 51–62. Cambridge: Cambridge Univ. Press, 2014.

McGee, Owen. *Arthur Griffith*. Dublin: Merrion Press, 2015.

McGee, Patrick. *Paperspace: Style as Ideology in Joyce's* Ulysses. Lincoln: Univ. of Nebraska Press, 1988.

McIntosh, Gillian, "Providing an Alternative to the Public House: The Irish Temperance League and the Creation of the First Coffee Chain in Belfast in the 1870s." Unpublished report for the Irish Temperance League, 2012.

McMahon, Timothy G. "Douglas Hyde and the Politics of the Gaelic League in 1914." *Éire-Ireland* 53, no. 1 (2018): 29–47.

McMahon, Timothy G. *Grand Opportunity: The Gaelic Revival and Irish Society, 1893–1910.* Syracuse, NY: Syracuse Univ. Press, 2008.

McNulty, Eugene. "Waiting for the Exceptional: Pearse's Drama and the Space between Law and Law." In *Patrick Pearse and the Theatre: Mac Piarais agus an Téatar,* edited by Eugene McNulty and Róisín Ní Ghairbhí, 79–95. Dublin: Four Courts Press, 2017.

McRuer, Robert. *Crip Theory: Cultural Signs of Queerness and Disability.* New York: New York Univ. Press, 2006.

Meehan, Ciara. "'The Prose of Logic and of Scorn': Arthur Griffith and *Sinn Féin,* 1906–1914." In *Irish Journalism before Independence: More a Disease Than a Profession,* edited by Kevin Rafter, 186–99. Manchester, UK: Manchester Univ. Press, 2011.

Memmi, Albert. *The Colonizer and the Colonized.* Expanded ed. Translated by Howard Greenfeld. Boston: Beacon Press, 1991.

Mitchell, Melanie. *Complexity: A Guided Tour.* Oxford: Oxford Univ. Press, 2009.

Moore, George. *Hail and Farewell: Ave, Salve, and Vale.* Edited by Richard Allen Cave. Gerrards Cross: Colin Smythe Ltd., 1976.

Moore, George. *Hail and Farewell: Ave, Salve, and Vale.* Edited by Richard Allen Cave. Gerrards Cross: Colin Smythe Ltd., 1985.

Moore, George. *Literature at Nurse, or Circulating Morals: A Polemic on Victorian Censorship.* Edited by Pierre Coustillas. Hassocks: The Harvester Press Limited, 1976.

Moore, George. "My Impressions of Zola." *The English Illustrated Magazine* (Feb. 1894): 477–89.

Moore, George. *The Untilled Field.* London: T. Fisher Unwin, 1903.

Moore, George. *The Untilled Field.* Edited by Richard Allen Cave. Gerrards Cross: Colin Smythe Limited, 2000. xxxii.

Moran, D. P. *The Philosophy of Irish Ireland.* 2nd ed. Dublin: James Duffy and Co., 1905.

Morash, Christopher. *A History of the Media in Ireland.* Cambridge, UK: Cambridge Univ. Press, 2010.

Morris, Catherine. *Alice Milligan and the Irish Cultural Revival.* Dublin: Four Courts, 2012.

Morrison, Mark. *The Public Face of Modernism: Little Magazines, Audiences, and Reception 1905–1920.* Madison: Univ. of Wisconsin Press 2001.

Morrissey, Thomas J. *William Martin Murphy*. Dundalk: Dundalgan Press, 1997.

Moses, Michael Valdez. "Irish Modernist Imaginaries." In *The Cambridge Companion to Irish Modernism*, edited by Joe Cleary, 193–220. Cambridge: Cambridge Univ. Press, 2014.

Mulholland, Rosa. *Father Tim*. London: Sands and Co., 1910.

Mulholland, Rosa. "Wanted: An Irish Novelist." *Irish Monthly* 19 (1891): 368–69.

Mullen, Patrick. *The Poor Bugger's Tool: Irish Modernism, Queer Labor, and Postcolonial History*. Oxford: Oxford Univ. Press, 2012.

Murphy, Andrew. *Ireland, Reading and Cultural Nationalism, 1790–1930: Bringing the Nation to Book*. Cambridge: Cambridge Univ. Press, 2018.

Ní Bheacháin, Caoilfhionn. "Seeing Ghosts: Gothic Discourses and State Formation," *Éire-Ireland* 47, no. 3 and 4 (2012), 37–63.

Nic Congáil, Ríona. *An Óige agus an Athbheochan*. Dublin: Cló Léann na Gaeilge, 2022.

Nic Congáil, Ríona. "'Fiction, Amusement, Instruction': The Irish Fireside Club and the Educational Ideology of the Gaelic League." *Éire-Ireland* 44, no. 1 and 2 (2009): 91–117.

Nic Congáil, Ríona. *Úna Ní Fhaircheallaigh agus an Fhís Utóipeach Ghaelach*. Dublin: Arlen House, 2011.

Nietzsche, Friedrich. "Truth and Lies in a Nonmoral Sense." In *Philosophy and Truth: Selections from Nietzsche's Notebooks of the Early 1870*. Edited and translated by Daniel Breazeale. Atlantic Highlands, NJ: Humanities Press, 1979. 79–97.

Nolan, Emer. "Modernism and the Irish Revival." In *The Cambridge Companion to Modern Irish Culture*, edited by Claire Connolly and Joe Cleary, 157–72. Cambridge: Cambridge Univ. Press, 2004.

Nordau, Max. *Degeneration*. New York: D. Appleton, 1895.

Norris, Margot, ed. *Dubliners: Authoritative Text, Contexts, Criticism*. New York: W. W. Norton, 2006.

Ó Baoighill, Pádraig. *Nally as Maigh Eo*. Dublin: Coiscéim, 1998.

O'Brien, Mark and Kevin Rafter, eds. *Independent Newspaper: A History*. Dublin: Four Courts Press, 2012.

O'Byrne, Robert. "Irish Modernism: The Early Decades." In *The Moderns*, edited by Enrique Juncosa and Christine Kennedy, 8–22. Dublin: Irish Museum of Modern Art, 2011.

Ó Ceallaigh Ritschel, Nelson. "William Rooney." *History Ireland* 15, no. 2 (Mar/Apr. 2007): 8.

Ó Conaire, Pádraic Óg. *Liam Ó Maolruanaidh 1897–1901*. Dublin: Clódhanna Teo., 1975.

Ó Conchubhair, Brian. "The Apotheosis of the Vernacular: Language, Dialects and the Irish Revival." In *Irish Literature in Transition, 1880–1940*, vol. 4, edited by Marjorie Howes, 21–38. Cambridge: Cambridge Univ. Press, 2020.

Ó Conchubhair, Brian. "Capturing the Trenches of Language: World War One, the Irish Language and the Gaelic League." *Modernist Cultures* 13, no. 3 (2018): 382–98.

Ó Conchubhair, Brian. *Fin de Siècle na Gaeilge: Darwin, an Athbheochan agus Smaointeoireacht na hEorpa*. Indreabhán: An Clóchomhar, 2009.

Ó Conchubhair, Brian. "The Irish Language Revival 1876–1922." In *Oxford History of Ireland*, vol. 4, edited by Thomas Bartlett, 198–222. Oxford: Oxford Univ. Press, 2018.

Ó Conchubhair, Brian. "William Rooney: The Celtic Literary Society and the Gaelic League.' In *Proceedings of the Harvard Celtic Colloquium*, vol. 38, edited by Celeste Andrews, Heather Newton, Shannon Parker, and Elizabeth Gipson, 144–72. Harvard: Harvard Univ. Press, 2018.

O'Connor, Maureen. "Eva Gore-Booth's Queer Art of War." In *Women Writing War: Ireland 1880–1922*, edited by Tina O'Toole and Muireann O'Cinnéide, 85–102. Dublin: University College Dublin Press, 2016.

O'Connor, Maureen. "Vegetable Love: The Syncretic Nation in the Writings of Margaret Cousins and Eva Gore-Booth." *Journal of Irish Studies* XXVIII (2013): 18–33.

O'Hanrahan, Cormac. "1917 Sinn Féin Convention (Day 1)." In *Remembering Arthur Griffith: Cut and Paste*, edited by Cormac O'Hanrahan, 11–18. Dublin: Printwell Design Ltd., 2020.

O'Leary, Philip. *The Prose Literature of the Gaelic Revival, 1881– 1921: Ideology and Innovation*. University Park, PA: Pennsylvania State Univ. Press, 1994.

Olson, Liesl. *Modernism and the Ordinary*. Oxford: Oxford Univ. Press, 2009.

Ó Luing, Seán. *Art Ó Gríofa*. Dublin: Sáirséal agus Dill, 1953.

O'Malley, Ernie. *On Another Man's Wound: A Personal History of Ireland's War of Independence*. Boulder: Roberts Rinehart, 1999.

Ó Murchú, Máirtín. *Cumann Buan—Choimeádta Na Gaeilge: Tús an Athréimnithe.* Dublin: Cois Life Teoranta, 2001.

O'Neill, T. P. "Window on the Past." *Irish Press*, Sept. 6, 1967, 8.

Ó Rathaille, Aodhagán. "An Heroic Poet." In *An Macaomh*, edited by P. H. Pearse. Rathfarnham: St. Enda's, 1913.

O'Toole, Tina. "George Egerton's Translocational Subjects." *Modernism/modernity* 21, no. 3 (2014): 827–42.

O'Toole, Tina. *The Irish New Woman.* Basingstoke: Palgrave Macmillan, 2013.

O'Toole, Tina. "The (Irish) New Woman: Political, Literary, and Sexual Experiments." In *The History of British Women's Writing*, vol. 7, edited by Holly Laird, 23–34. London: Palgrave Macmillan, 2016.

O'Toole, Tina. "The New Woman *Flâneuse* or Streetwalker? George Egerton's Urban Aestheticism." In *Reconnecting Aestheticism and Modernism: Continuities, Revisions, Speculations*, edited by Bénédicte Coste, Catherine Delyfer, and Christine Reynier, 19–30. London: Routledge, 2017.

Papacharissi, Zizi, and Emily Easton. "In the Habitus of the New: Structure, Agency, and the Social Media Habitus." In *A Companion to New Media Dynamics*, edited by John Hartley, Jean Burgess, and Axel Bruns, 167–84. Malden, MA: Wiley-Blackwell, 2013.

Pašeta, Senia. *Irish Nationalist Women, 1900–1918.* Cambridge: Cambridge Univ. Press, 2013.

Pašeta, Senia. "1798 in 1898: The Politics of Commemoration." *The Irish Review* 22 (Summer 1998): 46–53.

Pašeta, Senia. *Suffrage and Citizenship in Ireland, 1912–18.* London: Institute of Historical Research, 2019.

Pateman, Carole. "Three Questions about Womanhood Suffrage." In *Suffrage and Beyond: International Feminist Perspectives*, edited by Caroline Daley and Melanie Nolan, 331–48. Auckland: Auckland Univ. Press, 1994.

Pearse. P. H. *The Murder Machine.* Dublin: Whelan and Son, 1916.

Pearse, Padraic H. *Collected Works of Padraic H. Pearse: Plays, Stories, Poems.* Dublin: Phoenix, 1917.

Pearse, Padraic H. *Collected Works of Padraic H. Pearse: Political Writings and Speeches.* Dublin: Phoenix, 1924.

Pearse, Patrick. "By Way of Comment." *An Macaomh* 11, no. 2 (May 1913): 6.

Pearse, Patrick. *Collected Works of Padraic Pearse: Political Writings and Speeches.* London: Maunsel and Roberts, 1922.

Pearse, Patrick. *Poems/Stories/Plays.* Dublin: Talbot, 1916.

Pearse, Patrick. *A Significant Irish Educationalist: The Educational Writings of P. H. Pearse.* Edited by Séamas Ó Buachalla. Dublin: Mercier Press, 1980.

Pearse, Patrick. *Three Lectures on Gaelic Topics.* Dublin: M. H. Gill, 1898.

Phibbs, Henry C. Bureau of Military History. Witness Statement 0848.

Plunkett, Joseph Mary. "The little black rose will be red at last." In *The 1916 Poets,* edited by Desmond Ryan, 160. Dublin: Gill and MacMillan, 1995.

Politics of Print. Cork: Cork Univ. Press, 2001.

Potts, Donna. "Irish Poetry and the Modernist Canon: A Reappraisal of the Poetry of Katharine Tynan." In *Border Crossings: Irish Women Writers and Nationalism,* edited by Kathryn Kirkpatrick, 79–99. Tuscaloosa: Univ. of Alabama Press, 2000.

Prabhu, Anjali. "Eros in Infinity and Totality: A Reading of Levinas and Fanon." *Levinas Studies* 7 (2012): 127–46.

Putzel, Steven. *Reconstructing Yeats: The Secret Rose and* The Wind among the Reeds. Dublin: Gill and Macmillan, 1986.

Quigley, Megan. "Ireland." In *Cambridge Companion to European Modernism,* edited by Pericles Lewis, 170–90. Cambridge: Cambridge Univ. Press, 2011.

Quinn, Antoinette. "Ireland/Herland: Women and Literary Nationalism." In *The Field Day Anthology of Irish Writing: Irish Women Writers and Tradition,* vol. 5, edited by Angela Bourke, Siobhán Kilfeather, Maria Luddy, Margaret Mac Curtain, Gerardine Meaney, Máirín Ní Dhonnchadha, Mary O'Dowd, and Clair Wills, 889–98. New York: New York Univ. Press, 2002.

Quinn, Vincent. "Fostering the Nation: Patrick Pearse and Pedagogy." *New Formations* 42 (Winter 2001): 71–84.

Quirici, Marion. "*Cathleen Ni Houlihan* and the Disability Aesthetics of Irish National Culture." *Eire-Ireland* 50, no. 3–4 (Fall/Winter 2015): 74–93.

Rafter, Kevin. "Profits, Politics, and Personal Position: The Role of the Proprietor." In *Independent Newspapers: A History*, edited by Mark O'Brien and Kevin Rafter, 195–205. Dublin: Four Courts Press, 2012.

Rambuss, Richard. *Closet Devotions*. Durham: Duke Univ. Press, 1998.

Rendall, Jane. "Citizenship, Culture and Civilisation: The Languages of British Suffragists, 1866–1874." In *Suffrage and Beyond: International Feminist Perspectives*, edited by Caroline Daley and Melanie Nolan, 127–150. Auckland: Auckland Univ. Press, 1994.

Reynolds, Paige. *Modernism, Drama, and the Audience for Irish Spectacle*. Cambridge: Cambridge Univ. Press, 2007.

Reynolds, Paige. "Prose, Drama, and Poetry, 1891–1920." *A History of Modern Irish Women's Literature*, edited by Heather Ingman and Clíona Ó Gallchoir, 131–48. Cambridge: Cambridge Univ. Press, 2018.

Rich, Adrienne. *Of Woman Born: Motherhood as Experience and Institution*. New York: Norton, 1995.

Rickard, Aoife. "The Shame of Breast-Feeding? An Aspect of Irish Culture in Historical Perspective." *PaGes: Postgraduate Research in Progress* 4 (1997).

Ricoeur, Paul. "Life: A Story in Search of a Narrator." In *Facts and Values*, edited by M. C. Doeser and J. N. Kraay. Dordrecht: Martinus Nijhoff, 1986.

Riggs, Pádraigín. "*An T-Úr-Ghort* and *The Untilled Field*." In *George Moore: Artistic Visions and Literary Worlds*, edited by Mary Pierse, 130–41. Newcastle: Cambridge Scholars Press, 2006.

Riquelme, John Paul. "Toward a History of Gothic and Modernism: Dark Modernity from Bram Stoker to Samuel Beckett." *Modern Fiction Studies* 46, no. 3 (Fall 2000): 585–605.

Roche, Anthony. *The Irish Dramatic Revival, 1899–1939*. London: Bloomsbury Methuen Drama, 2015.

Ritschel Rodriguez-Ruiz, Blanca, and Ruth Rubio-Marín, "Introduction: Transition to Modernity: The Achievement of Female Suffrage and Women's Citizenship." In *The Struggle for Female Suffrage in Europe: Voting to Become Citizens*, edited by Blanca Rodriguez-Ruiz and Ruth Rubio-Marín, 1–46. Leiden: Brill, 2012.

Roiste, Liam de. "Witness Statement." Bureau Of Military History 1913–21. File BSM2.

Ruskin, John. *The Stones of Venice*, vol. 2: 1853; Project Gutenberg 2009. http://www.gutenberg.org/etext/30755.

Russell, George (A. E.). *Deirdre: A Legend in Three Acts*. Chicago: DePaul Univ. Press, 1970.

Russell, George (A. E.). *New Songs*. Dublin: O'Donoghue and Co, 1904.

Russell, George William. *The Candle of Vision*. In *The Descent of the Gods: The Mystical Writings of G. W. Russell—A. E.: Part Three of the Collected Works*. Edited by Raghavan Iyer and Nandini Iyer, 81–166. Gerrards Cross: Colin Smythe Ltd., 1988.

Russell, George William. "Concentration." In *The Descent of the Gods: The Mystical Writings of G. W. Russell—A. E.: Part Three of the Collected Works*. Edited by Raghavan Iyer and Nandini Iyer, 456–457. Gerrards Cross: Colin Smythe Ltd., 1988.

Russell, George William. *Imaginations and Reveries*. 2nd ed. Dublin: Maunsel and Roberts, 1921.

Russell, George William. *The Living Torch*. Edited by Monk Gibbon. London: Macmillan, 1937.

Russell, George William. *The National Being*. Dublin: Maunsel and Company, 1916.

Russell, George William. "Nationality and Cosmopolitanism." In *Imaginations and Reveries*. 2nd ed. Dublin: Maunsel and Roberts, 1921. 1–11.

Russell, George William. "The Story of a Star." In *The Descent of the Gods: The Mystical Writings of G. W. Russell—A. E.: Part Three of the Collected Works*. Edited by Raghavan Iyer and Nandini Iyer, 472–75. Gerrards Cross: Colin Smythe Ltd., 1988.

Ryan, Louise. *Winning the Vote for Women: The Irish Citizen Newspaper and the Suffrage Movement in Ireland*. Dublin: Four Courts Press, 2018.

Ryan, Louise and Margaret Ward, eds. *Irish Women and the Vote: Becoming Citizens*. Rev. ed. Dublin: Irish Academic Press, 2018.

Ryan, W. P. *The Irish Literary Revival: Its History, Pioneers and Possibilities*. London: Ward and Downey, 1894.

Salisbury, Lord. "Disintegration." In *Lord Salisbury on Politics: A Selection from His Articles in the Quarterly Review (1860–1883)*, edited by Paul Smith. Cambridge: Cambridge Univ. Press, 1977.

Sceilig (J. J. O'Kelly). Bureau of Military History, Witness Statement 384.

Schaffer, Talia. *The Forgotten Female Aesthetes: Literary Culture in Late-Victorian England*. Charlottesville: Univ. of Virginia Press.

Schmidt, Barbara Quinn. "The *Cornhill* Magazine: Celebrating Success." *Victorian Periodicals Review* 32, no. 3 (1999).

Schuchard, Ronald. "The Chanting of Yeats's *Deirdre*." *The Princeton University Chronicle* 68, no. 1–2 (2007): 201–52.

Scientific and Learned Societies of Great Britain: A Handbook Compiled from Official Sources. London: Allen and Unwin, 1901.

Sheehy, Jeanne. *The Rediscovery of Ireland's Past: The Celtic Revival 1830–1930*. London: Thames and Hudson, 1980.

Sheringham, Michael. *Everyday Life: Theories and Practices from Surrealism to the Present*. Oxford: Oxford Univ. Press, 2009.

Short, Ann Marie, Abigail L. Palko, and Dionne Irving, eds. *Breastfeeding and Culture: Discourses and Representation*. Ontario: Demeter Press, 2018.

Shovlin, Frank. "Who Was Father Conroy?: James Joyce, William Rooney, and 'The Priest of Adergool.'" *James Joyce Quarterly* 47, no. 2 (Winter 2010): 255–65.

Sinnett, A. P. *Incidents in the Life of Madame Blavatsky*. London: George Redway, 1886.

Skorpios, Antares (Jane Barlow). *History of a World of Immortals without a God: Translated from an Unpublished Manuscript in the Library of a Continental University*. Dublin: William McGee, 1891.

Smith, Andrew, and Jeff Wallace, eds. *Gothic Modernisms*. New York: Palgrave, 2001.

Smith, James M. *Ireland's Magdalen Laundries and the Nation's Architecture of Containment*. South Bend: Notre Dame Univ. Press, 1999.

Society for the Preservation of the Irish Language. Report of the Proceedings of the Congress Held in Dublin on the 15, 16 and 17th of August 1882.

Spenser, Edmund. *A View of the Present State of Ireland*. Edited by W. L. Renwick. Oxford: Clarendon Press, 1970.

Standage, Tom. *The Victorian Internet: The Remarkable Story of the Telegraph and the Nineteenth Century's On-Line Pioneers*. New York: Berkley Books, 1998.

Steele, Karen. *Women, Press and Politics during the Irish Literary Revival*. Syracuse, NY: Syracuse Univ. Press, 2007.

Stepan, Nancy. "Biology and Degeneration: Race and Proper Places." In *Degeneration: The Darker Side of Progress*, edited by J. Edward Chamberlain and Sander L. Gilman, 97–120. New York: Columbia Univ. Press, 1985.

Sullivan, Kelly. "Modernist Heresies: Irish Visual Culture and the Arts and Crafts Movement." In *The Edinburgh Companion to Irish Modernism*, edited by Maud Ellmann, Siân White, and Vicky Mahaffy, 234–51. Edinburgh: Edinburgh University Press, 2021.

Sullivan, Moynagh. "The Treachery of Wetness: Irish Studies, Seamus Heaney and the Politics of Parturition." *Irish Studies Review* 13, no. 4 (2005): 451–68.

Sweet, Paul R. *Wilhelm von Humboldt: A Biography*, vol. 2: 1808–35. Columbus: Ohio State Univ. Press, 1980.

Synge, J. M. *The Aran Islands*. Edited by Tim Robinson. 1907, Reprint London: Penguin, 1992.

Synge, J. M. *The Complete Plays*. London: Methuen Drama, 1963.

Synge, J. M. *The Complete Works of J. M. Synge*. New York: Random House, 1935.

Synge, John M. *The Playboy of the Western World*. In *Collected Plays and Poems and the Aran Islands*, edited by Alison Smith. London: J. M. Dent, 1996.

Teehan, Victoria, and Elizabeth Wincott Heckett. *The Honan Chapel: A Golden Vision*. Cork: Cork Univ. Press, 2004.

Thall, Hannah Freed. *Spoiled Distinctions: Aesthetics and the Ordinary in French Modernism*. Oxford: Oxford Univ. Press, 2015.

Tiernan, Sonja. "Challenging Presumptions of Heterosexuality: Eva Gore-Booth: A Biographical Case Study." *Historical Reflections/Refléxions Historiques*. Special Issue: Gender, History and Heritage in Ireland and Scotland 37, no. 2 (2011): 58–71.

Tiernan, Sonja. *Eva Gore-Booth: An Image of Such Politics*. Manchester: Manchester Univ. Press, 2012.

Tiernan, Sonja. "Tabloid Sensationalism or Revolutionary Feminism?: The First Wave Feminist Movement in an Irish Women's Periodical." *Irish Communications Review* 12, no. 1 (2010): 74–87.

Toomey, Deirdre. "'Both Beautiful, One a Gazelle': An Essay Reviewing Sonja Tiernan, *Eva Gore-Booth, An Image of Such Politics* and Lauren Arrington, *Revolutionary Lives: Constance and Casimir Markievicz*."

In *Yeats's Legacies: Yeats Annual No. 21*, edited by Warwick Gould, 545–46. London: Open Book Publishers in association with the Institute of Irish Studies, School of Advanced Study, Univ. of London, 2018.

Toomey, Deirdre, ed. *Yeats and Women*. Basingstoke: Palgrave Macmillan, 1997.

Trotter, Mary. *Ireland's National Theaters: Political Performance and the Origins of the Irish Dramatic Movement*. Syracuse, NY: Syracuse Univ. Press, 2001.

Trumpener, Katie. *Bardic Nationalism: The Romantic Novel and the British Empire*. Princeton: Princeton Univ. Press, 1997.

Tucker, Amanda, and Moira E. Casey, eds. *Where Motley Is Worn: Transnational Irish Literatures*. Cork: Cork Univ. Press, 2014.

Turner, Victor. *From Ritual to Theatre: The Human Seriousness of Play*. New York City: Performing Arts Journal Publications, 1982.

Turpin, John. "1798, 1898 and the Political Implications of Sheppard's Monuments." *History Ireland* 6, no. 2 (1998): 44–48. https://www.jstor.org/stable/27724561.

Tynan, Katharine. *Memories*. London: E. Nash and Grayson, 1924.

Tynan, Katharine. *Twenty-Five Years: Reminiscences*. London: Smith, Elder and Co, 1913.

Uí Fhaoláin, Aoife. "Language Revival and Conflicting Identities in the *Irish Independent*." *Irish Studies Review* 22, no. 1 (2014): 63–79.

"The Untilled Field." Anonymous review in *The English Review* (December 1914).

Valente, Joseph. "'Double Born': Bram Stoker and the Metrocolonial Gothic." In *Gothic and Modernism*, edited by John Paul Riquelme, 46–58. Baltimore: Johns Hopkins Univ. Press, 2008.

Valente, Joseph. *The Myth of Manliness in Irish National Culture, 1880–1922*. Urbana-Champaign: Univ. of Illinois Press, 2011.

Valente, Joseph. "Nation for Art's Sake: Aestheticist Afterwords in Yeats's Irish Revival." In *Yeats and Afterwords*, edited by Marjorie Howes and Joseph Valente, 100–126. Notre Dame: Univ. of Notre Dame Press, 2014.

Valente, Joseph. "Stoker's Vampire and the Vicissitudes of Biopower." In *Dracula* by Bram Stoker, edited by John Paul Riquelme, 649–65. Boston: Beford/St. Martin's, 2nd edition, 2012.

Victorian Periodicals Review, Special Issue: Victorian Networks and the Periodical Press 42, no. 2 (Summer 2011).

Viswanathan, Gauri. "Conversion and the Idea of the Secret." *Nineteenth-Century Literature* 73, no. 2 (2018), 161–86.

Viswanathan, Gauri. "In Search of Madame Blavatsky: Reading the Exoteric, Retrieving the Esoteric." *Representations* 141 (2018), 67–94.

Vladiv-Glover, Slobodanka, and Gerald Frederic. "Pierre Bourdieu's *Habitus*: A Critique in the Context of C. S. Peirce's Belief as Habit." In *Practicing Theory: Pierre Bourdieu and the Field of Cultural Production*, edited by Jeff Browitt and Brian Nelson, 31–38. Newark: Univ. of Delaware Press, 2004.

Voynich, E. L. *The Gadfly*. 1897, Reprint London: Mayflower, 1973.

Waldrop, M. Mitchell. *Complexity: The Emerging Science at the Edge of Order and Chaos*. New York: Simon and Schuster, 1992.

Walker, Dorothy. *Modern Art in Ireland*. Dublin: The Lilliput Press, 1997.

Washington, Peter. *Madame Blavatsky's Baboon: A History of the Mystics, Mediums, and Misfits Who Brought Spiritualism to America*. New York: Shocken Books, 1995.

Waters, Maureen. "Lady Gregory's 'Grania': A Feminist Voice." *Irish University Review* 25, no. 1 (Spring–Summer 1995): 11–24.

Weintraub, Stanley, ed. *The Savoy: Nineties Experiment*. University Park: Penn State Univ. Press, 1966.

Welch, Robert. "Moore's Way Back: *The Untilled Field* and *The Lake*." In *The Way Back: George Moore's* The Untilled Field *and* The Lake, edited by Robert Welch, 29–44. Totowa, New Jersey: Barnes and Noble Books, 1982.

Wells, Emma Jane. "Henry Williams and the 'Ymage of Deth' Roundel, Stanford-on-Avon, Northamptonshire." *Vidimus* 40 (May 2010) Panel of the Month. (ISSN 1752-0741, accessed Aug. 30, 2012.)

Whall, J. A. *Stained Glass Work: A Text-book for Students and Workers in Glass*. New York: D. Appleton and Co., 1905.

Whelan, Glen. "Appropriat(e)ing Wavelength: On Bourdieu's *On Television*." *ephemera* 2, no. 2 (2002): 131–48.

White, James, and Michael Wynne. *Irish Stained Glass*. Dublin: Gill and Son, 1963.

Wilde, Oscar. *The Picture of Dorian Gray*. New York: Norton, 2006.

Wolf, Joan. *Is Breast Best? Taking on the Breastfeeding Experts and the New High Stakes of Motherhood*. New York: New York Univ. Press, 2011.

"The Women's Suffrage Movement: Meeting at Drumcliffe." *Sligo Champion*, Dec. 26, 1896, 8. www.irishnewspapersarchive.com/. Accessed Apr. 14, 2020.

Wynne, Michael. *Irish Stained Glass*. The Irish Heritage Series: 1. Dublin: Eason and Son Ltd., 1977.

Wyse Power, Jenine. "The Political Influence of Women in Modern Ireland.'" In *The Voice of Ireland*, edited by W. G. Fitzgerald. Dublin: Virtue, 1924.

Yeates, Padraig. "The Life and Career of William Martin Murphy." In *Independent Newspapers: A History*, edited by Mark O'Brien and Kevin Rafter, 14–25. Dublin: Four Courts Press, 2012.

Yeats, W. B. *Autobiographies*. New York: Scribner, 1999.

Yeats, W. B. *The Autobiography of William Butler Yeats*. New York: Macmillan, 1965.

Yeats, W. B. *Cathleen Ni Houlihan*. In *The Collected Plays of W. B. Yeats*. New York: MacMillan, 1934.

Yeats, W. B. "The Celtic Element in Literature." In *Essays and Introductions*. London: Papermac, 1989. 173–88.

Yeats, W. B. "The Celtic Element in Literature." In *Ideas of Good and Evil*. London: A. H. Bullen, 1903. 270–95.

Yeats, W. B. *The Collected Letters of W. B. Yeats*, vol. 1: 1865–1895. Edited by John Kelly and Eric Domville. Oxford: Clarendon Press, 1986.

Yeats, W. B. *The Collected Poems of W. B. Yeats*. New York: Simon and Schuster, 1989.

Yeats, W. B. *The Irish Dramatic Movement*, vol. 8: *The Collected Works of W. B. Yeats*. Edited by Mary FitzGerald and Richard J. Finneran. New York: Scribner, 2003.

Yeats, W. B. "Irish National Literature, Contemporary Prose Writers: Mr. O'Grady, Miss Lawless, Miss Barlow, and the Folk-lorists." *The Bookman* 7–8 (Aug. 1895): 139.

Yeats, W. B. "Irish National Literature, IV: A List of the Best Irish Books." In *The Collected Works of W. B. Yeats, vol. 9: Early Articles and Reviews*, edited by John P. Frayne and Madeline Marchaterre. New York: Scribner, 2004.

Yeats, W. B. "Irish National Literature: Contemporary Prose Writers." *The Bookman* (Aug. 1895): 138–40.

Yeats, W. B. *The Letters of W. B. Yeats*. Edited by Allan Wade. London: R. Harte Davis, 1954.

Yeats, W. B. *Memoirs*. Edited by Denis Donoghue. London: Papermac, 1988.

Yeats, W. B. *The Poems*. Edited by Daniel Albright. London: Everyman, 1990.

Yeats, W. B., ed. *Representative Irish Tales*. 1891. Reprint, Dublin: Colin Smythe, 1979.

Yeats, W. B. *Representative Tales of Ireland*. In *W. B. Yeats Prefaces and Introductions*, edited by William H. O'Donnell. Basingstoke: Palgrave Macmillan, 1988.

Yeats, W. B. "The Trembling of the Veil." In *The Autobiography of William Butler Yeats*. New York: Collier Books, 1965.

Yeats, W. B. *Uncollected Prose*, vol. 1: 1886–1896. Edited by John P. Frayne. New York: Columbia Univ. Press, 1970.

Yeats, W. B. *A Vision: The Original 1925 Version*. New York: Scribner, 2008.

Yeats, W. B. *The Wind among the Reeds*. London: Elkin Mathews, 1899.

Younger, Carleton. *Arthur Griffith*. Dublin: Gill and Macmillan, 1981.

Žižek, Slavoj. *The Sublime Object of Ideology*. London: Verso, 1989.

Žižek, Slavoj. *Tarrying with the Negative: Kant, Hegel, and the Critique of Ideology*. Durham: Duke Univ. Press, 1993.

Zola, Émile. *The Experimental Novel, and Other Essays*. Translated by Belle M. Sherman. New York: Cassell Pub. Co, 1893.

Contributor Biographies

Abby Bender teaches in the languages and literatures department at Sacred Heart University, where she is the director of the Irish Studies minor. She is the author of *Israelites in Erin: Exodus, Revolution, and the Irish Revival* (Syracuse Univ. Press, 2015), as well as recent essays on James Joyce and citizenship and Ireland's Mother and Baby Homes. Her current book project examines the cultural and literary history of breastfeeding in Ireland.

Gregory Castle is a professor of British and Irish literature at Arizona State University. He has published *Modernism and the Celtic Revival* (2001), *Reading the Modernist Bildungsroman* (2006), and *The Literary Theory Handbook* (2013). His edited volumes include the *Encyclopedia of Literary and Cultural Theory*, vol. 1 (2011), and *A History of the Modernist Novel* (2015) and, with Patrick Bixby, *Standish O'Grady's Cuchulain: A Critical Edition* (2016) and *A History of Irish Modernism* (2019). He has published numerous articles and chapters on Joyce, Yeats, Wilde, Synge, Stoker, and other Irish writers.

Gregory Dobbins is an associate professor of English at the University of California, Davis. He is the author of *Lazy Idle Schemers: Irish Modernism and the Cultural Politics of Idleness* (Dublin: Field Day Publications, 2010) and essays about James Connolly, J. M. Synge, James Stephens, and Flann O'Brien. He is currently writing a book that seeks to propose and theorize Irish "Magic Naturalism."

Anne Fogarty is professor of James Joyce Studies at University College Dublin, codirector of the Dublin James Joyce Sumer School, and coeditor with Luca Crispi of the *Dublin James Joyce Journal*. She has coedited, with Timothy Martin, *Joyce on the Threshold* (2005), with Morris Beja, *Bloomsday 100: Essays on "Ulysses"* (2009), with Fran O'Rourke, *Voices on Joyce* (2015), and with Marisol Morales-Ladrón, *Deirdre Madden: New Critical Perspectives* (2022). She has published widely on aspects of twentieth and twenty-first century Irish writing and is currently completing a new edition of *Dubliners* for Penguin.

Marjorie Howes is associate professor of English at Boston College. She is the author of *Yeats's Nations: Gender, Class, and Irishness* (1996) and *Colonial Crossings: Figures in Irish Literary History* (2006). She is the coeditor of *Semicolonial Joyce* (2000), *The Cambridge Companion to W. B. Yeats* (2006), and *Yeats and Afterwords* (2014). She is also the series editor, with Claire Connolly, of *Irish Literature in Transition* (6 vols, 2020).

Mary L. Mullen is associate professor of English at Villanova University. She is the author of *Novel Institutions: Anachronism, Irish Novels, and Nineteenth-Century Realism* (Edinburgh, 2019), which won the Robert Rhodes Prize for Books on Literature from the American Conference for Irish Studies. She is currently writing a book on the colonial politics of public interest.

Brian Ó Conchubhair, a former president of the American Conference for Irish Studies, is an associate professor at the University of Notre Dame and a fellow of the Keough-Naughton Institute for Irish Studies. He has published on various aspects of the Irish-language revival, including print culture, Darwinian and racial theory, intellectual history, and cultural aesthetics. His biography of Flann O'Brien will appear in 2023.

Tina O'Toole is senior lecturer at the School of English, Irish, and Communication at the University of Limerick, Ireland. Her scholarship focuses on constructions of gender and sexuality in Irish literature; publications include *The Irish New Woman* (2013), essays for *Modernism/Modernity* (2014), *A History of Irish Women's Writing* (Cambridge Univ. Press, 2018), and *Irish Literature in Transition 1880–1940* (Cambridge Univ. Press, 2020). As editor, she has produced special issues of *Irish University Review* (2021; coedited with Anna Teekell), *Éire-Ireland* (2012; coedited with Piaras Mac Éinrí); essay collections including *Women Writing War* (2016;

coedited with Gillian McIntosh and Muireann O'Cinnéide), and *Irish Literature: Feminist Perspectives* (2008; coedited with Patricia Coughlan).

Paige Reynolds, professor of English at the College of the Holy Cross, has published on the subjects of revivalism, modernism, drama and performance, and modern and contemporary Irish literature. She is author of *Modernism, Drama, and the Audience for Irish Spectacle* (Cambridge Univ. Press, 2007) and editor of *Modernist Afterlives in Irish Literature and Culture* (Anthem Press, 2016), as well as of *The New Irish Studies* and *Irish Literature in Transition, Volume 6, 1980–2020* (with Eric Falci), both published in 2020 for Cambridge Univ. Press. Her current project is a monograph titled *The Stubborn Mode: Modernism in Irish Women's Contemporary Writing*.

Karen Steele is professor of English at Texas Christian University. She is the author of *Women, Press, and Politics during the Irish Revival* (Syracuse Univ. Press, 2007); coeditor, with Michael de Nie, of *Ireland and the New Journalism* (Palgrave, 2014) and editor of *Maud Gonne's Irish Nationalist Writings* (Irish Academic Press, 2003).

Kelly Sullivan is clinical associate professor in Irish Studies at Glucksman Ireland House, New York University. Her recent publications include "Elizabeth Bowen and 1916: An Architecture of Suspense" in *Modernism/modernity Print+*, "Yeats's Birds: Recognising the Animal" in *Modernist Cultures*, "Elizabeth Bowen and the Politics of Consent" in *Irish University Review*, and essays and book chapters on Irish visual culture and environmental writing. She recently coedited the "Ireland and the Environment" special issue of *Éire-Ireland* (Winter 2020). She teaches and researches late modernism, environmental humanities, Irish visual culture, and contemporary Irish poetry.

Joseph Valente is UB Distinguished Professor of English and Disability Studies at the University at Buffalo. He is vice president of the Northeastern Modern Language Association. He has authored *The Myth of Manliness in Irish Nationalist Culture, 1880–1922* (University of Illinois Press, 2011), *Dracula's Crypt: Bram Stoker, Irishness and the Question of Blood* (University of Illinois Press, 2002, 2012), and *James Joyce and the Problem of Justice: Negotiating Sexual and Colonial Difference* (Cambridge Univ. Press, 1995, 2009). Most recently, he coauthored *The Child Sex Scandal and Modern Irish Literature: Writing the Unspeakable* (with Margot Backus, Indiana Univ. Press, 2020). His edited collections include *Quare Joyce* (University of Michigan Press, 1997), *Disciplinarity at the Fin-de Siecle* (with Amanda Anderson, Princeton Univ. Press), *Urban Ireland* (a special issue of *Eire-Ireland*), *Joyce and Homosexuality* (a special issue of the *James Joyce Quarterly*), *Yeats and Afterwords* (with Marjorie Howes, Notre Dame Univ. Press, 2014), and *Ireland in Psychoanalysis* (with Seán Kennedy and Macy Todd, a special issue of *Breac*). In addition, he has published over seventy journal articles and book chapters in such venues as *Critical Inquiry, Diacritics, Novel, ELH, Narrative, Modern Fiction Studies, Journal of Modern Literature, Style, Contemporary Literature, Eire-Ireland, Irish University Review, James Joyce Quarterly, Joyce Studies Annual, Studies in Romanticism*, the *Journal of Literary and Cultural Disability*, and the *Journal of Critical and Religious Theory.*

Index